AMERICAN BALLET THEATRE

TEXT & COMMENTARY BY
CHARLES PAYNE

WITH ESSAYS BY
ALICIA ALONSO
ERIK BRUHN
LUCIA CHASE
NORA KAYE

ALFRED A. KNOPF
NEW YORK, 1978

AMERICAN BALLET THEATRE

FOR
LUCIA CHASE
AND IN MEMORY OF
JOHN KRIZA
WHO BY THEIR EXAMPLES SET THE
CHARACTER OF BALLET THEATRE

THIS IS A BORZOI BOOK PUBLISHED BY ALFRED A. KNOPF, INC.

COPYRIGHT © 1977 BY CHARLES PAYNE
ALL RIGHTS RESERVED UNDER INTERNATIONAL AND PAN-AMERICAN COPYRIGHT CONVENTIONS.
PUBLISHED IN THE UNITED STATES BY ALFRED A. KNOPF, INC., NEW YORK,
AND SIMULTANEOUSLY IN CANADA BY RANDOM HOUSE OF CANADA LIMITED,
TORONTO. DISTRIBUTED BY RANDOM HOUSE, INC., NEW YORK.

PHOTOGRAPHIC ACKNOWLEDGMENTS APPEAR ON PAGES 369–72.

LIBRARY OF CONGRESS CATALOGING IN PUBLICATION DATA
MAIN ENTRY UNDER TITLE: AMERICAN BALLET THEATRE.
INCLUDES INDEX. 1. AMERICAN BALLET THEATRE.   I. PAYNE, CHARLES.
GV1786.A43A44   792.8′4   77–75002
ISBN 0-394-49835-6

MANUFACTURED IN THE UNITED STATES OF AMERICA
FIRST EDITION

ACKNOWLEDGMENTS: This volume has been produced with the collaboration and assistance from the staffs of three organizations: American Ballet Theatre, The Dance Collection of the Performing Arts Research Center at Lincoln Center, and Alfred A. Knopf. Current information has been efficiently and cheerfully supplied by Ballet Theatre's executive secretary, Florence Pettan, by Daryl Dodson, and by Charles France and Elena Gorden of its publicity department. Genevieve Oswald, the curator of the Dance Collection has amassed so prodigious an aggregation of dance material (much of it unique) that it is now difficult to conceive of an authoritative volume on the dance that could be written without recourse to this material and without the assistance of her expert and dedicated staff. This author particularly appreciates the cooperation of Thor E. Wood, chief of the Research Center, in making available the uncatalogued materials from the Ballet Theatre Archives, one of its acquisitions. This volume became the fourth major picture book on the dance edited by Robert Gottlieb, and consequently the author was confident from the start that a book of the highest quality would be produced by Gottlieb and his talented and expert staff: his assistant Martha Kaplan; Knopf's art director Robert Scudellari; production manager Ellen McNeilly; and dance-informed copy editors and proofreaders under the direction of Neal Jones. Thanks are due to Mary Clarke, editor of The Dancing Times of London, for her assistance in tracking down pictures and information abroad, and finally to Selma Jeanne Cohen and A. J. Pischl, whose compilation in Dance Perspectives of the chronology of Ballet Theatre from 1940 through 1965 were of inestimable assistance in assembling this volume. —CHARLES PAYNE

Note: Throughout this text, American Ballet Theatre is identified simply as Ballet Theatre, although its original title was officially The Ballet Theatre and for a period of time it adopted the title American National Ballet Theatre.

LUCIA CHASE AND OLIVER SMITH BECAME ADMINISTRATIVE DIRECTORS IN 1945.

CONTENTS

INTRODUCTION: From the beginning, the element of chance has played a decisive role in the preparation of this book. Chance alone dictated that I should become associated with Ballet Theatre and thus be placed in a position to record its history. Had my friend George Ross Mackenzie Ewing not been in the class below me at the Yale Law School in the 1930s and had he not grown accustomed to rely on me for tutorial lectures of sorts before examinations, he would not have asked my quasi-legal advice whether or not to accept the offer of an executive position made by Lucia Chase in 1940, and thus I would never have become involved with Ballet Theatre.

Neither George nor I ended up as practicing lawyers. I became a member of the New York Bar (just to prove I could do it) but with no intention of practicing. Instead I accepted an offer from Street and Smith Publications and soon became the founding editor of PIC, a picture magazine covering sports, Hollywood, and Broadway.

George's philosophical outlook was not compatible with the practice of law. Like Rafael Sabatini's hero Scaramouche, "He was born with a gift for laughter and a sense that the world was mad." He abandoned the law and became an amateur connoisseur of the arts with the admission, "I don't know what I like, but I know art." When he came in contact with the ballet, he not only knew it was art, but he knew he liked dancers, whom he entertained with expensive dinners at 21 and the Marguery, acquiring thereby a reputation as a wealthy ballet patron. This was not entirely justified since he lived on a modest allowance from his father and was not wealthy by patron standards. In response to an appeal for money from a director of the Ballet Theatre corporation, he made his position clear with respect to contributing, but was equivocal in respect to fund-raising. The telegram read: "I am poor as seven church mice but will write notes beg people for favors and lick any boot that has money behind it." Neither was he a patron if the word was meant to describe one actively engaged in the support of the art of ballet. His sense that the world was mad—particularly the world of ballet—was therefore intensified when he was offered the presidency of a newly formed corporation that was to present Ballet Theatre in a season at the Majestic Theatre. He called on me for help in investigating what dangers lurked behind the offer and what responsibilities he might be committing himself to.

Accordingly, in December 1940 it was arranged for me to meet Lucia Chase Ewing (who, despite the last name, was in no way related to George), but it could not be in the offices because she appeared in the building occupied by Ballet Theatre only in the rehearsal studios as a ballerina: that she sometimes performed managerial functions was a secret she kept from everyone, almost including herself. We met, therefore, next door, in the lobby of the Museum of Modern Art, where she told me that the backers of a proposed season (one of whom was Dwight Deere Wiman) had urged the engagement of a president who could relieve the artistic director, Richard Pleasant, of all financial responsibility and could put the operation on a "sound business basis." There was no suggestion that George himself would be expected to make any substantial financial contribution or that it was contemplated that he could raise money from others.

I reported back to George that as the president of Ballet Theatre he would be in control of and responsible for considerable funds and that the directors of the corporation would certainly be at least hopeful that he could raise money from the wealthy Long Island polo-playing set at whose homes he was a frequent guest. George pointed out that his rich friends were more interested in "improving the breed" of the thoroughbred horse than in assisting the art of ballet. Miss Chase, perhaps because of her persistent belief that a stone could be made to yield blood if subjected to constant pressure, nevertheless continued to urge George to accept the presidency and suggested that if he feared it would entail too-great responsibility, he could bring me along to meetings as a watchdog to guard against Ballet Theatre's imposing on him or vice versa. As a consequence, I began to "sit in" on meetings of Ballet Presentations, the corporate entity which was to present Ballet Theatre at the Majestic Theatre.

At this point, chance again became a decisive factor. The publishers of PIC and I began to differ on policy. In due course I was fired, though the publishers subsequently insisted I had resigned. Within a year the magazine had failed—I like to believe it was a matter of cause and effect—and I had accepted the position of executive manager of Ballet Theatre (at a weekly salary of $75.00), which I retained until I joined the navy in 1943. After a sixty-day training course at Dartmouth College made me a lieutenant (junior grade), I was assigned to the Bureau of Aeronautics in Washington, where I remained throughout the war. (This experience in military bureaucracy was made bearable only by the chance that the desk next to me was occupied by James A. Michener for several years—until he was assigned to a special investigative operation whose principal mission would appear to have been a search for story plots which he employed later in his TALES OF THE SOUTH PACIFIC.)

After VJ Day, I returned to New York with the government's assurance that Ballet Theatre must restore me to my former position or buy me off at a fixed scale of compensation. I chose not to test the effectiveness of this government regulation and consequently never learned whether I would have been rehired. Instead, I took advantage of a situation which, again by chance, came into existence at that moment. Richard Davis, the editor and publisher of the Ballet Theatre souvenir program, had inserted in his most recent contract a precautionary stipulation that he would be relieved of all obligation to furnish programs if S. Hurok ceased to manage the company. In the spring of 1946, when I was released from the navy, Hurok did in fact withdraw as manager, and I was able to present a proposition to the directors: I would edit and publish the program, assuming complete financial responsibility; I would absorb any losses and retain any profits (under some circumstances paying a royalty to Ballet Theatre); I would also make my services available in a managerial capacity at no extra charge. This arrangement had two attractions for me: it allowed me to be my own boss, and, because I had not been hired, I could not be fired. (I even then entertained the suspicion—later confirmed—that being fired was an occupational hazard of ballet managers.) An agreement was reached, and as the souvenir-book publisher, I began to accumulate a collection of ballet photographs that I acquired for the program. I also became familiar with the operational papers of the company as I served in a number of administrative capacities carrying with them important-sounding but not always meaningful titles.

During one of the cyclic interregnums between presidents

(the one position I would never accept when offered), I was the senior officer in charge when the production stage manager (later general manager), Daryl Dodson, by chance decided to consult me before ordering the junking of a half-dozen filing cabinets in our Philadelphia warehouse to make room for some recently acquired scenery. An inspection revealed that the files contained all the correspondence, contracts, and financial records of the Mordkin Ballet from 1937 and for the first year of Ballet Theatre in 1940. Of those most actively engaged in the daily operations of the company at that time, Lucia Chase and I were string-savers, and Daryl Dodson and Florence Pettan (the office manager) were compulsive house-cleaners who believed that mental and physical sanitation dictated the periodic burning of all ancient and therefore irrelevant materials. The string-savers' compulsions won out, and not only were the Mordkin files preserved but unequivocal instructions were issued for all out-dated materials to be similarly preserved. As a consequence, the complete archives of Ballet Theatre are virtually intact, a situation unique in the ballet world. The records of the Diaghilev Ballets Russes, for example, were scattered throughout the world during its nomadic existence; a large portion of the New York City Ballet papers were destroyed in a fire; and the records of other companies have fallen victims of house-cleaners.

With all these materials—photographs and office records—on hand, it was inevitable that I should begin to think in terms of a book. The photographers who had photographed the company had, by the 1960s, attained international fame: Cecil Beaton, Gjon Mili, Richard Avedon, George Platt Lynes, Hurrell of Hollywood, Heinrich of the Argentine, Baron of London, Lido of Paris, et al. In 1964, therefore, I approached a dozen publishers with the suggestion that they consider a book that would outline the history of Ballet Theatre in photographs. All of them professed varying degrees of enthusiasm but all concluded there was not sufficient interest among the general public to make such a picture book marketable.

Subsequently, a detailed study of the rescued Mordkin files revealed that much of what had been written about the creation of Ballet Theatre was as fanciful as various widely accepted versions of the creation of the world. This led me to believe that a textual history of the company would prove instructive and interesting. But it also did not arouse the interest of publishers.

That any book on Ballet Theatre should have been published and that it should have taken its present form was because of an additional series of chance happenings,* the most decisive of which occurred several decades earlier when Robert Gottlieb was taken by his mother to see GISELLE (with Markova) at the Old Met and to see the "suitable-for-boys" ballets (BILLY THE KID and FANCY FREE) at the Rockefeller Center Theatre. This early exposure to ballet infected the future president of Alfred A. Knopf, Inc., with so virulent a strain of balletomania that he has since described himself as a publisher whose true vocation is attending dance performances. By 1976, his publication lists already contained a number of ballet books, including THE NEW YORK CITY BALLET, and he was ready to turn his attention to Ballet Theatre. The decision to publish a book that would survey its history in words and pictures was quickly and easily made. The decision as to what form the book should take was not so hastily arrived at.

Bob Gottlieb was confronted with the question of how to organize a book about a company seemingly so disorganized. Ballet Theatre has had no single creative choreographer whose development could be traced through the years. Neither was its artistic policy one that lent itself to a progressive analytical study. When its founders opted to present an eclectic repertory, they in effect declared that Ballet Theatre would not be bound by any set artistic policy in the generally accepted meaning of the words. Nor was it a company which readily suggested a visual pattern—one that could be viewed through the lens of a single photographer. Through the years, it had been served by as many—and as different—photographers as it had been by choreographers. Eventually, we faced the fact that Ballet Theatre had always been an aggregation of disparate personalities whose aims and accomplishments had been modified from decade to decade. Making a virtue out of necessity, we decided to let the book mirror the company's constantly kaleidoscopic image, to reproduce its infinite variety in photographs loosely grouped into four decades and interspersed with comments by several of the personalities who had contributed to the formation of its character.

While this book as it finally evolved contains more text than I had contemplated, it cannot pretend to offer an exhaustive, definitive history of the company or a critical appraisal of its artistic accomplishments and deficiencies. It is intended, rather, to offer one participant's explanation of how an American ballet company, despite its Topsy-like upbringing, succeeded in attaining maturity. To present in detail all the activities of the company during its four decades—its productions, performances, contract negotiations, financial accounts, et cetera (many of them of equal significance to those recorded here)—would require a text of prohibitive length for this volume. However, the archives remain available, and doubtless some day a more complete chronicle of events will be undertaken and an artistic evaluation made. The mere thought of such a project reminds me of an incident I witnessed when a British family was exiled here during the Second World War. The youngest son caused a panic by swallowing a safety pin. After it was dislodged from his throat and tragedy averted, his mother's relief was followed by mounting anger as she repeated endlessly, "Don't ever do that again!" The repentant youngster listened submissively until the mother's insistence called for a reply, which he offered with confidence: "You know, Mummy, it's not the sort of thing one does more than once!" That he never in fact did it again encourages me in the hope that the writing of a history of Ballet Theatre is not the sort of thing one does more than once, and that if the definitive history is ever written, it will not be by me.

—CHARLES PAYNE

---

*It was also by chance that the archives remained in New York, where they were readily available for research. I had given them to the Dance Collection of the New York Public Library in 1973, but before they were picked up, the possibility arose that the University of Texas might purchase them to add to their theater collection. Since I had not asked for or received approval from the Trustees, the lawyers for Ballet Theatre advised that the gift to the Public Library could be ethically withdrawn. Fortunately, the next president of the Ballet Theatre Foundation, Sherwin Goldman, persuaded the Library that the materials must remain in New York, and the purchase money was raised by New Yorkers. It was therefore only by chance that in writing the text of this volume I was able to make almost daily referrals to the archives, which remained uncatalogued in the basement storage of the Dance Collection instead of being interred in an inaccessible vault in Texas.

AMERICAN BALLET THEATRE

THE ERA OF MIKHAIL MORDKIN

The debut performance of Ballet Theatre on January 11, 1940, at the Rockefeller Center Theatre in Radio City, New York, marked the beginning of a season unique in the annals of ballet. For the first time, the post of choreographer-in-chief was eliminated from the organizational structure of a major ballet company: in the past, the choreographic activities of such companies had always been subject to the despotic control of a principal choreographer. To him was reserved the privilege of creating all new ballets and of selecting and restaging all existing works that were to be introduced into or returned to the repertory—a privilege he guarded jealously. Only occasionally did he permit an assistant or an associate to choreograph on his own, and when he did so, he continued to maintain close supervision over the creative process, thus discouraging originality. The founders of Ballet Theatre instead invited eleven choreographers to stage their ballets independently, with no overriding artistic supervision. The relationship between the choreographers was to be that of equals, and each was to be autonomous. Their activities were to be coordinated by a managing director who would not interfere in matters of choreography and would be prepared only to offer suggestions as to designers and, when required, composers.

This departure from the norm was dictated more by chance and circumstance than by artistic determination or conviction. Ballet Theatre's original organizational pattern was, in fact, designed to accomplish purposes only marginally concerned with artistic considerations. Subsequently, the first managing director, Richard Pleasant, proclaimed his artistic credo and predated a set of principles which, he insisted, had guided his actions in the founding of the company. Commentators and historians have continued to accept his protestations on faith, but in reality the first actions of his company had been instigated by individuals and events more compelling than any theories, however viable, that Pleasant may later have evolved. The influencing characteristics of these individuals included personal ambition, the drive for self-preservation, jealousy, and suspicion. The events included a revolution, the Great Depression, and two world wars. The explanation of why Ballet Theatre was fashioned as it was can best be determined by an examination of how these characteristics and events affected four colorful personalities as they fortuitously converged in New York during the years preceding 1940: Mikhail Mordkin, Rudolf Orthwine, Lucia Chase, and Richard Pleasant.

Mikhail Mordkin was born in Moscow, the son of a violinist in the orchestra at the Bolshoi Theater. He attended the Imperial Ballet School, where he studied under Vassily Tikhomirov, the teacher responsible for the lusty, effusive vigor of Moscow male dancing that was so in contrast to the more restrained and refined style of the dancers at the Maryinsky Theater in Saint Petersburg. Accepted into the Imperial Ballet at the Bolshoi, he rose rapidly to the rank of premier danseur and in 1909 was invited by Serge Diaghilev to appear in his first Saison Russe at the Théâtre du Châtelet in Paris. At the conclusion of this innovative and trend-setting season, he remained in Paris long enough to appear on July 25 with Anna Pavlova in a performance at the Opéra to benefit the victims of the Messina earthquake. This performance was attended by Otto Kahn, then chairman of the board of the Metropolitan Opera Association, who immediately engaged the pair to appear in America in the winter of 1910. Mordkin and Pavlova performed first in New York, dancing at a private party at which Mrs. Harry Payne Whitney entertained 200 guests in her Fifth Avenue home. Two nights later, on February 28, 1910, they made their official debut at the Metropolitan in a two-act version of COPPÉLIA. The ballet followed a performance of Massenet's WERTHER, with the curtain rising at 11 p.m. At the end of their five-week engagement, the couple signed a contract to return to the Metropolitan and to tour the United States for six months during each of the 1910–11 and 1911–12 seasons. Mordkin was to be paid 15,000 francs a month, or $18,000 for each of the six-month periods. As he was then receiving less than $2,000 a year at the Bolshoi, it is not surprising that he should have been quoted by VARIETY, the theater weekly, as asking, "Why should we go back to Russia when we can earn more money here in America in a year than we could earn in Russia in ten years?"

The association between Mordkin and Pavlova lasted two seasons only and was enlivened from the beginning by temperamental clashes on and off the stage. In 1910, at the Valencia Theatre in San Francisco, Pavlova left the stage and refused to return to complete the AUTUMN BACCHANALE with Mordkin. In 1911, at the Palace Theatre in London, it was Mordkin who left the stage and refused to join Pavlova in a performance of the same ballet. The bioscope screen was lowered, and, although the audience protested by walking in front of the projector and obliterating the news pictures with their shadows, no money was returned. However, the en-

gagement and the Pavlova-Mordkin partnership were terminated at the end of the week, with each dancer selecting a new partner from a troupe of Russian Imperial dancers appearing at the Alhambra Theatre: Pavlova engaged Laurent Novikoff, and Mordkin joined up with Catherine Geltzer. As if to demonstrate that their personality clashes could not be attributed exclusively to either partner, within two years Novikoff walked off the stage, not to return, when Pavlova slapped him on the shoulder, and Geltzer broke with Mordkin after only one season.

Mordkin elected to fulfill the Pavlova-Mordkin contract with the Metropolitan for the 1911–12 season, dancing SWAN LAKE, COPPÉLIA, and THE RUSSIAN WEDDING on tour and in New York. After his break with Geltzer, he appeared at the Winter Garden Theatre in New York on a variety bill that also featured Gaby Deslys and Annette Kellerman, who, in her diving act, introduced the one-piece bathing suit to the world of swimming fashion. With his wife, Bronislava Pojitskaya, and with Lydia Lopokova as his partner, he presented a mini-recital of dances that included the AUTUMN BACCHANALE, VALSE CAPRICE, GREEK VARIATIONS, and a GYPSY DANCE. Although the pay was good, the artistic satisfaction was poor; nothing could disguise the fact that his performance was merely an "act," a vaudeville "turn." Consequently, whenever possible, he returned to Moscow for spiritual restoration at the Bolshoi. In 1914 World War I and the Revolution prevented his returning from his last visit to Russia. Along with his fellow dancers, he was exempted from military service and was delegated to "entertaining the troops." At the outbreak of the Revolution, he remained at the Bolshoi (renamed the State Theater) but was soon maneuvered out of his position of authority by proletarian politics. He withdrew to Tiflis, in Georgia, where he was caught in the power struggle between the Bolsheviks and the White Russians. In 1922 a task force of the American Near East Relief Committee found him and his family starving in an abandoned boxcar. His return to Moscow was arranged, but he found that his school had been confiscated by the government and that he was no longer welcomed at the State Theater. Throughout the balance of the Lenin regime he worked successfully with the Moscow Art Theater, but his volatile temperament and egocentric nonconformance threatened his survival under the new Stalin dictatorship. In 1924 he obtained a six-month leave of absence to perform in New York for Morris Gest. He left Russia with his wife and son, Michael, Jr., never to return.

Morris Gest is remembered in theatrical circles as the impresario who was forced into bankruptcy with debts of more than $600,000 as a result of producing Max Reinhardt's THE MIRACLE in 1924, the year he brought Mordkin back to America. He should be, but rarely is, remembered by the dance community as the impresario who first introduced to New York the reformed style of ballet created by Michel Fokine for Serge Diaghilev. He did so in 1911, when he presented plagiarized versions of LES SYLPHIDES, CLEOPATRA,

and SCHÉHÉRAZADE at the Winter Garden with the American vaudeville artist Gertrude Hoffmann as his star. Gest combined the function of producer with that of press agent and, in a day when newspapers would print press releases without investigating their truthfulness, he became a master of colorful exploitation. For instance, earlier, when his client Hoffmann was performing THE VISION OF SALOME at the Hammerstein Roof, he sent out a story that the papers unblushingly printed. It reported that Miss Hoffmann had been on a Forty-second Street crosstown trolley when it caught fire and that in the confusion she had lost her purse. As the purse contained her entire Salome costume, the dance number had to be omitted from the first show.

MORDKIN AND ANNA PAVLOVA IN VALSE CAPRICE, 1912.

In his announcement of the engagement of Mordkin, Gest denied the rumor that the Soviet Union would share in the box-office receipts, tracing its origin to Berlin, where, he reported, Isadora Duncan had denounced Mordkin for deserting the Soviets. Mordkin had retorted, "Miss Duncan cannot dance. That is why she has become a politician." Doubtless, Isadora, who after her conversion to Communism had applied for Soviet citizenship, regarded Mordkin as a traitor to his native land, but at that date she was touring the eastern provinces of Russia and could not have denounced him from Berlin. Doubtless, also, Mordkin believed Duncan could not dance, especially since she had grown fat, but on the date of Gest's release Mordkin was still in the Soviet Union and would not have jeopardized his chances of obtaining an exit permit by maligning the darling of Anatole Lunacharsky, the Commissar of Education in charge of all theatrical arts.

Gest booked Mordkin into the current edition of the Greenwich Village Follies at the Winter Garden, where—as though ten years, a world war, and a revolution had not intervened—he once again performed AUTUMN BACCHANALE, VALSE CAPRICE, et cetera, this time with Lydia Semyonova. Meanwhile, as an outlet for Mordkin's energies and as an added source of income, Morris' brother Simeon Gest organized the Mikhail Mordkin Studio of the Dance Arts, a ballet school located on West Fifty-ninth Street. The inevitable sequence of events ensued: the school produced dancers, the trained dancers required jobs, a ballet company was formed to provide them with employment. During the 1926–27 season,

MIKHAIL MORDKIN IN THE THIRTIES.

the Mordkin Ballet toured the country with a cast of school pupils led by the stars, Mordkin, Vera Nemchinova and Pierre Vladimiroff (graduates of the Diaghilev company), and Hilda Butsova (the English Hilda Boot of the Pavlova company). The tour was arranged by a team of novice concert managers, Bloch and Endikoff, and was managed by Butsova's husband, Harry Mills. Performing a series of one-night stands, the company got as far as the West Coast before staggering home, plagued by poor houses, mounting debts, and sheriffs' attachments. At the beginning of the next season it set off again, this time collapsing only two weeks into the tour, following appearances in Toronto and Montreal. Thereafter, Mordkin confined himself to informal recitals in and around New York until he met Rudolf Orthwine, the father of one of his pupils, Lillian Orthwine.

Rudolf Orthwine's participation in the founding of Ballet Theatre was predetermined by a historical event that occurred seven years before his birth in 1893. In 1886 the Prussian army had invaded the Electorate of Hesse, where Orthwine was later born. Consequently, he was the subject of a militaristic nation dominated by Junkers, who decreed that all males, when they came of age, perform military service: three years in the regular army, four years in the regular reserve, twelve years in the Landwehr (the territorial reserve), and six years in the Landsturm (the local garrison reserve). Early in life, Orthwine resolved that he would be neither a butcher, like his father, nor a soldier. He ran away from home and apprenticed himself to the Schauspielhaus in Berlin, and from there he graduated to the Deutsches Theater of Max Reinhardt. As he approached the age of conscription, he was touring with a company that performed at the Bonn Military Academy. An officer at the academy warned him that with the Kaiser figuratively shaking an iron fist at the rest of Europe and

LUCIA CHASE (FOURTH FROM RIGHT) IN MORDKIN SCHOOL RECITAL.

literally changing uniforms five times a day, it was only a matter of time before he would provoke a war. Orthwine recognized that his acting career might be not only interrupted by military service but terminated by war. As soon as he could save the passage money and arrange for a visa, he sailed for the United States, arriving in New York penniless owing to a shipboard robbery. In New York, an examination of the German-language repertory theater on Irving Place decided him against continuing his acting career in the United States. He found a job in a bakery and, after earning enough money to buy a small hand press, went into the printing business for himself, working out of his home and supplying neighboring merchants such as J. C. Penney and W. T. Grant with billheads and stationery. As his customers' businesses prospered, his orders increased and in time he was operating a

full-scale printing press. Through his association with a new client, a Russian-language newspaper, the RUSSKAYA GAZETTA, he was introduced to the Russian refugee colony in New York City. Among those he met was Mikhail Mordkin, to whom he sent his daughter for ballet lessons when she was in need of physical therapy. In the course of lending support to the school, he made the acquaintance of one of his daughter's fellow students, Lucia Chase.

THE MORDKINS (IN CAR), CHASE, VIOLA ESSEN, AND RUDOLF ORTHWINE.

Lucia Chase was born in Waterbury, Connecticut, the daughter of a clockmaker, Irving Hall Chase. Her interest in the theater dated from her early participation in school dramatics and her weekly attendance at performances of the local stock company. Like two other girls from non-theatrical families, Rosalind Russell of Waterbury and Katharine Hepburn of nearby Hartford, she left her hometown after completing school and went to New York to prepare herself for a professional career in the theater. While attending the Theatre Guild School she also took lessons in singing and, again like Miss Hepburn, attended classes at the Mordkin ballet school. After a number of singing and acting engagements, including a tap-dancing role in a musical that closed on the road, her theatrical career was channeled exclusively toward the ballet. But in the 1930s few professional engagements were available for American dancers. A feature of New York life at the time was the socially sponsored concert series, the best known of which was the Albert Bagby Morning Musicales at the Waldorf Astoria. The Mordkin dancers were engaged by a number of such series, including The Metropolitan Players, which presented its programs in small concert halls: the Barbizon Plaza Concert Hall, the Chanin Theatre, and the Heckscher Theatre at Fifth Avenue and 104th Street. These recitals provided the dancers with an opportunity to appear professionally before a paying

audience and encouraged them to persist with their strenuous ballet training.

By this time Mordkin was training a large number of dancers who required encouragement; he was operating two schools in the city (at the Roerich Museum at 310 Riverside Drive and at the Barbizon Plaza on Fifty-eighth Street) and three in the suburbs. Late in 1935 he attempted his most ambitious school project, the production of a full-evening

LUCIA CHASE IN THE THIRTIES.

version of THE SLEEPING BEAUTY. To appear with himself and Miss Chase, he engaged two dancers with considerable professional experience: Leon Varkas and Dimitri Romanoff. Varkas was born in Kansas but had received his ballet training in the Soviet Union, later performing there for the Workers' Ballets. Romanoff, a native of Russia, emigrated to San Francisco, where he studied ballet with Theodore Kosloff and Maria Baldina. He had danced for Bronislava Nijinska in Max Reinhardt's film version of A MIDSUMMER NIGHT'S DREAM and was concluding a cross-country concert tour with Nina Theilade when Mordkin attended a performance and offered him the role of Prince Desire.

As the pressures mounted to keep his dancers occupied, Mordkin began to dream that there might once more be a Mordkin Ballet, and he was encouraged by Rudolf Orthwine, whose own dream of being active in the theater had not faded as he became successful in business. Even a cursory review of ballet activities in America during the previous twenty-five years should have triggered discouraging warnings. It was a story of repeated financial disaster, and Mordkin himself had been involved in two debacles. In 1911, when Otto Kahn brought him back from Moscow to reappear at the Metropolitan, he was sent out on a preliminary tour managed by Max Rabinoff. It had been contemplated that the tour would be resumed at the conclusion of the Metropolitan performances

in midwinter, but when the time came, Mordkin and Geltzer bowed out. The company continued on with Helena Schmoltz and Alexander Volinine as its stars and with a future ballerina, Lydia Sokolova, in the corps de ballet. After a series of one-night stands through Texas, the tour foundered at the Dauphine Theatre in New Orleans; the scenery and costumes were attached by creditors and the dancers were stranded. In the interval between that time and the collapse of the final Mordkin tour in 1927, the potent forces of Otto Kahn and Serge Diaghilev had combined in 1916 and 1917 to present two tours of Russian ballet headed by Vaslav Nijinsky, who was, in the language of today, a superstar. Both tours were financial disasters, and this despite the fact that they were managed by the tour-wise, experienced staff of the Metropolitan Opera organization. Even Anna Pavlova, the most popular of the touring ballerinas, avoided America during the last seven years of her career, making her final tour of the United States in 1924. For the next ten years, ballet was virtually nonexistent in America, and in 1935 the prospects for the success of a new company would have been forbiddingly bleak had not events of the past several years rekindled false hopes that ballet could pay its own way—or almost.

In December 1933 S. Hurok imported the Ballet Russe de Monte Carlo, successor to the Diaghilev company, and presented it at the St. James Theatre, where it was received by the press with critical reservations and was applauded by enthusiastic but <u>small</u> audiences. The season, with a subsequent short tour, was not a shattering financial disaster, but its American underwriters lost money. A return engagement the following year began at the Majestic Theatre and continued with a lengthened tour. Critical and public response was more favorable, but not until 1935, when it was first performed at the Metropolitan Opera House, did Russian

ballet register as an art form which would, as it had in Europe, amuse the chic set (known in New York as café society) and attract the financial support of wealthy art patrons. During the fourth season, in 1936, the company split in two. The half that proved to be the more stable called itself the Ballet Russe de Monte Carlo and survived until 1963, adhering to ballet tradition in two respects: it retained a choreographer-in-chief (Leonide Massine) and it catered to its principal financial backer. The presence of both these functionaries had always been considered indispensable to the survival of a ballet company. With the Imperial Ballet, the principal backer had been the Tsar, who from his privy purse financed the companies at the Maryinsky Theater and the Bolshoi. Diaghilev had been unsuccessful in finding a permanent principal backer. Forced to unceasingly seek out and enlist a series of backers, he died exhausted, penniless, and disenchanted with the ballet. More fortunately, the Ballet Russe de Monte Carlo was able to retain almost to the end the good will and financial support of Julius (Junkie) Fleischmann, heir to a yeast fortune.

This invasion of the Russian ballet was viewed with alarm and greeted with contempt by Lincoln Kirstein, who, while an undergraduate at Harvard, had developed a hero-worship of Serge Diaghilev and a passionate admiration for his erstwhile star, Vaslav Nijinsky, although he had never seen him in performance. When the Russians arrived in the 1930s, he was collaborating with Nijinsky's wife in the writing of the dancer's biography, and he announced publicly that he regarded the directors of the new companies as unworthy successors to Diaghilev (as an artistic director) or to Nijinsky (as an avant-garde choreographer). In a series of articles, later assembled into a pamphlet titled BLAST AT BALLET: A CORRECTIVE FOR THE AMERICAN AUDIENCE, he condemned these insensitive

DIMITRI ROMANOFF AND CHASE IN THE SEMI-PROFESSIONAL SLEEPING BEAUTY THAT PRECEDED THE FORMATION OF THE MORDKIN BALLET, ANNOUNCED ABOVE.

LEON DANIELIAN AND ADA VEROVA IN MORDKIN'S THE GOLDFISH
AND (TOP) LEON VARKAS AND CHASE IN HIS VERSION OF GISELLE.

heirs of the Russian ballet as ineffectual imitators, incapable of reproducing the masterpieces of the Imperial Ballet or preserving the tradition-breaking productions staged by Diaghilev. His "corrective" was the formation of a new company which would admit to the futility of attempting to preserve the choreographic masterpieces of the past and would concern itself only with new and progressive creations. He did, however, make two concessions to ballet tradition: he engaged a choreographer-in-chief (George Balanchine, a defector from the Ballet Russe de Monte Carlo) and acquired a principal backer (Edward M. M. Warburg). The company, named the American Ballet, made its official debut on March 1, 1935, at the Adelphi Theatre in New York.

These developments changed the picture for both Mordkin and Orthwine. Mordkin, in reviewing the careers of the various choreographers-in-chief, pointed out that, like him, they were all products of the Russian Imperial Ballet and had arrived in western Europe and America via the Diaghilev company. Leonide Massine of the Ballet Russe de Monte Carlo had been trained at the Bolshoi and been Diaghilev's second protégé; Michel Fokine of the Original Ballet Russe (the other half of the split company) and George Balanchine had been members of the ballet at the Maryinsky Theater and had joined Diaghilev as his first and last choreographer respectively. Their qualifications were similar and in no way superior to Mordkin's, or so Mordkin believed, never having admitted to the fact that his talent as a choreographer was minimal. He could boast of having been a star at the Bolshoi (when Victor Gorsky was choreographer-in-chief), and he had performed briefly with Diaghilev. Likewise, Orthwine, after studying the backgrounds of the various managing directors, judged himself to be as well qualified for the position as any of them. After all, Colonel de Basil of the Original Ballet Russe had been, so Hurok told him, a Cossack military policeman. Serge Denham of the Ballet Russe de Monte Carlo, also a Russian refugee, had only recently entered the ballet field after a sequence of business occupations that included those of automobile salesman and bank manager. Lincoln Kirstein had been a dilettante publisher, and Eddie Warburg, a classmate of Kirstein's at Harvard, was the son of the very rich banker, Felix Warburg. Orthwine, on the other hand, had not only been a successful businessman but he could lay claim to theater experience on the basis of his short career as a professional actor in Germany. Confident of their qualifications, Mordkin and Orthwine asked themselves, "Why not?" If the others were prepared to gamble on the American public's receptivity to ballet, why should they not do the same? Accordingly, they organized the Advanced Arts Ballets, Inc., to present the new Mordkin Ballet. The stationery, printed by the Rudolf Orthwine Corporation, listed Rudolf Orthwine as managing director, Frank Cruikshank as general manager, and Michael Mordkin, Jr., as business director. Mordkin took the title neither of choreographer-in-chief nor of artistic director. His name appeared as follows:

THE MORDKIN BALLET
CHOREOGRAPHY AND DIRECTION
MIKHAIL MORDKIN

The corporation engaged the Majestic Theatre in New York, where it presented performances on April 4, 6, 8, and 10, 1937. Two ballets were performed on each evening: Mordkin's version of GISELLE and his THE GOLDFISH, which was based on Victor Gorsky's choreographic rendition of a poem by Alexander Pushkin. The company of forty-seven was headed by Mordkin, Lucia Chase, Viola Essen (a youthful protégée of Mordkin), Dimitri Romanoff, and Leon Varkas. The reviews in the press were favorable, the receipts in the box office barely visible—for the second performance 105 tickets were sold to produce a gross of $161.50. After the New York engagement, the company toured as far south as Washington, D.C., giving six performances in as many cities. At no time did the gross receipts rise above $700 for a performance. The high expenses and low receipts might have discouraged the continuance of the venture had not the company been engaged to appear for a guaranteed fee with the Philharmonic Symphony Orchestra at Lewisohn Stadium of the College of the City of New York under the sponsorship of an organization headed by Mrs. Charles S. (Minnie) Guggenheimer. The program on the two evenings was made up of THE GOLDFISH and a series of divertissements—recital pieces similar to those that had been so successfully performed by Anna Pavlova on tour. Again the reviews were favorable, but even more encouraging was the attendance. The New York Times reported that more than 6,000 persons were present at the second performance, and there is nothing like the applause of an audience of that size to convince an impresario that the show must go on. Orthwine was convinced, but he realized that he and Mordkin required help. With Mordkin occupied with the rehearsals of new ballets and Mordkin, Jr., engaged as an employee in Orthwine's printing business, it became necessary to find someone who could direct his full attention to the Mordkin studio. Dimitri Romanoff recommended Richard Pleasant for the job.

IN REHEARSAL, MORDKIN (RIGHT) DEMONSTRATES HIS CHARACTERISTIC EBULLIENCE.

RICHARD PLEASANT IN THE THIRTIES.

Richard Pleasant was born in Denver, Colorado, and at the age of nine traveled across the Continental Divide to Maybell, in the northwest corner of the state, where his father became proprietor of a general merchandise store. An uncle who was an alumnus of Princeton sent him to that university, from which he was graduated with honors in architecture in 1932, at a time when there was little building in the country, still morassed in the Great Depression, and architectural firms offered no jobs. Pleasant worked where and as he could: as a cadet on the Matson Lines, running from Canada to Australia; as tutor in a wealthy California family; as a trainee with Shell Oil in San Francisco; and finally as an aspirant to movie fame. Dimitri Romanoff remembered him as a supernumerary performing with the San Francisco Opera Company and later around the movie studios in Hollywood, where he perhaps entertained the hope that some sharp-eyed director might "discover" him and start him off on a career similar to that of his classmate, James Stewart. Agnes de Mille remembers him only as a "lanky youth who answered the phone and kept the studio bookings" at the Perry Dance Studio. Pleasant himself spoke of more significant Hollywood activity when he wrote to Nana Gollner in 1937: "I doubt if you will remember me although you may remember the incident of my taking you and Dimitri Romanoff out to United Artists for an audition with Russell Lewis." (Years later, when he was asked to contribute to the Twenty-fifth Year Book of his class, Pleasant summed up his experience with: "I tried to straighten out the Motion Picture Industry, but instead flattened myself out.") After Hollywood he taught English for a year at the University of Wyoming. In the fall of 1937 he was in Chicago when the Mordkin Ballet gave two performances at the Studebaker Theatre and renewed his acquaintance with Dimitri Romanoff, who introduced him to Rudolf Orthwine and Lucia Chase. There was some vague talk about his joining the enterprise, talk that culminated a month later in a telegram from Orthwine asking whether he had been sincere in the

interest he had expressed in working with Mordkin. His reply is reproduced in full because it offers a first indication of his personality and of his intentions:

Hartsel, Colo.
9-IX-1937

Dear Mr. Orthwine:

I received your telegram last night after it had made, I am afraid, a very roundabout trip. For the past three weeks, since I left Chicago, I have been vacationing in the Southwest country in out-of-the-way parts and much of my mail has been lost or delayed.

The possiblity of working with the Mordkin company has interested me very much. So has your continued interest pleased me. However, I have been, and still am, unable to commit myself for lack of any definite information. I have never known whether the job you proposed was to be manager of the company while on tour or of the Carnegie Hall Studio during Mr. Mordkin's absence. Neither have I known what salary you propose to pay.

Much as I am interested in the "cause" I do not feel that I would be able to come to New York for less than $250 a month and a six-month guarantee—

With the split of the De Basil and the Massine-Blum companies and the increasing interest in ballet in the United States this promises to be an excellent year. Whether I am with you or not, I wish you and the company prosperity and a big success.

Yours very sincerely,
R. H. M. PLEASANT

Address until October first:
3040 Albion Street
Denver, Colorado

The use of the European-style date, the elegant handwriting, and the three-initial signature (which he abandoned immediately thereafter) made the letter appear more like a communication from "my noble lord" than from an applicant for a $60-a-week job tending a dance studio. It was the sort of stiff-upper-lip pose that jobless college graduates were forced to affect during the Depression, but with Pleasant the affectation approached pretension. What was indicated by his letter of September 9, 1937, was confirmed on actual acquaintance: he was reserved, dignified (when in full control of himself), shy, introverted, erudite, and somewhat stuffily self-important. He could not have been more different from his new colleagues, the ebullient and extroverted Mordkin, Orthwine, and Chase.

Pleasant accepted the job without any clear definition of its duties, which were kept vague intentionally in deference to Mordkin's paranoia. Having once had his school and company confiscated by the Soviets, Mordkin resisted the introduction of anyone who might be capable of executing another take-over. On the other hand, it was not Pleasant's intention to make a career of dance studio management; his ambitions were toward the directorship of a ballet company. That he might have been given some encouragement in this respect is indicated by a cryptic sentence in one of Orthwine's letters to Lucia Chase. He reports that Pleasant is very cordial and businesslike with everyone, that the school runs like clockwork, and that the classes are full, and then he adds: "So there are hopes that the boy will make a good man for us." During the first three months of his employment Pleasant

remained the efficient boy in the school while the company went on tour, to appear in thirty-three cities with gratifying artistic success and disastrous financial failure. In his spare time he prepared to assume the man's role foreseen for him by Orthwine. He assembled a dance library, including the flood of books on Diaghilev that had been published recently and from which would emerge the myth of the Great Director. Just as every sandlot player looked upon Babe Ruth as a model, and every street-corner punk dreamed of becoming an Al Capone, so did every aspiring ballet director pattern himself after Diaghilev. Pleasant was no exception, and by the time the Mordkin Ballet set out on its third tour of eight cities in January 1938, he considered himself fully equipped to assume the role of the American Diaghilev. But like Diaghilev, who had run into the opposition of the ballet establishment when he first became connected with the Imperial Ballet, Pleasant stirred up resentment when, for example, he issued his own press releases, thus stepping on the toes of the press agent (an old-timer who had managed the first Pavlova-Mordkin tour), and when he encroached on Mordkin's domain by sending instructions for the lighting of scenery directly to the stage electrician.

Unlike Diaghilev, who was dismissed as an assistant director of the Maryinsky Theater, Pleasant survived the attack by the establishment, and before the company began its fourth tour in October 1938, he had been elected secretary of Advanced Arts, Inc., and could speak with authority. He arranged for the company to appear in New York at the conclusion of the tour (which once again lost money). Six performances were given at the Hudson Theatre on consecutive Sunday evenings beginning on January 8, 1939. Scaled at a $3 top, the house could gross $2,352 per performance, about $14,000 for the season. In those days, when a stagehand was paid only $10.25 a performance and a corps de ballet dancer received $20 a week, the engagement could have broken even at 75 percent of capacity, or about $10,500. However, only 14 percent of the tickets were sold, to produce a total gross of not quite $2,000 for the six performances. At the next meeting of the directors of Advanced Arts Ballets, Inc., it came as no surprise to anyone when the lawyer for the principal backer announced that those activities of the Mordkin company that were not self-supporting could no longer be underwritten.

This decision was not made public because the principal backer had always insisted on anonymity. Other principal backers had been less reticent. It was common knowledge in the ballet world that the Original Ballet Russe was backed by Baron Frederic d'Erlanger, the Ballet Russe de Monte Carlo by Julius Fleischmann, and the American Ballet by Edward Warburg and Lincoln Kirstein himself, who was one of the heirs of the fortune derived from the Filene Department Store of Boston. But few people knew of the extent of Lucia Chase's financial contribution to the Mordkin Ballet, because Miss Chase wished it so.

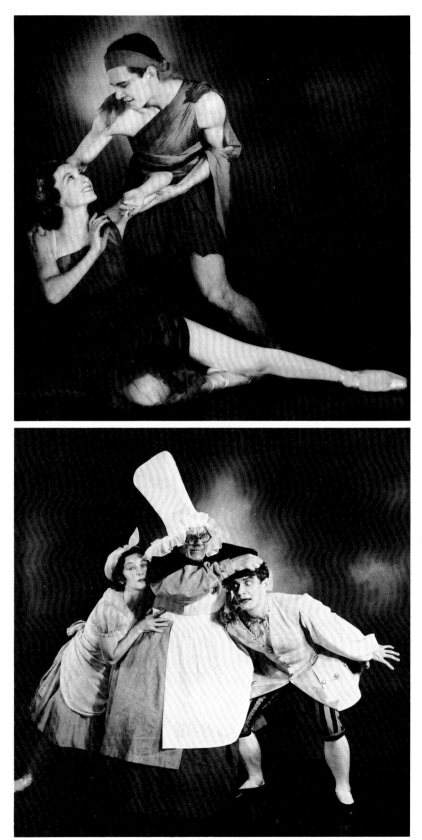

CHASE AND ROMANOFF WITH MORDKIN IN HIS VERSION OF
LA FILLE MAL GARDÉE AND (TOP) IN HIS OWN BALLET DIONYSIUS.

Miss Chase was obsessed with a single overriding wish—to become a professional dancer. And it was clear to her what constituted a professional in contrast to an amateur. A professional was one whose attention away from home was riveted on the dance: training, rehearsing, and performing—engaging in these activities with exclusive, almost compulsive, concentration and dedication. A professional attended classes regularly, arrived on time for rehearsals, and devoted unremitting attention to the choreographer's instructions. Before performances, she arrived early to warm up and to take scrupulous care in applying makeup and donning costumes, and during performances, she made entrances on cue and, above all, continually danced full out and strove to maintain a complete characterization as though every discriminating eye in the audience was constantly focused on her alone. Miss Chase was aware that her fellow professionals did not always act professionally—she witnessed Jerome Robbins, for example, behaving with levity at rehearsals,* she was there when Nana Gollner would arrive at the theater fifteen minutes before she was due to make her first entrance in SWAN LAKE, and she observed lapses from professional behavior when dancers dropped out of character in the erroneous belief that no one in the audience was watching them. And there were occasions when Miss Chase, being human, also lapsed from the professional and there would appear on the call board notices such as, "Chase and Orloff fined $2.00 for missing entrance in BLUEBEARD." But in general, throughout her dancing career her behavior in rehearsal halls and on stage earned from her fellow dancers the unquestioned acknowledgment of thorough professionalism.

Miss Chase's professionalism also expressed itself in a continuing drive toward the acquisition of new roles to be danced, or at least to be understudied. It may be assumed that all dancers are ambitious and are persistently demanding new roles, but this is not true. There are those who remain indifferent because they did not themselves choose the career of dancing but had it chosen for them, and there are those who are too modest, too lazy, or too easily content. Miss Chase was never one of these. She was prepared to try anything and she <u>was</u> demanding—but never more so than her confreres who were ambition-driven to advance their careers. Career-wise, she won some and lost some. Fokine, Tudor, and de Mille cast her in their ballets, Balanchine and Robbins did not.

There was one respect in which Miss Chase differed, though not uniquely so, from the large majority of her fellow dancers. Like her, a few others were wives and mothers and as such were faced with the problem of reserving an equal

*While a veteran Russian choreographer was creating a new work during the company's summer residency in Mexico, Payne was delegated to remonstrate with Robbins, then in the corps de ballet, over his inattentive and distracting behavior during rehearsals. Payne: "Some day you'll be a choreographer. How will you feel if dancers behave badly during your rehearsals?" Robbins: "If I give them such stupid choreography to dance, I won't blame them." His tolerance was never tested because he never produced stupid choreography.

MORDKIN, IN HIS PAJAMA-TOP REHEARSAL COSTUME, WITH NINA STROGANOVA, PATRICIA BOWMAN, LUCIA CHASE, KAREN CONRAD.

share of their attention for their families while their profession demanded their concentration during daytime rehearsals, evening performances, and periodic tours out of town.* They made the necessary adjustments, but Miss Chase went even further than most in her determination to keep her professional and private lives completely separate. There were moments when this gave rise to second thoughts. One Thanksgiving Day, for example, she called home from a drugstore phone booth in East Lansing, Michigan, when her family and guests were about to sit down to a traditional turkey dinner. After cheerful conversations with everyone, she hung up and seated herself at the counter, where she ordered a bacon-lettuce-and-tomato sandwich, thought unenthusiastically ahead to the evening's performance on the inadequate platform stage of the local high school, and wondered whether it was all worth it. Perhaps it was on one such occasion that a tentative suggestion was offered by her mother, who had brought her daughters up with the admonition that in whatever they undertook they should strive to be the best. She once (and only once) suggested that perhaps Lucia should modify her ambition to that of becoming the best amateur dancer. Lucia's reply was unequivocal. She would be a professional or nothing. As long as she remained a dancer

*On one tour, a ballerina attempted to solve her problem by taking her five-year-old son along with her. Things did not work out too badly but the impracticability of the solution became apparent when the house manager of the theater in Hartford came to Charles Payne with the complaint that a child from backstage was in the audience, crawling under seats to pinch the ladies' legs.

only (before she became a director), she acted like a dancer, rooming on tour with a fellow dancer and, like her roommate, living on her salary alone.

To be a professional dancer was the ultimate of Miss Chase's ambition: she had no suppressed desire to become a choreographer and no pretensions to becoming an artistic director. Comparatively few dancers think of themselves as potential choreographers, but a large portion of those who attain stardom believe they are qualified to perform at least some directorial functions. They will offer ideas as to what ballets the company should produce, what creative artists it should commission, and what dancers it should engage. Miss Chase did not believe such functions were within her competence and she would contentedly have left them to others had not circumstances forced her gradually to perform them. These circumstances arose from a combination of the facts of life in the ballet world in which she found herself:

Ballet companies could not be self-supporting.

Although many patrons were asked to contribute to the support of ballet, comparatively few responded (as compared to the number of those who contributed to hospitals, schools, or even opera companies).

As one of those comparatively few who contributed to the support of the Mordkin Ballet and later of Ballet Theatre, Miss Chase as an intelligent contributor was forced to concern herself with whether her contributions were wisely spent.

There was a limit to what Miss Chase could contribute and

there was no assurance that her support could continue indefinitely.*

Had the executives of the companies been more successful in their fund-raising, Miss Chase would have been willing, indeed eager, to disassociate herself from any concern with the artistic or financial management. In fact, during recurrent periods when sufficient independent financing materialized, she did disassociate herself. At such times she remained contentedly in the dark (except for the announcements and rumors available to any other dancer) as to the management's plans and as to how well it had things under control.

Unfortunately it all too often transpired that things had not been kept under control. Expenses had been underbudgeted while box-office receipts and contributions had been overestimated, with the inevitable result that funds would become exhausted and, after a brief period of existing on extended credit, the management would be left with no alternative but to close down operations. The responsibility for making this drastic decision took the same course as Harry Truman's buck—it stopped on Lucia Chase's desk. In passing the buck to her, the management in effect was announcing that, having investigated and exhausted all potential sources of support, it must now cease operations unless Miss Chase was once more prepared to bail them out. Miss Chase was never so prepared, but she has always allowed herself to be so persuaded.

On the other hand, her early training and New England background made her constitutionally incapable of permitting herself to contribute blindly. The instructions she received from her father and the examples he set for fiscal conservatism have always exerted a controlling influence on her. He had cautioned her never to sign a document without reading it and had shown his respect for money by making entries in a pocket notebook of even the smallest daily expenditure. In entering into agreements to finance Ballet Theatre projects, Miss Chase always carefully read the documents prepared by lawyers and, aside from passages written in legalese incomprehensible to laymen, she understood them. Similarly, in persuading herself that there was a reasonable prospect that

LEON DANIELIAN, LATER DIRECTOR OF THE BALLET THEATRE SCHOOL.

the money would be spent wisely, she meticulously examined proposed budgets and, again, except for some incomprehensible accountantese (depreciation, amortization, capital surplus, etc.) she was able to understand them. She diligently studied the figures (in the new accounting jargon always referred to as "numbers") with a considerable firsthand knowledge of the reasonableness of the proposed expenditures, but she did so resentfully and grudgingly because the process diluted her concentration on her career as a professional dancer. She discovered early in that career that when it became known that she was a substantial contributor, her dancing activities were intruded upon. There were always those importunate ones who would confront her with business questions that should have been addressed only to the management, and there were even some inexperienced members of the business staff who would commit the unpardonable error of having her called out of rehearsal to discuss a business decision. That this might compromise her professional status and set her apart from her fellow dancers was the principal motivation for her desire for anonymity as a contributor. But there were a number of other reasons that argued against any disclosure.

The knowledge of the extent of Miss Chase's contributions could not fail to have an effect on others. It could cause potential contributors to bow out with the excuse, "Let Lucia do it. She can afford it." And it could lead to an increased

---

*No one but Miss Chase herself and her lawyers have ever known with certainty the extent to which she was limited in her ability to make contributions. In the absence of any disclosure by her, the estimates that have appeared in print from time to time have necessarily been based on newspaper accounts. In 1929 the New York Times reported that Alexander Smith Cochrane, president of the Alexander Smith Carpet Company, had left an estate valued at $35 million, of which $19.6 million was willed to his eldest and favorite nephew, Thomas Ewing, Jr. When Mr. Ewing died, less than four years later, it was again reported by the press that the estate had shrunk considerably as a result of income taxes and the Depression: there remained only $4.5 million, which was divided by Mr. Ewing's will into three one-million-dollar trusts for his widow, Lucia Chase, and their two sons, with a proviso that the widow should also be the residuary heir. Presumably the Times was accurately informed, but it is impossible to estimate the amount of income available to Miss Chase at any one time without further information as to the effect on the estate of subsequent recessions and boomlets and of the success or failure of investments. Miss Chase will say only that her husband's forethought in establishing the trusts with untouchable assets has contributed to her peace of mind at times when the ballet's appetite became too voracious. But with respect to the residual estate she is not—like a number of other ballet backers of note—protected against the demands of ballet or against her own inclinations by the trustees of a private foundation or by the executors of a spendthrift trust. Though she may listen to advice, the final decision whether to make further contributions even if it involves the sale of capital assets always remains hers alone.

LEON VARKAS AS ALAIN IN LA FILLE MAL GARDÉE.

demand on her resources, since the customary procedure in preparing a contribution appeal is first to determine how much the donor can afford to give and then to budget the donee's needs accordingly. But perhaps one of Miss Chase's most compelling motives for retaining anonymity arose, once again, out of her New England background. To her friends and relatives in Waterbury, Connecticut, the ballet was a branch of the theater. To them, ballet was show business and they took the word "business" seriously. That one should continue to invest money in a losing business was, to a New Englander, if not sinful at least foolhardy, and a seemingly reckless dissipation of capital assets was almost un-American, a cause for embarrassment. When Miss Chase was forced to participate in the financial affairs of the company, she stressed fiscal conservatism but did so somewhat in the manner of Lyndon Johnson when he economized by going about the White House turning out lights before returning to his desk to sign an authorization for the spending of billions in Vietnam. An early letter to Richard Pleasant, in which she was in fact not interfering in business concerns but merely acting as an interpreting messenger, gives some indication of her thought processes as a businesswoman. The letter began, "Mr. Mordkin says Helene Pons Studio has sent costume contract to you and it's O.K.—so you can sign it." It concluded with, "You'd better make the agreement to start <u>when</u> she [Stroganova] returns to New York. No use paying her when

she is here and she has no expenses." The costumes were for a new production of LA FILLE MAL GARDÉE and would cost thousands. The ballerina, Nina Stroganova, was at Narragansett, Rhode Island, rehearsing with the principals in a barn owned by Miss Chase's mother. The saving on her rehearsal salary was in the neighborhood of $22 weekly.

Miss Chase's strivings toward anonymity were not wholly successful but they did serve to conceal from the public the extent to which her voice was decisive in the affairs of Ballet Theatre. Because financial crises arose with cyclic regularity she was repeatedly required to decide whether she would advance funds and on what terms. In stating the terms, she in effect, for better or worse, made most of the vital decisions that dictated the course of the company's progress through the years. It was for the better in 1942 (before she became a director) when she insisted that Tudor's PILLAR OF FIRE must proceed in production despite the objections of the general manager, German Sevastianov, and in face of the contempt of S. Hurok, who referred to it as PILLS OF FIRE. It was for the better in 1968 when she overruled an artistic committee (of which Agnes de Mille and Jerome Robbins were members) and insisted that the company should produce a complete SWAN LAKE. It was for the worse in 1947 when she turned down Morton Baum's invitation for the company to become the resident ballet company of the New York City Center. She opted instead for a return to the Metropolitan Opera House and thus lost out on the opportunity of later acquiring an official residency at the New York State Theater. Over the years, her unrealistic disavowal of the exercise of any managerial control has confused the picture. As a result, she has not always been charged with the company's mistakes and conversely has not always been accorded the credit for its successes.

At the meeting of Advanced Arts Ballets, Inc., in March 1939, when the decision to curtail its activities was announced by the treasurer, Harry M. Zuckert (who doubled as Miss Chase's lawyer), there was no doubt in the minds of Mordkin, Orthwine, or Pleasant that the decision had, in fact, been made by Lucia Chase. Orthwine was informed in a letter from Richard Pleasant which read, in part:

The Board of Directors has looked over the statement for 1938; and the prospects for 1939. The result of this and of Lucia's advisors has been that she cannot make any further investments beyond the settled running expenses without their approval.

This means that she will bear the expenses of studio, accompanists, insurance, etc., and the retaining salaries of 16 dancers between now and December 31, 1939—but that she cannot finance any other venture either in New York or on the road.

We have, therefore, a plant, scenery, costumes, music and 16 dancers which will be given free for us to work into any plan or type of production . . . that much headstart toward a new venture.

This was not the first time, and certainly not the last, when Miss Chase found herself in a quandary: determined not

to be committed to open-ended spending, but equally determined that a company that had been brought to an encouraging degree of excellence through the expenditure of much effort and money must be given one last chance to survive. The proposal was designed, in effect, to provide her with the protection of limited liability and it was readily approved by Pleasant, who may even have suggested the maintenance of the small group. His research had informed him that while the Diaghilev company was touring America in 1917 under the direction of Nijinsky, Diaghilev himself had retired to Spain with a small group that rehearsed new ballets with Massine. Orthwine regarded the proposal as reasonable and generous. Mordkin sulked, and his instincts for self-preservation urged him to seek out alternative sponsors.

It was agreed that approval would be forthcoming for a short tour in the fall or winter of 1939 provided it could be booked under a guaranteed arrangement whereby the company would receive a fixed fee for each performance. In other words, the Mordkin Ballet must gain entrance into the network system of community concert series, which alone offered some assurance that a tour could be undertaken with a reasonably accurate estimation and control of losses. This system had evolved through the efforts of groups of citizens in cities and towns across the country who were eager to have cultural attractions perform in their auditoriums. Usually there was one among these citizens whose interest in the attractions was enhanced by the prospect of making a personal profit out of them. He or she, who became known as a "local concert manager," approached his or her fellow citizens with the proposition: "If you will subscribe to all performances and pay for your tickets in advance, I will use the money to engage five or six concert attractions and to pay all the expenses involved." If no such enterprising citizen was available, a committee was appointed to perform the functions of the local manager. The national managers in New York were next approached. They were dominated by Hurok Attractions, which worked with the National Broadcasting Company, and the Columbia Concerts Corporation, owned by the Columbia Broadcasting System and managed by F. C. Coppicus. If the local manager or committee chairman was unenterprising or lazy, he would obtain all his attractions from one office by making the simple request, "Give me a soprano, a tenor, a violinist or pianist, a vocal group, and a dance attraction." If he was more knowledgeable and discriminating, he might approach Hurok, for example, with the demand, "All I want from you is the Ballet Russe de Monte Carlo," only to receive the reply, "From me you get the Ballet Russe de Monte Carlo only if you also take my very young pianist, John Doe, and my very old violinist, Ivan Ivanovitch." Or he might answer, "You can't have the Ballet Russe de Monte Carlo; it's fully booked. But I can let you have the Mordkin Ballet, which is just as good or better and will keep your subscribers just as happy." In later years the New York managers spoke less bluntly, having come under the threat of antitrust prosecutions.

The Mordkin Ballet had made previous attempts to gain entry into the system. Its tour in the fall of 1938 had, in fact, been managed by Columbia Concerts, but the agreement had been made too late for Columbia to place the company on concert series for all its engagements. Its artistic merit was not an important factor, because artistic merit did not exert a decisive influence in the system. When local managers were given the little latitude allowed them in choosing attractions, they chose on the basis of faith in the advice of the national manager or of reliance on the reviews of New York critics. Their subscribers were captive audiences at the single performance given in their city and were afforded no opportunity to express their approval or disapproval by attending or staying away from a second performance. Nor did they have the opportunity the following year, when an entirely new set of attractions would make up the series. Accordingly, when S. Hurok was approached with the request that he book the Mordkin Ballet for a series of guaranteed performances, he was not particularly concerned with the company's artistic merit. The Mordkin Ballet had received reviews from New York critics that, if not unqualifiedly enthusiastic, contained words of praise which could be effectively quoted. Also the company had the asset of the Mordkin name, which could be associated with Pavlova and the Imperial Russian Ballet. Hurok did not decline to take on the Mordkin company because he thought that he could not sell it or that it was not up to Hurok standards. Morris Permut, the company's lawyer who dealt with Hurok, recalls that negotiations broke down when Hurok was shown a copy of the first dancers' union agreement, which Pleasant was about to sign and which would have raised the fee the company would have required. Later experience suggests that Hurok's decision was influenced primarily by the fact that he was not yet convinced that Lucia Chase's advisors thoroughly understood the basic proposition that even when managed by Hurok, a ballet company could lose money, and that the loss must be borne by the company, not by Hurok. Two years later, when he entered into an agreement with the successor company, Ballet Theatre, and booked its first tour, he was grieved to discover that its lawyer-treasurer, Harry M. Zuckert, still did not understand that Hurok Attractions must not be expected to share any losses even though it appeared to be so obligated under the terms of the contract.

With its own dismissal of Columbia Concerts and its rejection by Hurok, the Mordkin Ballet was for all practical purposes excluded from the community concerts system. Pleasant, however, continued his efforts to arrange some sort of guaranteed engagements outside New York. He negotiated with Fortune Gallo, with the junior booking office Embree Concert Service, Inc., and with the Chicago Opera Company (suggesting that the Mordkin company serve as the opera ballet). And then, in 1939, while the search for engagements was still in progress, Orthwine met a Russian expatriate, Alexander Kahn, at a party at the Russian Tea Room.

Kahn had left Russia soon after his graduation from the university in Saint Petersburg and had worked first in London with the London Times, and during World War I in Boston with the Boston Post and the Boston Opera Company, and in Chicago with the Chicago Opera. At the conclusion of the war, he returned to Europe, remaining for the next twenty years in Paris, where he established himself as an agent-manager for concert artists, the most prominent of whom was Grace Moore. With a second world war looming in 1939, he came back to New York, where he was engaged as foreign editor of the concert weekly MUSICAL AMERICA. Pleasant hired Kahn as "a liaison and promotional officer" with a salary of $45 a week. Whether or not Pleasant foresaw it from the start, Kahn was to prove valuable to him in a number of areas: as a supporter in his negotiations with the directorate; as an ally in the developing power struggle with Mordkin; and as his envoy to the European and refugee Russian ballet circles to which Pleasant did not have easy access.

The directorate of Advanced Arts (the formal designation of Lucia Chase's advisors) had had no previous association with theatrical business and they were aware that Pleasant's experience was limited. When he expounded on his artistic theories, they were impressed and found no reason to quarrel, but their confidence in him did not extend to his business acumen. Kahn, on the other hand, was mature and had been associated with theatrical business for at least forty years. Further, he had been a classmate of Diaghilev, whose career in Paris he had followed at close range. This fact impressed Pleasant more than it did the directorate, to whom it was not particularly germane. To them the important factor was Kahn's Russian nationality. Before he began importing the English Royal Ballet, Hurok had been fond of pointing out, "When Americans want champagne, they want French champagne. When they want ballet, they want Russian ballet." There was truth in what he said, and he might have added, "When Americans want ballet managers, they want Russian ballet managers." In any event, when the time came in the summer of 1939 for the directorate to consider Pleasant's fantastic plan for Ballet Theatre, they might have rejected it out of hand had it not been seconded by Kahn, a Russian ballet expert who was also, as Pleasant described him, "a seasoned theatrical man."

Lucia Chase's professional relations with Mordkin had not always run smoothly. She deferred to him absolutely in artistic matters, but occasional conflicts ensued when she encroached, however deferentially, on what he considered to be his managerial or business preserves. In the artistic field Mordkin exercised the powers of a dictator. In management and business operations he professed a willingness to act under certain restrictions and limitations. However, he interpreted these restrictions as meaning that instead of issuing direct orders or making direct purchases, he must inform the business director, his son Michael, Jr., who would explain the request to the president, Rudolf Orthwine, who would in turn advise the principal backer, Lucia Chase, to issue the check that would increase the company's bank account. If there was any misfunctioning in the chain of command and his request was denied, Mordkin would turn sullen or, more likely, issue the order to make the purchase without authorization. When Richard Pleasant was added to the chain of command, Mordkin resisted and resented him. This is revealed in an early memorandum from Orthwine to Michael, Jr.:

The lawyer instructed and convinced Lucia that she had to have a man to watch her cash outlays in the ballet business. . . . So Lucia called me last week and said what the lawyer told her and she demanded that there be a man to look after her interests—and told me she told Mordkin she was getting the man, asking me to telegraph Pleasant which I did. . . . I have spent more time in the ballet studio and with the lawyers particularly, protecting Dad's [Mordkin, Sr.'s] interest than I did here [his own office] —yet war broke out this morning because your father seems annoyed that he did not know about Pleasant through me.

An easy rapport was never established between Mordkin and Pleasant. Mordkin's paranoia and Pleasant's inability to make friends easily kept them at arm's length. At one period of negotiations, Pleasant reported to Zuckert:

Miss Chase, Mr. Permut and Mr. Kahn spent almost five hours with Mickey Mordkin battling out the terms of a new contract with Mordkin Sr. . . . I did not take part in any of the discussion as Mickey says that my comments on his and his father's behavior in this matter were insulting and that therefore he can never talk to me again.

Once more Kahn proved his value to Pleasant. In refereeing a dispute between Mordkin and Pleasant, the directors were likely to take into consideration the latter's youthful impetuosity, his animosity toward Mordkin, and his personal ambitions, and these might have prejudiced them against his arguments. Such was not the case with Kahn. He was no brash, inexperienced young man seeking to dethrone a superior whom he held in contempt. He was a fellow Russian and a contemporary of Mordkin's and, at sixty-seven, was surely not impelled by personal ambition. When, therefore, he recommended in a memorandum of July 10 that Pleasant's power be increased, he was listened to. And Pleasant, submitting Kahn's memorandum, could convincingly comment:

The present memo is not only an up-to-date report on the state of the Mordkin Ballet, but also has value as the findings of a seasoned theatrical man who sees the Ballet with the fresh eyes of an efficiency expert.

The memo read in part:

I suggest further that the organization of the ballet administration be put on a thoroughly businesslike basis. The purely administrative end and the artistic direction should be distinct from one another although maintaining a thoroughly cooperative spirit. To this end I would suggest the naming of an executive secretary, responsible to the Board of Directors, but with power enough to put in force his coordinating duty.

Kahn did not presume to suggest who the executive secretary should be, but there could have been no doubt that Pleasant was his candidate.

The value of Kahn's acquaintanceships with artists abroad first became evident when he was able to inform Pleasant that Gordon Mendelssohn, member of a European banking family, was considering the organization of a small ballet company which would star the Polish dancer Yurek Shabelevski. Obviously an association between Mendelssohn and the Mordkin Ballet would be mutually beneficial. The former could present his protégé to better advantage with the full-scaled and already established Mordkin company, which in turn could more productively employ the capital that would have been invested in the small company. The mere possibility that Pleasant might be able to effect the association with Mendelssohn strengthened his position in the company and made it all the more likely that he would continue to receive support from Lucia Chase. For if anything could persuade her to remain as principal backer of the company, it would be the introduction of an additional backer whose contribution was sufficiently substantial to encourage the hope that someday she would be relieved of total financial responsibility. (This hope was destined to spring eternally during the next quarter of a century, but in 1939 it was a fresh hope.) Thus if Pleasant succeeded in associating Mendelssohn and his capital with the Mordkin Ballet, he would be everyone's fair-haired boy.

In addition, the association with Mendelssohn offered a fringe benefit of which Pleasant was not immediately aware: it could advance his ambition to become the American Diaghilev, a goal toward which he had been making little progress because of the barriers Mordkin, purposely or unconsciously, had been erecting in his path. It was, for example, a source of bitter frustration for a would-be Diaghilev that as late as mid-July, with rehearsals scheduled to commence momentarily, he had to urge Mordkin, Jr., to beg his father to forward a list of the ballets he intended to stage and a roster of the dancers he wished to engage. Kahn must have realized that there was little chance of Pleasant's exercising "power enough to put in force his coordinating duty" so long as he was confronted by an intransigent choreographer who was protected by monopolistic rights. Perhaps the time had come to revoke these rights. The opportunity to at least dilute them was presented by the association with Mendelssohn, since Shabelevski was known to have choreographic ambitions. In a carelessly dictated, convoluted paragraph of a letter to Lucia Chase, Orthwine passed on a suggestion—not too hopefully:

As I understand Shabelevski has an idea for presenting one of his own ballets. If this is the case, I think it would be a very good idea if we work on Shabelevski and Mendelssohn, to have him present one ballet with our company and have him pay for the expense of this ballet. If such a point could be worked, I am sure that we could convince Mr. Mordkin that it would be to the advantage of the company to have an extra choreographer as well as an addition to our repertoire, particularly since you would have nothing to do with it particularly.

THE TECHNIQUE AND TRADITIONS OF CLASSICAL BALLET CANNOT BE LEARNED FROM BOOKS; THEY MUST BE PASSED ON THROUGH PERSONAL CONTACT OF BALLET MASTER WITH STUDENT. THUS ALL CLASSICAL BALLET COMPANIES ARE RELATED, AND ALL, LIKE BALLET THEATRE, CAN TRACE THEIR ANCESTRY BACK TO THE COMPANY THAT STAGED DANCE SPECTACLES FOR LORENZO DE' MÉDICI IN RENAISSANCE ITALY.

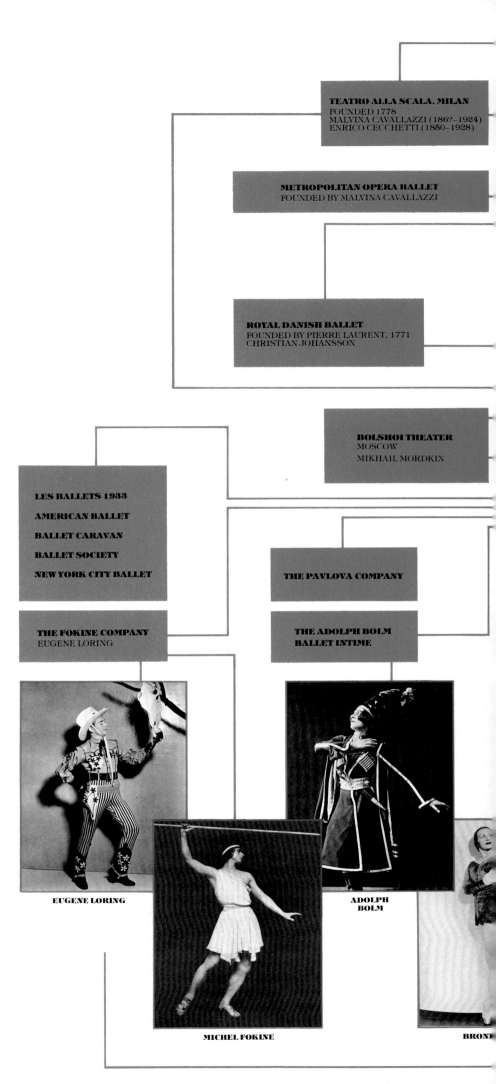

TEATRO ALLA SCALA, MILAN
FOUNDED 1778
MALVINA CAVALLAZZI (186?–1924)
ENRICO CECCHETTI (1850–1928)

METROPOLITAN OPERA BALLET
FOUNDED BY MALVINA CAVALLAZZI

ROYAL DANISH BALLET
FOUNDED BY PIERRE LAURENT, 1771
CHRISTIAN JOHANSSON

BOLSHOI THEATER
MOSCOW
MIKHAIL MORDKIN

LES BALLETS 1933
AMERICAN BALLET
BALLET CARAVAN
BALLET SOCIETY
NEW YORK CITY BALLET

THE PAVLOVA COMPANY

THE FOKINE COMPANY
EUGENE LORING

THE ADOLPH BOLM
BALLET INTIME

EUGENE LORING

ADOLPH BOLM

MICHEL FOKINE

BRON

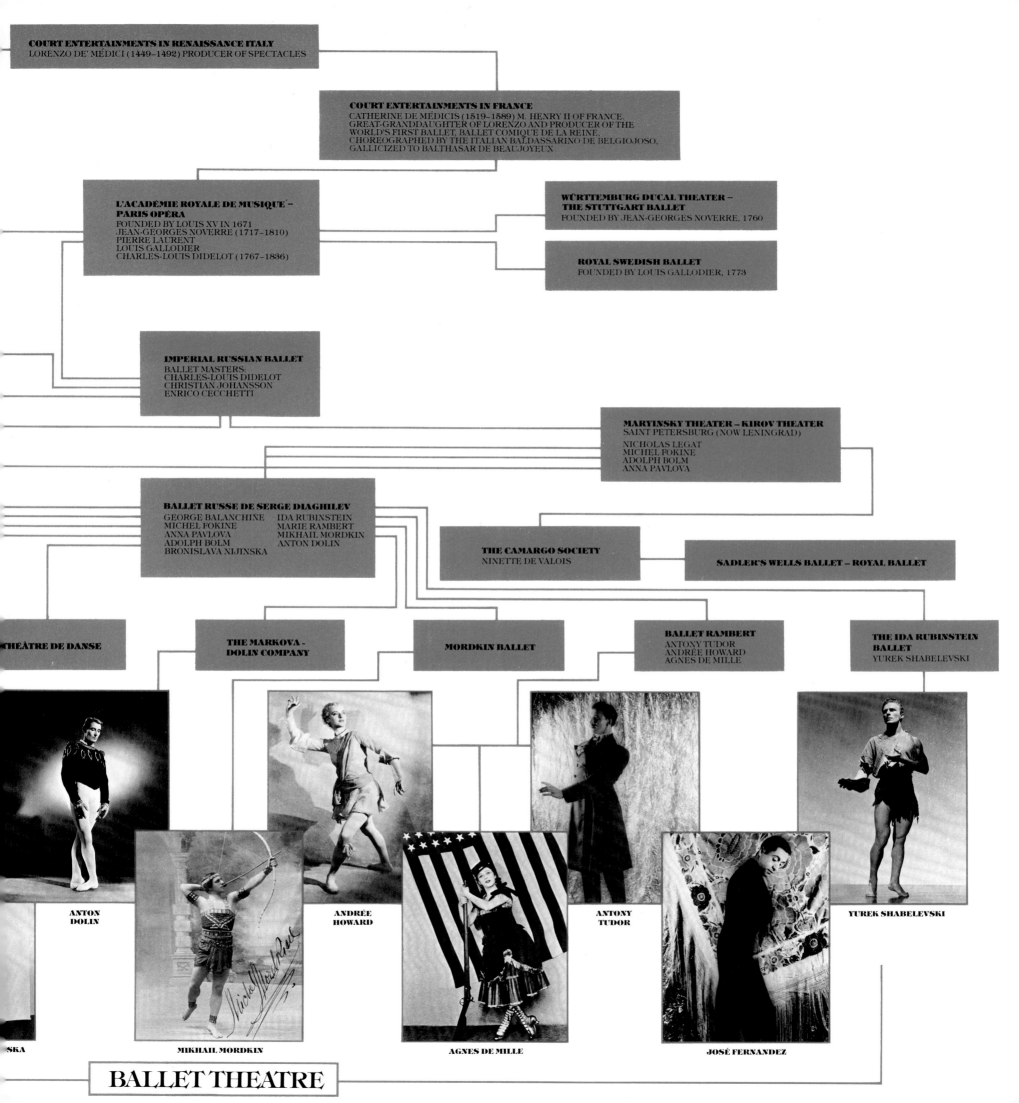

COURT ENTERTAINMENTS IN RENAISSANCE ITALY
LORENZO DE' MÉDICI (1449–1492) PRODUCER OF SPECTACLES

COURT ENTERTAINMENTS IN FRANCE
CATHERINE DE MÉDICIS (1519–1589) M. HENRY II OF FRANCE.
GREAT-GRANDDAUGHTER OF LORENZO AND PRODUCER OF THE
WORLD'S FIRST BALLET, BALLET COMIQUE DE LA REINE,
CHOREOGRAPHED BY THE ITALIAN BALDASSARINO DE BELGIOJOSO,
GALLICIZED TO BALTHASAR DE BEAUJOYEUX.

**L'ACADÉMIE ROYALE DE MUSIQUE –
PARIS OPÉRA**
FOUNDED BY LOUIS XV IN 1671
JEAN-GEORGES NOVERRE (1717–1810)
PIERRE LAURENT
LOUIS GALLODIER
CHARLES-LOUIS DIDELOT (1767–1836)

**WÜRTTEMBURG DUCAL THEATER –
THE STUTTGART BALLET**
FOUNDED BY JEAN-GEORGES NOVERRE, 1760

ROYAL SWEDISH BALLET
FOUNDED BY LOUIS GALLODIER, 1773

IMPERIAL RUSSIAN BALLET
BALLET MASTERS:
CHARLES-LOUIS DIDELOT
CHRISTIAN JOHANSSON
ENRICO CECCHETTI

MARYINSKY THEATER – KIROV THEATER
SAINT PETERSBURG (NOW LENINGRAD)

NICHOLAS LEGAT
MICHEL FOKINE
ADOLPH BOLM
ANNA PAVLOVA

BALLET RUSSE DE SERGE DIAGHILEV
GEORGE BALANCHINE   IDA RUBINSTEIN
MICHEL FOKINE   MARIE RAMBERT
ANNA PAVLOVA   MIKHAIL MORDKIN
ADOLPH BOLM   ANTON DOLIN
BRONISLAVA NIJINSKA

THE CAMARGO SOCIETY
NINETTE DE VALOIS

SADLER'S WELLS BALLET – ROYAL BALLET

THÉÂTRE DE DANSE

**THE MARKOVA -
DOLIN COMPANY**

MORDKIN BALLET

BALLET RAMBERT
ANTONY TUDOR
ANDRÉE HOWARD
AGNES DE MILLE

**THE IDA RUBINSTEIN
BALLET**
YUREK SHABELEVSKI

ANTON
DOLIN

ANDRÉE
HOWARD

ANTONY
TUDOR

YUREK SHABELEVSKI

SKA

MIKHAIL MORDKIN

AGNES DE MILLE

JOSÉ FERNANDEZ

BALLET THEATRE

Clearly no one was confident that Mordkin would accept the addition of a second choreographer. In these days of multi-choreographer companies, his reluctance is difficult to appreciate, but he had only to review the experiences of Michel Fokine, a friend from his old Imperial Ballet days, to make him wary. Fokine had been Diaghilev's choreographer-in-chief and only choreographer until Diaghilev had urged Nijinsky to try his hand at creating a ballet. Almost immediately Fokine became dispensable and was eased out of the company. Several years later, after Nijinsky himself had been expelled, Fokine was called back, only to be replaced within a year by Diaghilev's second choreographer-protégé, Leonide Massine. Thereafter Fokine became a nomad, wandering from one European opera house to another, with detours to New York movie palaces where he mounted stage shows. Not until 1936, when René Blum invited him to become choreographer-in-chief of his Ballets Russes de Monte Carlo, had he again worked with a major ballet company. In view of his friend's experience, it is not so surprising that Mordkin should have looked upon Shabelevski not merely as an extra choreographer but as a potential usurper. The issue was not pressed, but a question had been planted in a number of minds: "Was the temperamental and difficult Mordkin absolutely indispensable to the Mordkin Ballet?"

Meanwhile, steps were being taken in another direction, steps that though not designed to do so, were destined eventually to unseat Mordkin as choreographer-in-chief. In mid-May the directors had approved the booking of a four-week guaranteed tour, but the question of a New York appearance had been left in abeyance. Pleasant had concluded that it would be impractical to schedule performances on six successive Sunday nights (as at the Hudson Theatre). Sundays had come to be considered good nights for dance attractions since there was no competition from the legitimate theater, which was then forbidden by law from giving Sunday performances. But Pleasant had discovered that many of the costs for a single performance—advertising, moving the scenery in and out, installing the lighting equipment—were virtually the same as they would have been for a week of performances. There was, on the other hand, a disadvantage in compressing the six performances into one week: by the time the public had read the reviews or had heard of the company's excellence through word-of-mouth, the week was ended and the ballet had departed. A solution to this problem was first suggested in Alexander Kahn's memorandum of July 12,* which proposed a New York season that "could be prolonged in case of success," and continued:

We can have a theatre—for instance, the Belmont,—on a purely percentage arrangement with a very flexible option arrangement in case of prolongation and we could make the first serious attempt at creating a real dance centre in New York.

*It cannot be determined now with whom the idea originated. Kahn may have been asked to present Pleasant's idea as his own because coming from him it would carry more weight with the directors.

BALLET THEATRE'S ORIGINAL CORPS DE BALLET WAS PHOTOGRAPHED ON THE ROOFTOP FARM OF THE CHILDREN'S AID SOCIETY IN NEW YORK.

While the New York season and the leasing of the theatre would be primarily for the benefit of the Mordkin Ballet, I suggest that various dance groups should be asked to join us in maintaining such a dance centre. Should these groups agree to the plans that are to be worked out it would add big variety to the performances and would attract to the season dance lovers of every kind.

Under such an arrangement it is possible to envisage a very protracted engagement in New York, the time during the absence of the Mordkin Ballet on tour being taken up by such groups.

It cannot be emphasized strongly enough that the first step is the enlargement of the repertoire and the strengthening of the company so that the Mordkin Ballet should appear as a strong artistic organization, and not as an amateurish attempt at choreographic perfection.

A flaw in the proposal was quickly pointed out: no one would derive any significant benefit. The same costs were involved whether a theater was leased jointly or severally by a number of companies over an extended period. The participating dance groups effected no saving by subleasing the theater from the Mordkin company rather than renting it on their own. If there were to be substantial savings, other costs must

An evening's bill might be one Mordkin ballet, one Page ballet with Page choreography, artists, scenery and one ballet by the X ballet. Possibly a reciprocal arrangement could be worked out whereby the X artists could appear in a Page ballet, the Page artists in a Mordkin ballet, etc. Assuredly this ought to be both possible and economic for the corps de ballet. It is in this unity that economies can be effected. One orchestra, one theatre, one crew etc., the cost of which would be pro-rated among the participating companies.

Last winter we gave spaced performances in New York City for six weeks. The experiment was successful. On one night we would take in enough to pay for two or three nights [a misstatement but excusable as salesman's license] but at the same time our expenses ran for very little less than for a full week's performances. In order to give solid weeks of performance over an extended period of time variety is necessary . . . a wide repertory, different casts, different choreographers, designers, musicians, approaches to the problem.

Pleasant was no longer thinking merely of sharing the facilities of a theater and the services of dancers with other dance groups. What he now had in mind was a ballet spectacle of vaster scope than the one-man Mordkin Ballet had been presenting. The descriptive words were "variety," "wide repertory," "different casts," "different choreographers."

At this point there was no thought of changing the Mordkin company: it would be one of the components in an amalgamation of companies that would be presented under the all-inclusive title "America Dances." Mordkin was kept generally informed by his son, who had received a copy of Kahn's memorandum. Michael, Jr., puzzled as he must have been by the phrase "an amateurish attempt at choreographic perfection," could only have assumed it was directed at his father. He gave him what must have been an expurgated version of the memorandum together with a report of Pleasant's inquiries, and returned to report that his father had expressed no enthusiasm to associate with any of the choreographers approached by Pleasant: Maracci's balletic adaptation of Spanish technique was incomprehensible to him; Page was an American and therefore incapable of creating in the classical medium; José Fernandez was good only for staging dances for the movies, et cetera. He was prepared to make only one concession: he was willing to collaborate with Fokine, but this he knew to be impossible because Fokine was then producing ballets abroad for de Basil. Otherwise his attitude was defiant and uncooperative.

The response from the invited dance groups was no more enthusiastic; Maracci failed to reply and Page expressed only polite interest, referring Pleasant to her husband in Texas. No one was rushing to join forces with "America Dances," or the Dance Theatre as it was sometimes called. The entire scheme might have aborted had it not occurred to Pleasant or Kahn (or both) that the same goal could be reached without the collaboration of other dance groups. The alternative was to renovate and enlarge the Mordkin Ballet to the point where it could itself offer the public "variety, a wide repertory, different dancers, and different choreographers." In the course of a holiday at Miss Chase's summer home, Pleasant was able to arouse her enthusiasm and, more importantly, to convince

be shared, including those of the orchestra, the stage crews, the wardrobe personnel, and the press department. But these costs could not be shared if the Mordkin company went off on tour and took its personnel with it. On the other hand, if it remained in New York while other groups occupied the theater, how would it employ the time of its own dancers? The answer was suggested in a letter Pleasant wrote to Carmelita Maracci on July 17, which read in part:

It is in the first of these [New York seasons] that I would like to see you represented.

I should like to see the project worked this way: That you would come East personally and bring with you a small group of soloists that would be indispensable to your work. That you would produce several ballets of your own using your own key people and filling out with Mordkin-hired dancers. That the Mordkin Ballet would do likewise, using your people in its own ballets. That each evening throughout the series each company would give one or two of its own numbers.

A letter to Ruth Page written ten days later indicated a subtle change in Pleasant's thinking:

her that additional backers could more readily be found if the Mordkin Ballet were transformed into a major company with international scope. A few weeks after his return to New York, he wrote to report progress made in negotiations with artists (dancers and choreographers) and in the search for backers. His concluding paragraph reads:

From all of the above you know almost completely the details as well as the general outline to date. We can hardly touch another thing until we are actually ready to jump in. From this point on out the whole thing will begin to unravel again unless we act. Everything, as a matter of fact, must be done almost simultaneously and quickly. For example we can't tell Embree to go ahead [booking the tour] unless we can immediately advertise and announce exactly who we are going to have and what we are going to produce. Each thing is now dependent on the other . . . and, if I may use a mild expression, hell will break loose and no vacations for any of us for months. The one thing that now holds us back is money. The thing has assumed such proportions that you probably can't swing it alone. To date we have not been able to land anyone to help you.

There followed the most fateful question Miss Chase was ever called upon to answer (and her answer carried with it the most fateful consequences to ballet in America):

However, I wonder if you can see your way clear to finance the beginning of the program. It will be, as always, a gamble and a risk . . . but for the first time it will be a magnificent venture. Furthermore I am sure that it is the only plan that will stand a chance of attracting outside interest and help.

Given the word go Mr. Kahn and I would burn up the phones, cables, airplanes and every other invention to get our contracts signed in the shortest time.

That's that. It is now 11:15 and if you're not tired I am.

Miss Chase did see her way clear, and Pleasant and Kahn did burn up the phones and cables. While the answers were coming in, Mordkin was given a last offer to remain as choreographer-in-chief of the new company, which it was now proposed should be known as Ballet Theatre (Lincoln Kirstein, in announcing a 1937 project, had established proprietary right to the name Dance Theatre). The letter to Mordkin was over the signature of Rudolf Orthwine and was dated August 22. It outlined the following plan:

You have been told the parts of the new plan as they have been made. Now for the first time they have been developed far enough to admit of a more consecutive telling. These plans will probably not be complete for another two weeks. Until they are entirely so and until a highly detailed budget is decided and passed upon by this Board and by all of the sponsors, no single contract or part of the plan can be put into execution. However, we want to keep you informed from the beginning of every development.

To build up a New York City repertory which will be representative of every major period of ballet. As much of this repertory as possible must be ready for presentation at the opening in order to demonstrate that it is something more than a plan on paper. However, physical and financial reasons will cause some things to be delayed.

LA FILLE MAL GARDÉE: This represents the pre-19th century ballet and, fortunately, is already in production staged by Mordkin.

GISELLE: This represents the romantic ballet of the 1840s at its best. Fortunately again, it too is in production staged by Mordkin.

SLEEPING BEAUTY: This ballet would represent the Petipa period and the height of the Russian Imperial Ballet before 1900. Possibly Aurora's Wedding act might be feasible to produce this Fall. I am afraid the whole ballet cannot be produced for another year [presumably in the version Mordkin had staged in 1936].

EARLY DIAGHILEV PERIOD and the REVOLUTION OF 1909: This is a tremendously important period as all modern ballet stems directly from it. Four Fokine ballets sum up this pre-1920 period handsomely: PETROUCHKA, SYLPHIDES, PRINCE IGOR and SCHÉHÉRAZADE. Again it will be impossible to stage all four for this season. However, the first two seem feasible and would not only give variety to the repertoire, but also sketch in the main idea of representing this period. Fortunately again, Michel Fokine is available to revive his own masterpieces [if rehearsals did not conflict with his commitments to the Swedish Ballet].

LAST DIAGHILEV DECADE (1920s): This period is the period of activity of three Diaghilev choreographers: Massine, Nijinska, and Balanchine. Reproducing any of the repertory of this period presents numerous difficulties at the present [including the unavailability of the choreographers].

However, Adolph Bolm's BALLET MÉCANIQUE is available, inexpensive to produce and again has the virtue of being able to be set by its creator.

MODERN ERA: The repertory should have the great Mordkin 1938 masterpiece VOICES OF SPRING (already in production); TREPAK, too, has been produced. So have THE GOLDFISH and the Mordkin SWAN LAKE [a modernized version inspired by Gorsky's Bolshoi Theater production].

To give an element of variety, experimentation (since every one of the above-mentioned ballets is a sure-fire hit), and newness, there are the following projects: two new Mordkin ballets: RAYMOND SCOTT and LISZT. It is also possible to add two Spanish ballets by a Spanish choreographer, José Fernandez, and with an all-Spanish troupe.

Speaking through Orthwine, Pleasant could be said to have told the truth in his letter, but not the whole truth. There was no mention of negotiations that had been under way for several weeks to add the ballets of Ashton, Tudor, de Mille, and others as representatives of what he categorized as the Modern Era. Nor was there any reference to the matter of artistic direction. This subject was brought up a few days later in a memorandum for a proposed agreement, but in such a way that Mordkin was apparently unaware of its significance. The agreement was to cover the activities of two companies: the Mordkin company, which would tour, and Ballet Theatre, an amalgamation that would perform a season in New York City. In connection with the Mordkin company, the artistic direction, by whatever title, would presumably remain with Mordkin. The provisions with respect to Ballet Theatre read as follows:

The large group shall be known as The Ballet Theatre in which all ballets staged by Mikhail Mordkin shall bear the credit line "Choreography by Mikhail Mordkin." Any use of the name "Mikhail Mordkin" in printing, controlled by the company, shall be by mutual agreement.

It is understood that there shall be more than one choreographer for The Ballet Theatre, but that no one choreographer shall be artistic director and that each shall be responsible for his own work and not that of any other.

There is little reason why the phrase "no one choreographer shall be artistic director" should have alarmed Mordkin. As the works of the added choreographers had already been produced and performed by other companies,

Mordkin had no wish to concern himself with their staging. That he assumed he would maintain all the other powers of an artistic director was indicated by a condition he transmitted through Michael, Jr.:

Regarding personnel, of course, you know that he heartily approves of all those principals and corps de ballet who are now under contract, but he wishes to exercise sole right in the selection of the balance of the company and casting.

While these points were being argued, the Embree Concert Service decided to give up the attempt to book a tour for the Mordkin company, and so that part of the plan was abandoned. Meanwhile the formation of Ballet Theatre proceeded without the participation of Mordkin. Pleasant's actions from there on resembled the tactics employed in those days by the producers of musical revues. If a producer wished to free himself from a contract with a performer who, he thought, was not earning her salary, he began to eliminate, one by one, her songs, dances, and lines, until the role had been so drastically cut that the performer voluntarily withdrew in disgust. In successive letters Mordkin was informed that his services as teacher to the company would no longer be required; that the company would no longer use his studios for rehearsals; that he would no longer be required to stage GISELLE (to be staged instead by Anton Dolin); that he would not be required to rehearse LA FILLE MAL GARDÉE (to be staged instead by Bronislava Nijinska); that his modern version of SWAN LAKE was being removed from the repertory (the Diaghilev version would be staged by Dolin); and that TREPAK and THE GOLDFISH would not be performed. Pleasant also seized on an opinion expressed earlier by Mordkin, Jr., that "he did not believe his father was interested in creating new ballets that season" as an excuse for commissioning Dolin to choreograph the ballet QUINTET to Raymond Scott's music. And finally, on October 3, Pleasant sent by messenger a note to Mordkin that began:

At Mickey's request, I am enclosing a list of the company to date. I had hoped to have you participate actively in auditioning and choosing the corps de ballet and, as a courtesy, extended to you that privilege. Since, according to our basic agreement with the American Guild of Musical Artists, our options had to be exercised by Saturday, September 30th, the corps de ballet, as it now stands, is the work of [was selected by] Mr. Fokine and Mr. Gavrilov. However, out of consideration for you, I did interfere with their choices and put in as many members of the Mordkin Ballet as was possible.

Concurrently with negotiations concerning choreography, there was a series of communications discussing the roles Mordkin would dance. The result of all this was that whereas in accordance with the contract offered Mordkin on August 22, 1939, the repertory for the season under the title Ballet Theatre was to contain nine Mordkin ballets, in the majority of which he would appear as a dancer, in the actual season, which opened January 11, 1940, there was only one Mordkin ballet (VOICES OF SPRING) and Mordkin never appeared as a dancer.

Pleasant's actions arouse the suspicion that his convic-tion that a ballet company should not have a choreographer-in-chief as its artistic director was based less on objective artistic considerations than on the simple determination to remove Mordkin. Whatever his motives, Pleasant's effort to solve the Mordkin Ballet's financial problems by seeking to enlist the cooperation of other dance groups in a joint enterprise, together with the intransigence of Mikhail Mordkin, determined the eventual composition and functioning of Ballet Theatre. By accident Pleasant had made the discovery that a viable dance organization could be maintained even though it lacked the leadership of a single dominating choreographer who would provide the choreography to be performed by dancers trained, for the most part, at a single dance academy. The accidental nature of the discovery does not detract from the value of its contribution to ballet. In an art form in which creative genius is a rarity, it came as an important discovery that a company could function as a commune to which choreographers of diverse talents could bring their works to be performed by dancers who had received their training in many schools with differing methods and theories of dance education.

When Lucia Chase agreed to finance the start of Pleasant's program, she had no reason to believe that her commitment would involve an expenditure beyond the $25,000 she had set as the limit to her contribution. The capital required for new productions and for pre-opening rehearsal expenses was not expected to exceed this amount substantially, and Pleasant was confident he could obtain additional contributions: from Mendelssohn, who was interested in Shabelevski's career; from Laurance Rockefeller, who had been a classmate at Princeton; and from Dwight Deere Wiman, the millionaire Broadway producer whose musical comedy productions had featured ballets by George Balanchine. It was assumed that once performances began, the extraordinary attractions of the amalgamated season would earn a profit or, at worst, allow the venture to break even.

In these days of vast subsidization of ballet, it is difficult to imagine how anyone could ever have thought that a ballet season could be operated at a profit or even without a considerable loss, but such was the belief in 1939, fostered principally by the false assumption that Hurok was "making a fortune" out of ballet. Hurok, in fact, never made a fortune from ballet; he sometimes made a moderate profit from ballet companies. He did not himself own a company and, except on very rare occasions, contributed nothing to the production, general overhead, or rehearsal costs of the companies he presented. At the most, he guaranteed performing costs in the theater and transportation expenses on tour. At the conclusion of each tour he was again relieved of all financial responsibility for the continued existence of the company. If the box-office receipts had more than covered his limited expenses, he made a profit that was not diminished by the costs of maintaining the company between engagements (this

was the responsibility of the principal backers, who were at first individuals and later national and municipal governments, for instance, those of Great Britain, the Soviet Union, and the city of Stuttgart). But the fact that Hurok prospered (more through the management of soloists like Marian Anderson, Richard Tucker, and Isaac Stern than through ballet) left the principal backers with the illusion that, with efficient business administration, ballet could maintain itself on box-office receipts. Under this illusion, a budget drawn up by Pleasant, and knowledgeably analyzed by Miss Chase, indicated that the controlled loss should not be more than $25,000 and might be reduced if the sale of tickets exceeded expectations.

The budget called for a comparatively small investment in new productions and pre-season rehearsals. The backbone of the repertory would be seven Mordkin ballets that had already been produced, plus one or two new ballets to be selected from those he had proposed to create. The new ballets could be produced inexpensively because they required no scenery. Of the two ballets it was suggested Fokine should restage, LES SYLPHIDES and PETROUCHKA, the latter was almost immediately withdrawn from consideration because it could not be mounted cheaply, and CARNAVAL was substituted. Adolph Bolm's MECHANICAL BALLET, as it was now to be titled, had been revived recently in San Francisco, and Pleasant therefore assumed (wrongly, as it turned out) that the production could be acquired for a reasonable price. It was also assumed that other choreographers who had been invited to collaborate in the season—Maracci, Page, Fernandez, Shabelevski—would supply their own productions at no cost to Ballet Theatre. There remained only the ballets of Frederick Ashton and Antony Tudor. Any thought that they, too, might bring their own productions with them had to be dismissed with the threatened outbreak of World War II. However, both choreographers had created a number of simple ballets from which Pleasant could choose those that could be inexpensively re-produced. On the whole, then, Pleasant's was a modest production schedule which could be executed with no vast outlay of money.

The budgeted increase in rehearsal cost also gave no cause for alarm. It was recognized that the roster of dancers would have to be enlarged. The new figures called for a corps de ballet of between thirty-five and forty members, to which would be added approximately a dozen principals and soloists. But the expansion of the roster became of little concern when it was learned that the newly formed dancers' union, the American Guild of Musical Artists (AGMA), had set the minimum to be paid to corps dancers at $30 per week for rehearsing and $40 per week for performing; soloists such as Nora Kaye received the same rehearsal salaries but were paid $45 for performing. Even the addition of Fernandez' Spanish Group and of the Negro group (as it was then called) was not looked upon as an unwarranted extravagance. The Spanish dancers were paid $20 per week for both rehearsing and

performing, and the black dancers received $10 per week!

Only in the category of star dancers was there the danger that exorbitant demands might affect the budget, but Miss Chase was in full accord that this risk must be taken, as she believed in the essentiality of stars. As early as 1937, in the course of the second Mordkin tour, she had written Rudolf Orthwine from San Antonio, Texas, to discuss the chances of the company's survival, and had concluded:

We shall have to have two good ballerinas, I'm not good enough to hold the fort—neither is Viola [Essen] and certainly we can't rely on her [she was an emotionally unstable teenager] and you can still use us both for many things. We'll have to work on getting at least one hot ballerina immediately—the corps de ballet we can always get and much more easily now than last year before our reputation was made.

Immediately following receipt of this letter, attempts were made to engage the Russian Irina Baronova, then with the Covent Garden Ballet, and Nana Gollner, the American ballerina with the de Basil company, but without success. Arrangements were then concluded with the Norwegian Nina Stroganova of the Ballet Russe de Monte Carlo, and with the Americans Patricia Bowman, who had become a ballerina under the aegis of Michel Fokine, and Karen Conrad, the star of the Philadelphia Ballet. If Miss Chase was later to learn that good corps de ballet dancers are not so easy to find, to train, and to retain, and that they are as indispensable to a company as the leading dancers, she nevertheless continued in her conviction that a company must be headed by star dancers as well as by star choreographers.*

When, therefore, during the first week of August 1939 Pleasant was given the word to proceed, he took it as a mandate to engage star dancers as well as choreographers and, as he had promised, began to "burn up the telephones and cables."

A cable to Philip J. S. Richardson, the dean of English ballet publishers and editor of The Dancing Times, inquired about the availability of Ashton and Tudor. Cables also went to Margot Fonteyn at the Sadler's Wells Theatre and to Vera Verchinina, care of the de Basil company at Covent Garden. The replies were discouraging. Tudor could come to New York but must be back in London by October 8; Ashton was not free until possibly after the first of the year. Fonteyn was interested enough to ask about terms, but she warned that her contractual commitments to Sadler's Wells could prevent her from accepting. The cable to Verchinina was returned marked "Addressee not there." Pleasant persisted with Richardson, but his explorations in England made little progress, and Alexander Kahn's inquiries about the availability of French and Russian expatriate artists then residing in Paris were no more productive.

---

*To Miss Chase the word "star" has always been anathema, and the words "guest star" even more so. A star or a guest star by another name smelled sweeter. For this reason, the only title she has permitted herself (or others under her direction) to use has been "principal dancer."

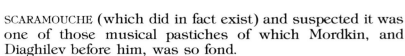

ADOLPH BOLM, FORMERLY ASSOCIATED WITH FOKINE
AND MORDKIN IN THE DIAGHILEV COMPANY, WAS
THE FIRST TO JOIN THE NEW BALLET THEATRE.

On the home front, matters were much the same; the burning up of telephone wires had little result. Fokine had recently returned from London, where his latest ballet, PAGANINI, had been given its premiere at the Covent Garden Opera House by the Educational Ballet Company. This was, in fact, the de Basil company, which had been reorganized and placed under the direction of Victor Dandré, Pavlova's widower. The reorganization proved only a device to ward off de Basil's creditors, and with his threatened return to full power, Fokine no longer wished to continue his association with the company. He was interested, therefore, in working with Ballet Theatre, but any affiliation with the new company would have to be postponed until he had honored a contract with the Royal Swedish Ballet that committed him to act as ballet master during the 1939–40 season.

Pleasant next turned to Adolph Bolm, with whose work he had become familiar when he was acting as a supernumerary in the production of COQ D'OR that Bolm had staged for the San Francisco Opera. Bolm, like Fokine, had been associated with the Imperial Ballet at the Maryinsky Theater and with Diaghilev during his first seasons. He was then teaching in Los Angeles and staging occasional productions at the Hollywood Bowl. The approach was made through Bolm's former son-in-law, Irving Deakin, an English music critic who since 1937 had been broadcasting a program titled MUSIC AND BALLET over station WQXR in New York. Bolm expressed immediate interest in reviving his MECHANICAL BALLET but was skeptical with regard to the suggestion that he create a ballet to a score purportedly by Sibelius. He had never heard of

SCARAMOUCHE (which did in fact exist) and suspected it was one of those musical pastiches of which Mordkin, and Diaghilev before him, was so fond.

Simultaneously, an effort was made to enlist the services of George Balanchine. In a postscript to a letter to Harry M. Zuckert, dated September 2, 1939, Pleasant wrote:

After leaving your office I spent over an hour with Dwight Deere Wiman and his business manager, Jack del Bondio, discussing the whole plan of "The Ballet Theatre" with them. They had planned to form an all-Balanchine Ballet, and I believe they were impressed with the impracticability of forming a company around one man and also with the added possibility such a scheme as our new one would have for Balanchine.

Balanchine, who with his wife, Vera Zorina, had been associated with Wiman in his stage production of I MARRIED AN ANGEL and in the filming of ON YOUR TOES, was anxious to return to ballet, and Wiman agreed to call Ballet Theatre to his attention. He was not, however, too hopeful that he could arouse Balanchine's interest.

With respect to the Americans on Pleasant's list of candidates, only the Mexican-born José Fernandez (with whom he and Romanoff had been friendly in Hollywood and whose group had recently performed on Broadway) was recruited without problems. There is no evidence that Carmelita Maracci ever replied to Pleasant's invitation to participate in his cooperative scheme. She did, however, bring her group to New York to appear in A HOLIDAY DANCE FESTIVAL, mounted at the St. James Theatre by Frances Hawkins, Lincoln Kirstein's business manager. Thus a month before the opening of Ballet Theatre, she shared the stage with Ballet Caravan, Sai Shoki, and Martha Graham under a collaborative arrangement similar to Pleasant's "America Dances" project.

Ruth Page, the second artist to be asked to join in the proposed collaboration, was still receiving enthusiastic letters from Pleasant in mid-August. Thereafter Pleasant's ardor appeared to cool. Perhaps he was disenchanted by performances of the Page Ballet he attended while on a visit to Chicago, but more likely he was influenced by Deakin, who had written disparagingly of Miss Page's association with Diaghilev. Miss Page had only recently pointed out factual errors in Deakin's account, and this indiscretion must surely have increased his antagonism.

Turning next to Agnes de Mille, Pleasant was able to sample her talents at the Guild Theatre on February 12, 1939, when she and her group of twelve dancers performed the works she had created during the past three years in London and Hollywood. Pleasant was impressed by the choreographer but not by what she had choreographed. True, the compositions were in the nature of concert pieces rather than ballets, but no more so than Andrée Howard's DEATH AND THE MAIDEN and Tudor's JUDGMENT OF PARIS, which Pleasant later accepted for the Ballet Theatre repertory. And although they were short, they could have been extended into regular-length ballets—as, in fact, one of them, RODEO, was a few years later

for the Ballet Russe de Monte Carlo. When Pleasant approached de Mille in July he made no commitment as to what ballet he would accept from her.

In search of an additional American choreographer, Pleasant attended performances of the American Lyric Theatre in mid-May at the Martin Beck Theatre, where in conjunction with the presentation of two short American operas, Ballet Caravan offered ballets by American choreographers. These included AIR AND VARIATIONS (Bach's GOLDBERG VARIATIONS) by William Dollar; POCAHONTAS and FILLING STATION by Lew Christensen; and BILLY THE KID by Eugene Loring. Pleasant immediately coveted the last of these, but Loring was precluded by contract from staging the ballet for another company, and Lincoln Kirstein, then director of Ballet Caravan, was understandably reluctant to share it. As with de Mille, Pleasant contemplated the engagement of Loring, but the question of what he would create was left in abeyance.

Thus while what has come to be known as the "Thirty Days in August" was proceeding fatefully in Europe, Pleasant's grand scheme had virtually stalled. Of the choreographers invited to participate, only Mordkin and Bolm had accepted, both with reservations. Mordkin's principal interest had been the survival of the Mordkin company. When, on August 22, this was placed in serious jeopardy by a registered letter from the Embree Concert Service informing Pleasant that it was abandoning any attempt to book a tour for the small group, Mordkin's interest in Ballet Theatre began to wane. Bolm had conveyed his reservations in a letter to Deakin: he was concerned that he had not been informed as to who his "boss" would be, and he was experiencing doubts that the ballets he had been asked to stage would enhance his reputation. And then on September 1 Hitler invaded Poland. This marked the beginning of Pleasant's and Ballet Theatre's fateful "Thirty Days in September."

Michel Fokine became immediately available. Hitler's action recalled to him a bitter period of personal history. In August 1914 he had left London and the Diaghilev Ballet to return to Saint Petersburg for temporary duty at the Maryinsky Theater only to find himself prevented from leaving there by the outbreak of World War I and the subsequent Revolution. During this enforced detention he had been exempted from military service and was able to continue creating ballets (even after the Maryinsky had become the State Theater), but it had not been a happy experience. Money and materials for new productions were scarce (not to mention heat, light, and food), and, to invert Mordkin's statement of 1910, he earned in ten years less than he could have earned in one year in the United States or Europe. He had no intention of reliving these frustrations. Rather than risk becoming stranded in Stockholm or at some point en route, he refused to fulfill his contract with the Royal Swedish Ballet and entered into serious, indeed eager, negotiations with Pleasant. By September 2, though no contract had yet

been signed, Pleasant was sufficiently confident to inquire of Augustus Vincent Tack whether he would be interested in designing the scenery for LES SYLPHIDES. On September 27 Fokine became the first choreographer to sign a contract with Ballet Theatre.

The acquisition of Fokine's signature was pivotal to Pleasant's plan. It enabled him to form the company envisioned in the plan and accorded a seal of approval to the new Ballet Theatre. As senior and dean of all choreographers, Fokine, and Fokine alone, was capable of disrupting Mordkin's choreographic monopoly without having to do so over his confrere's dead body. For even Mordkin himself had to admit that as a creator of original choreography he was scarcely in the same league with Fokine. Further, having incautiously suggested that Fokine be invited to associate himself with the Mordkin Ballet (at a time when he was confident Fokine could not accept), Mordkin must now welcome him to Ballet Theatre with as good grace as possible. The signing of Fokine also had a salutary effect on the board of directors and the principal backer. Fokine appeared to be a rational, dependable master of his craft, one whose businesslike attitude toward the ballet contrasted most favorably with Mordkin's wild-man, temperamental approach. His presence in the company would not only have a moderating influence but, more importantly, it would free both company and directors from total reliance on Mordkin. The board of directors immediately agreed with Miss Chase that the time had come for Pleasant to proceed with the signing of binding contracts with those who had been approached to join Ballet Theatre.

In contrast to today's multipaged choreographic contracts, which are styled by lawyers with pockets for every conceivable contingency, Fokine's first agreement with Ballet Theatre was a simple two-page document. Its brevity should not, however, be taken to mean that Fokine regarded its provisions lightly, particularly those which affected his status in the company. He did not insist that he be accorded a title such as ballet master or artistic director, but he refrained only because he was aware of Pleasant's dilemma. The granting of a title to Fokine would inevitably lead to a rupture with Mordkin, on whom Ballet Theatre had still to rely for seven ballets in its proposed repertory. However, in a similar situation with the de Basil company, Fokine had worked out a solution that was satisfactory both to himself and the company's choreographer-in-chief, David Lichine. In all advertisements and programs for the de Basil season at Covent Garden, the relative status of Fokine and David Lichine had been indicated by the following notice, prominently displayed:

BALLETS BY MICHEL FOKINE UNDER HIS PERSONAL SUPERVISION.
CHOREOGRAPHER: DAVID LICHINE

It was thus made clear that though Lichine was the choreographer-in-chief, he had nothing to do with the ballets of Fokine, to whom he was inferior in rank. To accomplish the

same purpose in Ballet Theatre, Fokine insisted on the inclusion of the following provision:

The name of Mr. Fokine must be mentioned in all the advertisements, billposters and other advertising matters and programs used in connection with said two ballets. If the names of other choreographers are mentioned, then the name of Mr. Fokine must not be printed in smaller type than any other choreographer and in the list of choreographers the following formula must be used at the head of said list:

"All ballets revived under the personal direction of Michel Fokine."

In no case shall it appear that Mr. Fokine works under the direction of any other choreographer.

When Fokine and Pleasant met for the formal signing of the agreement, Fokine requested the addition of three words to make the last sentence read: "In no case shall it appear that Mr. Fokine works under the direction of any other choreographer or other person." Pleasant acceded, inserting the phrase by hand and initialing it. He was probably unaware that he himself may very well have been the "other person" whom Fokine had in mind. Once again, the recollection of earlier experiences could have impelled Fokine to exercise extraordinary caution. In 1907, when he staged his first ballet for the Maryinsky, LE PAVILLON D'ARMIDE, he was forced to submit to the direction of Alexander Krupensky, a young, university-graduate aristocrat who had recently been appointed an assistant director of the Imperial Theaters and whose interference, so Fokine believed, almost resulted in the complete sabotage of the ballet. Fokine's suspicions of aristocratic dilettantes with their meddlesome ways had not been dissipated during his association with the aristocrat Diaghilev and were now naturally directed against the young graduate of Princeton University.

The provision, designed to protect Fokine's status, unwittingly provided Pleasant with a weapon in his struggle with Mordkin. It enabled him to maintain the contention that he could not in good conscience and with fairness deny to Bolm and Balanchine the same degree of autonomy he had promised to Fokine. Mordkin could not therefore expect to be designated choreographer-in-chief, ballet master, or artistic director, nor could he expect to exercise any artistic control over his fellow choreographers. By the same token, the addition of the words "or other person" had the effect of precluding Pleasant from himself assuming the title of artistic director, a step he would have been prevented from taking in any case by the operation of the Diaghilev mystique, which dictated that while everyone must look up to the Russian as the only model of the perfect impresario, no one must dare attempt to imitate him.

In the course of the contract negotiations, which extended through September, Pleasant continued his study of the ballet under three new masters: Fokine, Deakin, and Kahn. At the end of the month, in a letter to Julius Fleischmann, in which it was suggested that Leonide Massine associate himself with Ballet Theatre, Pleasant made it clear that he had either been taken in by his teachers or had misinterpreted or misapplied their teachings. He passed on the convictions he had acquired in what he described as "a fairly intensive ballet education." Among them were the following:

I believe it is possible to create during the coming year in New York City a ballet foundation (not merely a ballet company) which will be as the Maryinsky was in Petrograd or the Bolshoi was in Moscow.

As to the technique: Obviously no choreographer can be artistic director. Intentionally or unintentionally, any choreographer who has control over the work of another choreographer will sabotage it. Each choreographer, and there should be the widest variety of them, should come in, do his work, supervise the opening and depart. The symbol of the organization would be a repetiteur and a stage manager who would rehearse the works of each choreographer without discrimination.

None of his teachers, including Mordkin, could have told him anything which should have led him to believe that the Ballet Theatre he was in the process of forming would in any way resemble the Maryinsky or the Bolshoi of pre-Revolutionary times. The overall direction of these theaters (presenting both opera and ballet) was entrusted to a functionary who was chosen by the Tsar and who might or might not have been associated previously with the arts (the last appointee had been an officer in a regiment of the guards). To the extent that this director decided which operas and ballets should be produced and set their budgets and performing schedules, he could be said to have acted as the artistic director. However, when it came to the details of staging a ballet, his powers were limited. He had no choice but to delegate all control over the choreography to the ballet master, the title then applied to the choreographer-in-chief. The ballet master enjoyed a monopoly on the right to create new ballets, an exclusive right which he relinquished only occasionally to his assistant or a

MICHEL FOKINE ALTERED HIS CONTRACT TO MAKE CERTAIN THAT IT WAS NEVER MADE TO APPEAR HE WORKED UNDER ANYONE'S DIRECTION.

guest choreographer. His dictatorial powers included the right to alter any ballet in the repertory without the consent of the choreographer who had created it, and he even had the right to claim others' choreography as his own.

During Fokine's early association with the Maryinsky, Marius Petipa was a strong-willed ballet master who jealously guarded his prerogatives. Fokine was allowed no opportunity to choreograph for the company—only for school recitals and for charity performances not on the regular Maryinsky schedule. Pleasant's misconception may have been engendered when Fokine reminisced about his experiences during the atypical interim period that existed between Petipa's retirement and the appointment of a strong, competent successor. During this brief period, which continued until he himself became ballet master and assumed full dictatorial powers, Fokine was able to create ballets at the Maryinsky with little interference.

When Fokine discussed his contract with Pleasant, he was not concerned that another choreographer might sabotage any ballets he created or revived for Ballet Theatre. He may have been apprehensive of what might happen to his ballets when he was no longer on hand to oversee them, when spineless regisseurs (whom Pleasant referred to as "repetiteurs") might permit dancers to adapt his choreography to their special skills and make unauthorized alterations. To guard against these contingencies he took two steps. He had inserted in his contract a sentence reading, "The company must give the ballets as they are created by Mr. Fokine without any changes, cuts or additions," and he arranged that the regisseur of Ballet Theatre should be Alexander Gavrilov, who had been one of his favorite pupils at the Maryinsky.

Pleasant may honestly have believed that Fokine had told him that the Maryinsky and the Bolshoi had not been operated under the dominance of a single choreographer-in-chief, and he may have understood him to say that no choreographer should also occupy the post of artistic director, but if so he must surely have been mistaken. More likely, Fokine may have said, "I understand that you cannot give me the title of artistic director because of your problems with Mordkin, but if I cannot be artistic director, nobody can." And he would have insisted on this, not only to protect his artistic integrity but to maintain his status as a choreographer and ballet master second to none. It was a matter of prestige and of crass theatrical billing. Pleasant may also have been the victim of faulty interpretation from the Russian, provided by Kahn (Fokine spoke French and English but was more comfortable in Russian). It was then the practice among English-speaking Russians(at least in the ballet world) to translate into English not what the Russian actually said but what the interpreter thought he <u>should</u> have said or thought the listener would <u>like</u> the Russian to have said. (That many of these same refugees went on to interpret for generals and statesmen engaged in negotiating wartime and postwar agreements between the United States and the Soviet Union may account for the odd

nature of some of those agreements.) It may be that Kahn softened Fokine's ultimatum with talk of artistic autonomy, or that Pleasant on his own preferred to speak in terms of artistic integrity rather than admit that the whole question had arisen and been decided on the basis of rank and prestige. There was no doubt, however, that the use of the title "artistic director" was an important factor in Pleasant's reaching an agreement with Fokine, and it played a part also in his negotiations with Balanchine.

GEORGE BALANCHINE AND VERA ZORINA TURNED DOWN THE FIRST INVITATION TO JOIN BALLET THEATRE.

It is difficult to reconstruct the negotiations between Balanchine and Ballet Theatre because they were conducted orally (without the benefit of tape recordings) and perhaps even through intermediaries. Such evidence as exists is hearsay. When Balanchine was questioned on the subject by his official biographer, Bernard Taper, he recalled no 1939 negotiations. As a consequence, the biography reads:

Late the following year, Balanchine found himself left on the sidelines when the Ballet Theatre was organized. Eleven European and American choreographers were invited to contribute ballets to the new company; he was not. Balanchine was the only choreographer in the Western world who was not asked to contribute.

On the other hand, the papers of Irving Deakin reveal that Balanchine was invited to create a ballet to the PETER AND THE WOLF score of Prokofiev. An exchange of correspondence between Deakin and Bolm can be summarized as follows:

Deakin informed Bolm that discussions were in progress with a view to having Balanchine create the ballet PETER AND THE WOLF.

Bolm suggested that PETER be assigned to him as a substitute for SCARAMOUCHE should Balanchine decline the assignment.

Deakin reported: "It is more than likely that the Prokofieff work will be done by an English choreographer. Balanchine's insistence on certain things including his wife, acceptance of a corps de ballet exclusively from the School of American Ballet, does not meet with the approval of the direction which refuses to be bound to any individual school or artist."

Bolm protested: "Why by an Englishman?!"

Deakin replied on September 6: "Your point about this is well taken and if it were between you and an English choreographer we all feel there would be no question at all particularly in view of your past association with Prokofieff, but it would appear that differences are by way of being worked out between the direction and Balanchine. They told me they expect to have definite and final word from Balanchine by tomorrow. I might add that they are making no concessions or compromises with him on his being left a free hand entirely. Balanchine likes the Prokofieff work and under the circumstances, if he wishes to do it, I think it is a very good idea."

Deakin's report to Bolm is in itself no more than hearsay evidence that negotiations were conducted between Ballet Theatre and Balanchine, but Deakin was in a position to know the truth and there would appear to be no reasonable motive for his intentionally deceiving his former father-in-law. Of course, his whole account could have been a figment of the imagination, but the actions he attributes to Balanchine are not out of character for the Balanchine portrayed in Taper's biography. Taper describes Balanchine's mental state in 1939:

Undoubtedly, the worst and most fundamental of all his frustrations during that time was not having a ballet company. Those years without a company were years in which it was simply impossible for him to work at what he did best.

He describes also his relations with Zorina:

The bliss of Balanchine's conquest of Zorina did not last long. In fact, he found within a short time that, though he had won her hand, he had not conquered her affections.

If the accounts of Deakin and Taper are read in juxtaposition, three reasonable conclusions can be reached:

Balanchine, who had left Europe to establish the School of American Ballet, was determined that any ballet organization with which he associated himself should commit itself to the use of a quota of dancers from the school, at least those required to perform his ballets.

To enable him to persist in conquering Zorina's affections, Balanchine insisted that she be engaged as a ballerina by Ballet Theatre. Zorina, for her part, was not enthusiastic. She had already become a leading lady on Broadway with I MARRIED AN ANGEL and was confident of becoming a Hollywood star with the release of ON YOUR TOES, her second film. Only an intense, selfless affection for Balanchine could have induced her to abandon a more glamorous and profitable career to accompany her husband in the return to his first love, the ballet.

Faced with Balanchine's conditions, Pleasant had no objections to the inclusion of Zorina (three years later she was engaged as

ballerina), but having only recently freed himself from commitments to the Mordkin Ballet Studio, he was determined that no concessions for the employment of his pupils should be made to any other choreographer-teacher.

Any of these conclusions, alone or in combination, could explain the breakdown in negotiations, but there is perhaps a simpler explanation. Balanchine was prepared to sacrifice the rich rewards of Broadway and Hollywood for the greater satisfactions, as well as austerity, of ballet, but he could wait to do so on his own terms. That negotiations had in fact taken place, however, was further evidenced by a letter from Pleasant to Dwight Wiman, dated September 8, in which with a touch of condescension he assured the producer of his good intentions:

I am indeed sorry that Mr. Balanchine will not be a member of Ballet Theatre at its inception. It is obvious almost to the point of rudeness to say that a Balanchine ballet would be an ornament to any company.

Also—to coin a bromide—I think it much sounder to hang together than to hang separately.

One thing I insist upon: that the door of Ballet Theatre be continually open to Mr. Balanchine and Miss Zorina and the welcome mat out.

Addendum: Wiman became a substantial contributor to Ballet Theatre. Balanchine and Zorina remained with Broadway and Hollywood until 1941, when a new company organized by Lincoln Kirstein, the American Ballet, was sent to South America by Nelson Rockefeller, who was then co-ordinator of Inter-American Affairs for the State Department. PETER AND THE WOLF was choreographed by Bolm.

And so in the first week of Pleasant's "Thirty Days," he had won two (Fokine and Bolm) and lost one (Balanchine). He now returned his attention to the English contingent. On September 5 he wrote to Frederick Ashton:

Through Miss Rutherton and Mr. Richardson of The Dancing Times, I have had some communication with you about the possibility of your coming to New York to mount ballets for Ballet Theatre, a new organization which will absorb the Mordkin Ballet.

I am interested in having your work represented in our repertoire. At the time I first heard from Miss Rutherton you were not available at all. Now, with the declaration of war over last weekend, I don't know whether it will be totally impossible for you to leave the country or if by chance it might make you more available. We plan a great permanent organization in which there will be definitely a place for a person of your attainments.

Similar letters were dispatched the same day to Antony Tudor and Andrée Howard. Ashton's letter was returned stamped "No such address. Return to sender." A week later Tudor cabled Pleasant that he was free of contractual commitments and that he expected to soon receive official permission to sail.* He asked for details of a formal contract to cover the services of himself and his assistant, Hugh Laing. On the 23rd Pleasant cabled Tudor: "Please contact Margot Fonteyn, Gerd Larson and others. Advise immediately availability best terms you can arrange." At the same time he sent a cable directly to Fonteyn and received the reply: "Momentarily

---

*In accordance with a British government order of September 4, 1939, all citizens wishing to leave the country were required to obtain an exit permit.

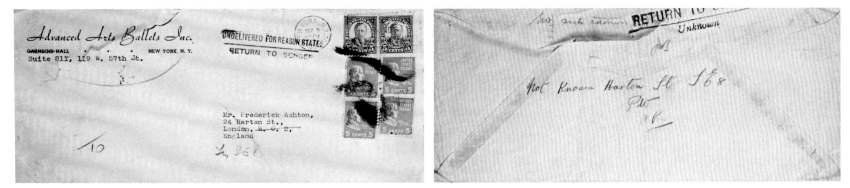

FREDERICK ASHTON MIGHT HAVE JOINED BALLET THEATRE IN 1939 HAD HIS INVITATION BEEN DIRECTED CORRECTLY TO WHARTON RATHER THAN TO HARTON ST.

impossible make arrangements for September. Wells yearly contract subject to war conditions. Can you send particulars." Presumably this meant that should the war continue, she would be released from her Sadler's Wells contract and might be available to Ballet Theatre. In an exchange of cables and letters, Pleasant came to terms with Tudor, Laing, and Andrée Howard, who arrived in New York aboard the S.S. WASHINGTON on October 12. The men were sent to Ellis Island because of a discrepancy in their documents: their passports had been issued to William Cook and Hugh Skinner while their labor-entry permits were made out to their stage names, Tudor and Laing.

Of the remaining choreographers, Pleasant came to agreements with Fernandez and de Mille within two days after Fokine's contract had been signed. Formal agreements with Shabelevski and Loring were delayed; Mendelssohn had gone ahead with his plan to form a company for Shabelevski and Loring had not yet freed himself of his commitment to Kirstein. They did not join Ballet Theatre until the third week of rehearsals. To complete the roster of choreographers, Pleasant entered into discussions with Gene Kelly, who was then the first-chorus-boy-on-the-right next to Mary Martin in her show-stopping number in LEAVE IT TO ME. He proposed that Kelly do the choreography for the ballet QUINTET to Raymond Scott's music, but this idea had to be abandoned when Kelly was cast as The Natural Born Hoofer in William Saroyan's THE TIME OF YOUR LIFE.

Pleasant's intensive ballet education continued into October and took a new turn when the S.S. WASHINGTON arrived in New York after a rough, twelve-day passage from Southampton. From one passenger—Lord Morley, Deputy Speaker of the House of Lords—the shipboard reporters learned that Britain would fight a defensive war, that it did not intend to break its back against a steel barrier and was reluctant to bomb German industries. They also learned that the ship carried fifty-four pedigreed dogs, which had been sent abroad as a precautionary measure against the impairment of championship strains. While the reporters remained unaware that the ship also carried Alicia Markova, Alexandra Danilova, Antony

Tudor, Hugh Laing, and Andrée Howard, they were informed of the presence of Anton Dolin, whose mission could have been to preserve the pure strain of the Imperial classic ballet as it had been transmitted to him through Diaghilev.

To Pleasant, Dolin's credentials were impeccable. He had been an intimate of Diaghilev, appearing first in 1921 at the age of seventeen as a royal page in his London production of THE SLEEPING BEAUTY. Two years later he joined the company as a regular member in Monte Carlo, but left in 1925 after a personal falling-out with Diaghilev. Later he returned and was with the company when it and Diaghilev died in 1929. By 1939 he had become recognized as the first Anglo-Irish ballet dancer to attain international stardom. In April of that year he had met with Irving Deakin in New York while en route from Australia to England with the de Basil company. In October, a few days out from Bordeaux on his way back to Australia via America, he received from Deakin the following cable: "Advise you sign nothing and commit yourself to nothing until I see you—will meet boat." Within a week after arriving in New York, Dolin decided against proceeding to Australia to join the de Basil company and signed with Ballet Theatre. Appended to the standard AGMA contract was a rider which set forth a number of special conditions, including: that he was engaged as a ballet master and choreographer and as a premier danseur; that he would choreograph SWAN LAKE and a new ballet to the music of Raymond Scott; and that he would dance the role of Albrecht in GISELLE. The last provision was further modified to give him the assurance that "whether the ballet [was] staged by Mordkin, Dolin, or another choreographer, the choreography for the said male leading part shall meet with Mr. Dolin's approval."

What Pleasant had been learning under the tutelage of Deakin was speedily confirmed by Dolin. Mordkin's restorations of the classics, he was told, were neither authentic nor in good taste—not surprising since Mordkin had received his ballet training at the Bolshoi under Alexander Gorsky, who had not inspired his pupils with a proper deference toward the sacrosanctity of original choreography. In 1911 Gorsky had staged a version of GISELLE that was set in the Directoire era of the 1790s and depicted Albrecht (danced by Mordkin) as a

villain. He had felt no more compunction at tampering with the ballet classics than do modern stage directors when they cut, reinterpret, and change the time of action of a play by Shakespeare. In 1938, when Mordkin staged a new one-act version of SWAN LAKE, he retained only the music. At the first performances the cast was listed as The Ideal, The Poet, the Protective Fates (the Black Maidens), et cetera. The critics were not horrified by Mordkin's choreographic license, nor were they favorably impressed. Representative of their opinions was that of Anatole Chujoy, who wrote, "For all I know, Mordkin's choreography may be superior to that of Petipa and Ivanoff, but ballet tradition is on the side of the latter." Dolin and Deakin were not so tolerant. They were purists, though their defense of purity extended no further back than the Diaghilev era, when excerpts from SWAN LAKE were presented in one act. Nor was this purity absolute. During performances at Lewisohn Stadium in the summer of 1940, Dolin altered his own version by transposing the pas de trois from the first to the second act, where it was danced not by three guests at the Prince's hunt breakfast, but by two cygnets and a huntsman (Nora Kaye, Karen Conrad, and Leon Danielian). However, when Dolin was negotiating his contract, he and Deakin had no difficulty in convincing Pleasant that Mordkin had taken unacceptable liberties in his version of SWAN LAKE. Pleasant readily agreed that if Dolin was to dance Prince Siegfried, he should be allowed to stage his own conception of the ballet. Accordingly, two days after Dolin signed his contract, Mordkin was informed by registered mail that "we shall not require your services in rehearsing last year's Mordkin version of SWAN LAKE."

Pleasant's confidence in Mordkin's ability to stage the classics was by then completely undermined. When the time came to consider GISELLE, he could appreciate Dolin's concern over the possible conflicts in the interpretation of the role of Albrecht. But in this case replacing Mordkin as choreographer could prove to be difficult and embarrassing. It was one thing to substitute the Diaghilev reduction of SWAN LAKE for the tone-poem version by Mordkin, which he had not intended should resemble the original. They were, in effect, two different ballets, and it was within the proper discretion of the management to decide which it preferred to present. With respect to GISELLE, on the other hand, the choice had already been made, Mordkin had rehearsed the corps de ballet of the new company, and it remained only for him and Pleasant to choose dancers for the leading roles. Consequently if Pleasant decided to substitute another choreographer, Mordkin would have <u>had</u> to regard it as a direct affront—regardless of how diplomatically Pleasant had attempted to phrase his announcement. Had he pointed out that Nicholas Sergeyev, the former ballet master of the Maryinsky Theater, had taught the authentic version to Dolin and Olga Spessivtseva, Mordkin would have protested that it surely could be no more authentic than the version he had danced with Pavlova, the greatest of

IN A FRENCH EMPIRE VERSION OF GISELLE AT THE BOLSHOI, MORDKIN PORTRAYED ALBRECHT AS A VILLAIN.

all the Maryinsky Giselles. Perhaps in the hope of avoiding such a confrontation, Pleasant ordered a run-through, which Dolin attended. When it was over, Dolin referred to his contract and gave notice that the choreography for the role of Albrecht did not meet with his approval.

Mordkin's choreography of GISELLE could not be dismissed as summarily as his SWAN LAKE had been. His version differed only in unimportant details from the one that had been presented recently at the Metropolitan by the Ballet Russe de Monte Carlo, with Alicia Markova and Serge Lifar. It was true that his production for the Mordkin Ballet could be faulted for the horrendous costumes that Lee Simonson had designed for the second act—the Wilis were swathed in cellophane (that year's "in" material for stage costumes), and their bodices and tulle skirts were sprinkled with sparkling paillettes—but the scenery and costumes could have been replaced without replacing Mordkin.

There were no diplomatic words with which Pleasant could inform Mordkin of his decision to entrust the staging of an Imperial Russian version of GISELLE to a young Irishman who had not yet graduated from knee pants when Mordkin was already performing the role of Albrecht on world stages. Had he assigned the staging to one of Mordkin's contemporaries (Fokine or Bolm), Mordkin would have regarded his decision as inexcusable but perhaps arguable. This alternative had been contemplated when the clause "whether the

MORDKIN'S SYMPHONIC VERSION OF SWAN LAKE (LEFT, WITH VARKAS AND BOWMAN) WAS REPLACED BY DOLIN'S ACT II WITH STROGANOVA (PUBLICITY PHOTO).

ballet is staged by Mordkin, Dolin, or another choreographer" was inserted in Dolin's contract, but it proved not to be a solution. Fokine had little respect for Mordkin as an artist (he vigorously opposed his engagement by Diaghilev in 1909), but he had even less respect for GISELLE as a ballet. In 1910 he had tried to dissuade Diaghilev from presenting it in Paris, and although as choreographer-in-chief he was credited with the staging, there is convincing evidence that he had little to do with the production, which starred Karsavina and Nijinsky. In 1939, much as he may have disapproved of Mordkin's version, he would have been equally determined not to offer one of his own. As for Bolm, even if he had not been fully occupied already with the staging of MECHANICAL BALLET and the creation of PETER AND THE WOLF, the staging of GISELLE could not have been assigned to him without jettisoning one of the pet publicity projects of Pleasant and Deakin, who, in a pre-opening release, had informed the press:

When Diaghileff opened at the Chatelet Theatre in Paris in 1909—that never-to-be-forgotten opening of ballet—he had four great men, undoubtedly the greatest assemblage ever seen at one time in the world. The four (and no one would ever say that there were three or five) were Fokine, Bolm, Mordkin, and Nijinsky. All four are alive, the first three are hale and available. Naturally the Ballet Theatre has engaged all three of them—and it is the first time they have been united in one effort for 30 years.

Deakin followed up with a letter to Bolm in which he urged him to put aside all past differences with Fokine. "Looked at from a purely mundane point of view," he wrote, "it would provide publicity of the finest type. What would be more effective than a photograph of Fokine, Bolm, and Mordkin with clasped hands?" The fact of the matter was that Fokine had more reason to harbor resentment than his two confreres. In 1909 Mordkin had carried off Fokine's partner Pavlova to amass all that American gold under the sponsorship of Otto Kahn, and in 1919, when Fokine was interned in Russia, Bolm mounted a pirated version of PETROUCHKA for the Metropolitan. But any chances of a grand reconciliation would have evaporated had Fokine or Bolm insulted Mordkin by presuming to improve on his choreography for GISELLE.

In the end, Pleasant never acquired his "clasped-hands" picture. Unable to hit on a tactful way of informing Mordkin about Dolin's GISELLE, he tactlessly said nothing, leaving Mordkin to find out about it for himself. He found out during a rehearsal of THE GOLDFISH, and in the presence of members of the company, including Lucia Chase. He heard the music of GISELLE being played in an adjoining studio, quickly learned that Dolin was conducting rehearsals of the ballet, and left the building in a fury. Although he returned to continue rehearsals of THE GOLDFISH, he began each session by elaborately placing a toy gun on the piano as a sign that a state of war existed. All face-to-face communication ceased between Mordkin and Pleasant (it had, in any case, to be conducted through an interpreter, since Mordkin spoke virtually no English), and the choreographer discontinued speaking to Miss Chase in any of her several capacities: as a pupil, a dancer, a principal backer, or a friend. Though it must be admitted that Mordkin was sorely provoked, it must also be admitted that, to say the least, he was being difficult.

Shortly after the declaration of the private war between Mordkin and Pleasant, the Russian was given additional reason for intensifying his resentment. Bronislava Nijinska arrived from Europe on one of the boats crammed with refugees and was engaged to restage Mordkin's version of LA FILLE MAL GARDÉE. Her qualifications for becoming a charter member of the new Ballet Theatre were persuasive to Pleasant and his associates: she was the sister of the heroic Vaslav Nijinsky; as a choreographer she had created LE TRAIN BLEU and LES FÂCHEUX—ballets that had propelled Dolin to international fame—as well as the dance sequences featuring Dimitri Romanoff in the film A MIDSUMMER NIGHT'S DREAM; and she was a personal friend and client of Irving Deakin. Her qualifications for becoming the choreographer of LA FILLE MAL GARDÉE were, on the other hand, somewhat less convincing. As a member of the corps de ballet at the Maryinsky Theater, she had doubtless appeared in, or at least attended, performances of that ballet. But the records do not reveal that she ever danced a soloist role, much less one of the leads, during the three years she performed with the Imperial Theaters before resigning to cast her lot with Diaghilev. Nor could she have appeared in more than six performances of FILLE, the total given at the Maryinsky between 1908 and 1911. In addition, while still a student she must surely have attended at least the two performances in 1907 in which her brother danced, but even had she attended all ten performances she could not have observed them with the analytical concentration that would have enabled her, thirty years later, to reproduce the choreography with any degree of accuracy. As it turned out, her version differed almost imperceptibly from Mordkin's, and for a good reason. From the start she enlisted Dimitri Romanoff's services as an interpreter (like Mordkin she spoke no decipherable English) and also relied on his memory and that of Miss Chase to reconstruct the action of the ballet. The three of them went over the score together, with Romanoff and Chase—who had danced the leading roles of Lisette and Colin dozens of times since 1938—recalling the pantomime and steps. As his later career proved, Romanoff possessed an exceptionally accurate photographic recall of choreography.

Once again, Mordkin could not regard the engagement of Nijinska as other than a direct affront. To him Nijinska remained the homely, ungainly corps de ballet girl whom Diaghilev had reluctantly accepted into his company as an accommodation to her brother Vaslav. As premier danseur and as a connoisseur of youthful beauty, Mordkin had scarcely noticed her at the time, nor had he been impressed when she went on to create what to him were ugly, avant-garde ballets. That she should be chosen to restage his production of LA FILLE MAL GARDÉE was the final insult. On December 18 he received a letter from Pleasant in which were enclosed the proofs of programs for THE GOLDFISH and VOICES OF SPRING. He was asked to proofread them and to give his preferences for the casts on opening night. He sent no reply.

Ten days later he received a check for $1,650, which represented the amount due him under his contract for conducting rehearsals from October 1 through December 16 at $150 per week. With his endorsement on the back of the check he acknowledged the termination of his active association with Ballet Theatre and, though he was not aware of it at the time, signed the death certificate for the last of the series of Mordkin companies that had succeeded one another since the first Pavlova-Mordkin company had been organized in 1910.

Of the choreographers engaged during the first week of December in the preparation of the repertory for the new American company, four were Russian (Mordkin, Fokine, Bolm, Nijinska), three English (Tudor, Howard, Dolin), and one Mexican (Fernandez). It was not until December 10 that the first American, Agnes de Mille, was able to start staging her ballet. Until then she had been busy choreographing the dances for SWINGIN' THE DREAM, an all-black musical version of A MIDSUMMER NIGHT'S DREAM, starring Maxine Sullivan. The show opened at the Center Theatre in Rockefeller Center on November 29. Unhappily for those associated with the venture—but happily for Ballet Theatre—it closed in ten days.

Its early demise solved two of Pleasant's most pressing problems: what to do about Agnes de Mille's ballet and where to find a suitable theater in which to launch the new company. From the start de Mille's commitment to SWINGIN' THE DREAM had presented difficulties. It meant that she could not be available for Ballet Theatre rehearsals until the musical opened, and Broadway openings were always subject to unforeseen delays. Pleasant had therefore hedged in his press release, which announced, "A negro ballet will be presented to the music of Darius Milhaud's LA CRÉATION DU MONDE." Several paragraphs later appeared the presumably unrelated item, "Agnes de Mille will stage a ballet to be announced." This arrangement allowed de Mille to follow her preferred modus operandi: to work out the choreography on a small group with whom she was familiar, and subsequently transfer it onto the dancers who were to perform the ballet. In this instance, while creating the dances for SWINGIN' THE DREAM, she sketched out the Milhaud ballet on Sybil Shearer, Marguerite de Anguerro, and Mirthe Ballance. With the early closing of the musical, she was able to deliver a nucleus of the black dance group to Ballet Theatre. The Milhaud ballet, now titled BLACK RITUAL, was completed on schedule, but only just so. In each of the three performances given during the season, Marguerite de Anguerro blackened her face and mingled with the dancers to direct dance traffic on stage.

The closing of SWINGIN' THE DREAM not only freed de Mille to concentrate on BLACK RITUAL but it made available to Pleasant the sole unoccupied theater in New York whose stage and auditorium could provide the atmosphere of grandeur appropriate to a major ballet company. On December 11, less than three weeks before the opening date, he signed a lease.

IN MORDKIN'S GISELLE, THE PEASANTS (MIMI GOMBER AND DODY GOODMAN) WORE SABOTS, AND THE WILIS WERE CLOTHED IN CELLOPHANE.

DOLIN STAGED A MORE CONVENTIONAL GISELLE WITH PATRICIA BOWMAN (LEFT) AND HIMSELF (SOARING ABOVE NORA KAYE, FOURTH FROM LEFT).

leasant made his last directorial decision with respect to the productions for the inaugural season when he reached an agreement with Eugene Loring. The American-born dancer-choreographer had come to New York from Milwaukee in 1934 with a letter of introduction to Lincoln Kirstein, which resulted in their entering upon a five-year association. He became a charter member of the American Ballet company and remained with it when it performed for three years as the resident ballet company of the Metropolitan Opera and then as Ballet Caravan, a small company that was to present American works on tour during the summer months. Loring was assigned to the Caravan, for which he choreographed HARLEQUIN FOR PRESIDENT, YANKEE CLIPPER, and BILLY THE KID. During the summer of 1939 he was working on a new ballet for Kirstein, CITY PORTRAIT, when Pleasant approached him with an offer he found difficult, if not impossible, to refuse. It was not a spectacular offer: rehearsal salary, $50; performance salary, $125; fee for the choreography of a new ballet, $1,000 –but it exceeded the payments being made by Kirstein. Loring had been receiving only the minimum salary stipulated by the dancers' union, and for remounting the choreography of BILLY THE KID he received a total payment of $250 for all rights in perpetuity, with no provision for royalty payments. (If this was perhaps the least favorable deal ever negotiated by a choreographer, perhaps the most favorable deal ever made by a ballet company was concluded in 1941 when Ballet Theatre purchased all choreographic rights to the ballet, together with the scenery and costumes, for a total payment of $2,500.) However, financial considerations aside, Loring was content in his association with Ballet Caravan. He suggested that Kirstein match Pleasant's offer, but Kirstein insisted he could not do so without setting a precedent that might upset the financial balances within his company. By today's standards, the sum under discussion was of no great significance, but to Loring the differences involved would make it possible for him to continue to support himself in New York. The increase in the choreographic fee, for example, would more than pay the yearly rental on his apartment. To him this was the deciding factor, and he was reassured in his decision by the knowledge that Fokine, whom he admired and for whom he had danced at Lewisohn Stadium and the Capitol Theatre, had associated himself with the new company. Accordingly, he signed with Ballet Theatre and concluded his obligations to Kirstein by completing CITY PORTRAIT.

Pleasant had discussed with Loring a number of possible librettos (including the one to the music of Raymond Scott, which later emerged as QUINTET) but none of them struck a responsive spark. As Loring had no proposals of his own, Pleasant suggested that a story be solicited from a playwright. (This was in furtherance of one of Pleasant's Diaghilev-inspired projects; in 1938 he had written a dozen playwrights, including Maxwell Anderson and Philip Barry, asking if they

BRONISLAVA NIJINSKA REHEARSED PATRICIA BOWMAN AND YUREK SHABELEVSKI IN LA FILLE MAL GARDÉE.

would be interested in collaborating on ballet scripts. There is no record of any replies having been received.) Loring welcomed this suggestion because he himself had been toying with the idea of creating a ballet in which the dancers were called upon to speak. Recently he had read William Saroyan's collection of short stories THE DARING YOUNG MAN ON THE FLYING TRAPEZE and recognized in him a kindred spirit. Pleasant's enthusiasm was instantly aroused. That season William Saroyan was the hero of the Broadway intelligentsia; the Group Theatre had produced his MY HEART'S IN THE HIGHLANDS, and his THE TIME OF YOUR LIFE was being praised during its tryout tour. Loring met with Saroyan, who was happy to cooperate but had no ideas for a libretto. However, in the course of their conversation Saroyan began to indulge his habit of observing character and personality traits, to be stored away and later drawn upon in creating the characters of his stories and plays. Although Loring's boyish face was frequently illuminated with a disarming smile, he did not look to Saroyan like a typical American boy. He was too earnest. He regarded life with deadly seriousness. His artistic theories were weighty, his philosophical observations professorial. He was convinced that the ballet could affect the course of American life. Like Saroyan himself, who dreamed of creating the great American novel, Loring dreamed of the great American ballet. Saroyan considered both dreams simplistic; dreams that could be dreamed only by a great American goof. The libretto for THE GREAT AMERICAN GOOF began to germinate in his mind. Perhaps Saroyan thought of himself as the Goof; Loring believed <u>he</u> was and cast himself in the role.*Saroyan's libretto included a description of each character, beginning

* When the libretto was later published in RAZZLE-DAZZLE, Saroyan recalled having told Loring that the character of the Goof had been in his mind for some time—which may possibly have been the fact.

with "The Great American Goof, the naïve white hope of the human race." Loring chose Henry Brant, who had composed the score for CITY PORTRAIT, to write the music.

To complete his roster of eleven choreographers, it remained only for Pleasant to accept Yurek Shabelevski's ODE TO GLORY, a pas de deux created for the Polish Ballet. The name of a twelfth choreographer, Alexander Gavrilov, appeared on the first billposter. He was scheduled to restage Vaslav Nijinsky's L'APRÈS-MIDI D'UN FAUNE for a Nijinsky benefit, but neither the benefit nor a performance of the ballet took place.

It may prove useful to examine Pleasant's accomplishments as a ballet producer up to December 20, 1939, when he signed a $3,000 check for the first deposit on the rental of the Center Theatre, and when all his dancers had been engaged and his choreographers were busy conducting rehearsals. A preliminary statement of what he did not accomplish and of what he did not intend to accomplish should clear away a number of misconceptions that have been permitted to survive or, indeed, have been promoted over the years.

Pleasant did not settle on the name Ballet Theatre because it was his intention that the company's repertory should stress both dance and theater, or that emphasis should be placed on the dramatic aspects of ballet. To him the title "Ballet Theatre" was the equivalent of "Art Museum": it designated the organization that presented ballets, just as the museum exhibited paintings. In his original plan, the organization would present a number of dance groups in the Theatre.

Pleasant did not consciously and deliberately arrive at the conclusion that no single choreographer should be the artistic director of the company. In his original conception of Ballet Theatre as an organization to which choreographers could bring their works to be performed by their own groups (sharing only theater facilities and personnel), the question of an artistic director did not arise. Not until he had revised his plan and decided that the Mordkin company should be enlarged, assume the name Ballet Theatre, and itself engage choreographers to stage ballets for it, did he discover that none of the established choreographers was willing to submit to the direction of a fellow choreographer. But in any case, he would not have been the first to ban a choreographer from the position of artistic director. Kirstein, not a choreographer, had been the artistic director of Ballet Caravan since 1936, while Balanchine, his attention concentrated on other projects, neither choreographed ballets for the company nor assumed any role in its direction. Only rarely did he make casual visits to the rehearsal halls where five choreographers were creating new works.

Pleasant did not preside over the great creative period of Ballet Theatre, though he is often credited with having done so. Of the twenty-eight ballets (including restagings, revisions, and pas de deux) produced by Ballet Theatre during the two seasons under his direction, only four—BLACK RITUAL, THE GREAT AMERICAN GOOF, PETER AND THE WOLF, and QUINTET— could be categorized as original works, that is, ballets that had not been performed previously by other dance groups. Of these four, only PETER AND THE WOLF was accorded popular and critical approval and survived beyond Pleasant's tenure of office. The only original musical score commissioned by Pleasant, Brant's THE GREAT AMERICAN GOOF, has disappeared from the theater and concert hall.

Finally, Pleasant did not rank as a prime discoverer and promoter of American talent. Both of his American choreographers, Agnes de Mille and Eugene Loring, had already demonstrated their talent with other dance groups before joining Ballet Theatre. It is true that he also engaged the future choreographers William Dollar, Edward Caton, Jerome Robbins, Michael Kidd, and Donald Saddler, but he used them only as dancers. And of the American dancers whom he recruited for the first seasons and who later emerged as stars, all had come to Ballet Theatre after performing in other dance groups.

This recital of Pleasant's "non-accomplishments" should not be allowed to detract from his achievements that were real and exerted a beneficial influence on the course of ballet in America.

Pleasant founded the first major ballet company which offered a diverse group of choreographers the opportunity to create or restage their ballets independently, free of pressure and interference from a supervising choreographer. Ballet Caravan could not claim this distinction because it was not a major company and did not present a diversity of choreography. Its choreographers—Lew Christensen, Douglas Coudy, William Dollar, Erick Hawkins, and Eugene Loring—were all Americans, and their librettos were derived predominantly from American themes. Though the choreographers themselves would insist that their several approaches to choreography were highly individualistic, the differences in style were scarcely discernible to the unschooled eyes of the audience. Nor were they discernible to the dancers, all of whose muscles had been conditioned at one training school, the School of American Ballet. Pleasant's assemblage of choreographers, on the other hand, worked in distinct and varied styles. Ballet Theatre offered variety both to its dancers and its audiences. The dancers found excitement and stimulus in adapting their muscles to the varied styles, and the audiences found increased enjoyment in programs of ballets that were diverse in story, dance style, and national flavor.

In evaluating this accomplishment, it matters little that Pleasant's choices of choreographers and star dancers were for the most part fortuitous and were made possible by the outbreak of the war, which confined artists like Michel Fokine and Nana Gollner to the United States and drove others to its protective, neutral shores. Thus in assembling his first company Pleasant was not guided by any determining artistic policy but simply selected from what was available—and

NANA GOLLNER AS GISELLE.

THE FIRST SEASON FEATURED TWO BALLETS BY AMERICANS: AGNES DE MILLE'S BLACK RITUAL WAS PERFORMED BY THE "NEGRO UNIT" (TOP RIGHT); EUGENE LORING'S THE GREAT AMERICAN GOOF BY THE ENTIRE COMPANY INCLUDING MIRIAM GOLDEN AND LORING HIMSELF.

availability became an increasingly common condition in September 1939. For example, as the Germans threatened the French border, Alexander Kahn received an intriguing proposition from his Paris correspondent, de Korvé. Serge Lifar could come to America with a small group to join Ballet Theatre. If a benefit for the Croix Rouge could be arranged, the French government would pay all the group's transportation expenses. Had Dolin not become available, Pleasant could have chosen Lifar to stage SWAN LAKE (he had danced in the Diaghilev version) and GISELLE (like Dolin he had danced the Sergeyev version with Spessivtseva at the Paris Opéra). Each of these dancers projected a strong presence on stage and danced in an exuberant manner, but in highly contrasted styles. Either would have left an impression on the dancing of the company, particularly that of the males, and when Pleasant made his choice he unknowingly determined to an extent the future dancing style of Ballet Theatre. Similarly, had Pleasant been forced to settle for Mordkin because Fokine chose to fulfill his commitment in Sweden, Ballet Theatre's initial style would have been that of the Moscow school, extroverted and free-wheeling. Still different would have been its style if Balanchine had come as the principal choreographer and brought with him his own form of neo-classicism.

It is interesting to speculate what Ballet Theatre might be like today had Pleasant's grab-bag system of selection provided him with a different set of choreographers and dancers. What if Ashton had been free to come to New York and Tudor had been forced to remain in England? What if Carmelita Maracci had accepted Pleasant's early invitation and precluded him from inviting Agnes de Mille? What if an immediate acceptance by Ruth Page had eliminated the need to engage Andrée Howard? What if Eugene Loring had come to terms with Kirstein, and Pleasant had reached an agreement with Gene Kelly? Also, what if Alexandra Danilova and Paul Petroff, to whom Pleasant had offered contracts, had been engaged and replaced Patricia Bowman and Anton Dolin before they had settled their contract differences with Pleasant? And what if Pleasant had been able to persuade Paul Haakon that he could support his wife and child on a Ballet Theatre salary and had engaged him instead of Hugh Laing? What if Nora Kaye had decided not to leave the International Casino, or if Alicia Alonso had remained loyal to Balanchine, or if THE STRAW HAT REVIEW had turned into a long-running hit and kept Jerome Robbins occupied on Broadway? It is interesting to speculate, but the element of chance does not diminish Pleasant's accomplishment. Whatever his method, or lack of method, he did succeed in bringing to life a ballet company whose distinguishing features were variety and versatility.

Pleasant's second, and perhaps greater, accomplishment was the mere fact of accomplishment itself—he pulled it off. In this he matched his prototype, Serge Diaghilev, but with a difference. Although, like the Russian impresario, he found himself unable to operate under the budgetary restrictions imposed on him by his backers, he approached his problems with a different temperament and was forced to conduct his business dealings under different regulative standards. Diaghilev, in his confident arrogance, never questioned his right to demand unlimited support from his backers. The privilege of associating with him in his artistic ventures must be paid for with unstinting generosity. While he accepted the reality that his demands would not always be fully satisfied, he experienced no embarrassment or temerity in advancing them. Pleasant, on the other hand, conceded that backers had the right to limit their contributions. If these proved to be insufficient, he requested further support with a feeling of humility, a sense of guilt, as though he had let them down, wasted their money, or even violated a fiduciary trust. When faced with obligations he could not meet, instead of proceeding with arrogance, as did Diaghilev, he panicked. Diaghilev, too, might have panicked had he had to operate under the same conditions as Pleasant. As it was, he was not constrained by any trade union that stipulated how much and when he must pay his artists. Nor did he hesitate to run up bills with theaters and theatrical supply houses, which he chose to regard as unwitting partners in his ventures and as creditors who should expect to be paid only by funds produced at the box office. Pleasant was required to proceed differently. For one thing, the American Guild of Musical Artists stipulated minimum salaries for dancers and enforced the regulation that the curtain could not rise on a performance until the payment of all salaries was guaranteed. For another, Pleasant's principal backers and their financial advisors maintained the conservative position that supply creditors must be paid with reasonable promptness, unless of course they were banks in the business of supplying credit. If the debt was not in dispute, the creditor must never be forced to go to law to collect it. It was unthinkable that any corporation with which Miss Chase was connected could ever declare bankruptcy. In 1909, when Diaghilev presented his company in its first season, he knew that at its conclusion he could, if necessary, leave Paris with bills and even salaries unpaid, and he in fact did so. In 1939, Pleasant knew that at the conclusion of Ballet Theatre's first season, all salaries must have been paid and arrangements made for all creditors to be satisfied in due and early course. His inability to cope with this situation set the stage for his eventual downfall.

THE INAUGURAL SEASON

When, on July 26, Pleasant had written Miss Chase asking her whether she could see her "way clear to finance the beginning of the program," he assured her that additional backing could be obtained from other sources. When Miss Chase answered in the affirmative, she qualified her assent with the provision that her contribution should not exceed $25,000. During August and September, disbursements were held down to $8,493. On October 1, with the start of rehearsals, dancers went on salary and choreographers received down-payments on their contracts. By the end of the month total disbursements had reached $23,452.60, still under Miss Chase's guarantee. By the end of November, however, Pleasant had paid out $41,639.61. Meanwhile, Miss Chase had increased her contribution, but in the form of loans that were to be repaid with moneys expected from other contributors and eventually from the box-office receipts. By December 31 Pleasant had signed checks totaling $92,820.65. The alarm bells in the financial advisors' offices began to sound too stridently to be ignored. Pleasant was removed as co-signer of checks, with Rudolf Orthwine, and replaced by Harry M. Zuckert, a legal consultant and treasurer of the presenting corporation. Orthwine made a stab at effecting economies by canceling the production of the ballet QUINTET.

The farcical aspects of the production of QUINTET are illustrative of the ease with which theatrical budgets can be compromised. On July 25, 1939, when Mordkin met with and charmed Raymond Scott, it appeared that the ballet could be produced inexpensively. Pleasant was able to report in his July 26 letter that Scott's royalty demands were modest and that Mordkin planned a production that required no scenery, merely the regular cyclorama, "with perhaps a bit of skeleton, indicative scenery here and there, more in the manner of props." All this changed when Dolin was substituted as choreographer. The ballet soon required scenery and costumes by Lucinda Ballard: six sets which cost $6,409 and were considerably more than skeletal and ninety-two costumes costing $7,293. The production, which had been budgeted at less than $5,000, was on its way to costing more than $17,000 when Orthwine attempted to call a halt. He argued that excess expenditures could be reduced most effectively by the cancellation of the production. In any case, he pointed out, the ballet could not be ready for performance until the final week of the season; its only four performances were, in fact, scheduled for the last weekend. If it was not presented, the public would not miss it and certainly would not protest. There were, however, others who objected vehemently. Pleasant later recalled (inaccurately in certain details) the course of events in a letter to Orthwine:

The idea of cutting out the Scott ballet was very dangerous as you and I found out when we tried to do it. Scott's was one of the first ballets we had planned and announced. Dolin had already set the choreography (it was the first thing he was engaged to do; his other two ballets had first been assigned to Mordkin); Ballard was originally engaged to do the Scott and then other things followed. On the basis of doing that, Ballard had made very special concessions to us on her fees and had supervised or lent her name for program credit for non-union designers. Both Dolin and Ballard set up a terrific howl; refused to go on with their other work unless our promises on Scott were kept.

Worst, however, were the very real and open threats of Mr. Best, Scott's manager. They had been most cooperative and had given us the music for almost nothing compared to Scott's regular royalties. . . . Further Best had bought 500 tickets (cash). . . . He threatened to sue for injury to Scott's name, throwing out his ballet at the last moment; using him to plug the whole season and then not using his ballet, etc.

Added to the protests of Dolin, Ballard, and Best were those of Elizabeth, the Countess von Furstenberg, whose nine-year-old daughter, Betsy, had been assigned the role of La Petite Fille in the Eighteenth-Century Ballroom scene. So determined was the Countess that her daughter should not be deprived of this opportunity that she made a contribution to Ballet Theatre in the form of a $2,500 stock purchase, and she obtained from Henry I. Harriman (no relation to the Harrimans) an advance of an additional $5,000. Mr. Harriman requested that his contribution be regarded as a temporary loan with the assurance that it would later be applied to the purchase of stock. Accordingly, Orthwine gave him a promissory note. It was the intention that the money be spent only on QUINTET, for the production of which Ballet Theatre would make no further payments. To assure segregation of the funds, Orthwine deposited the money in a separate account, and in making out the note to Harriman signed it "For the Raymond Scott Production," carelessly adding the abbreviation "Co." When Harriman later became disenchanted with ballet, he was able to point out that no corporation by that name had ever been registered. Charging Orthwine with fraud, he demanded payment of his note, denying that he had ever intended to convert the loan into a stock purchase. The lawyers eventually negotiated an out-of-court settlement for $3,500, but to accomplish this it was necessary to request Orthwine to disassociate himself from the company; he cooperated by resigning as president of Advanced Arts Ballets, Inc., the parent company of Ballet Theatre, and delivered the corporate papers contained in filing cabinets rediscovered a quarter of a century later in Ballet Theatre's Philadelphia warehouse. In an aide-mémoire prepared for the lawyers, Pleasant disclaimed responsibility: (continued on page 102)

THE FORTIES

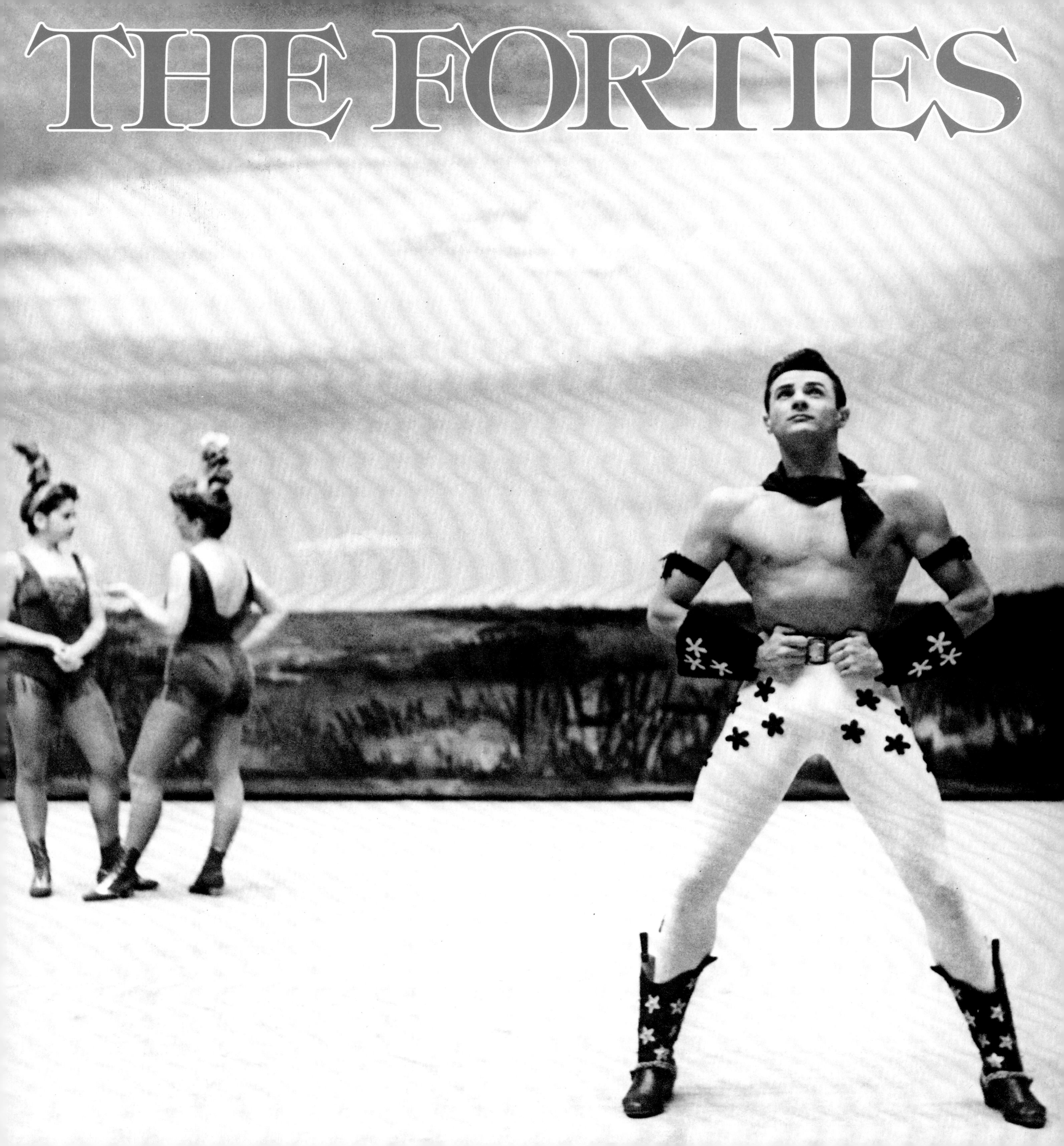

LES SYLPHIDES
KAREN CONRAD
WILLIAM DOLLAR
BILLY THE KID
(PREVIOUS PAGE)
JOHN KRIZA

THE EARLY YEARS
OPENING NIGHT

The opening-night program presented by Richard Pleasant, director of the newly founded Ballet Theatre, became the prototype of the thousands of programs that were offered during the succeeding four decades. Ideally, the evening began with an "opening ballet," usually a plotless work in the classical style that could be enjoyed even by latecomers and would gently prepare the audience for the more concentrated attention demanded of it by the thought-provoking "middle ballet" to follow. The evening would end with a gay, lighthearted "closing ballet," designed to send the audience home in a state of euphoria, eagerly resolving to return for more.

On the night of January 11, 1940, Michel Fokine's LES SYLPHIDES fulfilled the function of the opening ballet and Mikhail Mordkin's VOICES OF SPRING was the ideal choice for the closing ballet. The manner in which these ballets were presented also presaged future practice—the casts were not as had been announced in advance. Mordkin had quit the company in a huff and did not perform the role of the General in his own ballet. Nana Gollner

had left, too, ostensibly because an injury prevented her from dancing the Mazurka in LES SYLPHIDES but possibly because her agent had persuaded her that, by insisting on an alphabetical listing of the dancers' names in all advertisements and posters, the company was jeopardizing her status as a ballerina. Patricia Bowman threatened to depart in a similar huff until it was decided that the choreographer, Adolph Bolm, need not be listed in his dual capacity as a dancer, leaving Miss Bowman's name to head the list. (Four decades later, the roster was again headed by a dancer whose name began with B, and there was only the remotest possibility that anyone would be engaged whose name would alphabetically precede Baryshnikov's.)

THE GREAT AMERICAN GOOF by Eugene Loring admirably qualified as a thought-provoking middle ballet. It innovatively combined dancing with the surrealist dialogue written by William Saroyan and delivered by characters with enigmatic designations such as The Woman, the bright potential; Drunkard, a religious man; Praying Boy, a dreamer of kites and fishes; and Boy, With a Fever of 105.

VOICES OF SPRING
(OPPOSITE PAGE)
(TOP) PATRICIA BOWMAN WITH
MIKHAIL MORDKIN, AND
WITH NINA STROGANOVA.
(BELOW) MORDKIN,
STROGANOVA, DIMITRI ROMANOFF,
BOWMAN.
THE GREAT AMERICAN GOOF
ANTONY TUDOR
EUGENE LORING

THE FIRST AMERICANS

THREE VIRGINS AND A DEVIL
JEROME ROBBINS
LUCIA CHASE
MARIA KARNILOVA
JOHN KRIZA

Richard Pleasant made a valiant attempt to sponsor native choreographers in Ballet Theatre, which was being hailed as a new American company, though in fact it was American only with respect to its direction and financing. In addition to Loring's THE GREAT AMERICAN GOOF, he commissioned a work by Agnes de Mille titled BLACK RITUAL, which proved to be equally thought-provoking and innovative in its presentation of what Miss de Mille described as the "psychological atmosphere" of the ritual of blood sacrifice, as performed by an all-black cast of dancers.

LUCIA CHASE
ANNABELLE LYON
MARIA KARNILOVA

In the second season, these two choreographers scored unquestioned successes with the revivals of their works originally created for other companies. Loring staged BILLY THE KID from the repertory of the Ballet Caravan, and de Mille revised THREE VIRGINS AND A DEVIL, which had first appeared in a London musical. Both ballets have enjoyed frequent reappearances in the Ballet Theatre's list of active ballets.

BILLY THE KID
JOHN KRIZA DANCED THE ROLE
OF BILLY FOR TWO DECADES,
FIRST WITH ALICIA ALONSO
(OPPOSITE PAGE, UPPER LEFT),
AND LATER WITH RUTH ANN KOESUN.
(THIS PAGE TOP)
KRIZA WITH KOESUN,
AND WITH PAUL GODKIN.

SWAN LAKE
NANA GOLLNER
ANTON DOLIN

In 1940 no ballet company attempted to mount the full-evening classical or romantic ballets that had been so popular in the theaters of Imperial Russia, even though Russian choreographers capable of staging them were resident in the United States. No one was certain whether the interest of an American audience could be sustained during the four acts of a single ballet. It was clear to everyone, on the other hand, that the millions allotted for spectacular productions by the Tsar's privy purse could not be provided by even the richest American patron. Nor could Americans engage the large complement of dancers required to perform them. Hence, like Diaghilev before him, Pleasant had to be content with an abridged, one-act version of SWAN LAKE.

The case was different with ballets created for French opera-house companies and later transported to Russia. Originally these had been more modestly produced, and performed by smaller casts. Ballet Theatre could afford to produce, and could perform, such multiple-act ballets as LA FILLE MAL GARDÉE, COPPÉLIA, and GISELLE.

Giselle has always been the dream role of ballerinas. Virtually all of them have attempted it, including many who should not have. Until recently, the ballet was not popular with the public and was sparingly presented by impresarios. In its native France, it was not performed at all in the Paris Opéra during the forty years preceding its re-introduction by Diaghilev in 1910. Even in the Imperial Russian theaters it was presented only a few times each year, and then only in response to pressures exerted by the reigning ballerina. Pleasant's experience with the ballet was no more felicitous: it failed to sell tickets and gave rise to dissension and bitterness among the ballerinas. Nana Gollner rehearsed the title role, but withdrew from the company before the premiere. Patricia Bowman, who had previously performed the Mordkin version discarded by Pleasant, found herself in conflict with Anton Dolin's interpretation, and their differences could not be resolved in time for the first scheduled performance. As a consequence, Annabelle Lyon established what has since become almost a tradition with Ballet Theatre presentations of GISELLE: she took on the role with only a few days' notice.

The romantic ballet of the nineteenth century was further represented by Dolin's version of PAS DE QUATRE, which reconstructed a gala performance of the ballerinas Taglioni, Grisi, Grahn, and Cerrito.

LA FILLE MAL GARDÉE IRINA BARONOVA ON THE SHOULDERS OF DAVID NILLO AND DONALD SADDLER. AS PERFORMED IN THE 1942 MEXICAN FILM "YOLANDE."

LA FILLE MAL GARDÉE BARONOVA WITH DIMITRI ROMANOFF AND SIMON SEMENOFF.   **COPPÉLIA** DONALD SADDLER, MARIA KARNILOVA; BARONOVA, SEMENOFF, ANTON DOLIN.

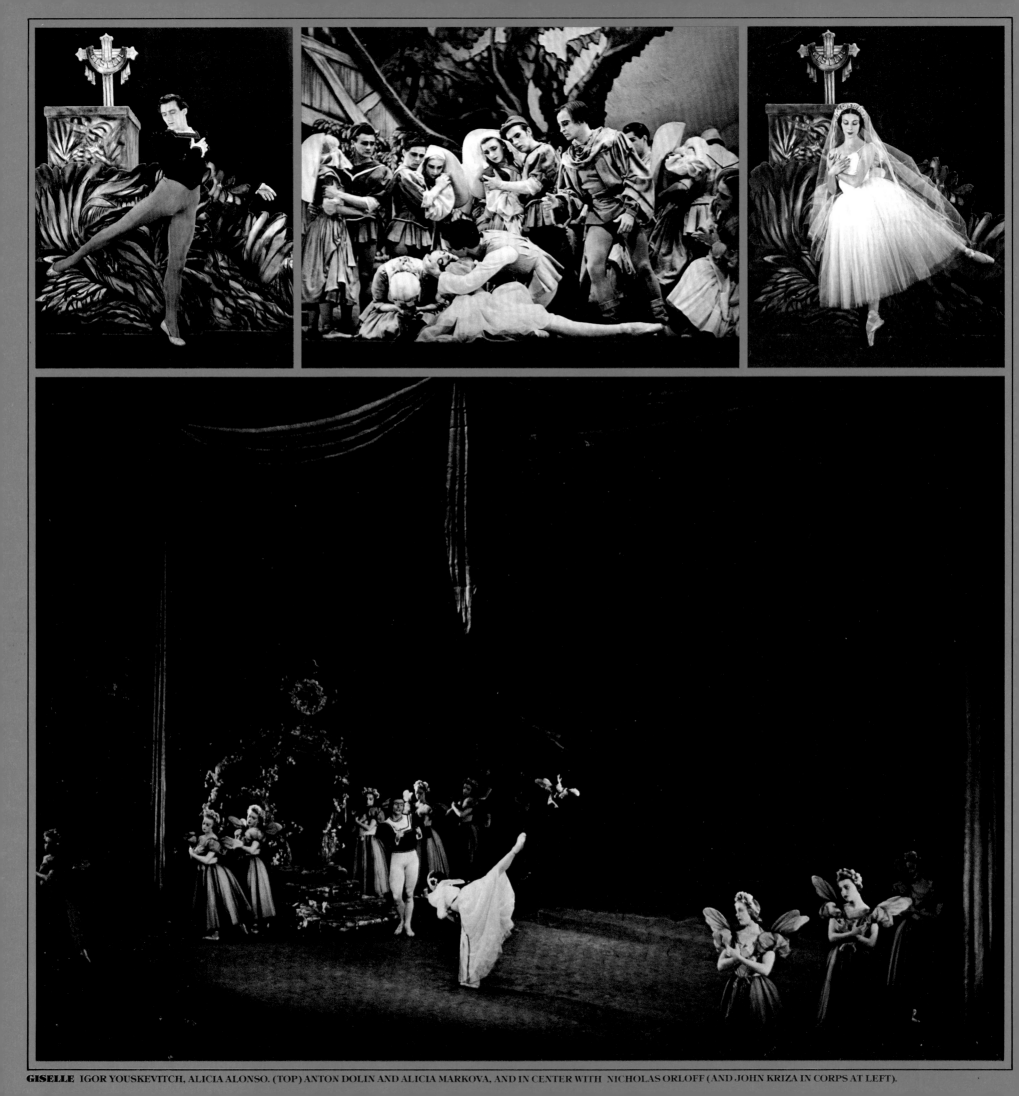

GISELLE IGOR YOUSKEVITCH, ALICIA ALONSO. (TOP) ANTON DOLIN AND ALICIA MARKOVA, AND IN CENTER WITH NICHOLAS ORLOFF (AND JOHN KRIZA IN CORPS AT LEFT).

PAS DE QUATRE ALICIA MARKOVA WITH NORA KAYE, ANNABELLE LYON, ROSELLA HIGHTOWER.

CAPRICCIOSO
ANNABELLE LYON
JOHN KRIZA

DARK ELEGIES
SEATED: MARIA KARNILOVA
KIRSTEN VALBOR
NORA KAYE
ANTONY TUDOR
STANDING: HUGH LAING
AND HUBERT BLAND
WITH LUCIA CHASE

THE ENGLISH

When Antony Tudor's JARDIN AUX LILAS was given its New York premiere on the fourth program of the season, America was introduced to a fresh style of choreography, one in which dance movement and action were controlled by psychological motivations.

Of all the ballets contributed for the first season by eleven choreographers, Fokine's LES SYLPHIDES and the works of Tudor most clearly set the style for the company and most profoundly influenced the creative approach of future Ballet Theatre choreographers. For the dancers, working with Tudor provided a continuing inspiration that was of particular significance to Nora Kaye. It was his approach that revived her flagging interest in ballet and directed her onto the path toward becoming America's leading dramatic ballerina.

With war threatening in Europe, Pleasant wrote to both Tudor and Frederick Ashton. The letter to Ashton was returned marked "Not at this address." It can only be conjectured what Ballet Theatre's dominant dancing style would be today had both Englishmen been engaged for the first season and exerted their divergent influences on the company in its formative stage.

For the company, Tudor staged three other works he had created in London: DARK ELEGIES, JUDGMENT OF PARIS, and GALA PERFORMANCE. They were all well received, but at first the not-unusual gaps in communication between English and American minds occurred: Americans saw nothing but slapstick comedy in what Tudor considered the bitterly tragic JUDGMENT OF PARIS, and as GALA PERFORMANCE unfolded, they mistakenly regarded it as Tudor's reconstruction of the golden age of ballet. When, halfway through this work, they realized that he was in fact ridiculing the style and techniques of conventional classic ballet, they were somewhat resentful at having been taken in. Anton Dolin added two works to the English contributions: CAPRICCIOSO and QUINTET, an Englishman's view of Capri and of the United States as observed on a trip from New York to California.

JARDIN AUX LILAS
PAULA LLOYD
DIANA ADAMS
MURIEL BENTLEY
HUGH LAING

(OPPOSITE PAGE)
NORA KAYE

GALA PERFORMANCE
(TOP)
ANTONY TUDOR
NORA KAYE
ALICIA ALONSO
NORMA VANCE
HUGH LAING

THE RUSSIAN OCCUPATION

PRINCESS AURORA
IRINA BARONOVA
ANTON DOLIN

THE "HAM-AND-EGGS" PROGRAM

At the beginning of Ballet Theatre's third season the direction of the company was assumed by German Sevastianov, and the management of its engagements in New York and on tour was undertaken by S. Hurok. Both were Russian and both confirmed in the belief that only Russians could create ballets. Consequently, from the several Ballet Russe companies Sevastianov engaged stars (not necessarily Russian by birth) and hired choreographers (to provide them with featured roles in new ballets) so that Hurok could begin to advertise Ballet Theatre as "The Greatest in Russian Ballet." Thus began the period that might aptly be described as the Russian Occupation.

Anton Dolin, who had acted as marriage broker in the union of Ballet Theatre and Hurok, organized the activities of the company in the summer of 1941 in preparation for its Russification. He leased Jacob's Pillow, vacant since the dissolution of Ted Shawn's all-male dance group, and invited a nucleus of the Ballet Theatre company to occupy the rustic cabins built by Shawn's men. The dancers were paid seven dollars a week for room and board (Ballet Theatre contributed two of each seven dollars). For the weekly recitals staged by Dolin, they received modest fees, and also rehearsed without compensation the works to be presented by Ballet Theatre in the fall.

The first of these, an adaptation of the last act of SLEEPING BEAUTY, was given the title PRINCESS AURORA. As with his production of one act of SWAN LAKE, Dolin was following the precedent set by Diaghilev, who had presented the one-act AURORA'S WEDDING after his complete BEAUTY had been impounded by creditors. Dolin's PAS DE QUATRE and Fokine's BLUEBEARD were added to PRINCESS AURORA to form the first "ham-and-eggs" program, so named because it was the staple on which the company subsisted on the tours booked by Hurok. On its first trans-

PRINCESS AURORA ALPHEUS KOON, MURIEL BENTLEY, FRANK HOBI; IRINA BARONOVA, GEORGE SKIBINE.

PETER AND THE WOLF YURA LAZOVSKY; VIOLA ESSEN, EUGENE LORING.

BLUEBEARD KENNETH DAVIS (PRINCE SAPPHIRE), LUCIA CHASE (QUEEN), BARBARA FALLIS (PRINCESS), DIMITRI ROMANOFF (BLUEBEARD), MELISSA HAYDEN (ANGELO).

continental tour, this program was seen in every one of the fifty-one cities of the United States and Canada where only one performance was given. In cities where a matinée was offered, a supplemental ham-and-eggs program was presented, which invariably featured Adolph Bolm's PETER AND THE WOLF—an irresistible magnet for children. Only in cities where the company remained for more than a single day were other ballets performed.

BLUEBEARD was made to order for the closing ballet of the program. Commissioned to create a comic ballet to the score of Offenbach's BARBE-BLEU (with additional danceable music selected by Antal Dorati from other Offenbach operas), Fokine employed the original libretto devised by Ludovic Halévy and Henri Meilhac, adjusting it somewhat to provide roles of equal importance for the ballerinas Irina Baronova and Alicia Markova and substantial roles for all the other stars and soloists. His creative processes were such that he did not require rehearsals with the company in Jacob's Pillow. In effect, he conducted the preliminary rehearsals in his head. Having mentally blocked out the choreography, before meeting with the dancers he was able to offer a detailed synopsis that Sevastianov translated into approximate English: "Entry of the King, 1 min.; Scene with daughter, 30 sec.; Bluebeard wants to marry bride of Prince...Scandal...Entry of Soldiers, 1 min.; Duel, 20 sec...."

(TOP) DOLIN WITH BARONOVA. (BOTTOM) ALICIA MARKOVA, GEORGE SKIBINE; JEROME ROBBINS, LUCIA CHASE, YURA LAZOVSKY.

Sevastianov met with Fokine at his Tudor-style house in Riverdale, on the banks of the Hudson River, and they cast the roles of the ballet, consulting occasionally with Charles Payne about the qualifications of those American dancers with whom they were not yet acquainted. Thereafter, Fokine transferred in private the choreographic images from his mind to the bodies of himself and his wife, Vera, who, according to Sevastianov, always participated in these creative sessions in the nude. (This can probably be dismissed as pure fiction, though it is true that August of 1941 was unusually warm.) By the time the company returned to New York, Fokine had worked out all the choreography and was able to transmit it to the dancers in fewer rehearsals than choreographers usually require for staging a major work.

Fokine successfully carried out his commission according to specifications, with one exception: the role he created for Markova was not equal to Baronova's and was soon passed on to a soloist understudy. BLUEBEARD was the first ballet created especially for Ballet Theatre that proved to be a critical and popular success. It was still in the repertory when the company visited the Soviet Union in 1960, where it was seen by Premier Nikita Khrushchev, who declared it to be his favorite of the evening's program.

RUSSIAN SOLDIER YURA LAZOVSKY WITH MIRIAM GOLDEN, JEANETTE LAURET, SONO OSATO, MURIEL BENTLEY. (OPPOSITE TOP) JEROME ROBBINS AS THE OFFICER IN COMMAND.

CARNAVAL ANTONY TUDOR, LUCIA CHASE, HAROLD LANG.

SPECTRE DE LA ROSE ANNABELLE LYON, IAN GIBSON.

MICHEL FOKINE

For his second work, Fokine acceded to the suggestion that he employ Prokofiev's score for the film LIEUTENANT KIJE. But he rejected the movie scenario, partly because it was unsuitable for dance interpretation, but principally because it ridiculed the idiocy of the military establishment under Tsar Paul I. He retained a sense of loyalty toward the House of Romanov, which had treated him well, and he nurtured resentment against the Soviet regime, which had spurned the terms under which he had offered to return to his native land in 1925. Consequently, the program note revealed, "When Fokine first listened to LIEUTENANT KIJE, he heard it not as satirical music but as an expression of the soul of a simple Russian peasant." In the ballet, the Russian peasant became a soldier who died bravely in defense of the motherland of the nineteenth century. Subsequently, the twentieth-century peasants were besieged at Stalingrad and the Soviet military achieved heroic world stature. Hurok insisted that they must be honored during a benefit performance at the Metropolitan. As Fokine's Russian soldier lay dying, a Soviet counterpart was spotlighted in the background above him, waving the hammer and sickle. (By then, Fokine was no longer alive to give or withhold his permission for this innovation, but it is doubtful whether he would have approved of the Hurok press releases, which dedicated the ballet "to the gallant Russian soldiers of World War II"—whereas in truth he had carefully written that "This ballet is dedicated to all suffering warriors.")

Fokine next created HELEN OF TROY, which was performed in Mexico, but was then withdrawn because he died before he could make the necessary revisions. During the last years of his association with Ballet Theatre, Fokine personally staged and rehearsed LES SYLPHIDES, PETROUCHKA, SPECTRE DE LA ROSE, and THE DYING SWAN.

PETROUCHKA
(OPPOSITE PAGE)
ANDRÉ EGLEVSKY
LUCIA CHASE
LEONIDE MASSINE

(TOP)
SIMON SEMENOFF
AS THE CHARLATAN

(MIDDLE)
SIMON SEMENOFF
DAVID NILLO
LUCIA CHASE
JEROME ROBBINS

(BOTTOM)
LUCIA CHASE
ANDRÉ EGLEVSKY
MICHAEL KIDD
STANLEY HERBERTT

MADEMOISELLE ANGOT ANDRÉ EGLEVSKY (JUMPING), JANET REED (CENTER), LEONIDE MASSINE HELD BY REX COOPER.

LEONIDE MASSINE

Leonide Massine's first work for Ballet Theatre, ALEKO, admirably advanced the cause of the Russian Occupation—it could not have been more Russian. All of its creators had been born subjects of the Tsar: the choreographer Massine, the composer Tchaikovsky, the librettist Alexander Pushkin, and the designer Marc Chagall. It delighted the moujik soul of S. Hurok, and during its initial run and subsequent revivals appeared to confirm his contention that, when given a choice, Americans preferred their wine French and their ballet Russian.

ALEKO SEATED BOYS: ROBBINS, KRIZA. (TOP) YOUSKEVITCH, ALONSO, KRIZA; MARKOVA, SKIBINE; LAING.

For his third contribution, Massine turned to the French opéra bouffe LA FILLE DE MADAME ANGOT, by Charles Lecocq, from which he created MADEMOISELLE ANGOT. The ballet was a popular success, and so impressed Ninette de Valois that she later asked Massine to stage it under the title MAM'ZELLE ANGOT as a starring vehicle for Margot Fonteyn in the Sadler's Wells Ballet.

Massine's second ballet, DON DOMINGO DE DON BLAS, demonstrated that the public, with respect to ethnic background, certainly did not want its ballets Mexican. His all-Mexican team of creators included the composer Silvestre Revueltas, the librettist Juan Ruiz de Alarcón, the designer Julio Castellanos, and several teachers of

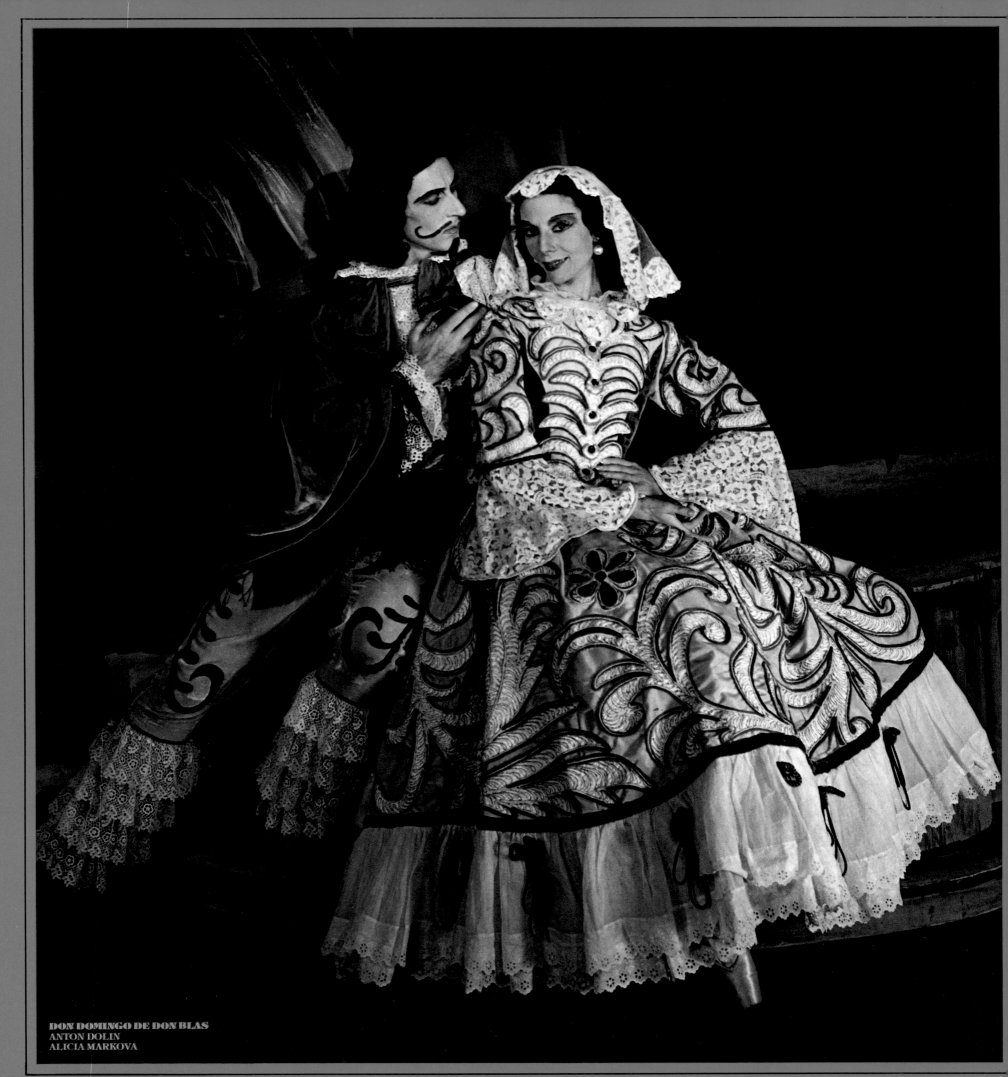

DON DOMINGO DE DON BLAS
ANTON DOLIN
ALICIA MARKOVA

THREE-CORNERED HAT LEONIDE MASSINE, ARGENTINITA.

THE FANTASTIC TOY SHOP KAREN CONRAD, LEONIDE MASSINE.

DON DOMINGO DUNCAN NOBL, KRIZA, ROBBINS, RICHARD REED. CAPRICCIO ESPAGNOL JEROME ROBBINS.

native dances. The ballet was designed as a flattering tribute to Mexico, which Sevastianov hoped would persuade its government officials to make the Palacio de Bellas Artes available to Ballet Theatre as its summer residence; it at least accomplished this purpose.

During his association with Ballet Theatre, Massine staged three other of his ballets, the physical décor and performing rights to which were his personal property: CAPRICCIO ESPAGNOL, THE FANTASTIC TOY SHOP, and THREE-CORNERED HAT. Although none of his ballets remain in the active repertory, and it is unlikely that any of them will be restored, Massine indirectly made a substantial contribution to Ballet Theatre in 1977. When the scenery and hand-painted costumes for ALEKO were being executed in Mexico City, Marc Chagall found it necessary to do much of the painting himself. Thirty-five years later, when Ballet Theatre was facing one of its recurrent financial crises, the décors were sold at the inflated prices commanded today for paintings by Chagall.

GEORGE BALANCHINE

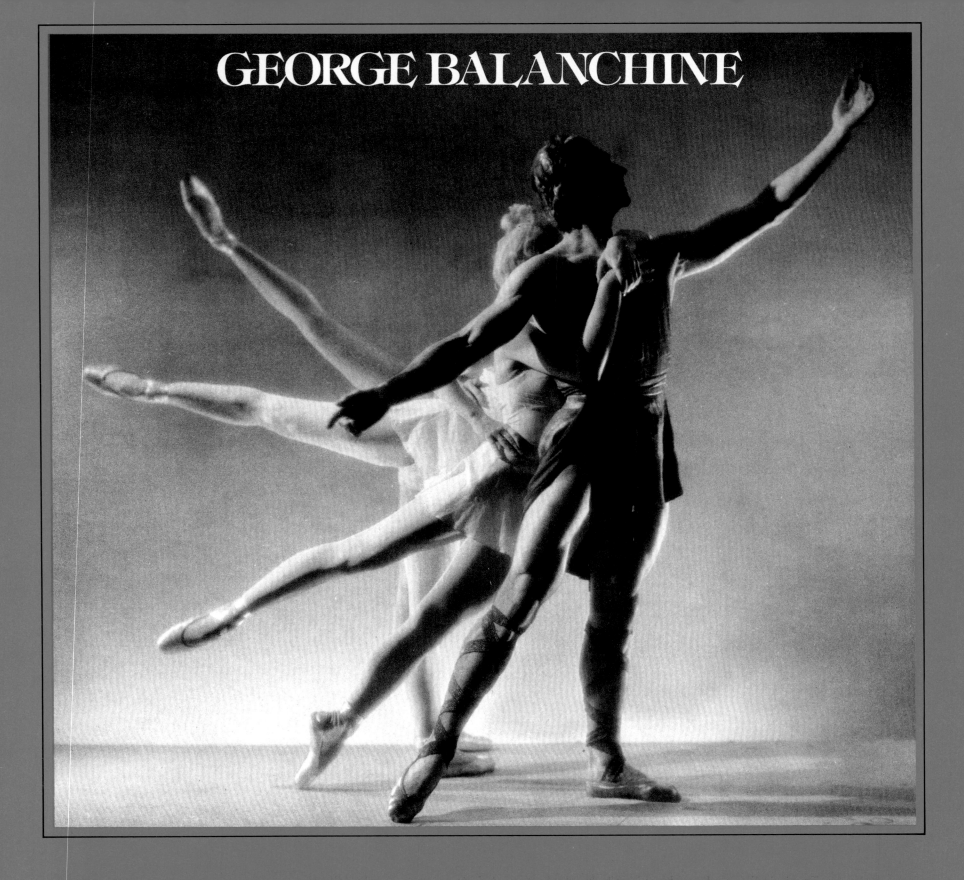

As the Russian Occupation continued into 1943, a star was added to the roster who was known by the Russian name Vera Zorina. (She was, in fact, a German-born Norwegian, Eva Brigitte Hartwig.) She brought into the company not only a glamorous Russian name but a distinguished Russian choreographer, George Balanchine, her husband. For Zorina he restaged two of his early creations, APOLLO and THE WANDERER, and he altered roles in such ballets as HELEN OF TROY to adapt them to her individual dancing style.

Balanchine continued his association with Ballet Theatre after Zorina's departure and in 1944 created for it a ballet titled WALTZ ACADEMY, which remained in the repertory until 1948. After it was temporarily withdrawn from the active repertory (all ballets are given a periodic rest), Balanchine was never able to arrange the time (or perhaps work up the enthusiasm) to restore it.

In 1947, Balanchine returned to create a work of genius in THEME AND VARIATIONS, designed to set off the special talents of Alicia Alonso and Igor Youskevitch.

APOLLO
DIANA ADAMS
NORA KAYE
NANA GOLLNER
IGOR YOUSKEVITCH

THEME AND VARIATIONS
IGOR YOUSKEVITCH
(TOP) YOUSKEVITCH WITH
ALICIA ALONSO
NORA KAYE
MARIA TALLCHIEF

GIFT OF THE MAGI MARJORIE TALLCHIEF, NORA KAYE.   FIREBIRD ALICIA MARKOVA, ANTON DOLIN.   FAIR AT SOROCHINSK DOLIN, LUCIA CHASE.

THE BELOVED ANTON DOLIN, ALICIA MARKOVA, ROSELLA HIGHTOWER (SECOND FROM RIGHT ON PLATFORM).

GRADUATION BALL TATIANA RIABOUCHINSKA; HAROLD LANG.

OTHER RUSSIANS

In addition to Fokine, Massine, and Balanchine, the Russian forces engaged by Sevastianov included half-a-dozen other Slavic choreographers whose works aided S. Hurok in selling "The Greatest in Russian Ballet" to the American public: Adolph Bolm (FIREBIRD), Yura Lazovsky (AFTERNOON OF A FAUN), David Lichine HELEN OF TROY, FAIR AT SOROCHINSK and GRADUATION BALL), Bronislava Nijinska (THE BELOVED), Vania Psota (SLAVONIKA), and Simon Semenoff (GIFT OF THE MAGI).

HELEN OF TROY
DIANA ADAMS (HELEN)
IGOR YOUSKEVITCH (PARIS)

(OPPOSITE PAGE)
JOHN KRIZA (HERMES)
IGOR YOUSKEVITCH (PARIS)

PILLAR OF FIRE HUGH LAING AND DIANA ADAMS. (ORIGINAL CAST AT THE RIGHT) HUGH LAING, NORA KAYE, LUCIA CHASE, ANNABELLE LYON, ANTONY TUDOR.

THE ENGLISH SURVIVAL

While the Russian Occupation remained in force, Antony Tudor was given little cooperation or encouragement in his efforts to create ballets, although he continued to preside over what Pleasant had labeled the English Wing. However, with the determination of an English bulldog and the British penchant for muddling through, he persisted in producing ballets as English as his untainted accent, which he steadfastly retained along with his British citizenship.

Tudor's PILLAR OF FIRE, the first successful <u>dramatic</u> ballet created especially for Ballet Theatre, projected Nora Kaye and Hugh Laing into immediate stardom. The décor was designed by the American Jo Mielziner and to some suggested a New England locale, but as Tudor had conceived the libretto before he left Old England, he could not have intended it as an American ballet. His next creation, ROMEO AND JULIET, was as English as

ALICIA MARKOVA

SONO OSATO, HUGH LAING

LAING, MARKOVA

MARKOVA, ANTONY TUDOR, LAING

Shakespeare had been able to make it. Strangely, critics both here and abroad deplored his use of a score compiled from the music of Frederick Delius, apparently in the belief that music by an Englishman was not an appropriate accompaniment to a tale of star-crossed Italian lovers. DIM LUSTRE was danced to Richard Strauss' BURLESKE, but its setting was clearly Edwardian Brighton, not an Austrian spa. And even SHADOW OF THE WIND, with its oriental screen sets and costumes, could be said to represent a British imperialist's view of the China of Li Po.

TUDOR, NICHOLAS ORLOFF, LAING

LAING, TUDOR, DIMITRI ROMANOFF, LUCIA CHASE, MARKOVA

LAING, MARKOVA

ROMEO AND JULIET
(OPPOSITE PAGE) FIRST MEETING OF JULIET AND ROMEO.
(ABOVE) ROMEO ENCOUNTERS THE FUNERAL CORTEGE:
NORA KAYE
HUGH LAING

UNDERTOW (OPPOSITE PAGE) DIANA ADAMS, HUGH LAING. (TOP) SHELLIE FARREL, RICHARD BEARD; HUGH LAING, ALICIA ALONSO; MURIEL BENTLEY, HUGH LAING; STANLEY HERBERTT, SHIRLEY ECKLE. (BOTTOM) DIANA ADAMS, JOHN KRIZA; NANA GOLLNER, HUGH LAING.

Perhaps the most English of Tudor's works was his UNDERTOW. Although the setting, designed by the Chicago artist Raymond Breinin, may have been intended to represent an American city, it more closely resembled the slums of Liverpool or Newcastle, and the people who inhabited it, though named for figures in Greek mythology, were clearly those with whom Tudor had grown up in London. If Tudor had hoped to establish a universality of locale and personae, he failed to disguise the English accent. In these permissive days, UNDERTOW remains a striking example of ballet's ability to animate highly erotic themes, bordering on pornography, incurring the censure of only the most puritanical. The plot for the ballet of "psychological murder" was passed on to Tudor by John Van Druten, perhaps because he realized it could not be employed for a play on the legitimate stage. Where but in the dance theatre could one have then enacted such sequences as the following: a woman painfully gives birth to a boy and instantly rejects him; a nose-picking old man molests a child; juvenile delinquents rape a provocative nymphomaniac; a Salvation Army lass gropes the timid protagonist, who later murders a predatory female determined to rob him of his virginity. In an era when sex-oriented plays were still being banned in Boston, UNDERTOW was performed with impunity; it was forbidden only in Los Angeles, at Philharmonic Hall, which was also used as a church by the religious group that owned it.

Further additions to the English Wing included Dolin's ROMANTIC AGE and Frederick Ashton's LES PATINEURS, which the company brought back from London as a souvenir of its first appearance at the Royal Opera House in Covent Garden.

DIM LUSTRE
HUGH LAING
NORA KAYE
NORMA VANCE
HARRY ASMUS

LES PATINEURS
(OPPOSITE PAGE)
BARBARA LLOYD

(TOP TWO)
JOHN KRIZA

(BOTTOM TWO)
TOMMY RALL

FALL RIVER LEGEND
(OPPOSITE PAGE) LUCIA CHASE, ALICIA ALONSO.
(ABOVE) NORA KAYE; NORA KAYE, LUCIA CHASE.

AGNES DE MILLE

While the Russian contingent under Sevastianov maintained control over the artistic activities of Ballet Theatre, Americans were given no serious consideration as contributing choreographers. Not until Sevastianov was drafted into the army and was succeeded by an American, Alden Talbot, was native talent once more encouraged. For the first time in three years, a new Agnes de Mille ballet, TALLY-HO, was added to the repertory—it proved American in no respect. Set in eighteenth-century France to the music of Gluck, it dealt with a hunting party during which the bored wife of a scholarly genius flirts with a reprobate prince.

The ballets of de Mille are alternately inspired by two contrasting facets of her nature: her devastating wit, and her ever-present awareness of impending doom. TALLY-HO was witty; her next ballet, FALL RIVER LEGEND, was doom-laden. Throughout her career, Miss de Mille has been convinced that theatrical directors and producers, like Lizzie Borden's wicked stepmother, are bent on sabotaging her efforts to attain artistic fulfillment. If this were indeed true, it would have to be said that the direction and management were defeated with respect to these ballets: both opened to enthusiastic acclaim, and their success has persisted through repeated revivals.

FALL RIVER LEGEND (TOP) NORA KAYE, PETER GLADKE, LUCIA CHASE. (BOTTOM) ENRIQUE MARTINEZ AND ERIC BRAUN (CENTER), JOHN KRIZA AND KAYE (RIGHT).

TALLY-HO (TOP) JOHN KRIZA, JEAN SULLIVAN. (BOTTOM) STANLEY HERBERTT, KRIZA, MURIEL BENTLEY (ON GROUND), MELISSA HAYDEN (BEHIND HER,) LUCIA CHASE, DIMITRI ROMANOFF. 97

FANCY FREE
(CENTER PICTURE)
JEROME ROBBINS
JOHN KRIZA
HAROLD LANG
JANET REED
MURIEL BENTLEY
(REX COOPER, BARTENDER)

JEROME ROBBINS

FANCY FREE was a ballet of fortunate second choices. It was the second ballet Robbins submitted for the consideration of the direction, and Leonard Bernstein and Oliver Smith were his second choices for composer and designer respectively. A contract was first offered to Herbert Kingsley to compose a score for a ballet tentatively titled "Shore Leave Interlude," and several designers were considered before the choice fell on Smith.

Because Robbins was on tour with the company, the ballet had to be created through correspondence. Bernstein in Boston would mail several bars of music to which Robbins would devise the choreography in Kansas City while writing suggestions for the alteration of the set designs Smith had sent him from Brooklyn Heights.

These second choices proved as beneficial for the world of ballet as for the individual participants. FANCY FREE demonstrated once and for all the viability of choreography by Americans, and it catapulted its creators to fame in the theater. The characters were portraits of the choreographer himself and of his friends. It is as though Robbins

INTERPLAY JOHN KRIZA, JANET REED.

FACSIMILE JEROME ROBBINS, JOHN KRIZA, NORA KAYE.

SUMMER DAY RUTH ANN KOESUN, JOHN KRIZA.

INTERPLAY ZACHERY SOLOV, ERIK KRISTEN, PAULA LLOYD, JOHN KRIZA, MELISSA HAYDEN, MURIEL BENTLEY, FERNANDO ALONSO, ANNA CHESELKA.

had asked himself: "If Johnny [Kriza], Harold [Lang], and myself joined the Navy, how would we behave?" Had he chosen to create the roles on other dancers and had his choreography limned their individual characteristics, the actions, movements, comedy, the ballet as a whole, would have been quite different. In this respect, he was fortunate that Janet Reed and Harold Lang joined the company just at the time when he was a choreographer in search of characters who could join his old friends, John Kriza and Muriel Bentley, in acting as catalysts for his first work for Ballet Theatre.

MICHAEL KIDD

ALICIA ALONSO, MICHAEL KIDD

RUTH ANN KOESUN, JOHN KRIZA

ON STAGE! ALICIA ALONSO (SEATED LEFT), DIANA ADAMS (ON LADDER), JOHN KRIZA AND NORA KAYE (CENTER), MICHAEL KIDD (FAR RIGHT).

Because Robbins has not staged the ballet for another company, it has become a signature work for Ballet Theatre. What with the confusions caused by the great proliferation of ballet companies, it can always be said to one in doubt that "If you've seen FANCY FREE, you can be sure you've seen Ballet Theatre."

With the sensational success of FANCY FREE, the new American directors were encouraged to seek more works by Americans. Robbins added INTERPLAY, FACSIMILE, and SUMMER DAY, and in rapid succession, ballets by other Americans were produced: Michael Kidd's ON STAGE!, Catherine Littlefield's BARN DANCE, and John Taras' GRAZIANA.

At the time of this business I had been relieved of all business authority or responsibility and Mr. Lundberg [an accountant engaged by Mr. Zuckert] was OKing all bills and making all payments. I was not even signing checks at the time.

In a similar memorandum, Orthwine gave the lawyer his version of the events leading up to the Harriman affair:

I don't want to bother you too much with details but I suppose you do remember what a mess that Ballet Company was in after the second day it opened, starting with Dick Pleasant's hysteria, and a complete break-down of the management, which as you know, took me some days and nights to straighten out, and right on top of it they threw the mess of the Raymond Scott Ballet at me, which had so many angles to it, that I couldn't begin to tell you all the ramifications.

It seemed that between Kahn and Pleasant, so many verbal agreements had been made, and authorizations had been given for music, scenery, and publicity, etc., that the Advanced Ballet was involving themselves in lawsuits from different angles.

As you know, I called off the production of QUINTET twice, and on the heels of it, almost had a public scandal in the theatre between the representative of the Scott interests who seems to have ganged up with the scenery builders and everybody else. It looked as if everybody was giving me a Blitzkrieg.

DOLIN AND BETSY FURSTENBERG VIEW STAGE-BOX OCCUPANTS MEANT TO REPRESENT JEROME ZERBE, LINCOLN KIRSTEIN, AND DWIGHT WIMAN IN QUINTET.

The three-week season was completed as scheduled but with an unscheduled loss of more than $200,000. The excess of actual costs over budgetary estimates was due to the enlargement of the scope of the venture and the application of higher and more costly artistic standards. Although the principal backer and the corporate officers had not intended to spend so large a sum, it cannot be denied that they received a fair return for their money. At the end of the season they were left in possession of complete productions for eighteen ballets—thirteen of which were to be performed during the second season, and ten of which were to remain in the repertory for a dozen or more years. Close to a hundred people had been on the weekly payroll, and this expenditure could not be regarded as a complete waste of money, particularly not by the employees. In this connection Pleasant could boast of an accomplishment that has never since been matched, even by the astute S. Hurok: he succeeded in keeping the payrolls for stagehands and musicians lower than that for the dancers: stagehands, approximately $16,000; musicians, $21,500; dancers, $23,000.

What, then, was Pleasant's most noteworthy achievement? In what respect did he most successfully emulate Diaghilev? Like him he had the impudence, the "unmitigated gall" (to use the language of the 1940s), to incur financial obligations without knowing where he could obtain the money to discharge them, but only that it could not be derived from his own, nonexistent private resources. What Pleasant in effect did was to obligate Miss Chase for expenditures that were far in excess of her most generous intentions, but without this irresponsible course of action there would have been no Ballet Theatre. Miss Chase enthusiastically approved of and supported the project, but had she been accurately informed of the probable cost, she would never have provided the sums that proved necessary to convert the minor Mordkin company (with its dubious prospects for survival) into Ballet Theatre, a major company whose advent was noted on the editorial page of the New York Herald Tribune on January 30, 1940:

Here at last is a solidly American organization that has brought together a wealth of talents from many countries and put their creations, old and new, on the stage with a freshness and an intelligence that have honestly earned the enthusiastic support of its performance.

Fortunately, in view of future developments, Pleasant and only Pleasant was on hand to lead the not too unwilling but fiercely resisting lamb to the slaughter, thus playing the role of the Judas-goat, which is unaware of the fate in store for those it leads. The short-term fate was painful for Miss Chase, who for years was called upon to make large contributions, but the long run proved that it was Pleasant who was basically responsible for the birth of Ballet Theatre—no mean accomplishment.

ANTONY TUDOR, WHO WAS INTRODUCED TO AMERICA WITH HIS JARDIN AUX LILAS, APPEARS WITH (FROM LEFT) MARIA KARNILOVA, HUGH LAING, AND NORA KAYE.

At the end of the engagement at the Center Theatre, Anatole Chujoy wrote in the March issue of Dance Magazine:

The first season of the Ballet Theatre is an undisputed outstanding artistic and financial success . . . a new page in the history of ballet in America.

In 1940, Chujoy's judgments were accorded considerable weight. He was Russian, and in line with Hurok's dictum, those Americans who wanted their ballet Russian also wanted their critics Russian. Others who might question his judgments nevertheless had to admit that he was the only critic writing about ballet in America who had attended performances of the Imperial Ballet at the Maryinsky Theater in Saint Petersburg. But even if judged by today's more exacting standards, Ballet Theatre's first season would still have to be considered an undisputed artistic success.

Of the eighteen ballets presented, at least ten must be ranked as noteworthy achievements. Heading the list were Fokine's personally directed CARNAVAL and LES SYLPHIDES. The latter was to become the definitive version of this work and was to continue to improve over the years as the technical skill of the corps de ballet dancers advanced in excellence. Two of Tudor's ballets, JARDIN AUX LILAS and JUDGMENT OF PARIS, were immediate successes with American audiences, while his DARK ELEGIES was at once appreciated by the connoisseurs, who continue to savor it. Successful, though less distinguished, were Mordkin's VOICES OF SPRING and Bolm's PETER AND THE WOLF. VOICES provided Patricia Bowman (and two years later, Irina Baronova) with a vehicle in which she could display her soubrette charm. For many years PETER sold out

matinée performances. (Parents thought they had found the perfect ballet for children, who may, in fact, have preferred the slapstick of THREE VIRGINS AND A DEVIL or the gore of FALL RIVER LEGEND.) The classics were represented by serviceable versions of SWAN LAKE, GISELLE, and LA FILLE MAL GARDÉE, which remained in the repertory until being replaced by restagings or new productions.

Neither of the two experimental works, BLACK RITUAL and THE GREAT AMERICAN GOOF, could be classified as an unqualified success, though perhaps they were ahead of their time and were never given an opportunity to prove themselves. Loring soon left the company to found Dance Players, and his ballet was dropped from the repertory. De Mille missed her chance to restage BLACK RITUAL with white dancers when she chose instead to present an American version of her THREE VIRGINS AND A DEVIL as her contribution to the second season. The remaining ballets found favor with neither the critics nor the public. With the departure of the Spanish group, GOYESCAS was revised by Tudor and survived in that form for two seasons. Dolin's QUINTET was repeated through the 1941 engagement at the Majestic Theatre and then disappeared. Only five of the eighteen ballets—Bolm's MECHANICAL BALLET, Shabelevski's ODE TO GLORY, and Andrée Howard's two works, LADY INTO FOX and DEATH AND THE MAIDEN—did not survive into the second season, and this was perhaps because of the unavailability of the choreographers. Pleasant's score for the 1939–40 season could be said to have tallied fourteen successes and four qualified failures.

For the 1940–41 season, Pleasant played it safe. In addition to the thirteen ballets repeated from the first season, six works that had previously been staged by other organizations were inexpensively produced, in some cases with revisions: CAPRIC- CIOSO by Anton Dolin (created for the Nemchinova-Dolin company in 1938), BILLY THE KID by Eugene Loring (created for Ballet Caravan in 1938), GALA PERFORMANCE by Antony Tudor (created for the London Ballet in 1938), THREE VIRGINS AND A DEVIL by Agnes de Mille (created in its original version in 1934 for the London musical revue WHY NOT TONIGHT?), PAS DE QUATRE by Anton Dolin (the original version by Keith Lester was created for the Markova-Dolin company in 1936), and THE LOVE SONG by Adeline Genée (composed for a Royal Command Performance in London in 1932).

THE LOVE SONG was presented for a few performances only as a gesture of respect toward the celebrated Danish ballerina, who was visiting America in behalf of British War Relief. BILLY THE KID did not yet belong to Ballet Theatre; it was on lend-lease while off-and-on negotiations were in progress for its purchase. No one knows, perhaps not even Lincoln Kirstein himself, why he finally consented to parting with the ballet. In his book THE NEW YORK CITY BALLET, he wrote only that:

BILLY THE KID worked well; when I went into the army, it was assigned to the Ballet Theatre, through my friendship with Oliver Smith, its cofounder.

The leasing agreement was signed by Kirstein, as president of Ballet Caravan, Inc., on November 28, 1940. It gave Ballet Theatre the right to perform the ballet upon the payment of $100 per performance and to purchase it outright on January 1, 1942, for $2,500. Doubtless Kirstein placed a high value on his friendship with Oliver Smith, but this could have had nothing to do with the sale of the ballet. Smith had not been a co-founder of Ballet Theatre in 1940, and in January 1942 he was in no way connected with the company.* To the contrary, on the latter date he was working on the scenery sketches for RODEO, which was being produced by Ballet Theatre's rival, the Ballet Russe de Monte Carlo. He would not have regarded as an act of friendship Kirstein's assignment to Ballet Theatre of Loring's competing "cowboy" ballet. CAPRICCIOSO, with delightful Neapolitan scenery and costumes by Nicolas de Molas, remained in the repertory for two seasons, but passed out of it when the décor was stored in Mexico City and subsequently became "lost." The remaining three ballets continue to be periodically revived.

At the end of Pleasant's two-and-a-half-year regime, which terminated on March 1, 1941, his production tally could be set, subject to dispute, at eighteen successes and six failures—an average of 75 percent success. Few Broadway producers and even fewer ballet directors could boast of such a record.

*Kirstein may have confused the negotiations for the sale of BILLY THE KID with negotiations which he did in fact conduct with Smith for the sale of CONCERTO BAROCCO and PASTORELA in 1945.

FIRST-YEAR CONTRIBUTIONS BY THE ENGLISH CHOREOGRAPHERS WERE DOLIN'S CAPRICCIOSO AND (TOP) TUDOR'S JUDGMENT OF PARIS, WITH VIOLA ESSEN, AGNES DE MILLE, LUCIA CHASE, HUGH LAING, AND TUDOR.

Chujoy's verdict that Ballet Theatre's first season was an "undisputed artistic success" has remained undisputed. But his report that it was a "financial success" should have been disputed long ago. He was in the same position as those who witnessed the full houses at the Théâtre du Châtelet during Diaghilev's first Paris engagement and assumed that it had been highly profitable. That the engagement had, in fact, lost heavily at the box office was not revealed until thirty years later, when the records of the impresario, Gabriel Astruc, were made public. Similarly, the myth of Ballet Theatre's initial financial success has persisted down the years because the records were not made available to historians or requested by them. Thus the entire issue that the quarterly Dance Perspectives devoted in 1960 to an account of Ballet Theatre's first twenty years, while otherwise detailed and accurate, erred in reporting that

On January 12, the Center Theatre had to provide extra help at the box-office. The huge auditorium could hold hundreds of standees. And it did—at every performance for three weeks.

This statement is based on hearsay; the facts could not have been within the firsthand knowledge of the editors. It will do little to raise the reader's confidence in this volume to be told that the editors of Dance Perspectives acknowledged: "Lucia Chase and Charles Payne, of the American Ballet Theatre, helped fill in numerous gaps in our information and to clear up a number of apparent discrepancies."

The authenticated facts are contained in the Center Theatre box-office statements, which were attested to and signed by the manager of the theater and the company manager of Ballet Theatre. Admissions were sold to standees only for the two performances on the last day of the season. And even these might not have been sold had not an excessive number of seats in the orchestra been distributed at no charge. At the matinée, for which 126 standee admissions had been sold, 191 orchestra seats were occupied by the press or guests of Ballet Theatre. At the evening performance, although tickets for 70 standing places were sold, 423 orchestra seats remained unsold. If standees were seen at other performances, it was because they were admitted free of charge or had moved down from seats in the upper balconies of the house.

It is perhaps quibbling to maintain that the last two performances were not sellouts; they probably would have sold out had not free tickets been distributed in advance. But no other performances came even close to selling out. Therefore, if "the Center Theatre had to provide extra help at the box-office," it was not to expedite the <u>sale</u> of tickets but rather to handle the distribution of tickets worth $35,268 that were issued free of charge in order to "paper the house" (that is, to give the impression that the house had been sold out). The official box-office statements reveal the percentage of sales to have been: first (half) week, 48 percent; second week, 47; third week, 51; fourth week, 66. For the entire engagement, 56 percent of the seats were sold. In no week were the receipts at the box office sufficient to cover the payrolls, and

the payrolls constituted only 60 percent of the cost of operating the company (exclusive of production expenses: scenery, costumes, music and choreographic royalties, et cetera).

It was Pleasant's contention (subsequently given wide credence) that had the Center Theater not committed itself to a showing of Walt Disney's PINOCCHIO beginning on February 5, the Ballet Theatre engagement could have been extended and an eventual financial success would have been assured. Aside from the fact that general theater experience indicates that extended engagements rarely prosper, the figures argue that additional performances would not have transformed the season into a financial success. Even in the unlikely event that all performances were completely sold out, the operating expenses were such that at the most a break-even point could be reached with no excess remaining which could be applied to the already existing operating deficit of $60,000.

It could be argued that considering the circumstances under which the season was operated, it should not be labeled a financial disaster. The American company (and what made Americans think they could perform a Russian art?) was an unknown quantity and no subscriptions were sold in advance. There had been some pre-season publicity but the first advertisement did not appear until three weeks before the opening. There were no mail orders and the box office was not opened until sixteen days before the first performance. Not until a week later were the first week's programs announced, while those for subsequent weeks remained tentative. And yet despite this lack of cooperation with the public, purchasers of 51,100 tickets came to the box office during three and a half weeks. Granted there was a deficit, but with receipts of $60,000 who could speak of financial <u>disaster</u>? Well, for one, Lucia Chase could. And she did so as she reached for her checkbook on the cluttered Queen Anne desk in her penthouse bedroom each time Mr. Zuckert informed her of the bad news, of the amount of money that would be required to get Ballet Theatre through the season. The checks were not signed dispassionately and philosophically with the assurance that the money was being invested in the establishment of one of the great ballet institutions of the twentieth century. Vehement protests accompanied the signing of every check, and Miss Chase reacted as one subject to the ancient Chinese water torture. Each demand for money represented another drop of water, individually not too painful but with an overwhelming cumulative effect. The checks signed while the season at the Center Theatre was in progress were less painful because of the palliative counterpoint of audience enthusiasm and the unstinted praise of the critics, which conveyed a sense of worthwhile accomplishment. When, however, the season was past and the drops of water continued to fall, their cumulative power became affective, and Miss Chase called a halt.

It was one of those rare occasions in the history of Ballet Theatre when a halt could have been executed without

incurring exorbitant termination costs. The dancers' contracts provided for a layoff, which automatically became permanent if the company failed to exercise an option. There were no outstanding obligations for the production of new ballets or for the fulfilling of performance engagements. If no further action was taken, the company would die a natural death. But as in 1939, the halt called by Miss Chase was not to all of the company's activities but only to the practice of open-ended spending. She left it up to Pleasant and her advisors to devise a method of operation that would employ the surviving assets—scenery, costumes, choreographic rights—without relying solely on her for financial support.

With the hope of accomplishing this, a new corporation was formed under the title The Ballet Theatre, Inc., with Harry M. Zuckert as president. No commitments could be made or expenditures incurred without the approval and express permission of the president and the six directors of the company. It must again be emphasized that the restrictions placed on the disposal of Miss Chase's contributions were entirely voluntary on her part. Had she wished, she could have diverted to the support of Ballet Theatre the entire income from her trust as well as the capital derived from the residue estate, and she could have directed how it should be spent. She was not, as was the principal contributor to another company, constrained by a "spendthrift trust," but she did in effect attempt to impose one on herself. Her arrangement with Mr. Zuckert was similar to that arrived at between theatrical stars and their agent-managers. It was then, as it is today, a common practice for a star to enter an agreement whereby all his pay checks were deposited into an account controlled by the agent, who then paid the bills and doled out an allowance. As a practical matter, if the star chose to violate the agreement and incur unauthorized expenditures, the manager's only recourse was to drop him as a client. Mr. Zuckert was not, of course, an agent-manager. He was counsel for the Alexander Smith Carpet Company, and acted as president of Ballet Theatre at no salary purely as a public service and as an accommodation to Miss Chase, a friend and an important stockholder of the carpet company. Like the stars, who were often heard to complain, "I would like very much to do such-and-such, but my manager won't give me the money to pay for it," Miss Chase could and did include in her letters such phrases as, "Mr. Zuckert will never OK it," "There's no one I can talk to and nothing I can do because it's up to Mr. Zuckert," et cetera. There was nothing she could do, not because she couldn't, but because if she did, she might be running the risk of losing Zuckert as an advisor and as a buffer against those who would be extravagant with her resources.

Under this organizational setup, it was proposed to solve Ballet Theatre's problems by seeking additional contributions and by contracting with impresarios who were prepared to present the company in performances for which it would be guaranteed against loss. As regards the search for new contributors, it appeared for a while that H. I. Harriman might organize "his friends" as backers, but after extensive discussions it became clear that his only real interest was to recoup the $5,000 he had advanced toward the production of QUINTET. Dwight Deere Wiman, stimulated by the inclusion of ballets in his Broadway musicals, made a substantial contribution. His enthusiasm was perhaps enhanced by the fact that his daughter was engaged as a member of the corps de ballet. A number of philanthropists who might conceivably be interested in contributing to the support of ballet were approached by the several existing companies, but they proved to be more liberal with their advice than their money: "Why," they frequently suggested, "don't you fellows combine into one strong company instead of competing with each other for the patronage of so limited a public?" But they gave no assurance that, even should such an amalgamated company be formed, contributions would be forthcoming. Discouraged, the various principal backers extended feelers toward one another: Fleischmann toward Chase, Denham toward Kirstein, de Basil (through Hurok) toward Chase, and Chase toward Kirstein. The discussions between the last of these were characterized by Kirstein in his THE NEW YORK CITY BALLET: "We also had skittish conversations about being absorbed by the Ballet Theatre, which Lucia Chase was now directing away from the original Russian orientation of Mikhail Mordkin, her teacher. Our aimless flirtation with the Ballet Theatre continued until I went into the army." "Aimless flirtation" were the mots justes. The conversations were cordial and enthusiastic, but when held in Miss Chase's drawing room they often came to resemble the Mad Hatter's Tea Party, as the strongly held opinions of the Harvard-educated Renaissance man were deferentially countered by the strong-willed Connecticut Yankee who nevertheless appeared to concede his superior knowledge and wisdom. They shared many of the same problems and were in agreement on many issues, but an active association between them was doomed from the start.

A proposal had been made that Kirstein should become an independent producer within the Ballet Theatre organization, that he should select the creators of a new ballet (choreographer, composer, librettist, designers), direct them, and arrange for the financing of the work. The ballet would be performed by the Ballet Theatre company. But this left too many unresolved questions: who would select the dancers for the company, who would control the choice of program, who would decide when and where performances would be given—in short, who would have the final say? That Kirstein was indeed merely flirting was made evident immediately. For instance, in the course of considering Proposition Six of an agenda that included a number of proposals, it would be discovered that Kirstein had shifted his position and backed down on an agreement to Proposition Two expressed only half an hour previously. It was then that Alice would pause to pour another cup of tea for the Mad Hatter. In the end, Chase and Kirstein proceeded with their un-integrated activities, even-

tually establishing separate but equal companies.

Negotiations with other companies were no more productive. Hurok offered to book Ballet Theatre if it would strengthen its repertory by purchasing the ballets of Colonel de Basil. But it soon developed that de Basil must be part of the package, he must have a role to play in Ballet Theatre. Again the question arose, who will be the boss? Fleischmann's interest in the amalgamation of the Ballet Russe de Monte Carlo with Ballet Theatre was conditional on Ballet Theatre's agreement to engage Leonide Massine as its artistic director. Once again, who would be the boss? Lucia Chase agreed with her directors that Ballet Theatre must find someone who could manage the business affairs of the company efficiently. Artistically, she was prepared to go along with Pleasant and his "dance gallery" concept. The company did not need a Kirstein (with his conviction that American ballet must be American), nor a de Basil (with his conviction that there was no good ballet but Russian ballet), nor a Massine (with his conviction that all ballet must be Massine ballet). No one, it appeared, was interested in an amalgamation that might effect fiscal stability but at the same time result in a lessening of artistic control. Everyone wanted to be the artistic boss in the ideal amalgamated company to which could be channeled all the resources of all the potential money-contributors.

Meanwhile, on the booking front Pleasant seemed to be operating with greater success. He signed contracts for eight performances in July and August at the Robin Hood Dell in Philadelphia and the Lewisohn Stadium in New York for which Ballet Theatre received a set fee. The success only seemed to be so, however, as the fees did not cover the entire cost of preparing for the performances. Pleasant wrote prophetically, if somewhat pretentiously, to Mrs. Charles S. (Minnie) Guggenheimer that when Ballet Theatre became a great American institution she would gain recognition as having been "a patron in the very real sense of Lorenzo the Magnificent."

Pleasant next signed what appeared to be a loss-proof contract for Ballet Theatre to appear with the Chicago Opera Company in November and December 1940. Ballet Theatre was to receive a weekly fee for staging and performing the ballet sequences in the operas and was to share with the Opera the profits or losses on eleven evenings of performances of ballets from its own repertory. Optimism in connection with this contract was based on two misconceptions: that the Chicago public would flock to American ballet as it had to the Russian, and that an organization under the chairmanship of Chauncey McCormick was financially responsible. Both suppositions proved false. The cost of presenting the ballet evenings totaled nearly $36,000, but the box-office receipts were only $15,000. Except for the opening-night, society-sponsored benefit, the Chicago public stayed home, and fewer than 500 people attended each subsequent ballet performance. This would not have been too disastrous had the

Chicago Opera made good on its weekly guarantee and assumed its share of the losses on the ballet evenings, but when Pleasant's business manager protested the non-payment he was told by an Opera representative, "You can quote me. The Opera Company doesn't have any money. It's broke, and we can't help it."

Although Ballet Theatre had repeated its artistic success in Chicago, the board of directors again grumbled about Pleasant's lack of business acumen. At the same time, they allowed themselves to be talked into endorsing a venture that was to prove to be as ill-advised as any ever undertaken by Ballet Theatre. Upon its return from Chicago at the beginning of its second year, the company had an enviable collection of press notices and critical evaluations. In its warehouse were some twenty ballet productions in fresh condition, and in its files were unexercised options on the services of the dancers who had performed them. That the options were not imperishable was noted by Miss Chase in a letter to one of her directors in which she pointed out a fact of ballet life, using Kirstein as an authority, "As Lincoln said, dancers are not paintings that you can lock up and hold." If Ballet Theatre did not provide them with work on a salary basis, they would seek it elsewhere. Dwight Wiman understood this and agreed that performances must be resumed. He offered a suggestion that was accepted by the board of directors as coming from a theater professional and businessman. With the legal advice of John Wharton, the eminent theatrical lawyer, a new corporation was formed under the title Ballet Presentations, Inc. It entered into an agreement with Ballet Theatre, Inc., whereby it would lease its properties, assume its contract

JEROME ROBBINS, DAVID NILLO, DONALD SADDLER, AND JOHN KRIZA
RELAX BEFORE A 1940 PERFORMANCE AT THE LEWISOHN STADIUM.

rights, and present performances. Ballet Theatre would receive a share of the profits, and even if there were no profits, at the termination of the lease it would come into full possession of any ballets produced by Ballet Presentations. Ballet Theatre could not lose. Ballet Presentations, Inc., could, but under John Wharton's plan the loss would be comparatively painless. At any convenient point, Ballet Presentations, Inc., could be dissolved and the stockholders would be permitted to deduct their losses in computing their income taxes. Further, a loss could be deducted by anyone who loaned money to the corporation (as did Miss Chase), since loans could obviously not be recovered from a dissolved corporation. And these losses were business losses, an unlimited and more sacrosanct deduction than a charitable contribution. A number of high-bracketed businessmen (including Wiman) were induced to buy stock and Miss Chase was persuaded to make loans.

Also at Dwight Wiman's suggestion, the corporation rented the Majestic Theatre for four weeks beginning February 11, 1941, where it presented Ballet Theatre. The critical notices were again most favorable but the audiences were still small, in fact, much smaller. Only 20 percent of the tickets were sold. Ballet Presentations, Inc., was dissolved and its stockholders took their tax deduction. Even the deduction taken by Miss Chase for unpaid loans, which was challenged by the Internal Revenue Service, was allowed by a Federal jury in New York. However, subsequent courts held that Miss Chase's investments in ballet were frivolous, and it became necessary to form the Ballet Theatre Foundation, a charitable, educational trust. As a business loss could no longer be taken, businessmen were less interested in investing in ballet. The additional tax revenues that the government has collected over the years by not permitting business losses to supporters of Ballet Theatre are minuscule compared with the amounts it now contributes to the support of that same company through the National Endowment for the Arts.

After the last performance at the Majestic Theatre on March 9, Pleasant assembled the company in the theater's lounge. He informed them that he had been unable to raise the money needed to continue operations and as a result both he and they had been dismissed. This might well have been the end of Ballet Theatre; it was indeed the end of Pleasant's career as a ballet director—five days later he made it official on stationery of the New York Athletic Club:

Dear Mr. Zuckert,

At your request, I herewith tender you my resignation as a Director and as Vice-President of the Ballet Theatre, Inc.

Yours very truly,
RICHARD PLEASANT

Presumably Pleasant had been dismissed because of his inability to raise funds. Had this been so, then the board of directors had unwittingly treated him unfairly—unwittingly, because they had no way of knowing that throughout the forties and fifties no one would succeed in raising substantial contributions for the ballet. Only during the past decade have private philanthropists, foundations, and government agencies come to the support of ballet with the same generosity they had shown toward opera and symphony orchestras. But Pleasant was not, in fact, dismissed because of his inability to combine his artistic taste with business skill, but rather because when he was faced with business failure or was placed under pressure to perform fund-raising miracles, he panicked. And more and more he sought relief from this panic in all-night drinking bouts and soul-searching nocturnal walks through Central Park that ill-equipped him to cope with his daytime problems. Had he been less sensitive and only a trifle more Machiavellian, his ballet career need not have ended so prematurely. At a time when he should have remained cool and adopted a stance of compromise, he continued to oppose contemptuously any association with S. Hurok, even after everyone else had become convinced that only Hurok could salvage Ballet Theatre. In what was perhaps a clumsy attempt at Machiavellianism, Pleasant wrote a letter to Morris Permut, who was handling negotiations with Hurok, and sent copies to the directors, which it was not his custom to do. It contained the paragraphs:

Do not pull any punches with Hurok with a thought of me in mind. I am all for the best external management we can get and today, as we all know, the most skillful manager has been Mr. Hurok.

We need not, I feel, be afraid of Mr. Hurok. This company is strong and youthful and if worst comes to worst, in order to insure continuance through a New York season I am sure we can sell stock to all of the dancers to cover their salaries. There is that much vitality in the Ballet Theatre.

If the copies to the directors were intended to convince them that Pleasant was reconciled to working with Hurok, they had the opposite effect. Patently he was not prepared to work with Hurok in a spirit of all-out cooperation, and all-out cooperation was the least Hurok demanded. It became a question of an uncompromising choice—Pleasant or Hurok—of a battle between Pleasant and the ballet establishment. Pleasant lost. It might have given him some satisfaction to know that his idol, Diaghilev, had lost a similar battle with the establishment of the Imperial Ballet. But whereas it had taken the establishment only a little over a year to oust Diaghilev from his post as an associate director of the Maryinsky Theater, Pleasant had survived for more than three years as an active force in the Mordkin–Ballet Theatre company.

THE ERA OF GERMAN SEVASTIANOV

While Pleasant was allowing himself to be destroyed by the establishment, Lucia Chase was learning not only to deal with it but to use it to advantage. The ballet establishment in America was then largely under the control of S. Hurok, who had been connected with the ballet off and on since the 1920s, when as a fledgling impresario he had subcontracted from Max Rabinoff the right to present the New England portion of one of Pavlova's transcontinental tours. By 1941 he was managing the American tours of all the visiting Russian companies and held an exclusive lease on the Metropolitan Opera House during the spring and fall, when the opera itself was not performing. Over the years, he had accumulated the largest mailing list in New York, and he could count on the patronage of the leaders of what was then known as café society—the chic set—who brought glamour to his opening nights and assured him a sellout season. Kirstein pamphleteered against him in his BLAST AT BALLET and influenced many of his confreres, including Pleasant and John Martin. The latter, who was only gradually being converted from modern dance to ballet, particularly resented the alien nature of the establishment. After Ballet Theatre's opening, he wrote in the New York Times:

The Ballet Theatre, whether by accident or design, has hit on the answer to the question of what constitutes an American ballet. It is not a regard for the citizenship of its personnel nor an insistence on exclusively national topics; it is rather a consideration for what constitutes the native American taste. It is a fine thing to have one's novelties and experiments designed to please one's own self instead of being created with the approval of Paris and the Riviera in mind.

If activity at the box office could be taken as an indicator, Hurok appeared to have a more perceptive answer to the question of what constituted American taste. It was his conviction that America's taste in ballet, like its taste in haute couture, was still molded by Paris. The public came to performances presented by Hurok in the assurance that it would be entertained by spectacles with "real" dancing, spectacular settings, and rich costumes of which Paris would approve. On the other hand, audiences stayed away from Kirstein's and Pleasant's ballets in the belief that they were avoiding homespun or avant-garde ballets designed as intellectual stimuli rather than as glamorous entertainments. Further, a large portion of the American public had not yet developed any taste in ballet; it was in no position to distinguish good from bad. For these people, "S. Hurok Presents" was the seal of approval. And his authority extended throughout the country thanks to a cadre of local managers who spread the good word through their extensive mailing lists.

The avant-gardists who expressed contempt for Hurok's commercial approach to the arts could bolster their arguments against him with the charge that he was guilty of sharp business dealings. The charge appeared to have some merit. Anyone who could survive for several decades in so high-risk a gambling business and go bankrupt only twice must indeed be sharp. And so it was that at both the conferences of Ballet Theatre's artistic staff and the meetings of its board of directors the name Hurok was a dirty word. Any association with him, it was believed, would contaminate Ballet Theatre's artistic purity and business integrity.

There was, however, one member of the company who dared speak in Hurok's defense. Unlike Pleasant (who was deceiving others and perhaps himself when he boasted, "Who's afraid of the big bad wolf?"), Anton Dolin was truly not afraid of Hurok nor contemptuous of the ballet establishment. He had, in fact, himself been part of the establishment in Europe, where he had been associated with Serge de Diaghilev, Ninette de Valois, and Vassily de Basil (all of whom had adopted the "de" to enhance their establishment status) and where he had directed his own companies, the Nemchinova-Dolin company and the Markova-Dolin company. He admired Hurok, agreed with his judgment of what the public wanted, and, as his advocate, succeeded in impressing both Mr. Zuckert and Miss Chase. He also proposed as business manager a former associate whose experience in ballet management had equipped him not only to solve Ballet Theatre's fiscal problems but also, should it prove necessary, to outsharp Hurok. His candidate was German Sevastianov. With his arrival on the scene, Ballet Theatre became party to a series of old-world ballet intrigues of which its directors were not fully aware until the company was made codefendant in a conspiracy suit brought by Colonel de Basil.

Born in Moscow, Sevastianov attended the Russian Officers Training School before moving to what was then the kingdom of Yugoslavia to enter the University of Ljubljana. Later he emigrated to Paris, where, because of his theatrical connections (he claimed to be a nephew of Constantine Stanislavsky), he found employment with Colonel de Basil, with whom he held the position of executive secretary from 1934 through 1937. His apprenticeship with the Colonel proved most enlightening and provided him with the opportunity to become informed about all the operations of a ballet company in their most cunning aspects. With Pavlova's widower, Victor Dandré, he served as director of the company during an interim period in 1938 when de Basil had ostensibly retired but had in reality, as the court decided, withdrawn only temporarily in order to evade his creditors. When the Colonel resumed control, Sevastianov resigned rather than return to a secondary position, and in 1939 he joined the Hurok office with the comprehensive title of promotion manager. In this capacity he conducted negotiations for the purchase by Ballet Theatre of the de Basil repertory, which was being held under creditors' liens in Australia. This was typical of his assignments, in which he served as a negotiator and mediator between Hurok and those who distrusted, feared, or simply disliked the old man.

GERMAN SEVASTIANOV   IRINA BARONOVA

In 1936 Sevastianov had married Irina Baronova, one of de Basil's "baby ballerinas," thereby acquiring another and most important client. During succeeding years he devoted much of his energy to the promotion of her career, both in the movies and the ballet. In 1938 he organized the Ballet Arts Associates, which was to parent a company starring Baronova, and in 1939 he arranged for her to star in the Metro-Goldwyn-Mayer film FLORIAN. In 1940 he wrote to movie producer Winfield Sheehan proposing a series of ballet shorts, and adding, "I have at present the possibility of forming a ballet company for her along the lines of the Anna Pavlova Company. I have acquired the rights and properties to nine good ballets and have offers of engagements for such an IRINA BARONOVA BALLET RUSSE from Australia, South America and the United States." Had he been able to raise the capital for this Baronova company, he would never have joined Ballet Theatre.

The Sevastianovs worked well as a team. Handsome, vivacious, multilingual, they were a much sought-after couple. Oddly, it was Sevastianov who somewhere along the line had acquired the nickname "Beautiful," the use of which he understandably did not encourage. But his looks played an important part in his success as a negotiator. In a branch of the arts cluttered with Erich von Stroheims and mad-Russian Mischa Auers, he was a slavic-accented Cary Grant. And who could suspect a Cary Grant of chicanery and sharp practice? A tall and powerful-appearing man, Sevastianov's most effective weapons were his soft eyes, gentle smile, and quiet voice. In conversations, both business and social, he was an attentive and understanding listener and most sympathetic to talk with, since he always seemed to be agreeing. Only those who grew to know him better became aware that when he was in disagreement he rarely employed the direct retort, having discovered that the desired ends could be attained by avoiding arguments and thus lulling opponents into unwariness.

By the time Sevastianov first came in contact with Ballet Theatre, late in 1940, his course of action was directed by three resolutions in an indeterminable order of importance: to avoid any involvement with the war in Europe, to turn down any work with or for Colonel de Basil, and to advance Baronova's status from baby ballerina to undisputed international ballerina assoluta. With reference to the war, there was no country to which he owed a patriotic duty, and after his experience with the Russian Revolution he retained no illusions that his personal welfare would be greatly affected by the form of government under which he was forced to live. He was convinced that, should it prove necessary, he could do business with Hitler, just as he later demonstrated that even a White Russian like himself could do business with Stalin and end up with a substantial Swiss bank account. He was determined, therefore, to sit out the war in the United States, or in Mexico and South America should America be so foolish as to become involved in the conflict. He abandoned all plans that would take him to Europe or to countries of the British Commonwealth where he might become entrapped in the fighting. As for de Basil, his was a form of dictatorship that affected him personally and with which he could no longer do business. And with respect to Baronova, her career was as important to him as his own.

By chance Sevastianov became associated with Hurok at a time when the impresario shared a number of these resolutions. Hurok, too, was determined to disengage himself from all European entanglements before the war would restrict his activities to the Western Hemisphere. Dealings with the de Basil company constituted a form of foreign entanglement because its properties were subject to liens of creditors in England and Australia and its male dancers were subject to conscription into foreign armed forces. The Ballet Russe de Monte Carlo was also not entirely free of foreign entanglements; it was European-oriented, though at least its

principal backing came from an American with American-based capital. For Hurok's purposes, Ballet Theatre was the ideal company if it could become convinced that what the public really wanted was Russian ballets with Russian ballerinas. And Sevastianov was the ideal person to persuade Ballet Theatre to accept these facts and, as managing director, to put them into operation. Only recently, during de Basil's absence, he had demonstrated his preference for Russian-style ballet with his production for the Ballet Russe of PAGANINI, choreographed by Fokine to a score by Sergei Rachmaninoff. That he was predisposed to Russian ballerinas and that he would engage Baronova went without saying, and as a favor to Dolin, who had introduced him to Ballet Theatre, he would also engage Alicia Markova, Dolin's erstwhile partner. He would do so without trepidation because Markova's style of dancing was so different from his wife's that she would be a complementary rather than a rival talent. The acquiring of these Russian or Russianized ballerinas was favored by Hurok for another reason, which he disclosed only to Sevastianov: it would make Baronova unavailable to the de Basil company, whose contract he intended to breach, and it would remove Markova from the roster of the Ballet Russe de Monte Carlo, whose contract he did not intend to renew. If this appears to be in the nature of Balkan intrigue, it was as innocent as the politics of a New England town-meeting compared to the machinations subsequently set in motion during the spring of 1941.

If Hurok was to sign a management contract with Ballet Theatre, it was imperative that he immediately be freed of all contractual obligations to the de Basil company and to the Ballet Russe de Monte Carlo, since it was not feasible for him to book three ballet companies in the limited world market left untouched by the war. It cannot be stated with certainty whether he obtained his objective through a series of coincidental occurrences, as he himself maintained, or through the operation of a conscious plot to destroy the de Basil company, as the Colonel charged. The sequence of events in the spring of 1941 lends itself to either interpretation.

There is evidence that as early as November 1940 Hurok was planning to unload one or both of the Russian companies. On the 23rd Harry Zuckert dictated the following memorandum:

Permut [Morris Permut, Ballet Theatre's counsel] reported on his conversation with Hurok. Monte Carlo will open for one week in Chicago December 26th. After short stops to the Coast until March when he feels that it will be ready for the burying ground.

DeBasil grossed $31,000 in Chicago for 8 performances. . . . New York poor at first better now. Here until Christmas week, though not making any money.

Believes our Company [Ballet Theatre] would be No. 1 with a few additions. Open to a proposition.

For its New York season that year, the de Basil company appeared at the Fifty-first Street Theatre with a cast headed by its three baby ballerinas, Irina Baronova, Tamara Toumanova, and Tatiana Riabouchinska. At the end of the season, the company made a short tour of New England and Canada before embarking on a Latin American tour booked by Hurok. Baronova had been transferred to the payroll of Hurok Attractions and was not scheduled to appear in Latin America. However, at the last moment Toumanova withdrew from the company, leaving de Basil with only Riabouchinska. Presumably to protect his own interests as well as de Basil's, Hurok offered Baronova as a substitute ballerina. She flew to Mexico City with Sevastianov, who accompanied her not only as a concerned husband but as a precautionary representative of Hurok.

S. HUROK WITH ALICIA MARKOVA AND LUCIA CHASE (THE NURSE)
BEFORE THE CURTAIN RISES ON ROMEO AND JULIET.

At the conclusion of the successful Mexico City engagement, Sevastianov and Baronova flew to Havana while the rest of the company proceeded by boat. En route, a disgruntled faction of eighteen dancers banded together and pledged to strike unless the Colonel returned their salaries to the level at which they had been paid in the United States. They maintained that they had never knowingly agreed to accept reduced salaries in consideration of the fact that living costs in Latin America were substantially lower. The Colonel refused to make any concessions and a strike was called. Performances were given by the remaining non-striking twenty-six dancers, but when the day arrived on which the company was scheduled to depart for Lima, Peru, the strike still had not been settled. Sevastianov later described the situation in a colorful broken-English letter to Philip Richardson of the London Dancing Times:

I and secretary to Hurok who flew from New York tried our best to persuade Basil not to make major issue out of this strike, to negotiate and settle. He refused as he stated that Europeans have no country where to go so they have no rights whatsoever and have to take what he gives them, etc. He failed to deliver the company for sailing to Peru, then he insulted Irina who refused to continue on and threatened that if I insisted she would immediately return to her mother. So the company had no more Ballerina and Hurok had only alternative to cancel contract at great loss to himself and Quesada [the Hurok of Latin America].

He concluded his letter with an afterthought bit of further news, "Ballet Theatre suddenly cracked and fell to pieces at the end of the season." Back in New York, Sevastianov pressed the strikers' case with AGMA and continued, through correspondence, to direct their activities in Havana.

Meanwhile, Morris Permut carried on conversations with Hurok. On April 9, 1941, while the de Basil company was still stranded in Cuba, he reported on one of his meetings:

> I asked Mr. Hurok why the information had been given to the newspapers that the arrangements between Ballet Theatre and Mr. Hurok had been concluded and the plans of an enlarged company. He said that the writer of either the Mirror or the News, and also Mr. Martin of the Times, had told him of various releases which had previously been given and were circulated that the Ballet Theatre, in addition to having lost Richard Pleasant, was definitely through, and he felt that in order not to cause irreparable hurt to our Company, that he should say something about the plans of trying to take over the management of our company.

At the time, Ballet Theatre was not aware that it was from the Hurok office that word of its collapse was being spread in letters such as Sevastianov's to Richardson (dated April 2). Nor was it aware that Hurok was assuring local managers that as a patriotic duty he was rescuing and enlarging Ballet Theatre and would substitute it for the de Basil company, which he had booked with them for the 1941–42 season. He was forced to do this with precipitate haste before the local managers should sign contracts for de Basil's appearance with his new manager, Fortune Gallo. Though puzzled by Hurok's actions, Zuckert continued negotiations. On April 12 he wired Lucia Chase in Palm Beach:

> Have seen Dolin and Sevastianov and am impressed. Have given latter opportunity to develop more detailed plan for submission to you on Monday. Broad aspects seem good but there are many factors requiring careful consideration, most important being whether we can rely on him to represent both sides.

Within a month a personal employment contract had been worked out with Sevastianov whereby he would become general manager of Ballet Theatre, but at his request it contained a provision that the contract would not become effective until the company had concluded an agreement with Hurok. After considerable legalistic bickering, the contract between Ballet Theatre and Hurok was signed in mid-June.

De Basil brought his threatened lawsuit but did not remain on hand long enough to see it through. Hurok's first reaction was to express a preference for settling the case out of court because, as Sevastianov explained, he had a phobia about appearing on the witness stand. Zuckert was sympathetic but he insisted that since Ballet Theatre (and presumably Hurok) was innocent of the charges, it could not admit to even partial guilt, which would be implicit in a settlement. The case proceeded with ponderous slowness, and it was not until 1945 that the court discovered a technical error in the drawing up of the complaint. By then de Basil's activities were confined to South America, where he had gone after the unsuccessful American tour booked by Fortune Gallo. War

hysteria had made him and his company personae non gratae in all the participating countries—the Colonel because of a perhaps unjustified reputation for having acted as a double-agent spy, and the dancers because of their Russian-refugee, stateless status. At one juncture, the court issued the unrealistic order that a disposition must be taken from de Basil in South America, and thus any serious action was forestalled until the Colonel could return at the conclusion of the war. By then, Hurok had broken with Ballet Theatre and once more managed the de Basil company. The lawsuit was allowed to expire and there was no official determination handed down as to whether Hurok and Ballet Theatre had conspired in the instigation of the strike that had crippled de Basil and placed him in the position of appearing to have defaulted on his contract.

The court, however, must have been given cause to wonder when it was informed of subsequent events. Sevastianov, who had so vigorously espoused the cause of the strikers and organized a protest in their behalf with the dancers' union, was shortly thereafter engaged as general manager of Ballet Theatre, and among his first official acts was the hiring of a dozen of the striking dancers, including their authorized representative, George Skibine, and a number of de Basil's key staff members: his conductors, stage manager, and wardrobe mistress. Then Hurok, without waiting to determine whether de Basil could replace the striking dancers and come up with a refurbished company capable of fulfilling his contract, offered Ballet Theatre (since joined by Baronova) to local managers as a replacement for the de Basil company in their Hurok Attractions contract for the 1941–42 season. Looking back at these facts and the sequence of events, it seems incredible that such astute lawyers as Harry M. Zuckert, Morris Permut, and John Wharton should have been confident that the court would decide in favor of Ballet Theatre. It seems even more incredible that lawyer Charles Payne, who was then secretary and treasurer of the company and in almost daily contact with Sevastianov, should have accepted his version of the affair and been convinced that Ballet Theatre was not even unknowingly involved in a conspiracy.

When Sevastianov assumed the post of managing director of Ballet Theatre he found a great deal which in his judgment and that of Mr. Hurok required renovating. Whereas during the debut season at the Center Theatre the company had operated encouragingly with what appeared to be a proper respect for Russian ballet, by the time it reached the Majestic Theatre it had fallen under the artistic control of a group that might be categorized loosely as Anglo-Saxon: Anton Dolin (Irish), Antony Tudor (English), Eugene Loring (German-American), and Agnes de Mille (American). None of the Russians (Mordkin, Bolm, Nijinska, or Fokine) remained actively associated with the company, although the last had dropped in to conduct a brief and unsatisfactory rehearsal of LES SYLPHIDES and CARNAVAL for the Lewisohn Stadium perform-

ALICIA MARKOVA (OPPOSITE PAGE IN THE MAD SCENE FROM GISELLE) WAS ONE OF THE LEADERS OF THE 1941 RUSSIAN INVASION.

ances in August 1940. Nor had the regisseur, Alexander Gavrilov, continued on the staff. Instead his functions had been parceled out in an arbitrary and somewhat ridiculous fashion. The program billing read as follows: "Anton Dolin, Regisseur of the Classical Wing; Eugene Loring, Regisseur of the American Wing; Antony Tudor, Regisseur of the New English Wing." This represented a compromise arrived at in order to conform to Pleasant's original concept that a choreographer should "come in, do his work, supervise the opening and depart" and that thereafter the works of each choreographer should be rehearsed by a regisseur "without discrimination." The now artificial structure created a number of anomalies. Was Tudor, the regisseur of the New English Wing, expected to rehearse the new ballets by the Irish choreographer, Dolin? Would Dolin, as regisseur of the Classical Wing, rehearse the ballets of Fokine and Nijinska? (These choreographers were quick to lodge protests with Pleasant.) And did Loring, as regisseur of the American Wing, rehearse the ballets of Agnes de Mille? Over her dead body! The regisseurs were, in practice, a not very well-matched troika over which the driver, Pleasant, was able to exercise only a semblance of control.

The ballets produced under this system were unsatisfactory to Hurok. To the most substantial of these works, BILLY THE KID, he took an instant dislike (which continued to the point where, in 1960, he frustrated Lucia Chase's persistent efforts to present it in the Soviet Union during Ballet Theatre's first tour). To him, THREE VIRGINS AND A DEVIL was modern dance, a form of art that should have been abandoned after he had managed Isadora Duncan's last tour. GALA PERFORMANCE was a satire on the ballet of Imperial Russia and as such an insult to the art. Dolin's PAS DE QUATRE and CAPRICCIOSO were concert pieces, not ballet. These were his opinions, but, it might be asked, why was anyone interested in his opinion? Those who had to be were interested.

The importance of Hurok's opinion was spelled out in the terms of his management contract. He had agreed to pay Ballet Theatre a weekly fee and to continue paying it even in those weeks when the box-office receipts were not sufficient to reimburse him. In return for this guarantee, Ballet Theatre agreed to engage a set number of international stars and to mount two major and two minor productions a year. Ballet Theatre was free to engage the stars and produce the ballets of its choice, but in as much as Hurok was assuming all the financial risks, he reserved the right of "approval." This arrangement has often been misconstrued by ballet historians, Hurok's biographers, and even Hurok himself, who has been quoted as saying, "When I managed Ballet Theatre I produced such-and-such a ballet, or I hired so-and-so as ballerina." There were one or two cases in which Hurok was so anxious to have Ballet Theatre produce a particular ballet (FIREBIRD) or to have it engage a particular ballerina (Zorina) that the company was able to say, "If you insist on having it (or her), you pay for it." But in 99 percent of the cases, the

THE RUSSIAN FORCES INCLUDED (TOP) DAVID LICHINE, TATIANA RIABOUCHINSKA, LEONIDE MASSINE, AND MICHEL FOKINE; (BOTTOM) TAMARA TOUMANOVA, IRINA BARONOVA, AND ANDRÉ EGLEVSKY.

directors (or choreographers) of Ballet Theatre conceived, created, and produced each ballet in all its details, and chose the dancers to perform it. It remained only for Hurok to say, "I accept it as one of the major (or minor) ballets called for by the terms of our contract."

Sevastianov, too, was discontented with the trend of ballet-making being followed by Pleasant and his troika; it was not productive of vehicles for his newly engaged stars, particularly Baronova. Of the entire existing Ballet Theatre repertory, there were only three ballets she could dance with any enthusiasm: SWAN LAKE, LA FILLE MAL GARDÉE, and LES SYLPHIDES. She made token appearances in GALA PERFORMANCE, PAS DE QUATRE, and VOICES OF SPRING but she could not regard them as true ballerina roles. Markova found the repertory only slightly more to her liking. In addition to GISELLE, SWAN LAKE, and LES SYLPHIDES, there were CAPRICCIOSO and PAS DE QUATRE, which had been originally created for her, and also JARDIN AUX LILAS, in which the role of Caroline should have been perfect for her but for some unfathomable reason was not. Sevastianov's plans for his first season were therefore dominated by two objectives: to produce vehicle ballets for his three stars, Markova, Dolin, and Baronova, and to create spectacle works (preferably Russian) that Hurok would accept as fulfilling the requirements of his contract. To accomplish this, he re-enlisted Fokine, Nijinska, and Mordkin, with whom he spoke the same language, both figuratively and literally. Fokine, who had been at odds with Pleasant over the scenery for LES SYLPHIDES and the casting of CARNAVAL, readily came to terms with Sevastianov on an agreement to create two major works, BLUEBEARD and ROMEO AND JULIET (to the Prokofiev score), and to revive his LE SPECTRE DE LA ROSE. Nijinska, an old friend and associate, returned to revive THE BELOVED, which she had last staged for the Markova-Dolin company, and to rehearse LA FILLE MAL GARDÉE. Even Mordkin was lured back to adapt his VOICES OF SPRING to the distinctive comic talents of Baronova.

How did Lucia Chase, as dancer and sometime performer of managerial functions, fit into this freshly painted picture? Inconspicuously and very happily. As a dancer she willingly accepted fourth billing after Baronova (whom she came to adore), Markova, and Karen Conrad. As a reluctant manager, for the first time (and it proved to be the last) she was able to retire into the background and entrust all responsibility to Sevastianov, an experienced professional. For several years she was permitted to concentrate on her career as a dancer—and these were very good years, made all the more rewarding because she was able to participate in the creation of new ballets and new roles by two of the geniuses of the twentieth century, Michel Fokine and Antony Tudor. To her, the arrival of Sevastianov marked the division between an earlier period in which she was educated in the ways of dancers and choreographers by observation and a later one in which she learned about management through direct participation. In the ways of dancer-choreographers, she was taught

by experts of her own choosing: Dolin and Tudor. Almost immediately following the engagement at the Center Theatre, when there was a cessation of all activities (except free classes to a nucleus of the company), she sent a message of advice to her directors: "Make a contract to June 1st with Dolin and Tudor so that they will be a part of Ballet Theatre and it will not be just Pleasant and Chase as it is now. . . . If Tudor and Dolin are enthusiastic about a Spring season and think it can be done with $25,000, go ahead with it. If not, don't do it." Having put her faith in Dolin and Tudor, she quickly discovered that they were not as ready to put their faith in her. She received the return message: "Tudor is not willing to discuss any connection with the Company until he has a good talk with Lucia, Edward Carmody [a director], and Pleasant. One or two things are happening that he doesn't agree with." Even after the contracts were signed, Carmody received and noted a message from Miss Chase: "Dolin stampeded into the office and demanded a release from his contract so that he can sign a two-year contract with Hurok."

These two incidents, insignificant in themselves, were part of Miss Chase's experience in dealing with dancers and choreographers, a "how-to" course that was to prepare her for her future role as director. During that spring of 1941 she learned that dancers, and dancers-turned-choreographers, were egocentric to the point of egomania, with an added touch of paranoia. Not only were they interested solely in their own careers but they looked upon all other dancers as rivals intent on destroying them. Miss Chase was not unsympathetic with these idiosyncrasies. As a dancer, she had been there herself. She knew, too, that a certain amount of irrational egoism was essential in the formation of a confident artist. Therefore, though she recognized the baselessness, or indeed foolishness, of many of the dancers' claims and complaints, she nevertheless heard them out, preferring to persuade them of the error of their positions rather than appear to dismiss them with too little consideration. This careful attention to the dancers' protests sometimes led them to conclude in error that their demands had been acceded to, but in the long run it earned her the reputation of a director to whom one could talk. But with the signing of the contracts with Sevastianov and Hurok in the spring of 1941, she began a three-year vacation from daily personal involvement in the dancers' and choreographers' problems.

One of the first problems confronting Sevastianov was the question of who should be accorded first billing, Markova or Baronova? Both had been prima ballerinas of Ballet Russe companies, and although Markova was the senior, Baronova's international reputation was equally great. Sevastianov solved the problem by persuading Markova to share first billing with Baronova in all advertising and publicity. For example, the souvenir program would be printed so that Markova's picture appeared first in half the copies, Baronova's first in the other half. Everyone praised Sevastianov for his Solomon-wise solution and everyone lost patience with

PILLAR OF FIRE, THE FIRST BALLET CREATED BY TUDOR IN AMERICA, RAISED NORA KAYE AND HUGH LAING TO STAR STATUS.

Markova for her constantly voiced suspicion that every souvenir book offered for her autograph had Baronova's picture in first place. (This may well have been because the printer of the program, an old and dear friend of the Sevastianovs', had interpreted the sharing agreement to mean that Markova's picture should appear first in one-third of the copies and that in the other two-thirds it should be preceded by Baronova's.)

With respect to the choreographers, Sevastianov was explicit. In a telegram from Mexico, he instructed the printer of the souvenir program, "Be sure Dolin's name as well as picture as choreographer placed before Tudor; order is Fokine Nijinska Mordkin Bolm Dolin Tudor." The order of listing corresponded exactly to Sevastianov's artistic convictions. His reverence for Russian ballet was even more devout than Hurok's. It was not that he was chauvinistic; he simply believed that only Russians were capable of producing ballet, just as only Americans were capable of producing musical comedy. He conceded that Americans could on occasion create amusing Americana ballets, such as Catherine Littlefield's BARN DANCE, and accordingly went so far as to urge Ballet Theatre's American choreographers to consider basing a ballet on the songs of Stephen Foster. The right kind of American ballet might be viable, but who could take seriously a ballet by an Englishman! He rated Dolin above Tudor purely because Dolin had restaged Russian ballets, not because his original creations deserved recognition. Having enthusiastically entrusted to Dolin the restaging of Petipa's PRINCESS AURORA (THE SLEEPING BEAUTY) during his first season as director, Sevastianov stalled until his second season before permitting Dolin to stage an original work (ROMANTIC AGE)— and then only on condition that the ballet be financed by money raised by the choreographer.

Tudor's ballets failed to command Sevastianov's respect on three grounds: they were not Russian, they could not serve as vehicles for his stars, and they did not sell tickets. As vehicles they proved neither serviceable for his Russian ballerina wife nor adaptable to the styles of Markova and Dolin, despite their being English. Against his better judgment, he permitted Baronova to assume the role of the Russian Ballerina in GALA PERFORMANCE for a few performances, and he watched while Markova attempted the role of Caroline in JARDIN AUX LILAS with little satisfaction to herself or Tudor. If Tudor was not for ballerinas, he was also not for the public. Sevastianov had read the critics' rave reviews but he had also examined the box-office statements of the Chicago Civic Opera House and the Majestic Theatre. Tudor's public, he concluded, might be greatly enthusiastic but it was exceedingly small. The requirement of the Hurok contract for two new major ballets could be satisfied with the production of PRINCESS AURORA and of Fokine's projected BLUEBEARD or ROMEO AND JULIET, while for minor works there would be Nijinska's THE BELOVED and Fokine's LE SPECTRE DE LA ROSE. Thus a ballet by Tudor was not a necessity but an indulgent luxury.

However, as a pragmatist, Sevastianov recognized that he could not completely follow his personal preferences. He was aware that Lucia Chase regarded Tudor as an indispensable member of Ballet Theatre, one whose participation was as essential to the fulfillment of the company's artistic policy as was Dolin's, or even Fokine's. Accordingly, one of Sevastianov's first acts upon assuming the directorship was to sign a contract with Tudor, dated July 1, 1941, engaging him to stage a ballet tentatively titled "I Dedicate." This was the ballet to Schönberg's VERKLÄRTE NACHT that Tudor had first conceived while still in England in 1939 and had worked on intermittently in this country. The contract provided that rehearsals were to begin on or about September 1, 1941, but significantly no date was specified for its completion or first performance. With any luck, thought Sevastianov, the date might never arrive.

During succeeding months rehearsals were called occasionally and conducted in an atmosphere devoid of urgency. Tudor unwittingly cooperated in creating the air of a minor work in progress by choosing to use none of the major stars; his leading women were the fourth-, sixth-, and eighth-ranked Chase, Annabelle Lyon, and Nora Kaye, and his male leads the fourth- and ninth-ranked Tudor and Hugh Laing. Sevastianov did not intend to offer the ballet as a "major" work in the language of the Hurok contract. In fact, both he and Hurok hoped that its status would never have to be determined, that if ignored it would simply go away. The ballet's title was soon changed to PILLAR OF FIRE, and Sevastianov and Hurok began to refer to it as PILLS OF FIRE. But the time arrived when it could no longer be ignored. A decision had to be reached: would the ballet be presented during the spring season at the Metropolitan or postponed indefinitely and perhaps abandoned? A run-through of those portions that Tudor was prepared to exhibit was given at the Goldfarb rehearsal studios. Hurok attended, accompanied by his executive secretary, Mae Frohman, his most persuasive assistant and advisor. They saw, among other passages, the sensational street scene in which Hagar is mauled by the Lovers in Experience and rejected by the Young Man from the House Opposite. Following the audition, Hurok, Frohman, Chase, and Sevastianov conferred in one of the dressing rooms. The dancers were apprehensive. There had been rumors that the ballet would be jettisoned. They were concerned, as Nora Kaye reports, that Miss Chase might fail to assert herself lest it appear that she was pressing for continuance of the production only because the ballet provided her with a meaty role. Inasmuch as all the participants in the conference have since died—except Miss Chase, whose memory of the event is by now somewhat hazy—it cannot be known for certain what was said. But afterward Sevastianov emerged sunk in gloom to announce with irritation to Payne, the executive director, "Lucia insists it has to go on," and to add incredulously, "Mae was no help. She likes it!" This was one of the few occasions, if not the only one, on which Miss Chase directly overruled Sevastianov.

IRINA BARONOVA (CENTER, WITH NORA KAYE AND KAREN CONRAD) MADE
TOKEN APPEARANCES AS THE RUSSIAN BALLERINA IN GALA PERFORMANCE.

BARONOVA (HERE WITH DOLIN IN PRINCESS AURORA) PREFERRED
THE CLASSICS OR NEW BALLETS BY HER RUSSIAN COMPATRIOTS.

Otherwise he had his own way, and his way was to transform Ballet Theatre into a company that was barely distinguishable from the various Ballets Russes.

During the Sevastianov regime not a single ballet by an American choreographer was produced, but it must be said that the projects proposed made it easy for him to turn them down: Loring offered THE MAN FROM MIDIAN (a ballet about Moses), de Mille spoke vaguely about a ballet to music by Mozart, and Robbins outlined a psychological love-hate relationship between Cain and Abel. Of the eighteen works produced, only one, PILLAR OF FIRE, was by a non-Russian, and thanks to its enormous success, Tudor was entrusted with ROMEO AND JULIET (though it was not premiered until after Sevastianov had entered the army).

It was not only with respect to repertory that Ballet Theatre became Russianized; the company's personnel was altered when Sevastianov engaged dancers as well as staff members from the Russian companies. In doing so, he was influenced by two considerations. First, he considered European-trained dancers to be superior to the native product, and, second, he believed he would be helping Hurok, and indirectly Ballet Theatre, if by raiding the rival companies he weakened them (Hurok had already discarded one while contemplating the demise of the other). More than a quarter of the dancers from the Majestic season, most of them eager to remain with Ballet Theatre, were replaced with dancers from the Original Ballet Russe or the Ballet Russe de Monte Carlo. The entire staff (company manager, stage manager, wardrobe supervisors, regisseur, et cetera) was completely Russianized; only Charles Payne was retained (until he entered the navy in 1943). However questionable his biases, Sevastianov did succeed in assembling an excellent company and in making additions to the repertory that increased the stature of Ballet Theatre, which was now recognized by the critics and accepted by the public as the equal (or almost) of the Ballets Russes. In the process he did no violence to the company's founding principles as stated by Pleasant. He engaged a number of different choreographers and entrusted no one of them with the artistic direction. Variety and versatility remained the key words.

oubtless time, with an assist from Lucia Chase, would have forced Sevastianov to recognize the talents of American choreographers, at least to a limited extent. But the day might have been postponed considerably had he not been drafted into the army in May 1943 as the result of an ironic twist of fate, one of a number of such twists that dogged his own personal Americanization. In the 1930s, when he was wooing Baronova, her parents expressed no enthusiasm for the match because of the difference in their ages: she had not yet reached seventeen and he was in his thirties, almost twice her age. As others under similar circumstances might change their names or religions to mollify their prospective in-laws, Sevastianov changed his age. He made the necessary alteration in whatever official document he was carrying at the time, probably Nansen papers or possibly a British passport, and he did this with an easy conscience, never having held official names, dates, or documents in finical regard. When the Germans became unpopular in America at the outbreak of the war, he changed his first name to Gerald. Subsequently, with the signing of the Stalin-Hitler pact, he changed the Sevastianov to Severn. When proof of innoculation was required before the dancers could embark for Mexico, he sent a list of names to a New York–based Russian physician friend who obligingly returned a set of certificates without requiring the dancers to interrupt their rehearsals for superfluous needle-sticking. By comparison, the changing of a birth date cannot be regarded as more than an innocent white lie.

And it might indeed have remained an insignificant error had not the United States gone to war and started to draft males under the age of thirty-eight. The date Sevastianov had chosen was 1906, which made him twenty-nine in 1935, when he became engaged to Baronova. This date had been transferred from his old documents to his new American passport, perhaps unnoted at the time by Sevastianov himself. As one after another of the dancers and staff members were called up for military service, he remained unperturbed; he knew something the draft board didn't know. When he received the fatal summons in 1944 he hastened to point out that he was, in fact, ineligible since he had passed the age of thirty-eight, assuring the officials that he had been born in 1904 and not, as the records indicated, in 1906. The unimaginative and unsympathetic bureaucrats reminded him that when his passport had been issued he had sworn to the accuracy of the statements contained therein, including the birth date. Did he now wish to swear differently? Faced with the alternative of a possible conviction for perjury or with service in the armed forces, he chose the latter. In the army, he served as a Russo-English interpreter, and it is to be hoped he was able to avenge himself on the bureaucrats by thoroughly confusing both the Russian and the American military staffs. The significance to Ballet Theatre lies in the fact that had Sevastianov not been drafted he would have

remained as managing director during an indeterminate number of years through the company's formative period and he might well have molded an organization quite different from the one that survives today.

Also, during his term of office with Ballet Theatre, Sevastianov became Americanized to the extent of devoting all his waking hours to business, so much so that he neglected Baronova, who left him and later married another. When he was demobilized, the prospect of re-entering the ballet field held little attraction for him. It had never been a business in which one could expect to prosper financially, and now, without a ballerina wife to share its pleasures, the fun had gone out of it. Instead he returned to Europe, where he took advantage of his language facility and of the foreign military contacts he had made during the war and began to sell heavy industrial machinery to the Soviet Union via Yugoslavia. By the time he died a millionaire at the age of 68?/70?, he had been reunited at his villa on Malta with Baronova, who was by then a widow.

SEVASTIANOV'S LAST PRODUCTION, HELEN OF TROY, CHOREOGRAPHED BY FOKINE (AND LATER BY LICHINE) STARRED BARONOVA AND DOLIN.

(OPPOSITE PAGE) HUGH LAING AND NORA KAYE IN ALEKO.

THE ERA OF J. ALDEN TALBOT

When Ballet Theatre embarked on its fourth season in September 1943, there was every reason to believe that before another year had passed it would have become a casualty of the war. If fighting continued, the time might come when any male who was capable of dancing would also be considered able to serve in the armed forces. The time might also come when the rolling stock of the railroad would be restricted to the transportation of troops and war supplies, making it impossible for ballet companies to tour. With its tours canceled, Ballet Theatre could not long continue to give performances only in New York City, which in those days could absorb but a few weeks of ballet each season. Finally, as gas rationing became more stringent and in the event that strict blackouts and a curfew were imposed, the size of audiences would be greatly reduced.

As it turned out, the company's worst fears never materialized. Though many of the dancers were drafted, an equal number were rejected because the services' physical standards differed from those of the ballet. Poor eyesight, athlete's heart (normal in dancers), or other physical deficiencies that had proved no impediment to dancing were considered cause for disqualification by the military's examining doctors. Nor could all service psychiatrists convince themselves that men who chose ballet dancing as a career would be sufficiently stable to undergo the rigors of military discipline. As a result, a quota of male dancers remained available, at least during periods of prolonged deferments.

Access to transportation, though severely limited, was never completely restricted. In spite of adverse conditions, Ballet Theatre continued to tour the country during the war years. Because these tours demonstrated for the first time the viability of an American company and encouraged the backers to continue their support, today's dancers owe a tremendous debt of gratitude to the pioneering accomplishments of the wartime dancers. The dancers of the 1970s would not be enjoying the satisfaction of international acclaim had the dancers of 1943 not been willing to undergo abnormal hardships—as shown by the following comparative schedules.

FOR THE PERIOD FROM OCTOBER 1
THROUGH AUGUST 30

	1943–44	1974–75
TOTAL NUMBER OF PERFORMANCES	226	174
PERFORMANCES IN NEW YORK CITY	80	96
PERFORMANCES IN WASHINGTON, D.C.	3	32
PERFORMANCES ON TRANSCONTINENTAL TOUR	143	46
NUMBER OF CITIES VISITED ON TOUR	73	8
NUMBER OF ONE-NIGHT STANDS	48	0

These figures provide only the barest indication of the difference in life-styles and working conditions. On Saturday, February 15, 1975, the dancers were given the day off from rehearsals to prepare for the trip to California. On Sunday afternoon they deposited their baggage on the sidewalk outside the New York State Theater; they would not see or handle it again until it was delivered to the rooms reserved for them by the ballet management in a hotel in Los Angeles. Chartered buses took them to the airport (had it been a chartered flight, the buses would have driven directly to the plane, parked on the runway). Dinner was served on board the plane. From the airport in Los Angeles buses delivered the dancers to the door of their hotel, where they remained for fourteen days, during which they appeared in fifteen performances. At the conclusion of their stay, buses again picked them up and delivered them to the airport. The same transportation procedure was repeated between the remaining six cities of the tour. In accordance with a union regulation, transportation and performing schedules were arranged so that in each week there would be a period of twenty-four hours in which the dancers were not required either to travel or perform.

In contrast, the dancers of 1943 fared only slightly better than cattle on the drive from Albuquerque to the Chicago stockyards. On Saturday and Sunday, November 6 and 7, 1943, they danced in the final four performances of a four-week engagement at the Metropolitan Opera House. Early on the morning of the 8th, they assembled at Grand Central Station, carrying their own luggage on to the two reserved coaches attached to a train bound through Worcester, Massachusetts. At the Worcester station they found porters and taxicabs (or themselves carried their bags to public transportation) and proceeded on their own to their hotels. Some of the dancers had personally made hotel reservations by mail (the ballet management supplied them only with a list of hotels). Others preferred to take their chances on hotel vacancies or to stay at the local YMCA. They performed that evening at the Worcester Auditorium. Early the next morning they paid for their hotel rooms with part of their regular salary. (Today dancers receive an extra per diem allowance that more than covers the cost of room and board on tour.) Then they found and paid for transportation to the railroad station, where they waited for the train to Springfield.

TOURING WAS ARDUOUS IN THE FORTIES, WHEN KAYE AND ROBBINS CLOWNED AND LAZOVSKY AND MARKOVA SAT GRIMLY AS THEY WAITED FOR A TRAIN. IN THE FIFTIES, BEFORE THE COMPANY TOOK TO PLANES, A GROUP ASSEMBLED IN THE OLD PENN STATION: FERNANDO SCHAFFEN, PRISCILLA ALLEN, RICHARD GOLTRA, LIANE PLANE, RUTH GILBERT, MARGARET CRASKE, AND JACK BEABER.

(Usually, but not always, two coaches were stationed in the yards, to be boarded in advance and later hooked on to a scheduled train.) Tuesday evening they performed at the Springfield Auditorium. Early Wednesday morning they boarded the train for the six-hour trip to Philadelphia, where they performed that evening at the Academy of Music. Thursday and Friday were days of luxury and sloth—they remained in Philadelphia, giving only one performance on each evening. Saturday morning they jumped to Baltimore for matinée and evening performances at the Lyric Theatre. Early Sunday they moved on to Washington, D.C., performing twice that day at the DAR's Constitution Hall. Thus in the first week of the tour they danced every day, giving nine performances in five cities. The following week they again danced every day, but appeared in only eight performances in six cities from Washington to Buffalo. And so it continued for the next nineteen weeks, except for Christmas week, in Chicago, when they were laid off without salary, receiving only an inadequate sustenance allowance of three dollars a day.

Again, this sketch gives only the merest hint of the hardships the dancers underwent during the war years. As war activities intensified, the early-morning search for taxis became more hectic, the railway coaches more crowded and uncomfortable, the hotel accommodations more precarious. So many of the transportation facilities were commandeered for troop movements that the ballet management was forced to post Travel Regulations, one paragraph of which read:

> Whenever it is humanly possible, the Company will be notified as to the conditions of travel on each jump, i.e., whether there will be one or two cars, where they will be spotted and when they can be boarded. Therefore, one rule that must be observed is that EACH MEMBER OF THE COMPANY AND ORCHESTRA TAKE BUT ONE SEAT IN EACH CAR UNTIL THE ENTIRE COMPANY IS SEATED. LUGGAGE MUST NOT BE PLACED ON SEAT. In this way every member of Ballet Theatre will be assured of a seat without confusion and the resulting ill-temper on every single trip.

Consequently, the phrase "One body, one seat!" became a company byword. (On the rare occasions when the distance between cities made night travel necessary, each Pullman berth had to be occupied by two bodies.) Another byword forced upon the company, this one originated by the military, was "Hurry up and wait!" The dancers hurried to the railroad station only to wait, sometimes for hours, for a civilian train that had been sidetracked by troop movements. After a ride in a crowded, often unheated coach (to which a diner was almost never attached), they arrived late and stood in long lines for transportation to their hotels, where they were told they must wait until the priority-occupants of their rooms moved out and their beds could be made up (there was no promise that the rooms would be cleaned). Unwashed and unrested, they looked for a restaurant, again standing in line in the hope (usually vain) that the menu that day would feature some form of the rationed and hard-to-find red meat. The day after the Travel Regulations were posted, Lucia Chase wrote from Seattle to one of her directors. The letter began, "We're waiting for our rooms so I'll start a letter." Six pages and some hours

later she concluded, "Now we have our rooms [she was rooming with Nora Kaye] so I must bathe and be ready for class at 7."

But if trains, hotels, and restaurants were crowded, so were theaters. Despite gas rationing and blackouts, audiences were larger than ever before. Overtime payments and the greater profits of wartime industry had boosted personal incomes, and this excess cash, which could not be spent on scarce and tightly rationed consumer goods, was used to buy a few hours' surcease from the anxieties of war.

The difficulties of operating a ballet company while a world war raged were counterbalanced by certain unforeseen advantages. First of all, competition was relaxed. As has been noted, Colonel de Basil's Original Ballet Russe remained exiled in South America, and the activities of the Kirstein-Balanchine enterprises, American Ballet and Ballet Caravan, were suspended while Kirstein served in the army. On the national market the only serious competitor to Ballet Theatre was Serge Denham's Ballet Russe de Monte Carlo, which booked its own tours. Thus Ballet Theatre was Hurok's sole major ballet attraction.

Another advantage was that the drafting of Russian-born executives gave Americans a chance to gain experience in the conduct of a hitherto Russian-dominated art form and business—and, in the process, they changed the character of Ballet Theatre.

BALLET ASSOCIATES HELPED MOUNT ROMEO AND JULIET WITH MARKOVA.

AT THE RUSSIAN TEA ROOM, HUROK ENTERTAINED JANET REED,
NANA GOLLNER, NORA KAYE, ALDEN TALBOT, AND ALICIA MARKOVA.

When German Sevastianov departed for Fort McClellan, Alabama, in May 1943, his functions as managing director were assumed by John Alden Talbot, a native-born New Yorker whose prosperous family had occupied a house on the Washington Square South of Henry James. An engineer by profession, a widower and father of two children, Talbot had recently retired to Butler, New Jersey, where he became engaged in real-estate activity: the subdivision into smaller estates of a huge tract of land known as Smoke Rise that a friend had inherited as heir to the Sweet Caporelle cigarette fortune. During his retirement years he developed an interest in music, particularly opera. Active participation in the Metropolitan Opera Guild led to his introduction to its counterpart, the Ballet Associates, an organization, headed by Countess Mercati (the mother of Michael Arlen), whose membership consisted of café society balletomanes who brought enthusiasm and spotless amateurism to their support of ballet.

With his Old New York background, and more especially with his personal financial independence, Talbot brought a new element to the management of Ballet Theatre that was in sharp contrast to the career-building ambitions of Pleasant and the esoteric Russianisms of Mordkin and Sevastianov. There was no need for him to temper his actions with a view to protecting his ballet career, for he contemplated no such career—at least not at the start. He regarded his ballet activities as a public-spirited avocation to be indulged in in conjunction with his work as a civilian volunteer in a New Jersey munitions plant. Nor did he feel compelled to adopt the subtle Slavic thought processes customarily applied to the operation of the essentially Russian art form. His approach was American: unsubtle, direct, and frank to the point of naïveté. Shortly after assuming office, he received advice from his predecessor concerning the sensible and effective method of solving a ballet problem. Sevastianov wrote from his barracks:

I gather you have trouble so far with Alicia [Markova] and Anton [Dolin]. If Irina [Baronova] or Slavenska or Danilova will be on the way to join Ballet Theatre, I imagine it will be much easier to sign both Alicia and Anton on our terms. My advice is to start negotiations with Slavenska—preferably in the Russian Tea Room—so that rumors reach Alicia right away.

The advice did not come as a surprise to Talbot; he was by then familiar through ballet lore with the chicaneries of de Basil, Hurok, Denham, et al. But their tactics were not for him. When he experienced difficulties with Leonide Massine, Talbot did not (as Sevastianov would have advised) arrange to be seen having lunch with Balanchine at the Russian Tea Room. Instead, he reported his reactions in a letter to Harry M. Zuckert:

Every time Massine calls me up on the telephone, he threatens that if I don't do this, he won't do that, usually that he won't open at the Met in the new ballet [MADEMOISELLE ANGOT]. He called me up this morning to ask whether "Tricorne" [THREE-CORNERED HAT] had been put back in the repertory and I told him I had spoken to Mr. Hurok but that nothing definite had been settled and there was a chance that it would go on later in the season and that we had no chance to rehearse it now anyway. [Hurok had no intention of including TRICORNE in the Met repertory, but by telling Massine there was a chance he got the choreographer off his back onto Talbot's.] He said he wanted to give me formal assurance that unless it was established in the program before his rehearsals in the Met started, he would not go on in his new ballet and that it would not go on. I told him that as far as I knew, there was nothing in the contract that forced us to give "Tricorne" and that anyway the contract was worked out between his lawyers and ours and signed by you and him and I had nothing to do with it. Furthermore, I told him that threats never interested me very much and I was damned sick of him constantly telephoning and threatening me. Fun is fun, but I have had quite enough of that particular type of fun.

Talbot had yet to learn that in the world of ballet, threats fell into the category of "fun is fun," and that, armed with a binding contract, he could lead a dancer or a choreographer to the stage but he could not necessarily make him dance or choreograph. His education in these respects was soon to be advanced by some of Ballet Theatre's non-Russian choreographers, de Mille, Tudor, and Robbins. Before assuming his official position Talbot had been acquainted with them on a casual social basis: as invitees to the Ballet Balls sponsored by Ballet Associates, as weekend visitors to the cottage he rented for the Berkshire Festival, and as his guests for luncheons, dinners, and after-performance parties. He was enchanted by de Mille's unmatched wit, intrigued by Tudor's dour disdain of everyone (except, of course, Talbot), and charmed by Jerome Robbins' malicious imitations of Fokine and Massine, who emerged as figures of fun possessed of minimal talents. Tudor with his triumph, PILLAR OF FIRE, and de Mille with her RODEO, recently produced for the Ballet Russe de Monte Carlo, were the toast of the ballet intellectuals. Consequently, Talbot offered them every cooperation and encouragement. The management's previous condescension toward Tudor was replaced by a recognition of his genius, currently being applied to the creation of ROMEO AND JULIET. De Mille's Mozart ballet, once rejected by Sevastianov, was reincarnated as a Gluck ballet, tentatively titled TALLY-HO, and

WITH FANCY FREE, JEROME ROBBINS PROVIDED AMERICAN ROLES FOR HIS FRIENDS TIRED OF PLAYING FRENCH ACTRESSES (JANET REED WITH ANDRÉ EGLEVSKY IN MADEMOISELLE ANGOT), GREEK GODS (JOHN KRIZA WITH KAREN CONRAD IN ROMANTIC AGE), SPANISH ARISTOCRATS (MURIEL BENTLEY WITH ROBBINS IN GOYESCAS), AND EVEN A SHEAF OF WHEAT (HAROLD LANG IN RUSSIAN SOLDIER).

enthusiastically backed by Talbot. Robbins at last found someone in management who would listen, and replaced his Cain and Abel story with a ballet about three sailors on shore leave. Doubtless Robbins would have brought a touch of genius to his Cain and Abel work, but fortunately for Ballet Theatre and for American ballet in general, he had tired of performing Fokine's peasants (even in one case appearing as a sheaf of wheat), Massine's gypsies, Lichine's Greek gods, et cetera. He asked himself why American dancers could not perform the roles of Americans, and the most colorful Americans of that period were the sailors who could be observed in the restaurants and bars where Ballet Theatre dancers congregated after performances in port cities on both coasts.

Talbot was determined to advance the interests of these charming new friends, whose approach to the ballet—being frank, open, and as healthy as his own—contrasted with that of the Russians. But before long, he discovered that wit, humor, and camaraderie were quickly discarded when an artist entered the rehearsal hall or the office of the managing director. He also began to wonder whether the strategic maneuvering he so deplored in the Russians was perhaps a necessary evil in the conduct of ballet affairs. Within five months of his letter of complaint about Massine's blackmailing, he again wrote to Harry M. Zuckert:

I am beginning to change my opinion very strongly about the advisability of having Mr. Hurok sign up Dolin and Markova, which might be a bad precedent to start and Tudor has been behaving so badly for the last month that I am now of the opinion that it is a very good thing to have Markova and Dolin within the company to counteract his influence. Tudor thinks he is a little [dictator] and gives every indication of behaving like a big one, if he had the power. It is really amazing the nonsense he can think up to cause trouble.

The de Mille ballet [TALLY-HO] is going to take up a lot of money this week, as she is another one who thinks she is a little [dictator] and we are going to have to work out some way of curbing our choreographers, just how I am at a loss to know at the present. After many trials and tribulations, threats and what not, it looks as though the ballet will really go on tonight. The additional expense has been considerable. Lucia has come out on the small end with her part, and I am going to have a serious talk with de Mille before I leave here, as she must do something about the part before it opens in New York. Lucia is really being a brick about the whole thing and I must say that my stay here in California has increased my admiration and affection for her very much. Also I realize that she deserves better treatment than she gets a good part of the time, and she certainly is a good trouper.

If Talbot did, in fact, have a "serious talk" with de Mille before he left Hollywood, it is regrettable the conversation was not recorded. What words does a parvenu dilettante use to convince a seasoned show-woman, the scion of an illustrious theatrical family, that she has erred in failing to make the role of a rival dancer as important as her own? Miss de Mille has not as yet reported on the conversation, but if it took place it undoubtedly marked the beginning of the dissolution of the de Mille–Talbot mutual admiration society.

Talbot never did work out a way of "curbing" his choreographers. This is not surprising since no director ever has, not even Diaghilev. Even directors who are experienced and highly respected choreographers themselves have still discovered no acceptable method for guiding, let alone curbing, other choreographers. Thus Talbot, no choreographer himself and, at most, an amateur at artistic direction, should have been chary of offering suggestions to choreographers, but he believed in speaking his mind. Miss Chase reported on this belief in a letter to Zuckert: "I have just come from a very good lunch talk with Alden. Found him a different person to talk to and am quite encouraged over it. He told me I should have been frank and blunt." Talbot meant she should have been "blunt" about her objections to his committing Ballet Theatre to new productions with no prospects of raising the money to pay for them. His own frankness with Miss Chase was appreciated by her but it was taken amiss by George Balanchine when Talbot discussed with him his new ballets: WALTZ ACADEMY, created for Ballet Theatre in 1944, and DANSES CONCERTANTES, created simultaneously for the Ballet Russe de Monte Carlo. Talbot bluntly informed Balanchine that it was obvious to all that he had lavished his best steps and most inventive choreography on DANSES CONCERTANTES, leaving WALTZ ACADEMY a poor relation. It would have been fruitless for Balanchine to explain that his choreographic inventions were directly inspired by the music, and therefore the steps devised to Stravinsky's DANSES CONCERTANTES score could not be interchanged for those suggested by Vittorio Rieti's waltzes, or vice versa. He chose instead to resist all urgings to create another ballet for Ballet Theatre until 1947, when Chase and Smith commissioned THEME AND VARIATIONS.

AGNES DE MILLE'S TALLY-HO FEATURED HERSELF AND HUGH LAING.

THE CAST ALSO INCLUDED ANTON DOLIN AND LUCIA CHASE.

GEORGE BALANCHINE CREATED WALTZ ACADEMY FOR BALLET THEATRE WITH A SERIES OF PAS DE DEUX FOR SOLOISTS INCLUDING ALONSO AND ROMANOFF.

More often than not Talbot's decisions were dictated by considerations that had little to do with an established artistic policy. He had to contend, for instance, with the unreliability of ballerinas and premiers danseurs and Hurok's somewhat confused predilection for things Russian. Thus in the spring of 1943, when Markova and Baronova were alternately ill, unable to dance, and scarcely well enough to deny persistent rumors that they were about to sign with another company, it became necessary for Ballet Theatre to engage a standby ballerina so as not to risk breaching its contract with Hurok, which provided that Markova and Baronova, or an acceptable substitute, should be available to appear in all performances booked by him. Qualified and available ballerinas were in short supply, and the choice was made more difficult because it had to be approved by Hurok, whose judgment was based on vague and highly individualistic standards. He would readily have approved of the very Russian Tamara Toumanova, one of de Basil's baby ballerinas, but she was unavailable. With misgivings, he was prepared to accept Nana Gollner, who, though an American, had ranked as a ballerina with the Original Ballet Russe, but she too was unavailable. He would not listen to the suggestion that Nora Kaye serve as stand-in even though she had earned ballerina status by her performance in PILLAR OF FIRE the previous spring. Alicia Alonso, who was to make her debut as Giselle a few months later, was not even mentioned, and Tatiana Riabouchinska was rejected because in the eyes of Hurok's advisors she ranked only as a soubrette, not as a ballerina. Alexandra Danilova remained happily and loyally committed to the Ballet Russe de Monte Carlo. There remained only Vera Zorina, who instantly won Hurok's approval not only as a Russian ballerina but as a star of stage and screen.

The German-born Norwegian Eva Brigitte Hartwig (Zorina) was less Russian than Nora Kaye (Koreff), who might have been Russian-born had not her parents caught the last boat from Siberia, but the public would not be let into the secret. Zorina was engaged as guest artist. A ballerina must have a partner, and André Eglevsky was induced to return to the company, also as a guest artist. Further, a ballerina must have ballerina roles, and the choreographer George Balanchine was called in. He revised the title part in Lichine's HELEN OF TROY to suit Zorina's individual style, and restaged two of his early works, APOLLO, created for Diaghilev in 1928 under the title APOLLON MUSAGÈTE, and THE WANDERER, first performed with the title L'ERRANTE in Balanchine's own company, Les Ballets 1933. Neither was any more Russian than Zorina but they satisfied Hurok: Balanchine was Russian, the composer of APOLLO (Stravinsky) was Russian, and although the score for THE WANDERER was Germanic (Schubert-Liszt), the designer (Pavel Tchelitchev) was Russian.

To Hurok, the Russian aspect was a matter of vital importance, one over which he was prepared, if necessary, to break with Ballet Theatre. Apprehensive right from the start about managing an American company, by now he had seen his worst fears realized. Although the first two-month tour, beginning in January 1942, had been a financial disaster, astonishingly, Ballet Theatre had not hastened to make good his losses. After prolonged negotiations the company did agree to share them, but only on condition that for the following season he guarantee it more performances on more favorable terms. This was not Hurok's first experience in presenting American dance. But when American audiences had failed to support the appearances of Isadora Duncan, Paris Singer, the sewing machine heir, had eagerly volunteered to cover the costs—and Hurok had expected no less from the backers of Ballet Theatre. As soon as it became apparent that no one was going to pay for American ballet, he decided that henceforth he would not present <u>American</u> ballet. Instead, as the advertisements from 1943 on declared, S. Hurok presented "The Greatest in Russian Ballet by the Ballet Theatre." The wording and the size of the type in these advertisements provoked a running battle that was waged unremittingly throughout the last years of the association between Hurok and Ballet Theatre. A typical advertisement appeared in the Seattle Star on August 3, 1943:

If this was not enough to raise the hackles of the directors, who were hoping to establish "Ballet Theatre" as the immediately recognizable name of an <u>American</u> company, the advertisement (right) inserted in the same paper the next day infuriated not only them but also the dancers.*

*As an indication of how little is new in the world of ballet and how little Hurok and his successors have changed, this advertisement should be compared with one in 1973 that announced: "S. Hurok presents THE CANADIAN NATIONAL BALLET **RUDOLF NUREYEV**, Guest Artist."

Because by contract Hurok had been given the right to determine what constituted a "major" ballet (two of which must be produced each year) and because, in effect, he was empowered to decide whether a star dancer who was proposed as a substitute for one named in the original contract was of equivalent stature, he was able virtually to exercise a veto power over the production and hiring policies of Ballet Theatre even though he was not empowered to initiate them. Consequently, it is difficult through independent evidence to distinguish between what the Ballet Theatre management chose to do of its own volition and what it was forced to do during the five years it operated under the Hurok contract. Many of the decisions were arrived at in the course of Russian Tea Room luncheons or during conferences at the Hurok offices. These conversations were unrecorded, and it is to be expected that in later years the only-human participants would clearly recall their opposition to works that proved to be failures and their ardent championing (in the face of bitter opposition) of those ballets that became hits. However, enough correspondence has survived to establish these two assertions: that Hurok preferred Russian ballets, and that Talbot (backed by Miss Chase) desired the development of Anglo-American choreographers. Naturally there were exceptions, and the demarcation between the Russian and Anglo-American camps was never clean-cut. One of the first Amer-

ican ballets to attract Talbot's interest, Catherine Littlefield's BARN DANCE, was brought to his attention by the Russian editor Anatole Chujoy, who persuaded Hurok during Russian-speaking lunches to accept it as a major ballet under the terms of the contract. Further, one of the last ballets planned by Talbot (it was produced after his departure) was O'Henry's GIFT OF THE MAGI, which could have been categorized as American had it not been choreographed by the Latvian-

Russian Simon Semenoff, who was even less American than Hurok.

An examination of the Sevastianov production record leaves no doubt that he went along enthusiastically with Hurok's demands for Russian ballets. Talbot, under pressure from Hurok, produced a preponderant number of ballets by Russians but did so under protest.* Talbot and Miss Chase remained in agreement on artistic policies, but Hurok, with his exorbitant demands and insatiable appetite for new ballets, forced them into conflict over financial affairs. This predicament was not of Talbot's own making; it had been predetermined by the signing of the original Hurok contract and its subsequent options.

Ballet Theatre had entered into the Hurok agreement with self-deceiving hopes. Hurok was to guarantee it against performing losses and was to allow it a share in the profits, which, he assured it, would be ample to cover production and rehearsal costs. Perhaps not _all_ those costs, but enough so that the balance could be taken care of with Miss Chase's annual contribution of $25,000, together with additional funds that Sevastianov, and subsequently Talbot, should find it easy to solicit from the increasing number of balletomanes. Talbot counted on the Ballet Associates in America, Inc., to act as a tax-exempt conduit for such contributions, and, to a certain extent, it did. But the participation of the Associates was limited—though played up with a view to encouraging donors. The Associates, for example, were credited in the program with having paid for ROMEO AND JULIET when, in fact, they had contributed only a fraction of its costs. Later they did raise enough money to pay for the entire costs of the less elaborate ballet ON STAGE!, but more often than not promised funds failed to materialize, and bills were paid when Harry M. Zuckert forwarded a check to Miss Chase for her signature. Zuckert frequently added the warning, "If you persist in showing your enthusiasm for a new ballet before the funds are on hand with which to produce it, you will be stuck with the costs." Belatedly, Miss Chase heeded his warning in connection with the proposed purchase of Balanchine's CONCERTO BAROCCO, and this led to strained relations between her and Talbot.

On January 18, 1945, Talbot telegraphed Miss Chase at the Fox Theatre in Spokane, Washington:

Have had two long talks with Smith and Colt who have firm offer from Kirstein's representative for Balanchine's CONCERTO BAROCCO which Monte Carlo wants and am now trying to get Balanchine's OK and price. We could do it quickly for about six thousand including fifteen hundred for first-year royalty for Kirstein and one thousand to Balanchine and using present Berman set and costumes said to be in good condition. This seems like best proposition for Spring.

During the preceding fall Ballet Theatre had produced Lichine's GRADUATION BALL and Balanchine's WALTZ ACADEMY,

rated as minor ballets by Hurok. For the season, it still owed him two major ballets, to be presented in April at the Metropolitan. Tudor's UNDERTOW was in rehearsal, but Hurok had not agreed to accept it as a major ballet. Ballet Theatre therefore had to come up with two additional works. Oliver Smith and Alvin Colt, who had worked closely with Balanchine in designing the scenery and costumes for his WALTZ ACADEMY, were acting as intermediaries between Ballet Theatre and Kirstein, who was interested in disposing of some ballet properties now that he was no longer operating a company. CONCERTO BAROCCO and PASTORELA, created in 1941 for the American Ballet's South American tour, had been previewed at the Hunter College Playhouse, where they were seen by Miss Chase. She was enthusiastic about the Balanchine work but less so about PASTORELA, the joint creation of Lew Christensen and José Fernandez (the choreographer of Ballet Theatre's first-year GOYESCAS). Hurok immediately rejected PASTORELA, which was Mexican-American, but found BAROCCO, in the Imperial Russian style, acceptable on two grounds. On January 19 Talbot wired Miss Chase at the Capitol Theatre in Yakima, Washington:

Hurok willing to invest maximum half because he feels it will counteract large Balanchine repertory in Monte Carlo and that we need ballets.

Once again, Hurok was as concerned with weakening the competition, the Ballet Russe de Monte Carlo, as he was with strengthening Ballet Theatre's repertory. Meanwhile, Miss Chase, having initially expressed enthusiasm for BAROCCO, had been brought up short by Zuckert's warning. When Talbot pressed her for a reply, she wired him on January 23 that she did not understand why he was waiting further word from her about the purchase of BAROCCO— meaning that if he could raise the money from Hurok and others, she would be delighted to see the ballet added to the repertory, but that she had already reached the limit of her contribution for the season. The negotiations came to nothing, with misunderstandings and hard feelings on all sides.

By the spring of 1945 Talbot found himself subjected to intolerable pressures from two directions: from Hurok, who demanded more and bigger ballets, and from Miss Chase's advisors, who insisted that she must be relieved of the sole responsibility for furnishing Hurok with ballets that, they were convinced, were earning him huge personal profits. Talbot succeeded in inducing Hurok to assume a portion of the costs, but the only way he could have placated both sides would have been to discover untapped sources for the capital required to produce a yearly minimum of two major and two minor ballets. In 1945 such sources remained undiscovered. Recognizing his inability to raise money and the hopelessness of his position, Talbot resigned as president of Ballet Theatre and retired into the ranks of the Ballet Associates. During his tenure as director of Ballet Theatre, he raised American choreographers to a status of dignity and was responsible for keeping the company alive during the war years.

---

*Sevastianov produced twelve ballets by Russian choreographers and three by Englishmen: Tudor's PILLAR OF FIRE and ROMEO AND JULIET, and Dolin's ROMANTIC AGE. Alden Talbot produced fourteen ballets by Russians, three by Englishmen, and four by Americans.

GUEST STARS ENGAGED IN THE FORTIES AT THE INSISTENCE OF HUROK INCLUDED TAMARA TOUMANOVA, IN PETROUCHKA (TOP) WITH JEROME ROBBINS, AND VERA ZORINA, IN HELEN OF TROY (BELOW) WITH ANDRÉ EGLEVSKY, ROBBINS, DONALD SADDLER, AND SIMON SEMENOFF.

Neither the break between Ballet Theatre and Alden Talbot nor that between it and Hurok Attractions was caused by a single disagreement or confrontation. Both were brought about by a series of small, sometimes petty, squabbles that arose inevitably from misconceptions with regard to undiscovered truths about the business of ballet.

Talbot possessed limited qualifications for the two posts he had acquired as president of Ballet Theatre, Inc., and managing director of the Ballet Theatre company. To the latter post he brought no previous experience, and circumstances prevented him from devoting sufficient attention to the performance of his duties. His time was divided between his volunteer work at a munitions factory in New Jersey and the ballet, which was on tour outside New York during most of the year. As a consequence, he could make only rare and hurried visits to the company, and the largest portion of his managing activities had to be conducted by mail and telegram (long-distance telephone was not always available for non-war business use). It has since been proved that a ballet company cannot continue to function smoothly and efficiently unless a determined master is continually on hand to snap the whip. When the task master relaxes or interrupts his daily supervision, rehearsal and performance discipline grows lax. When he is absent, disputes multiply among the seconds-in-command, and they remain unrefereed and unresolved. Inertia spreads through the company, down to the corps de ballet, depressing morale. Talbot attempted to minimize the effect of his absences by delegating authority to his assistant, Alexis Tcherkassky, but this did not work. Everyone was aware that Tcherkassky had little authority on his own and that his decisions might be reversed when Talbot's private ear could be reached during his next visit. In the meanwhile, essential day-to-day decisions (such as emergency program and casting changes, which even at best cannot be made to everyone's satisfaction), because they were not made immediately and irrevocably by the one with the ultimate authority, became a source of endless quarrels and bitterness.

If circumstances vitiated Talbot's effectiveness as a manager and disciplinarian of the company, his lack of experience as an active participant in _any_ form of the arts left him unprepared to act as artistic director. Neither the choreographers nor the dancers could regard him as anything but an amateur, however charming and enthusiastic. During this century only a few directors have been able to assert an authority that is accepted by _all_ the members of a company: Diaghilev (because of his irresistible arrogance), Fokine (before his declining, querulous years), the indomitable Ninette de Valois, and Balanchine (because of his recognized genius). There are others, such as Tudor and Robbins, whose authority is accepted by their disciples but not universally. Talbot had none of the qualifications for artistic authority: knowledge, creativity, or a determination supported by self-confidence.

THE COMPANY UNDER THE DIRECTION OF LUCIA CHASE AND OLIVER SMITH: (SEATED ON SCAFFOLD) HUGH LAING, JOHN KRIZA, IGOR YOUSKEVITCH; (BELOW) MURIEL BENTLEY, ALICIA ALONSO, ANTONY TUDOR, SMITH, DIMITRI ROMANOFF, CHASE, NORA KAYE, MAX GOBERMAN.

In his post as president of Ballet Theatre, Inc., Talbot succeeded only partially. He did bring an apparent businesslike order to the production and operating expenses and he vigilantly pressed for all that was due to Ballet Theatre under the terms of the Hurok contract. With Hurok himself he was able to maintain a cordial relationship—up to a point.*

Keeping accounts in order and getting along with Hurok could not be considered the principal functions of the president of Ballet Theatre. The board of directors expected him to assume responsibility for the solvency of the corporation, to raise any money required over and above the limited contribution pledged by Miss Chase. This expectation was based on the misconception that a ballet company could eventually operate at a profit and that should minor deficits still persist, a growing number of ballet enthusiasts would be eager to make good the losses. Talbot came no closer than his predecessors to operating at a profit, nor was he any better at raising money. Like Richard Pleasant, who discovered that his Princeton friendship with Laurance Rockefeller was of no avail in eliciting funds from the Rockefeller Foundation, Talbot found that his fund-raising associate, John D. Barrett, Jr., could not obtain any contribution from the Mellon Foundation despite his Yale friendship with Paul Mellon. And his friend Lauder Greenway was no more successful, in spite of the fact that he was a trustee of the Mellon Foundation. In those days it could never be determined whether the boards of charitable foundations were deciding that Ballet Theatre already had a backer in Lucia Chase and therefore needed no other, or whether they cautiously agreed that ballet was something they wouldn't touch with a ten-dollar check. They could understand that a hospital could have every bed filled, or a university have every desk occupied, and still lose money, but they could not fathom how a theater presenting ballet could sell every seat and still not show a profit. Back then it was even questionable whether a foundation should support the arts—but if it did venture into that suspect area it should go no further than the staid Metropolitan Opera House or the publicly owned National (formerly Mellon) Gallery.

Talbot did succeed in raising some money through the Ballet Associates, particularly after it was reorganized so that donors could take a tax deduction for their contributions. The directors of the Associates were persons of substantial wealth, but their contributions (the larger portion of which was channeled to Ballet Theatre), although in their minds generous, amounted to no more than a token gesture toward the payment of Ballet Theatre's never-decreasing deficits. With no significant contributions coming in, the board of directors became impatient and Miss Chase grew desperate. On September 21, 1944, in a rare moment of letting her distress show, Miss Chase conveyed her desperation to one of the officers of the company following an unproductive meeting of the board:

What do we do now? I agreed to go for the summer [on tour] and report. I wrote every week to Mr. Zuckert saying the situation was intolerable. . . . I told my story on arrival [in New York on September 5]—I must wait for a Directors' meeting. . . . In September after two weeks I get a hearing—adjourned till October. . . . Money flows and I must go to Mr. Smith [George Smith, Mr. Zuckert's assistant] tomorrow to fix the money. I signed for 10M last week, but they need more. Money was never mentioned today. One meeting in three months and we must repeat for two hours everything that was discussed in the Executive meeting . . . no word was mentioned of pushing Ballet Associates to raise money. I think the whole set-up is idiotic. I can pour in money but so as not to hurt Alden's feelings, hours and hours are spent and we get nowhere.

The words "hurt feelings" are the key to the ineffectiveness of the meetings and actions (or rather, the lack of action) of the board of directors. The officers of the company were not paid salaries on which they depended for their livelihood, the directors held no stock in the company from which they hoped to earn dividends, and there were no small stockholders who could ask embarrassing questions at annual meetings. The participants were volunteer ladies and gentlemen who were discharging their civic responsibilities by devoting a portion of their time and energy to the support of the art of ballet, for which they had developed a fine appreciation. No one could be so ungentlemanly, so unladylike, or so crass as to demand, "How much social prestige do you derive from your association with the Ballet Theatre management, and how much pleasure do you derive from contacts with the glamorous artists? How much are you willing to pay for the privilege?" Nor would anyone come forward and directly assert, "What we need more than your advice and counsel is your money."

Miss Chase was equally perturbed by the state of the financial arrangements with Hurok. Her letter continues:

Peter [Lawrence] showed me Variety. Hurok announced in nine performances they took in $124,000. It was 50-50, so he got $62,000. He magnanimously paid us $6,000 for those nine performances and we lost plenty of money. Has anyone else looked into that or worried about it? In 7 months I had "loaned" $52,000; in 8 months I have "loaned" $72,000.

---

*Later it was discovered that anyone, including Lucia Chase and Oliver Smith, could "get along" with the "old man" up to a point. Hurok had a genuine affection for the arts and for artists. Like Samuel Goldwyn, he was self-educated in his appreciation of the arts and had developed an uncanny instinct for predicting what the public would accept. Like Goldwyn, too, he was in business to make money and not to please the critics and elitists, but he did not underestimate the elasticity of taste of the general ticket buyer. Just as Goldwyn could produce and make money out of THE CHILDRENS' HOUR, which the more cultured producers had labeled box-office poison, so Hurok could present the Sadler's Wells Ballet in THE SLEEPING BEAUTY at a time when all other experts insisted that no American audience could be induced to sit through a full evening of classical ballet. As an individual Hurok was crude but jovial, blessed with a broad, sometimes devastating, sense of humor that made him a charming social companion. If anyone could get along with him up to a point, that point was reached when he was crossed, usually by a threat to his business interests. At that juncture he began to resemble his compatriot Nikita Khrushchev. The resemblance was noted at a supper party for a half-dozen members of American Ballet Theatre in the club rooms of Moscow's Sports Palace after a ballet performance. Khrushchev, as host, was being crude, jovial, and broadly humorous—not at all the ogre he had been painted—until something was said that he took to be critical of his tact and good manners. His face flushed and his eyes flashed as he angrily defended himself. Hurok, when crossed, also flushed and glared and expostulated almost incoherently. But on the day following such an outburst, from the offices of Hurok Attractions would issue a letter in polished English written by one of his several literate associates. When future historians examine these letters at Lincoln Center's Library for the Performing Arts, Hurok will emerge as a man of moderation, reasonableness, and even temper who perhaps missed his calling when he chose to become an impresario rather than a literary figure.

In October 1944 Talbot threatened to relinquish one of his posts, that of managing director. The search was on for a successor who would operate with a large degree of autonomous power. Miss Chase again wrote:

Mr. Zuckert said I had chosen three right words, "professional," "theatre," "business" man. . . . I wrote Charlie [Payne] about looking for a Managing Director. Once before, I guess when Jerry Sevastianov left, he had suggested Eddie Hambleton—Yale man from Baltimore, young producer [T. Edward Hambleton, later founder of the Phoenix Theatre]. I told Mr. Z someone would fall from heaven and he said, "Well, you know, they sometimes do!" So I have my eyes on the sky.

Nobody fell from the sky and, hesitatingly, Miss Chase put forward her own candidate, Peter Lawrence. Lawrence had been borrowed from the Theatre Guild to fill in as stage manager after the departure of Serge Sokolov, whom Sevastianov had acquired in one of his raids on the de Basil company. Throughout his association with Ballet Theatre, Lawrence was an activist who triggered every casual thought into instant action. One had only to speculate idly on how nice it would be if the American President and his wife were to follow the example set by Queen Elizabeth (now the Queen Mother) in her solicitude for the Sadler's Wells Ballet, and he would pick up the nearest telephone to call the White House. When he first joined Ballet Theatre and learned of its management problems and of Miss Chase's distress over the financial situation, he did not, as had others, "sit around for hours" to discuss what <u>could</u> be done <u>if</u> the right man could be found to serve as managing director. Instead, he immediately drew up a chart that illustrated how the company should be reorganized so that it could operate on a sound theatrical and business basis. In so doing, he was confident that no one could suspect him of trying to feather his own nest, since he was committed to returning to the Theatre Guild in the fall. To Miss Chase, his positive-thinking and activist attitude were a breath of fresh air. She became even more impressed when he took her to the office of Lawrence Langner, where they explored the possibility of Ballet Theatre's becoming a subscription attraction on the road-tour series presented by the Theatre Guild.

Lawrence would not have been so sure of his actions being regarded as objective, altruistic, and above suspicion had he been more familiar with the potency and inaccuracy of rumors in a ballet organization. And, indeed, rumors were soon afloat to the effect that a conspiracy was in operation to substitute Lawrence for Talbot as managing director. Almost immediately it became apparent that Lawrence was not the only activist in the organization. On November 3 a petition in the form of identical letters addressed to Talbot and the board of directors was presented to Talbot. The letter addressed to the board of directors is reproduced here and analyzed in some detail because it is pertinent in accounting for the inauguration of the Lucia Chase–Oliver Smith era, which has continued to the present.

To the Board of Directors of
Ballet Theatre, Inc.

Ladies and Gentlemen:

Rumors have reached us that our Managing Director J. Alden Talbot is planning to resign, and that his resignation may bring a complete change in the present management. We sincerely hope that these rumors are without foundation.

It is vital to the success of our Company and our welfare to have mutual understanding and co-operation between artists and management. Artists need a sympathetic management to produce their fullest work. We feel that the present management has done much good for the Company. Our younger dancers have progressed only through the interest and encouragement of the management.

For the sake of morale and peaceful continuation of our season, we hope that you will be able to persuade Mr. Talbot to remain with us, at least to the end of our contracts, and not to make any changes in the present management.

Very sincerely yours,

The letter was signed by all but two of the dancers in the company.

The same letter was addressed to Talbot, substituting "you" for his name. Talbot passed both letters on to the board of directors with the following covering letter:

Mr. Harry M. Zuckert
475 Fifth Avenue
New York, N.Y.

November 6, 1944

Dear Harry,

On Friday November third the members of Ballet Theatre, at a meeting, composed two letters, one addressed to the Board of Directors, the other to me, and the originals were given to me Saturday night at the Metropolitan Opera House. I am enclosing photostatic copies of these letters and, as you will note, both were signed by all dancers in the company excepting Miss Chase and Mr. Orloff who refused to sign.

During the past ten days at least ten members of the company have spoken to me about rumors of a change and stated that the members of the company wished to hold a meeting to make a protest against any such change. I persuaded them for a week not to take any action, but they did so finally regardless of my request. It is apparent that they feel strongly on the matter and especially against the particular person mentioned as coming in to take charge as Managing Director, and all who spoke to me mentioned the name of Peter Lawrence and stated they would definitely turn in resignations if the change were made. I pointed out to them that they were under contract until August 31, 1945.

I believe that these letters are not only an expression by the members of the company of their feeling that they have received fair treatment under me but also express protest against bringing in Peter Lawrence to run the company.

Sincerely yours,
J. ALDEN TALBOT, President

Though these letters perhaps represented a sincere concern on the part of some of the dancers about a rumored change in management, no one who has been around a ballet company for any length of time could possibly mistake them for a spontaneous outburst of unanimity. The circumstances

as reported by Talbot do not ring true. It is of course <u>possible</u> that the entire company assembled for the meeting of November 3, but if so it was the first and last meeting in the history of ballet to record perfect attendance. But even in the unprecedented event that <u>all</u> members attended, it remains highly unlikely that everyone's attention was sustained for as long as it would have taken to compose the letters and reach unanimous agreement on their content. When the time came for the dancers to line up and append their signatures, at least a few would have slipped out. The gathering of all forty-one signatures could not have been a simple task; dancers are traditionally indifferent to or wary of requests for signatures. There is rarely, if ever, a request for signatures that does not require a followup. And in the case of the November 3 letter, the followup had to be made by a determined and persuasive activist if the completed document was to be presented to Talbot within twenty-four hours of the meeting.

If the spontaneity and eagerness with which the signatures were appended are suspect, so was Talbot's insistence that he attempted to dissuade the dancers from writing the letter. Talbot's interpretation of the letter is also questionable. He chose to characterize it as a protest against the engagement of Lawrence as managing director when, in fact, Lawrence was not mentioned in the dancers' letter. The letter, as actually worded, asks only that Talbot be retained, and this could explain the unanimity. The dancers liked Talbot personally and thought he was doing no worse a job than most managing directors, so why not sign a letter expressing their approval? The real import of the letter may have been understood by only the "at least ten members," the activists referred to in Talbot's letter. Nor was there any special significance in the fact that Nicholas Orloff and Lucia Chase were the only dancers who had "refused" to sign. Orloff was an eccentric, utterly anti-majority and anti-establishment. Miss Chase did not sign because she was one of the directors to whom the letter was addressed. And finally, the board of directors had only Talbot's word for it that the dancers had made the unrealistic threat of mass resignation; the threat does not appear in their letter.

A large majority of the members of the board of directors could not bring themselves to regard the letter seriously, but if the letters were designed to dispose of Lawrence, they indirectly achieved their purpose. The board, though impressed by his initiative and aggressiveness, had reservations concerning his youth and inexperience. Moreover, his record as a stage manager for the Theatre Guild did not in itself entitle him to the magic words "professional," "theater," "business" man. Now that it appeared he might be assuming the post of managing director without the full support of the entire company, it seemed advisable to postpone his appointment while the search for the <u>right</u> man was extended.

Meanwhile, Lucia Chase alternated between realistic appraisal of her situation and irrepressible optimism. She wrote, "David [the choreographer Lichine] said he thought I

was the biggest sucker he'd ever seen and I agreed with him. I believe my brain is clearing and I hope the 'biggest sucker' is not permanent." She believed she was a sucker not only because of her open-ended support of Ballet Theatre but because she was its <u>only</u> support. Nevertheless, her hopes sprang eternal—and within a few months of the letter incident she found the <u>right</u> man, Oliver Smith. He had been associated with the company for more than a year.

Oliver Smith's first work for the professional theater was the scenery for Agnes de Mille's RODEO, first performed at the Metropolitan Opera House on October 16, 1942, by the Ballet Russe de Monte Carlo. A fortnight later the New Opera Company premiered a long-run production of ROSALINDA, a new version of Johann Strauss' DIE FLEDERMAUS, with scenery by Oliver Smith and choreography by George Balanchine. Within a year Smith was collaborating with Jerome Robbins in Ballet Theatre's production of FANCY FREE, which received its first performance at the Metropolitan Opera House on April 18, 1944. By the following October, when he was chosen by Balanchine to design the scenery for WALTZ ACADEMY, Smith had attained full recognition as a designer, and without question he qualified for the magic descriptive words "professional" and "theater" man. On December 28, 1944, the musical comedy ON THE TOWN opened on Broadway. It was based on FANCY FREE and, like the ballet, had music by Leonard Bernstein, choreography by Jerome Robbins, and scenery by Oliver Smith. It was a hit, a successful business venture. As it was produced by Oliver Smith (in partnership with Paul Feigay), it immediately qualified him for the final magic descriptive word. Now he was not only a professional theater designer; he had become a professional theater businessman. At the next meeting of the board of directors of Ballet Theatre, Inc., he was elected a director, and was immediately accepted by Talbot and Hurok as a force to be recognized, and consulted with, in the implementation of the company's artistic policies.

All those engaged in the operation of Ballet Theatre— Talbot, Chase, Hurok—were confident that Smith would act the role of the "reasonable man," reconciling their differences by substituting good sense for emotionalism in the discussions. As each of the participants was further convinced that <u>his</u> position would be the one the reasonable man recognized as valid, it was inevitable that several would be disappointed.

The further issue between Chase and Talbot concerning the financing of the company was put on the line at the directors' meeting of December 11, 1944. Talbot opened the meeting by reading a letter addressed to him by Miss Chase and dated November 6, 1944, which contained the introductory sentence, "This is to confirm my statement at the last two meetings of the board of directors of Ballet Theatre, that having underwritten the total of twenty-five thousand dollars ($25,000.00) [the parenthetical figures make it evident the letter was prepared by counsel] which I agreed to advance

GJON MILI PHOTOGRAPHED A CRASKE CLASS WITH NORA KAYE (ADJUSTING RIBBONS)
AND LEAPING DANCERS JOHN KRIZA, MICHAEL MAULE, PETER GLADKE.

either toward the cost of the two new productions TALLY-HO and WALTZ ACADEMY, or for other general purposes of the company as seemed best, I can do no more for this 1944–1945 season." Talbot followed the reading with his own announcement to the effect, "Unless Lucia tears up the letter and agrees to continue her contributions, I will resign as president and managing director of the Ballet Theatre." He had no suggestions for new sources of financing. John D. Barrett, Jr., the president of Ballet Associates, who was also on the Ballet Theatre board, thought the Associates might be able to increase its contribution, perhaps raising it to $700.

Three weeks later, at the meeting of January 3, Talbot reiterated his determination to resign unless Miss Chase assumed all responsibility for the financing required to meet the operating costs and to complete the production of Tudor's new ballet UNDERTOW. In any case he would not remain in office after the annual meeting scheduled for April 1, and in contract discussions with the dancers he would so inform them. There was every indication that in the 1944–45 season the fiscal affairs of the company would repeat the pattern set the previous season, when the deficit was covered by contributions from Miss Chase totaling $132,032 and the only other source of support had been the Ballet Associates, which

produced a total of $3,375. Miss Chase offered a counter-proposition: if by April 21 Talbot could obtain the backing that would enable him to assume complete financial responsibility, she would relinquish any proprietary interest in Ballet Theatre and retire from the field, perhaps to return to acting or to try producing plays with Oliver Smith.

Miss Chase might not then have been aware of the addictiveness of the ballet habit, or may have believed she could kick it, but in a letter to Charles Payne in Washington she indicated that she didn't really expect to be put to the test. She wrote of the meeting, "I came out looking like a G-d fool as usual. . . . Oliver Smith was elected a director—he is delighted and so am I because it gives me someone, a successful producer, to bring out into the open. . . . I'm hoping for a strong Board of Directors—to add one or two good theatrical producers—then Chase and Smith can be administrative directors if you all think it a good idea, like Langner and Helburn [of the Theatre Guild]." Talbot did make an effort to obtain backing from ballet enthusiasts and from among his personal friends, including members of the Du Pont family, but without success. At the annual meeting on April 21, 1945, Chase and Smith were appointed administrative directors.

THE ERA OF LUCIA CHASE AND OLIVER SMITH

The issues between Talbot and Chase on the one side and Hurok on the other concerned publicity, stars, and new productions. Hurok still maintained that it was impossible to sell Ballet Theatre without billing it as "The Greatest in Russian Ballet." As for the stars, he refused to accept Nora Kaye and Hugh Laing as substitutes for Markova and Dolin and demanded that the latter pair be re-engaged (they had withdrawn to appear in Billy Rose's SEVEN LIVELY ARTS) regardless of the cost to Ballet Theatre. With respect to new productions, he continued to exercise his right of approval, notifying Miss Chase by official letter that he rejected UNDERTOW and insisted instead on either FIREBIRD or SCHÉHÉRAZADE. He was confident that Smith, as a Broadway producer, would sympathize with his demands for the kind of publicity that sold tickets and for stars and productions with popular appeal. However, his confidence was misplaced. Smith pointed out that FANCY FREE had become a hit without being publicized as "The Greatest in Russian Ballet"; that he had produced the Broadway success ON THE TOWN without a star (though Miss Chase's objection was not to stars per se but to their being chosen and controlled by Hurok); and that he had no prejudice against popular Russian ballets provided they were produced with taste. In the end, it was one special attitude of Smith's toward ballet that most surprised Hurok and led indirectly to the breach between him and Ballet Theatre.

Smith's decisions with respect to ballet are governed by an artistic standard that can be epitomized by the adjective "distinguished," a word that has cropped up unceasingly in his conversations over the past thirty years. For Hurok the adjective chosen to express approval of a ballet was most often "entertaining"; for Diaghilev it was "astonishing." But for Smith it has remained "distinguished." He uses the word somewhat as it is generally applied to a person and with the same lack of definition. What makes a man distinguished? His accomplishments, his intelligence, his manners? Or could it be simply the cut of his clothes, the gray in his hair, his cultured or Ivy League accent? Smith would feel no compulsion to be specific. He would recognize a distinguished man when he saw one. Similarly, what makes a distinguished ballet? Is it the libretto, the choreography, the designs? Or is it the status of the composer, the choreographer, or the designer? What, for example, makes LES NOCES a distinguished work, and what relegates GRADUATION BALL to the category of a ballet that can be presented by Ballet Theatre only with a blush of embarrassment? Is it a matter of the intrinsic value of the two ballets, or did LES NOCES earn the accolade "distinguished" because it was created by Stravinsky and Robbins, with an assist by Smith, while GRADUATION BALL was the product of Strauss (the less distinguished Johann) and David Lichine, with an unimaginative and necessarily restricted contribution from the designer Rolf Gerard?

Hurok first became aware of Smith's dedication to the "distinguished" in connection with FIREBIRD, the Fokine ballet that Hurok had suggested to Talbot as early as January 1945, after he received a report that their competitor, the Ballet Russe de Monte Carlo, was considering a production with choreography by George Balanchine and décor by Eugene Berman. Although Hurok had finally been persuaded to accept UNDERTOW as one of the ballets for the 1944–45 season, within a week after its premiere at the Metropolitan in April 1945 he wrote Miss Chase that it would not qualify as one of the ballets for the summer tour of the West Coast. He demanded that Ballet Theatre immediately produce either SCHÉHÉRAZADE or FIREBIRD. In view of the position taken by Miss Chase at the last directors' meeting, Talbot could only reply that he could make no commitment for the production of FIREBIRD until the financing had been assured and that he had no idea where the money could be found. Hurok had an idea where it could be found (where it had always been found), but fearful that it might be found too late for the fall season, he began on his own negotiations with Bolm and Stravinsky. Hurok's intermediary, Irving Deakin, soon reported that his former father-in-law was insisting that this time the design of the décors must be entrusted to Nicholas Remisoff. In 1940 Bolm had made the same demand with respect to the designs for MECHANICAL BALLET and PETER AND THE WOLF but had been overruled by Richard Pleasant. More recently, however, Remisoff's décor for Ballet Theatre's THE FAIR AT SOROCHINSK had delighted Hurok and not totally displeased the critical elite. Accordingly, Hurok entered personal agreements with Bolm, Remisoff, and Stravinsky (to revise his score).

Work progressed and time passed but still Ballet Theatre remained uncommitted to producing and paying for the ballet. The project became a factor in the negotiations for the summer season. The Hurok–Ballet Theatre contract provided that summer engagements would be covered by a separate agreement; Hurok was not obligated to offer summer work nor was Ballet Theatre required to accept it. Ballet Theatre injected the FIREBIRD matter into the negotiations in order to gain concessions from Hurok in the unrelated dispute on publicity and stars. The company's lawyers drew up a

proposed letter of agreement which provided that in advertising, the words "Ballet Theatre" must always appear before the words "Russian Ballet" and in type one point larger; that Ballet Theatre would employ Markova and Dolin at a cost not to exceed $1,200 per week (with the understanding that they would regard themselves as members of the company, not as independent guest stars); and that Ballet Theatre would produce FIREBIRD provided Hurok contributed to the costs. By then it was June 20, with performances scheduled to start in San Francisco on August 5. Hurok was desperate to reach an agreement. He had committed himself to the rental of theaters and of the Hollywood Bowl, and he controlled no other ballet attraction that could be substituted for Ballet Theatre. Further, his commitments to Bolm, Stravinsky, and Remisoff left him in danger of becoming the purchaser of a ballet for which he would have no use. So desperate was he that he signed the letter submitted by Ballet Theatre. It is almost inconceivable that such an astute businessman, usually so astutely advised, could have committed such an incredible boner. He put his signature in the blank after ACCEPTED AND AGREED TO in a letter whose fourth paragraph read:

While FIREBIRD is more of an expense than our contract calls for, we [Ballet Theatre] agree to your proposition that we produce it provided you pay all cost of production in excess of $15,000.

Preliminary budget discussions had estimated the costs of producing FIREBIRD at between $15,000 and $17,000. Accordingly, Hurok believed he was risking no more than $2,000, give or take a few hundred. But that is not how the agreement read. In his haste to obtain the FIREBIRD production from Ballet Theatre, he inadvertently entered an open-end street (one on which Miss Chase had long lived). He legally committed himself to pay all costs in excess of $15,000—and, as he soon discovered, he had not retained any control over such costs.

The day after the letter of agreement was signed, Miss Chase wrote to Bolm, Stravinsky, and Remisoff advising them that Ballet Theatre would produce FIREBIRD and would honor the agreements Hurok had previously negotiated with them. However, the letter to Remisoff contained a qualifying paragraph:

Oliver Smith is away at the moment or he would write you, but we discussed this whole question before he left and he asked me to write for him. He will be back July 1st and if we have some word and sketches from you by then we can get into action. We are both coming to Hollywood August 13th. He will be there for a week so it will give us a good opportunity for discussing everything. We are looking forward to seeing you then and to a most interesting collaboration.

When Smith arrived in Hollywood in August, his discussions with Remisoff did not lead to a "most interesting collaboration." He looked at the scenery that had already been painted, and at the sketches for the costumes, and found them unacceptable. They were conventional and serviceable but most certainly not "distinguished." Only Marc Chagall, he

decided, could create décor that would be truly distinguished. Remisoff's scenery and costume designs were discarded and Chagall was engaged. Hurok did not object. He and Chagall had been born in the same province of Russia, and the artist had created the décor for ALEKO, one of Hurok's favorite ballets. Presumably Hurok did not, as he should have done, rush back to his office to examine the agreement and determine his responsibility for the additional costs resulting from the substitution. In due course Ballet Theatre presented a bill for more than $34,000, of which Hurok was responsible for $19,000. Ballet Theatre continued to advance the monies for the production until October 23, the day before the scheduled opening at the Met. By then bills totaling $11,825 remained unpaid and a demand was made on Hurok in a letter that contained the sentence, "We must therefore insist that there be in our hands not later than tomorrow morning (Wednesday, October 24th) a remittance from you to pay the above stated obligations, or else the first performance, scheduled for tomorrow evening, will have to be postponed until such time as such payment has been made." In other words, no pay no play, a traditional theater ultimatum often threatened but seldom executed. Hurok chose not to call Ballet Theatre's bluff; a check was delivered on the morning of the 24th.

Although the Hurok–Ballet Theatre contract, with its options, bound Ballet Theatre to the exclusive management of Hurok until October 10, 1947, it can be said that a contractual relationship ceased to exist after the morning of October 24, 1945; there was no longer what the legal profession characterizes as "a meeting of the minds." Chase and Smith no longer regarded Hurok as the omniscient and omnipotent tsar of ballet in America; he had all too clearly demonstrated his fallibility and vulnerability. For his part, Hurok faced the fact that he could no longer rely on Ballet Theatre to supply the unlimited capital required if he was to manage it at a profit to himself. He was not convinced that the wells of capital had dried up, but he was convinced that a capping device had been installed that might eventually cut the flow to a trickle. During the next six months each side maneuvered to place itself in a position of advantage when the inevitable dissolution of the contract occurred. Soon Hurok's lawyers were accusing Ballet Theatre of having "designed a plan to bring about a breach of the present contract." The company, the lawyers alleged, was making unjustified claims under its contract; conspiring with local managers to undermine Hurok; and informing its dancers that Ballet Theatre would not be under Hurok's management the following year. There was some truth in these allegations. Further, when Peter Lawrence returned from managing a tour of the play DEAR RUTH, he was engaged as executive manager and began to dispatch an almost daily series of complaints and protests that increasingly exacerbated Hurok. The Ballet Theatre lawyers countered by accusing Hurok of violating his management contract when he began to organize the

OLIVER SMITH AND LUCIA CHASE POSED IN HIS WASHINGTON SQUARE APARTMENT FOR THEIR 1951 SOUVENIR-PROGRAM PORTRAITS.

Markova-Dolin company, when he agreed to manage Martha Graham, and when he opened discussions with de Basil, all in contravention of the provision that he manage no other major dance company.

Eventually Ballet Theatre began an action at law to have the contract voided. Viewed from a detached legal point of view, the actions of both parties were so murky and equivocal that neither set of lawyers was eager to present a case before a judge. Further, neither party could bide the law's delay; they demanded an early decision. Hurok was under pressure from his local managers to inform them as to which ballet he was sending on tour in October 1946. Ballet Theatre was negotiating with David Webster, the general administrator of the Covent Garden Opera Trust, a contract for a guaranteed season at Covent Garden that could not be signed until the company obtained its release from Hurok. In April 1946 a settlement was reached which removed Hurok as the exclusive manager of Ballet Theatre and awarded him the scenery and costumes of FIREBIRD and four other ballets that he had paid for in part or in toto: GRADUATION BALL and the failures MOONLIGHT SONATA by Massine and HARVEST TIME and RENDEZVOUS by Nijinska.

Each side thought it had scored a victory, but a realistic analysis indicates that though both were happy, neither had won. In the settlement Hurok received some valueless properties (the FIREBIRD scenery later found its way into the New York City Ballet production, where it is hung, virtually unseen, in the deepest shadows), and Ballet Theatre received its freedom, which it proceeded to exchange for an equally unsatisfactory booking contract with the Musical Corporation of America. Hurok and Ballet Theatre were to reassociate to their mutual benefit on future occasions, but when Hurok published his S. HUROK PRESENTS he did not foresee this possibility. He wrote:

The future of Ballet Theatre as a serious institution in our cultural life is questionable, in my opinion, because Miss Chase, after all these years, has not yet learned how to conduct or discipline a ballet company; has not learned that important policy decisions are not made because of whims.

Thirty years later, with Lucia Chase and Oliver Smith still directing Ballet Theatre, the prophecy rings hollow. So does another prophecy contained in Hurok's IMPRESARIO, which reads, "I believe we shall see the day when the American public will spend as much as two million dollars a year to see ballet performances." In six midsummer weeks of 1975 the American public spent more than $2 million in one New York City block when it bought tickets at Lincoln Center (in the New York State Theater and the Metropolitan Opera House) to see American Ballet Theatre (more than a million dollars worth) and the Stuttgart and Canadian National ballet companies.

Though neither contestant could be said to have won more than a Pyrrhic victory, each derived fringe benefits from the settlement. While negotiations were still in progress, Hurok had visited London, where the most Russian and most classical of the Russian classics had just been produced by a company that, while it could not be billed as "The Greatest in Russian Ballet," could be relied on to commit itself well in advance to arranging financing through its principal backer, the Exchequer of the British Empire. Hurok's separation from Ballet Theatre left him free to establish what proved to be a long and profitable association with the Sadler's Wells (now the Royal) Ballet.

The most satisfying of the fringe benefits that accrued to the directors of Ballet Theatre as a result of the rupture with Hurok was the attainment of complete artistic and financial autonomy—a satisfaction somewhat diminished by the concomitant requirement that they assume all the risks. The directors were no longer obligated to defer to Hurok's judgment as to what the public wanted in the way of ballets, or accept his unconfirmed reports of the local managers' demands with respect to the composition of programs. From the start of Ballet Theatre's association with Hurok there had been disagreements concerning what ballets the company should produce. In more recent years the composition of the programs had been an increasing source of contention. Hurok would report that the local manager in a Midwestern city, for example, was insisting that HELEN OF TROY with Zorina must be included in the performance and that UNDERTOW must definitely not be scheduled. When the company arrived in the city, the local manager would assure Miss Chase that he had made no such demand, and she would be convinced that Hurok had once more been caught in a lie. However, it is just as possible that she had been the victim of the local manager's deceit. If he felt that his insistence on HELEN OF TROY and his veto of UNDERTOW would make him look like a crass commercialist in the eyes of Miss Chase, he may have decided to improve his image, and at the same time give pleasure to his charming guest by confirming her suspicions of Hurok's duplicity. The break with Hurok did not solve all of Ballet Theatre's production problems. The directors could still guess wrong as to what ballets would please the public, the critics, or even themselves, but at least their productions were their own. And though they continued to be under pressure from local managers, they could now deal with these exigencies directly, without confusions introduced by a third, prejudiced party.

Fortunately for the future of Ballet Theatre, the directors' first independent venture proved to be one of the most successful and beneficial in the company's entire history. In the spring of 1946 Chase and Smith signed the contract for an eight-and-a-half-week season at the Royal Opera House in Covent Garden, London.

On June 20, 1946, at 7 p.m., Ballet Theatre, a company of fifty, sailed with 925 other passengers aboard the QUEEN MARY. Only a portion of the first class had been reconverted from troop accommodations. The ballet was assigned to cabin class and occupied staterooms originally designed for four occupants but rearranged to accommodate nine GIs with the

installation of three sets of triple-tiered metal bunks equipped with mattresses that from their earliest service could not have been lumpless. However, the sea was smooth and the sun shining. The dancers, accustomed to rail-coach travel under wartime conditions, enjoyed the six-day passage as though it were a luxury cruise. The debarkation in Southampton, followed by the train ride up to London through the neatly divided fields of incredible green, provided some of the excitements of travel that today's dancers never experience. To fulfill an engagement abroad, dancers now board a plane for a flight that seems to take scarcely longer than one from New York to Denver. When they arrive in the foreign city after a ride through the outskirts in an American-style bus, they might as well be in Denver; the inhabitants dress, eat, shop, and in general live much the same as the citizens of Colorado. But the dancers of 1946, after six days on the ocean, were conscious of the distance they had traveled and could not help being impressed with England's "foreignness" from the moment they stepped into the compartmented railroad cars. On arrival in London, they were quickly convinced that Londoners, though they spoke a similar language, were very different from New Yorkers.

This difference was impressed on Nora Kaye and Muriel Bentley during their first evening at the Savoy Hotel (where the rates were six dollars a day). After unpacking, they set off up the Strand in search of a restaurant, dressed as they would have been for the same sort of expedition on Broadway: with high heels, nylon stockings, silk dresses, fox-fur jackets, and John Frederick's hats. They soon became aware of suggestive leers, flattering whistles, and admiring suggestions from male passersby mistaking their profession. Having learned something of the Englishman's attitude toward what he considered chic in dress, they scampered back to the hotel, where they were to receive pointers regarding London's postwar eating habits. Forewarned of acute food shortages, they asked the room-service waiter what they could have for next morning's breakfast. "Anything you wish," he replied. "How about eggs?" "Certainly, how do you wish them prepared?" "Boiled three minutes." "Very good." As he was about to leave the room, the waiter added, "Oh yes, and may I have the eggs, please?" By the time the misunderstanding was cleared up, Kaye and Bentley had been informed that hotel guests could have powdered eggs in various forms. But if they wanted boiled eggs they were expected to supply the raw material themselves—and if they were cautious they would initial the shells with indelible ink to assure that the same eggs returned on their tray.

The deprivations of living in London—the almost complete absence of fresh fruit, the non-discovery of hamburgers, and the delayed introduction of milk shakes—were but minor irritations to the dancers in view of the joy of working in the historic opera house before what proved to be a warmly enthusiastic audience of both public and critics. The season opened on the Fourth of July with LES SYLPHIDES, danced by Nora Kaye, Alicia Alonso, Barbara Fallis, and André Eglevsky.

The choice of the opening ballet in a foreign city is crucial. Whatever the choice, the critics will almost invariably pronounce it to have been mistaken, wrongheaded, or even insulting. The first of the touring companies, Diaghilev's Ballet Russe, opened in Paris in 1909 with the wrong ballet, LE PAVILLON D'ARMIDE. It was wrong because it was pseudo-French, something which Parisians thought could be much better performed by their own dancers at the Opéra. The experiences of American companies in London have been much the same. In 1950 the New York City Ballet's least successful production at Covent Garden was Balanchine's version of FIREBIRD, with the Chagall décor originally commissioned by Ballet Theatre. London had first seen Fokine's FIREBIRD at the same Royal Opera House in June 1912, with Karsavina, Bolm, and Cecchetti in the leading roles and with conventional décor by Alexander Golovine. Balanchine's neo-classic choreography and Chagall's Russian-muzhik surrealism shocked the audience and critics. When the company returned to London two years later, Balanchine, with the impudence of genius, insisted, over protests from Webster, that the second season open with FIREBIRD. And in 1970, when Ballet Theatre made its return to London, it chose to open with a new full-length SWAN LAKE. At a reception in the opera bar after the performance, Webster (by then Sir David) made a welcoming speech that consisted principally of an expression of regret that the company had not presented American works in its opening program, as it had done so successfully in 1946. Webster's close friend, James Cleveland Belle, turned to Payne to concur. "He's quite right, you know. It's the American ballets we want to see. Why did you insist on SWAN LAKE?" Payne: "Perhaps for the same reason you offered THE SLEEPING BEAUTY for your debut in New York instead of Robert Helpmann's MIRACLE OF THE GORBALS or de Valois' JOB." Belle: "But BEAUTY is our signature ballet." Payne: "But it is Russian, not English." Belle: "Well, in any case, it's more English than American."

Chase and Smith had, in fact, chosen the opening ballet for the 1970 engagement with careful deliberation. The choice had fallen on SWAN LAKE because it would demonstrate instantly to the London public that since Ballet Theatre's previous visit to Covent Garden it had advanced to the status of a "major" company capable of duplicating the full-length classics as they had been performed in Imperial Russia. Similarly, in 1946 they had chosen to open with LES SYLPHIDES so that the public would be made aware at once that this American company was trained and skilled in the classic technique. That the critics recognized their intention was evident in the Times review:

The company presented its credentials according to established custom in LES SYLPHIDES. This to our notion seemed an athletic rather than a romantic interpretation: the dancers appeared to be an inch or two above the average height, and while their footwork was admirable their arms were lacking in beckoning grace.

The critic was accustomed to the delicately featured, wispy sylphs of the English pantomime shows and ballet. Surviving photographs of Diaghilev's first Paris production of LES SYLPHIDES indicate that his peasant-type dancers more nearly resembled Americans than English, but to say that LES SYLPHIDES was more American than English would have been as fatuous as the assertion of Webster's friend. The inclusion of LES SYLPHIDES, however, had served its purpose. It was followed by FANCY FREE, which, though acclaimed, was labeled "music hall." The program concluded with a miscast and lethargic performance of Fokine's BLUEBEARD, which was regarded as a farce comedy somewhat too light to be accorded serious consideration as a ballet. It can be assumed, therefore, that had there been no SYLPHIDES, Ballet Theatre would have been categorized as a semiclassical dance company, presenting American musical comedy in pseudo-ballet style. But perhaps the opening-night key to the success of the season (and an opening night can determine success or failure) was the Black Swan pas de deux, inserted between FANCY FREE and BLUEBEARD, which was given a bravura performance by Nora Kaye and André Eglevsky. The Times again reported:

Miss Kaye accomplished the 32 fouettés with a final touch of exultant brillance that excelled anything seen here in years, including performances before the war by the various Monte Carlo companies. . . .

It was the sort of performance that so often arouses Ballet Theatre audiences to demonstrations of noisy enthusiasm that the purists find irritating and objectionable. The critic in The Observer wrote:

After the third item of the opening performance at Covent Garden the visitors had an ovation which must have rid them of any preconceptions about the cold, phlegmatic English. . . . Grace, gusto and virility are the qualities I would specify in trying to define the virtues this company possesses. They gave us an unusually exciting evening, they had a tremendous success and if their other 17 ballets live up to the first night nobody with any taste for the art should miss Covent Garden now.

The season was indeed a success and its influence on the later development of ballet dancing in England and Europe was incalculable. The words chosen by the Observer critic were apt. The ballet previously enjoyed by Londoners had been strong on "grace" but weak on "gusto" and "virility" and not exactly brimming with "excitement." The remaining seventeen ballets did not in every case meet with the approval of the critics or the public, but the overall response was such as to instill in Chase and Smith a confidence in the repertory assembled during the company's first half-dozen years. It had earned the company a place in the top ranks of the world's ballet troupes.

An interesting sidelight of the engagement had to do with the company's name. Webster had insisted that the words "Ballet Theatre" would convey nothing to London audiences, and he urged that the name be changed. There were those in the organization who agreed and suggested changing the name to New York Ballet or, as a compromise, New York Ballet Theatre. But Lucia Chase, who develops sentimental ties to old cars and carefully preserved dresses, had become attached to the name Ballet Theatre, partly because of the meaning and significance it had acquired by chance over the years. Accordingly, the posters at Covent Garden were made to read:

THE

BALLET THEATRE

NEW YORK

Thus it was that when, a few years later, Morton Baum pointed out to Lincoln Kirstein that Ballet Society was a meaningless name for a performing company, the name New York City Ballet was still available and in the public domain.

The success of the London season gave Chase and Smith confidence in their ability to direct a ballet company. However, in implementing their production plans for the 1946–47 season they could not proceed with complete freedom of action; at least some portion of authority had earlier been maneuvered by Antony Tudor into the hands of an artistic advisory committee. In 1944, while J. Alden Talbot was still managing director, a supplementary agreement was attached to Tudor's employment contract that contained provisions for his billing in publicity, the location of his theater dressing room, the size of his picture in the souvenir program, and so on. It also provided the following:

There will be an Artistic Advisory Committee of not less than five members nor more than seven members whose duties shall be to advise the Board of Directors on all matters of artistic policy, including discussion and selection of new ballets, advising on all policies within the company, including such matters as consideration and merits of artists wishing to perform roles in the ballets of the repertory, new artists for the company, plans for rehearsals, setting definite curtain calls, and so forth. Meetings shall be held at least four times a year. Antony Tudor will be on the committee and the other members are Mr. Talbot, Miss Chase, Mr. Dorati and Mr. Clifford, the additional members to be chosen by the majority at a later date.

IN 1946, LONDON KNEW THE COMPANY AS THE BALLET THEATRE—NEW YORK.

In the spring of 1946 the committee consisted of Aaron Copland, Henry Clifford, Antony Tudor, Agnes de Mille, Jerome Robbins, and Chase and Smith. Several of the members were not completely satisfied that the committee's advice and, in some instances, its instructions were being faithfully followed by the administrative directors, and they insisted on the establishment of the post of artistic director, with Tudor as the first appointee. As this appointment would have been at variance with one of the company's founding principles (that no choreographer should also serve as artistic director) and as the title itself was a verbal contradiction of the fact that in Chase and Smith the company already had a set of codirectors (even though they eschewed the presumption of the word "artistic"), it was necessary to invent a compromise title. And so, Tudor became "artistic administrator." Thus it was that in planning the new season Smith and Chase were obligated to at very least <u>consult</u> with Tudor and the artistic committee. The projects of that season and their progress are reported here in some detail because they set the pattern for the artistic activities of Ballet Theatre during the coming years and because they illustrate the inevitable discrepancies between plans, however well-conceived, and actual achievements.

The first ballets to reach the contractual stage were two works by Jerome Robbins, FACSIMILE and an abstract ballet to the music of Vivaldi. Next in line was Agnes de Mille with a ballet titled HARVEST REEL, for which she requested that a score be commissioned from Leonard Bernstein. The contracts for the fourth and fifth works, LES PATINEURS by Frederick Ashton and SCÈNES DE BALLET by George Balanchine, were being negotiated by Chase in London and by Smith in California. The sixth novelty of the season was to be a new production of GISELLE, which would provide a stellar role for the company's new premier danseur, Igor Youskevitch, who had been released from the navy too late to be engaged for Covent Garden. If all these plans had come to fruition, and had Hurok and Pleasant still been associated with the company, they would have been delighted, the former with the salability of the ballets, the latter that the balance was being maintained among the Classical, English, and American wings. Unhappily, the projects did not all reach maturity.

The first casualty in the production prospectus was the Vivaldi ballet. Robbins' contract provided that he be allotted forty-five hours of rehearsal time. The hours were not made available to him in London, where so many rehearsals had to be devoted to the preparation of the twenty-one works presented at Covent Garden. In July, after remaining in London long enough to give a final performance of the title role in PETROUCHKA, Robbins returned to New York to collaborate with Bernstein on the second work, FACSIMILE. Progress was slow and erratic, in part a consequence of the choreographer's chronic indecisiveness, though other factors contributed, particularly the late arrival home of the dancers. David Webster, unable to find transportation for the company as a group, had dispatched the dancers a few at a time: by plane, on a ten-day freighter, and on the ACQUITANIA, which landed its passengers in Halifax, a thirty-six-hour train ride from New York. The last contingent of dancers, which included the cast of FACSIMILE, once more boarded the still unconverted QUEEN MARY. This time the seas were rough and the ship was overstuffed with war brides whose offspring not only mewled and puked in their arms but bawled and vomited throughout the public rooms and the decks. The FACSIMILE cast arrived in a humor unconducive to cooperative creativity.

FACSIMILE was intended to explore and elaborate an observation by the medical researcher Santiago Ramon y Cajol, who wrote, "Small inward treasure does he possess who, to feel alive, needs every hour the tumult of the street, the emotion of the theater, and the small talk of society." At the start of rehearsals the participants were listed as A Woman (Nora Kaye), A Man (Hugh Laing), Another Man (John Kriza), a Third Man (Donald Saddler), and Some Integrated People (eighteen corps de ballet). There was an alternate cast of Alicia Alonso (A Woman) and Igor Youskevitch (Another Man), with Robbins himself prepared to assume the role of A Man. The ballet was scheduled to open on October 18, but as the date approached, Robbins advised Chase and Smith that it would not be ready. In this instance there could be no question of his having been allotted too few rehearsal hours. As of September 17, dancers had been placed at his disposal for almost eighty-eight hours. A rule of thumb for estimating the number of hours required for the creation of a ballet had been established somewhat arbitrarily by Ninette de Valois: the choreographer should be allowed one hour of rehearsal time for each minute of the musical score. According to this rule, which admittedly was not always accurate, Robbins had already consumed more than four times the number of hours due him for nineteen minutes of music. The daily call sheets reveal that between September 17 and the postponed opening, on October 24, Robbins rehearsed for another thirty-two hours. Not since the creation of L'APRÈS-MIDI D'UN FAUNE by Vaslav Nijinsky had so many hours been devoted to the rehearsal of so few dancers in so short a ballet. Robbins, it is true, was faced with a number of problems, many of them of his own making. Early on, Alonso, Youskevitch, and Saddler withdrew from the cast for reasons that, at this late date, can only be a matter of speculation. On October 16, seven days before the premiere, Robbins instructed Bernstein to rewrite the mezzo-soprano's role so that it could be performed instead by a horn, a change requiring the reorchestration of ten pages of manuscript score. The Integrated People, who had begun as a chorus of eighteen, had been whittled down to ten, and reported in that number for the dress rehearsal at two o'clock on the afternoon of the premiere. Sometime during the next three hours they were eliminated from the ballet, together with the Third Man. In the end, only three dancers appeared on stage, Kaye, Robbins, and Kriza. The critics, who had hoped for a duplication of the Robbins-Bernstein-Smith FANCY

THE ARTISTIC COMMITTEE, 1947: JEROME ROBBINS, LUCIA CHASE, AGNES DE MILLE, OLIVER SMITH, AND AARON COPLAND.

FREE triumph, were disappointed. The more serious ones were confident that the "flaws could be eliminated" (Walter Terry) and that the almost burlesque aura could "no doubt be rectified" (John Martin), but the less reverent were derisive. In the Journal-American, Robert Garland wrote, "If you find out what FACSIMILE is about, write and tell me. I promise not to make it public." In the World-Telegram, Robert Sylvester produced a review that has become a collector's item of devastating ridicule:

First Nora Kaye wanders around the stage swinging a rose on a string. Or maybe it was a lobster. Then Jerome Robbins bounces in. He's swinging a red shawl. Poor Nora is stuffed into a striped leotard not quite big enough for Margaret O'Brien. Robbins takes a long look. Natch.

Robbins kisses Nora's hand. He kisses her on the kisser. She kisses back. He kisses her knee. She jumps around and falls down. He kisses her foot. She gets coy. He sulks. She kisses the back of his neck. Then they both fall down and play dead for a while.

In comes John Kriza, in red underwear. Everybody gets all mixed up, kissing Nora some more, until at one point Kriza nearly kisses Robbins. Then Robbins kisses Nora's foot while Kriza kisses her on the kisser and runs her around Robbins like he was a maypole.

All this is set to some very thin music by the sainted Leonard Bernstein. It's the new Bernstein-Robbins-Oliver Smith ballet called FACSIMILE, which Ballet Theatre made the mistake of offering at the Broadway last night. There is a typical Oliver Smith setting, which means that it cost about four dollars and manages to feature some terrific perspective and fine lighting.

Long before the acrobatics are over, Miss Kaye's costume leaves her rather indecently exposed. And the way the boys grab and manhandle her may be art, but it ain't gentlemanly. Where the title comes from nobody knows, unless from one brief sequence when Nora's shadow is outlined against a panel of backlighted burlap.

A minute or so before the finale, after the boys have tied her in a tight knot, dumped her on the floor and then fallen on her head, Miss Kaye raises her voice in agonizing appeal.

"Stop!" she cried plaintively. Ballet Theatre should have listened to her at the first rehearsal.

The second casualty was de Mille's HARVEST REEL. In mid-July, Smith had reported to her:

I spent the weekend with Leonard [Bernstein] and Aaron [Copland] and, after considerable discussion with Lennie, reached the conclusion that he would rather do FACSIMILE than HARVEST REEL. He has great admiration for you and I know would like to do a ballet with you, but he seems to feel this material is not his cup of tea. . . .

Smith next approached Benjamin Britten, who agreed to supply the score but not in time for the ballet to be included in the season. HARVEST REEL did not in fact ever materialize as such, but as it was "based on Irish folk matter with a generous use of bagpipes," perhaps it ended up in BRIGADOON, for which de Mille later supplied the choreography.

SCÈNES DE BALLET* was the next project to be abandoned despite ardent enthusiasm on the part of all concerned. When Smith began negotiations for this ballet in California, Chase had immediately communicated her delight from London, and it was only with the passage of time that her ardor somewhat cooled. Smith kept her informed in a series of letters and cables that conveyed the following information: Balanchine

was insisting Toumanova be engaged to dance the lead . . . Toumanova asked too much money. . . Balanchine suggested Mary Ellen Moylan. . . Tudor, who had used Moylan in the flop musical THE DAY BEFORE SPRING, said, "Over my dead body!". . . Balanchine was prepared to settle for Diana Adams.

In each of her replies Chase asked the question, "How about Kaye or Alonso in the lead?" but she never received an answer. She sat frustrated in London with two of her stars who would be outraged when they found out they had been passed over for the lead in a new ballet. Before the issue could be brought to a head, however, the project died of financial malnutrition. Dwight Deere Wiman had been pondering the "investment" of $25,000 in the 1946–47 season, and it occurred to Chase that he might be nudged into a favorable decision if he were informed that his participation would make possible the creation of a new Balanchine ballet. She cabled Smith, "Cannot afford Balanchine unless Dwight gives." Dwight did eventually give, but too late to rescue SCÈNES DE BALLET. Meanwhile, in a step that could only be described as desperate, it was decided to appeal to Lincoln Kirstein for financial assistance. It is not clear why Payne was chosen to approach him; perhaps because he had been involved in previous conferences concerning the possibility of Kirstein's acting as an independent producer under the Ballet Theatre umbrella. Payne's letter included the following proposition:

As Lucia has made every effort to raise additional funds but has exhausted all possible sources of immediate financial backing, it occurred to me that you might know where you could raise the money for the production and be willing to produce it and allow Ballet Theatre to perform it on a rental-purchase or other basis. Further, Lucia and Oliver would of course be most happy to entrust to you the complete supervision of the production so that it would be a Kirstein production artistically as well as financially. Ballet Theatre would carry it in its repertory with billing and publicity—"Produced by Lincoln Kirstein for Ballet Theatre."

Kirstein's reply, a week later, was cordial, but rejected the offer:

For a long time, I have realized that our kids don't get any training until they go into a company. For this reason, we are starting this year a series of school performances, under Balanchine's direction. These will be quite intensive and involve commissioned works. All the spare cash I have will go into them. I asked George if he would prefer to sacrifice part of this program and do SCÈNES DE BALLET and after consideration, he decided not.

SCÈNES DE BALLET, with choreography by Balanchine and décor (already sketched) by Eugene Berman, never saw the light of day, but the following month Kirstein announced the founding of Ballet Society, and a few days later Chase received a letter from Thomas Hart Fisher (husband of Ruth Page) informing her:

The new Ballet Society announced by Lincoln Kirstein is designed to pave the way for a full commercial ballet company two years from now when he receives his inheritance from his father's estate of about $1,500,000. Part of his plan is the construction of a new theatre in New York City, for which he has already had architects' sketches prepared.

Fisher enjoyed gossip, and his rumors were not always based on verifiable fact, but this made them none the less fascinat-

---

*The score by Stravinsky was written for Billy Rose's SEVEN LIVELY ARTS, with choreography supplied by Dolin for himself and Markova.

EUGENE BERMAN'S GISELLE COSTUMES MADE THE CORPS LOOK HEAVY.

ing, and in this case, perhaps by coincidence, the New York City Ballet <u>was</u> founded two years later.

The new GISELLE, which did reach the stage—though after a postponement due to the delayed delivery of the scenery and costumes from the workshops in California—could not be said to have been conventionally staged. Six choreographers contributed pieces of choreography. The only one to receive program credit, Jean Coralli, had been dead almost a hundred years. The other five—Dolin, Tudor, Dimitri Romanoff, Boris Romanoff, and George Balanchine—in the future claimed or disclaimed responsibility in varying degrees. Anton Dolin, who had staged Ballet Theatre's preceding version of GISELLE, was then unavailable for rehearsals as he was dancing for the de Basil company in Hurok's competing season at the Metropolitan. (The press made much of what they termed the "Battle of the Ballets.") When he was informed that the choreography was being tampered with, he asked that his name be removed from the program, which, to his surprise, it was. Meanwhile, at the suggestion of Igor Youskevitch, Boris Romanoff was engaged to coach the principals. Romanoff thus became re-associated with Balanchine, his Imperial Ballet schoolmate, who was then rehearsing WALTZ ACADEMY and APOLLO with Ballet Theatre. Together they restored to GISELLE some features that Dolin had eliminated: Giselle now made her graveyard appearance on the lowering branch of a tree and at the end sank into a bed of flowers where Albrecht had placed her. Balanchine and Romanoff also restored some bars of music, inserting choreography that they recalled from the Maryinsky version. Tudor, as artistic administrator, and Dimitri Romanoff, as associate regisseur, made additional contributions in the course of rehearsal, but the end product differed in few respects from the other GISELLE seen in this century. The Balanchine-Romanoff "innovations" were deleted after a few

performances, so that by the time Dolin's lawyers threatened suit, most of his version had been restored and Ballet Theatre's lawyers could reply that his name would be put back on the programs provided that he never again complained about changes, inasmuch as Ballet Theatre rejected his claim to proprietary rights in the choreography of GISELLE. For his part, Balanchine's remembrance of occasional attendance at rehearsals of GISELLE caused him to inadvertently lead his amanuensis to write in BALANCHINE'S COMPLETE STORIES OF THE GREAT BALLETS, "I staged a new version of GISELLE for the Ballet Theatre, October 15, 1946, at the Broadway Theatre. . . ."

Choreographically, the new GISELLE was a normal production abnormally arrived at. The décor was another matter. Smith was following the example set by Diaghilev when he engaged a distinguished easel painter, Eugene Berman, to design the scenery and costumes, and Berman was also acting in the Diaghilev tradition when he refrained from designing realistic replicas of the clothes, houses, and vineyards of medieval Germany. His individualistic, almost surrealistic style of painting was not inappropriate for GISELLE. The stylized scenery was not incongruous. The vivid orange costumes and straw hats of the peasants in the first act were not alien to Rhineland grape pickers, nor were the Wilis' dresses, with their black tulle and Berman-blue underskirts, completely out of character when worn by vengeful spirits intent on driving feckless youths to their doom. All would have been well had the costumes not been so heavy-looking and had the designer not been such a stubborn man. He agreed to tone down the bright orange in Act I but insisted on retaining the black and blue in the second act. More importantly, he refused to permit any alteration in the basic design. As a consequence, the peasants could have been mistaken for actual German vineyard workers—of the grossest and sturdiest sort. The Wilis in the second act resembled vengeful spirits but were no longer the airy, sylph-like creatures to which audiences had grown accustomed. For the next two decades the public wondered why the same corps de ballet that was so ethereal in LES SYLPHIDES was so heavy and plodding in GISELLE. This heaviness was especially conspicuous because it was viewed in contrast to the lightness and effortlessness of successive Giselles and Albrechts. What the public did not know was that the immovable Eugene Berman had been budged by the irresistible Alicia Alonso and Igor Youskevitch. <u>Their</u> costumes in both acts emerged traditional in design, well-fitted, and executed in featherweight materials with only a suggestion of Berman blue. Berman suffered his final defeat when Youskevitch calmly but firmly refused to appear on stage in the last act in the canary-yellow tights that Berman insisted would have been worn to Giselle's graveyard by the mourning Albrecht. Over the years the décor was staunchly defended by Chase and Smith, but had it been less costly to stage a new production, their defense might have been less staunch.

IN HIS BALLET FACSIMILE, JEROME ROBBINS TRIES TO AROUSE NORA KAYE
WITH KISSES ON HER NECK, HER KNEE, HER TOE, AND HER LIPS.
WHEN KAYE BECOMES ENTWINED WITH ROBBINS AND JOHN KRIZA,
SHE DESPERATELY SHOUTS ALOUD THE WORD "STOP!"

On the whole, Chase and Smith's first season out from under the pressures exerted by Hurok could be considered eminently successful. The Covent Garden engagement was an unquestioned triumph. And in the Battle of the Ballets in New York between Ballet Theatre and the Original Ballet Russe, while the former had to content itself with the smaller share of the monies the public brought to the box offices, it could boast of having garnered the larger share of critical honors. LES PATINEURS was instantly popular and remains in the repertory today. The new production of GISELLE, while only tolerated by the public and the critics, nevertheless enabled the company to preserve this romantic classic over the years. After its premiere, FACSIMILE was given an unusually large number of performances for a new work: it was performed twelve times during the last seventeen days of the engagement at the Broadway Theatre and was included in the repertory of the ensuing cross-country tour. A serious work, perhaps ahead of its time, FACSIMILE, as touched by Robbins' genius, was certainly superior to other sex-psychological ballets that it spawned. It was revived in 1950 to provide an additional new work for the repertory of the second Covent Garden season (with James Mitchell in Robbins' role), but has not since been returned to the stage—nor has Bernstein's score become a popular fixture of concert halls.

The failure of Robbins' Vivaldi ballet to materialize and the difficulties attending the creation of his FACSIMILE advanced Miss Chase's education in the responsibilities and initiatives that must be exercised by the director of a ballet company. With the elimination of the Russian dominance of the company's repertory, she found herself confronted with a new breed of choreographer—one that functioned very differently from the kind with which she had first worked. The differences between them were not a matter of ethnic backgrounds but rather the result of training and early professional experience. The Russians—Fokine, Massine, Bolm, Nijinska, and Balanchine—had been trained at the Russian Imperial Ballet Schools and had created ballets for Diaghilev and the successor Russian ballet companies. They had entered the schools as children and had been promoted from class to class only as they improved in their ability to perform the physical dancing exercises required of them. Their education was designed to make them skilled in a craft, and many of the students, even after they had become professional dancers, continued to regard their occupation as no more than a craft for which they had become equipped by chance of circumstances. Some of the students, particularly those listed above, came to regard their craft of choreography as an art. But even as they strove to raise their craft to the status of art, they never forgot that they remained craftsmen. As artists they responded to self-inspired creativity, but as craftsmen they were not averse to creating on order. Fokine, as an artist, was self-inspired to create CHOPINIANA (LES SYLPHIDES), but he did not feel he was demeaning himself when, as a craftsman, he agreed to furnish the choreography for a ballet for which Diaghilev had already adapted the libretto and for which Stravinsky had already completed the score. Nor did he feel he was being imposed upon when Diaghilev informed him that the ballet, FIREBIRD, must be ready for performance by June 25, 1910. The 25th was an exact, unalterable date. It was the evening upon which the fourth program of the subscription series had been scheduled at the Paris Opéra. The subscribers had reserved that Saturday for the ballet and had bought tickets on the assurance that they would witness the Paris premiere of a new ballet. If the ballet was not presented as scheduled, the subscribers would be indignant and Diaghilev would face legal proceedings. The public would not be appeased with the announcement that Fokine had run into choreographic difficulties that necessitated a postponement. Fokine did not question the management's right to insist on a fixed delivery date. He completed his works on schedule even under difficult circumstances—as when, in the case of DAPHNIS AND CHLOË, he had to force himself to devise overnight the choreography for the last twenty pages of Ravel's score.

In contrast, the training of the new breed of choreographers had been haphazard. Beginning in their late teens, they had, it is true, studied with qualified masters, but they had in effect conducted their own education. They had made their own choice of teachers and had decided for themselves when the time had come to move on to other teachers and other classes. The Russians had submitted to rigid discipline in exchange for being well-fed, well-clothed, and educated academically through the munificence of the Tsar's privy purse. The new breed were, to use an old-fashioned phrase with which they were not familiar, beholden to no one. In exchange for their education they had performed such menial tasks as sweeping out studios, and they had eaten little and cheaply. To them the ballet for which they had made great sacrifices was not merely a craft, it was a passion, and their exercise of it became a crusade. They were aware, too, that they must continue to make sacrifices even if they proved to be successful in their chosen field, for success in the ballet could never earn the dividends paid in other branches of the theater. Such small material rewards could only be compensated for by a belief that theirs was not just a craft but art with a capital A. As professionals they admitted there were problems of program scheduling, premiere dates, demands for new productions, et cetera. But these were problems to be solved by management, not by them. As artists they denied that time schedules could be applied to inspiration, or to the polishing and perfecting of a work of art.

In choreography, as in all fields of the arts, there are fast workers and slow workers, and there are even occasions on which fast workers are slowed down. But in other fields the artist works on his own: the painter in his studio, the writer at

ALICIA ALONSO AND IGOR YOUSKEVITCH IN THE NUTCRACKER PAS DE DEUX.

his desk, and the composer at his piano. Not so with a choreographer. If his ballet is not completed, the management cannot at the last minute call upon another choreographer to supply a substitute work as a world-premiere. New ballets are created, polished, and perfected on the bodies of the dancers who are to perform them. A choreographer cannot in an emergency fish an unproduced ballet out of his bottom bureau drawer.

Miss Chase had always been familiar with this fact of ballet life, but it was impressed on her much more deeply when she became a director. As a dancer rehearsing the role of the Nurse in ROMEO AND JULIET she observed the hours of rehearsal time that Antony Tudor spent molding the arms of the Attendants into Botticelli-like poses. She observed, too, the periods when choreographic inspiration failed. But when the premiere date approached and a ballet was still incomplete, it was not her concern or responsibility. It remained for Talbot and Hurok, in consultation with Tudor, to make the decision not to delay the opening but to present the ballet on schedule minus the last uncreated scenes. Even as late as 1946, after Miss Chase had become administrative director, the scheduling of rehearsals and performances was not her exclusive responsibility but one she shared with the artistic administrator and the artistic committee.

During the season at Covent Garden, the principal responsibility for scheduling rehearsals devolved upon Antony Tudor as artistic administrator. He was faced with the problem of finding the forty-five rehearsal hours that had somewhat unrealistically been promised to Robbins for the creation of the Vivaldi ballet. On July 15 Chase wrote to Smith, "Jerry did an excellent Petrouchka and is in a very good humor. He will get his Vivaldi rehearsals before he leaves on the 28th." However, when Robbins left London he had been allotted only fifteen hours and forty-five minutes of rehearsals, and his agent informed the company that his contract had been breached. Meanwhile, in New York, de Mille was writing a furious letter to Smith. She had heard from Muriel Bentley that THREE VIRGINS AND A DEVIL had been put on at Covent Garden without sufficient rehearsals, and her own London friends had written her that GISELLE, which was on the same program, was obviously under-rehearsed. What then had happened to all the rehearsal hours (which in those days, before the introduction of stern and costly union regulations, were virtually limitless)? Perhaps a hint can be found in a remark that Chase made to Smith on August 6: "Will let you know how UNDERTOW comes out tonight. Tudor has had fifty-two hours of rehearsal, but it is not quite ready!" The count, according to the call sheets preserved in the archives, was accurate. Fifty-two hours rehearsal of a ballet that had been performed frequently for more than a year! No one could be sure what Tudor's intention was, but certainly there were no complaints that his ballets had been under-rehearsed. It was becoming clear to Chase, however, that the administration of rehearsal scheduling was due for a change.

Soon after the company's return to New York, it also became apparent to Chase and Smith that adjustments had to be made in the division of powers between the administrative directors and the artistic committee. A meeting was held in Miss Chase's dining room, attended by Tudor, de Mille, Robbins, Chase, Smith, and Copland. Payne, though not a member of the artistic committee, was unaccountably asked to sit in. The discussions were devoted almost exclusively to complaints voiced by the choreographers, each speaking on his or her own behalf. For his part, Robbins complained that he had not been allotted sufficient hours to complete the Vivaldi ballet or to perfect FACSIMILE. He asked that the Vivaldi ballet be canceled and that FACSIMILE be postponed to another season. The other choreographers, when their attention could be diverted from their own complaints, sided with Robbins with respect to Vivaldi and agreed that FACSIMILE must be postponed, but only for a week, not for a season. This was cold comfort for the directors with a season to put on at the Broadway Theatre.

After the meeting, Robbins continued to protest that the system under which Ballet Theatre operated was not motivated by a desire to pursue excellence in art but was controlled by considerations of finance (he did not go so far as to use the inappropriate words "profit motive"). Because tickets had been sold with the promise of a new production, his ballet had to be presented on the 24th regardless of whether it was ready for public viewing.*

FACSIMILE was indeed given its premiere on the 24th, and it must be noted that Robbins did resume rehearsals the following day, taking eighteen more hours over the next two weeks. If he made any significant changes, they were not discernible to the critics, who reviewed the ballet again toward the end of the season when Hugh Laing had stepped into Robbins' role. The grand total of 138 hours devoted to the preparation of the nineteen-minute ballet was squeezed out of a heavy rehearsal schedule, but only at the expense of other ballets and with what a Prevention Society would term Cruelty to Dancers. During the days preceding the premiere, Kaye and Kriza were required to rehearse FACSIMILE, go for costume fittings, rehearse other ballets, and perform in the evenings. In addition, on the last two nights they were summoned to rehearse FACSIMILE for an hour and a half after the performance, from 11:30 p.m. to 1 a.m.

---

*Years later, during its first visit to the Soviet Union, Ballet Theatre was informed of an incident that might have provided the answer to Robbins' contention. The story, perhaps apocryphal, concerned a new production of HAMLET that the Moscow Art Theater was mounting for one of its veteran actors—also a power in the administration—who was to perform the title role. The rehearsals dragged on for two years without attaining to a state of perfection that satisfied the star and his director. Finally it was agreed that the time had come for a formal dress rehearsal and perhaps a preview performance. On the eve of the first performance, the actor died in his sleep, and rehearsals were resumed with the veteran-next-in-line in the title role.

It would of course be ridiculous to suggest that a rigid time schedule for the creation of a ballet can be specified in advance. There are too many variable factors, including the choreographer's work patterns, the complexity of the libretto, the intricacy of the music, and the proficiency of the dancers. Nor can it be determined whether a work of genius could have been improved with reworking, or whether what might have been a work of genius was whittled away by too much tampering and revising. However, in the course of the production that followed FACSIMILE, Miss Chase once more had the experience of working with a Russian artist-craftsman who demonstrated not only that a ballet could be created on order but also that it could be completed on schedule with a specified number of rehearsals.

As might have been predicted, Igor Youskevitch did not find himself attuned to the psychological approach of the new school of choreography, and it soon became apparent that a role must be created for him that would set off his premier-danseur skills to their best advantage. Coincidentally, the company's musical director, Max Goberman, had been reading through Tchaikovsky's Suite Number 3 in G Minor and had been struck with the thought that the fourth movement might well serve as the music for a ballet in the Petipa style, one that would fill the same function in the repertory as did PRINCESS AURORA. He passed on the suggestion to Chase and Smith, who approached Balanchine with the question, "Could you do an opening ballet for Youskevitch to this music?" Balanchine took the score and returned shortly with the answer, "But of course." Four days before the company departed on tour, he auditioned and chose the female soloists and corps de ballet. In the next three days he set the first movement in seven hours of rehearsal. While the company was on tour, Nora Kaye conducted three one-hour rehearsals to keep the choreography fresh in the dancers' minds. Balanchine rejoined the company in Wilmington, Delaware, and contined rehearsing during the next few weeks until the opening at the New York City Center on November 11, 1947. In all, he had taken thirty-nine hours to create a thirty-two-minute ballet, thus conforming reasonably closely to de Valois' formula. The ballet, designated simply as "Tchaikovsky" during rehearsal, was formally named THEME AND VARIATIONS and opened on schedule. It not only provided Youskevitch with a stellar role, but it became, and has remained, one of the undimming gems in the Ballet Theatre repertory. It is safe to say that additional hours expended on its creation would not have improved this work of genius.

Working with Balanchine made Chase and Smith conscious, by contrast, of the change in the relationship of the ballet director with his choreographers. No longer could directors order a new ballet as Diaghilev had ordered SCHÉHÉRAZADE from Fokine, as Kirstein had commanded a ballet about Billy the Kid from Loring, or as Sevastianov had presented Lichine with a libretto and score for a ballet about Helen of Troy. When a choreographer of the new breed was approached by a director, he expected to be asked whether he had in mind a ballet he wished to create. Uusually the choreographer had a store of librettos and ideas germinating in his head and would bring forth one he was willing to entrust to Ballet Theatre. If not, he would answer, "I'll see if I can come up with something." Never was there a hint that the suggestion of a collaborating librettist or composer would be welcome. Perhaps the choreographers feared that their status as creative artists would be threatened if they had to share the credit for creative ideas with others or if they seemed unable to devise their own libretto and choose their own score. Or perhaps they sincerely believed that their own ideas were superior to any of the suggestions that might be offered, some of which were indeed fatuous. Tudor, for example, perennially pretended to give serious thought to the suggestion that he create a ballet based on the writings of Proust, when he must have been saying to himself, "Don't they realize I've already done the ballet? What could be more Proustian than JARDIN AUX LILAS, or DIM LUSTRE, or even UNDERTOW!"

The new breed of choreographers' view of themselves as artists rather than craftsmen might not have had as much effect on the quality of the ballets as they would have liked to think, but it did have a noticeable effect on the quantity produced. It also affected the role of the director as a projector of production plans. Chase and Smith now had to await the moment when the artist-choreographer was visited by an inspiration. They then had to accept on faith his assurance that his inspiration would produce a viable, let alone a successful ballet, for customarily they received only a vague description of the project. Having settled on the production, they could only cross their fingers and hope that the choreographer's inspiration would continue to flow uninterruptedly and the ballet would emerge on schedule. How often they must have questioned the wisdom of Pleasant's insistence that Ballet Theatre should not have a dominant, resident choreographer! How often they must have envied Kirstein, who could always remain confident that some morning Balanchine would wake up and say to himself, "I must take time off this week to create the ballets we promised for this season or Lincoln will be very angry!" For their part, Chase and Smith could lead their choreographers to the rehearsal studio but they couldn't make them choreograph—a fact that the critics have continually refused to acknowledge when assessing Chase's and Smith's capabilities as directors. At the close of their first independently produced season, for example, the dance editor Rosalyn Krokover wrote in the Musical Courier:

The final score of Ballet Theatre's season adds up to one new ballet (FACSIMILE), two revivals seen for the first time in this country (LES PATINEURS and the Lester version of PAS DE QUATRE) and a newly—and badly, we might add—dressed GISELLE. Not a very good artistic record for a company of its potentialities. The fault rests squarely on the management. Considering the high standard of performance that was achieved, the selection of new ballets should have shown more originality and enterprise.

Had Miss Krokover herself shown more enterprise as an editor-reporter, she could have uncovered the following facts.

In London, Chase first asked Ashton to create a new ballet on the company during the Covent Garden engagement, but he pleaded exhaustion after the Sadler's Wells season and an unwillingness to interrupt his holidays. Chase next asked for SYMPHONIC VARIATIONS, his most recent creation. This request was vetoed by David Webster, who decided the ballet must be reserved for the planned visit of Sadler's Wells to New York. It was finally agreed that Ballet Theatre could have LES PATINEURS, which could be rehearsed by Joy Newton and need not be included in the Wells' first New York repertory.

Keith Lester's PAS DE QUATRE had been created originally for the Markova-Dolin company. Chase and Smith acquired it to replace Dolin's version solely because their lawyers advised them that it might prove to be a legal fact that Lester owned all rights to the ballet.

As noted, Chase and Smith had intended to present two new ballets by Robbins. Robbins claimed that the Vivaldi ballet could not be completed because he had not been allotted forty-five hours of rehearsal. The records show that he did in fact rehearse for thirty-three hours. He could have acceded to the directors' persistent request that he complete the work had he chosen to divert twelve of the 138 hours from FACSIMILE to Vivaldi. Had he done so he could have completed both ballets. The choice was his and his alone. This was clearly an example of the fact that the directors' control ceased once they had led the choreographer to the rehearsal studio.

The proposed ballet by Agnes de Mille could have been made ready for the season had she not insisted on the composition of an original score. Doubtless Max Goberman could have found an existing score with "a generous use of bagpipes," but this would have contravened the choreographer's recently acquired right to dictate and approve all the details of the ballet, including the score, the sets, and the costumes.

At Tudor's request, Chase and Smith had purchased the ballet rights to a score by Béla Bartók. However, Tudor delayed choreographing a ballet to it, preferring to concentrate his energies on repeated rehearsals of ROMEO AND JULIET, UNDERTOW, and DIM LUSTRE, all of which were already in the repertory.

Had Chase and Smith immediately acceded to Toumanova's demands (which included the exclusive right to dance Giselle in New York and on tour), and had they immediately diverted funds to its production, they could have staged Balanchine's SCÈNES DE BALLET. (If they wished to indulge in the same hindsight employed by their critics they could now say that had there been a SCÈNES DE BALLET there might never have been a THEME AND VARIATIONS.)

A new production of GISELLE was long overdue. From the start, the second-act set had been makeshift, economy-dictated. A raggedly cut drop, designed to give the impression of an overgrown, deserted graveyard, instead made it appear as though Albrecht had lost his way in a Mississippi bayou. It could be maintained that the choice of Berman as designer of the new production was a mistake, but three years earlier no one considered it a mistake when he was chosen to design the much-praised décor for Tudor's ROMEO AND JULIET.

Had all of Chase's and Smith's plans been realized they would have produced five new ballets by Balanchine, de Mille, Robbins, and Tudor; a new ballet by Ashton (or at least a near-simultaneous American production of SYMPHONIC VARIATIONS); a staging of the original version of PAS DE QUATRE; and a new and restudied production of GISELLE. In making these plans they surely could not be faulted for not having shown "more originality," and they could be charged with a lack of "enterprise" only in their failure to have controlled their choreographers with the use of chains and whips.

During their first season as administrative directors, Chase and Smith not only had learned much about the degree of dependability of choreographers but also about the limitations in the functioning of an artistic administrator and of an artistic committee. In particular, they discovered that the tasks of scheduling rehearsals and casting ballets were too complex and time-consuming to be undertaken by a choreographer, whose energies were better directed toward creating ballets. Devising rehearsal schedules is an intricate, jigsaw-puzzle operation that requires fitting the right dancer into the right time slot with the right choreographer so as to most fully utilize his services during the largest number of available hours. When a schedule is at last complete and ready for posting, all too often it is discovered that a key dancer has been scheduled for two rehearsals at the same hour, with the result that the whole puzzle must be reassembled. Similarly, in the process of casting, special care must be exercised to assure that a dancer who has learned a role is given the opportunity to perform it. Only thus is his enthusiasm aroused and his morale sustained. (Sustaining morale among a company of seventy is a formidable task and one of the prime responsibilities of a director.) Consequently, Miss Chase soon began to personally supervise the preparation of schedules. Over the years she has relaxed her concentration on this function only at times when she is satisfied that an assistant has reached the point in his training where he can be relied on to allocate the rehearsal hours fairly and efficiently. The casting, down to even the most minor roles and the composition of the corps de ballet, she has reserved exclusively to herself, subject only to the approval of the choreographer.

Chase and Smith also learned that important artistic decisions that might affect the season or the entire future of the company could not always be put off until the quarterly meeting of the artistic committee. And when committee members showed signs of being less concerned with general artistic policy than with the advancement of their individual

careers, their reliability as knowledgeable advisors came into question. In 1948 the committee was allowed to expire, along with the post of artistic administrator.

At the same time that it was becoming evident to Chase and Smith that they must seek ways to more effectively influence and control choreographers, the supply of choreographic talent was reduced still further during the next several seasons as the American choreographers became more and more immersed in their activities on Broadway. Michael Kidd left the company to stage the dances for FINIAN'S RAINBOW; Robbins and de Mille withdrew to stage HIGH BUTTON SHOES and BRIGADOON, respectively. They were in the big money. Soon they were in the even bigger money when they moved on to Hollywood to transfer their choreographic creations to the screen. They had to think twice now before committing themselves to the creation of a ballet, lest it interfere with a more lucrative Broadway or Hollywood assignment. And even when Ballet Theatre could adjust its production schedule to the choreographer's availability, it was made clear that the choreographers were performing a labor of love. Under these circumstances their independence was intensified, and they demanded complete control over every aspect of the production. But even on these terms projects rarely moved beyond the discussion stage. Kidd lost all interest in ballet and declined numerous invitations to return briefly to revive his ON STAGE! For the 1947 season at the City Center, Robbins loaned a pas de deux, SUMMER DAY (originally staged for the American-Soviet Musical Society), and Balanchine created THEME AND VARIATIONS, his last work for the company. De Mille was available during the interlude between BRIGADOON and GENTLEMEN PREFER BLONDES and created FALL RIVER LEGEND for the 1948 season at the Metropolitan. Tudor, who alone remained as an active resident choreographer, produced SHADOW OF THE WIND for the same engagement. These were the last two new ballets produced by Ballet Theatre during the next two years. However, in this instance the decline in productivity was owing not so much to a scarcity of choreographers as to a shortage of money.

In the spring of 1948 the well ran dry; the last of the leaves dropped off the money tree. On July 29 copies of the following letter were sent to all the members of the company:

Since we closed at the Metropolitan we have concentrated on raising the necessary funds but have found that this is taking longer than we anticipated. We all feel that sufficient money can be raised by January 1st to permit the resumption of operations at that time.

I hoped until the last minute that it would be possible to keep to our October schedule and assure you I have done my utmost, realizing how much it means to you. I have every confidence that this comparatively short delay will result in a healthier and stronger Ballet Theatre.

Despite Miss Chase's confidence, there was every indication that in the absence of a fresh gold strike or the intervention of a miracle, to mix a few more metaphors, Ballet Theatre was doomed in its ninth season. Why should the demise of ballet's "Fabulous Invalid" have occurred in this particular year?

IN 1947 BALANCHINE RETURNED TO CREATE THEME AND VARIATIONS FOR ALICIA ALONSO AND IGOR YOUSKEVITCH.

Partly because of a disastrous season at the Metropolitan and partly because of the hard-headedness of a philistine cell in the Bureau of Internal Revenue.

Since 1935 S. Hurok had been presenting at a profit a spring season at the Metropolitan Opera House; since 1942 his principal attraction had been Ballet Theatre. Business had been good, averaging about 75 percent of capacity (he would do better later with the Royal Ballet, but this percentage was good enough to more than cover the excessive operating costs at the opera house). In 1948 Hurok temporarily bowed out of the ballet business (he did not introduce the Royal Ballet to New York until the following season), and for the spring season he relinquished to Ballet Theatre his exclusive right to rent the Metropolitan. For the first time, Ballet Theatre presented itself at the Metropolitan, and attendance dropped to 47 percent of capacity. This disaster followed hard upon a successful two-week engagement in Chicago, during which Ballet Theatre had broken the Civic Opera House's box-office record for New Year's Eve. Why had it struck so suddenly?

In the theater many reasons are offered to account for poor attendance, most of them extraneous and intended to disguise the fact that the public is simply not interested in a particular attraction. If business is bad on a rainy day, for example, it will be said that the bad weather kept the public away. If business is equally bad on a clear, sunny day, it will be said that the public, preferring to remain outdoors, flocked to a football stadium rather than a stuffy theater. Another excuse for poor attendance is the lack of publicity. This explanation persists although it should have been discarded for all time after Hurok had spoken out of wisdom and experience, "If the public wants to see an attraction, no amount of publicity will keep it away." In the ballet field a special reason is advanced: attendance was poor because the company offered no new ballets. This reasoning is based on a conviction that ballet companies can retain the interest of the public only by presenting a number of new works (new as distinguished from revivals or fresh productions of old ballets) each season. This production of novelties is not required to the same extent from other performing organizations: the opera, the symphony orchestra, or the repertory theater. Nor was it expected of the ballet when it prospered in the Russian Imperial Theaters. The tradition was perhaps first established by Diaghilev, whose company performed in Europe not as a permanent, year-round institution but as a traveling troupe making short annual visits to a capital city. He could not wait for the public to learn of his presence through word-of-mouth; by then he would have left town. He required instant attention from the press and particularly from the critics. The ballet, he discovered, was reviewed by music critics, who regarded it as a second-class citizen and went to see each work only once. Subsequent performances of the work, even in later seasons, were ignored unless they were placed on the same program with a new ballet. To lure the critics to the theater on the opening night or for subsequent performances, he had to offer them new works to review, and the process had to be repeated each season. The same applied to the "tout Paris" audience he was determined to attract. He found that they could be induced to interrupt their busy social activities to attend the ballet more than once only if they could subscribe for a series of performances at each of which a new ballet was presented. Today critics will review performances that include no new ballets, and the companies' dependence on pre-season subscription sales is not so absolute, but the belief still persists that a ballet company cannot remain viable at the box office unless it satisfies the demand for novelties during every season. The demand from whom? From the general public, the ballet public, the balletomanes, the dancers, or the critics?

The general public, even what might be termed the theater public, is not attracted to the ballet more than occasionally, and usually only when a bright new star is so much talked about that it becomes embarrassing to have to admit one hasn't seen her or him. These people attend a performance without knowing or caring whether the ballet is old or new.

The ballet public consists for the most part of casual balletgoers who attend not more than a dozen times a year but nevertheless buy by far the greater proportion of the tickets. With the increase in ballet activity their demand for new ballets, never strong, has dropped off. If none of the many resident and visiting ballet companies produced a new ballet for the next five years, the members of the ballet public could still attend their dozen performances and at each of them see an old ballet that was new to them. Also, like their children, who attend THE NUTCRACKER for at least half a dozen years without expressing a desire to be taken to something new, they attend repeat performances of such ballets as SWAN LAKE with pleasure.

The balletomanes most certainly do demand new ballets. They view them as trophies to add to their collection: "I've seen everything she's ever danced, even THE NEW BALLET, which was only done three times!" But the demands of balletomanes can be put in perspective by another word of wisdom from Hurok, who described them thus, "Balletomanes are people who demand new ballets and free tickets." They are also people who ticket-shop wisely. If the management carelessly schedules two novelties on the same program, it is that performance which will sell.

The dancers welcome new works to varying degrees. For the lesser dancers there is always the possibility that a role in a new ballet will propel them into stardom. For the stars a new role may earn them additional kudos from the critics. And for the corps de ballet a new ballet relieves the tedium, although rehearsals are hard work.

In the last analysis, it is the critics' demands for new works that are the most insistent. Today they can, and do, review performances of old works, but these offer limited targets. What can the critic write, for example, about the music, libretto, choreography, and décor of a SWAN LAKE production in its second year? Unless he wishes to retract the previous season's evaluation of the production, only the dancers' performances remain to be discussed. Only with a completely new work can the ballet critic exercise his powers to the full in passing judgment on the choreography, the score, the libretto, the décor, the lighting, and the dancing, to make a first-time-in-this-paper appraisal of their worth. If this opportunity is not frequently afforded, the ballet critic feels resentful.

For a ballet company, or the art of ballet itself, to continue to grow there must, of course, be constant creative activity. But if the activity is aimed at satisfying the critics' appetites rather than at building up an enduring repertory, it may prove to be counterproductive. In the early seventies the New York City Ballet delighted critics (and balletomanes) by producing festivals dedicated to Stravinsky and Ravel. In summing up the Ravel Festival, Arlene Croce wrote in The New Yorker:

Of sixteen premieres, there are five that deserve to enter the repertory: RAPSODIE ESPAGNOLE, TZIGANE, LE TOMBEAU DE COUPERIN, and SONATINE—all by Balanchine—and MA MÈRE L'OYE by Robbins. Perhaps also CONCERTO IN G, and certainly, if the right conditions for performing it can be found, L'ENFANT ET LES SORTILÈGES. GASPARD DE LA NUIT will probably be around for another season or two. At a maximum, that gives us eight out of sixteen tries, which is a better average than the eight out of twenty-one ballets that remain from the Stravinsky Festival three years ago.

Considering that Miss Croce's discriminating taste is not necessarily matched by that of the general public, her prediction of 43 percent success will probably be reduced when it comes time for audiences to determine the durability of the new works. And at what cost was this concentrated spate of creativity accomplished? It not only brought the company to the brink of financial ruin but, in absorbing all the energies of the dancers and ballet masters, it left the regular repertory in ill-repair and so spiritlessly performed as to have at least temporarily alienated the public.

In 1948 Chase and Smith were in the ranks of those who believed that new ballets in abundance were essential to a company's survival. They had been persuaded to this belief by Hurok, and he, in turn, had proved his own commitment to it by going so far on occasion as to contribute to the cost of new works. At the time it occurred to no one to make a comparative study of box-office figures. Had this been done, some doubts might have been raised as to the drawing power of seasonal novelties. In the fall of 1946 Ballet Theatre produced four new ballets at the Broadway Theatre to audiences that averaged only 55 percent of capacity. Six months later, in the spring of 1947, the company performed a few blocks away, at the City Center Theatre, to audiences that averaged 75 percent of capacity. For that engagement it presented not a single new production. Similarly, in the spring of 1948 two world premieres, Tudor's SHADOW OF THE WIND and de Mille's FALL RIVER LEGEND, were presented at the Metropolitan Opera House to sparse audiences that averaged no more than 47 percent of capacity. The following spring, again at the Metropolitan, no new productions were presented, yet the audience increased to 63 percent of capacity. Clearly factors other than new productions accounted for the size of the audiences. Perhaps it was that the ticket prices at the City Center were lower than at the Broadway, just as at the Metropolitan they were lower for the second, better-attended engagement than for the first. Another explanation for the greater success of the 1949 engagement may have been that it marked the first appearance of Maria Tallchief with Ballet Theatre. She was indeed a unique box-office attraction for indefinable reasons above and beyond her dancing skills. But whatever brought the public to the theater during one engagement and kept it away during the other, it was certainly not the presence or absence of new productions.

For the Metropolitan season in 1948, Chase and Smith had planned to offer a number of novelties, including Doris

Humphrey's WITH MY RED FIRES, but only two new productions, SHADOW OF THE WIND and FALL RIVER LEGEND, reached the stage. Neither of them even began to rescue the season from disaster. Antony Tudor's SHADOW OF THE WIND was received only moderately well by the critics and could not be termed a success. Perhaps this ballet was ahead of its time or perhaps Tudor was uncomfortable when, for the first time, he created roles for established, non-malleable stars. It was not, as John Martin surmised, that SHADOW OF THE WIND was rushed on without sufficient rehearsals—Tudor had rehearsed for 358 hours from January through April 14. The public, for its part, showed little interest; at no performance did the audience reach 51 percent of capacity. For the ballet's fifth and last performance during the concluding week of the engagement, when word-of-mouth should have been showing its effect, attendance dropped to 24 percent of capacity. Agnes de Mille's FALL RIVER LEGEND fared better. John Martin began his New York Times review with, "To come to the point at once, the Ballet Theatre has a new hit on its hands." If he meant that the company had acquired a ballet that would still be a strong attraction in the repertory more than a quarter of a century later, he was quite right. If he meant that the ballet would blow fresh gusts of cash into the doldrums at the Metropolitan box office, he was wrong. Only on three Saturday nights did it come even close to selling out, and half of its performances were given to half-filled houses.

From a long-run point of view, Chase and Smith's production ventures during the entire 1947–48 season scored a high percentage of success, two out of three, and the costs were comparatively moderate: THEME AND VARIATIONS, $23,682; SHADOW OF THE WIND, $31,432; and FALL RIVER LEGEND, $24,812. Two of the ballets could be said to have earned back their investment over the years, but during the 1948 Metropolitan season they had little effect on the dismal profit-and-loss figures. The weekly operating expenses averaged $39,450, and the receipts $27,400; some $12,000 had to be found each week to make up the deficit. Not surprisingly the money was found in Lucia Chase's bank account, and not surprisingly she decided that another nadir had been reached, and that for the third time she would have to call a halt.

To the extent that Ballet Theatre can be said to owe its survival to Miss Chase's financial assistance, the credit must be shared with Herbert Hoover and his Depression, Adolf Hitler and his World War II, and Andrew Mellon and his solicitude for those who aided in the growth of the country's wealth by risking capital in investments. At the time when Miss Chase became a beneficiary of her husband's will, the Hoover economy was still depressed; the assets of the Ewing estate were at their lowest value and were accordingly moderately taxed. By the time Miss Chase was called upon to advance sums to save Ballet Theatre, Hitler's war had improved America's economy, with a resulting increase in the value and yield of the Ewing estate. And when the needs of

MARIA TALLCHIEF IN THEME AND VARIATIONS.

Ballet Theatre could no longer be supplied out of Miss Chase's income alone and the sale of capital assets became necessary, the assets could be sold under the advantageous regulations that the Mellon Treasury had set up for capital gains. The stocks, which had appreciated greatly since their purchase, were not subject when sold to a full income tax, and consequently larger sums could go to the ballet, the sole beneficiary of Miss Chase's increased prosperity. This, as any lover of the arts will agree, was as it should be.

However, not <u>all</u> events or <u>all</u> branches of the government conspired to enable Miss Chase to maintain the existence of Ballet Theatre. There were those in all three branches of the government who believed that support of the arts was the responsibility of those who loved them, not of the government. The entry of the United States into the war called for the imposition of Victory Taxes, which, in the theater, took the form of a 10- to 20-percent increase in the admission tax. In applying this tax, no distinction was made between non-profit-making ballet and commercial theater. This meant that when Ballet Theatre charged $3.00 for a ticket, it, in fact, received only $2.50. It also meant that in some weeks the admission taxes due the government constituted one-half of the deficit. But while the philistines in the Bureau of Internal Revenue placed ballet in the same category as the commercial theater with respect to admission taxes, they placed it in a very different category when considering it as an investment project. In each year in which Miss Chase advanced sums in excess of her original $25,000 pledge, she did so in the form of loans. Her lawyers arranged for her to do this through various forms of corporate structures, of the sort employed by investors in the commercial theater. These corporations, as with Broadway investment companies, were periodically dissolved and the loans that had not been repaid were written off as bad debts on Miss Chase's income tax returns. Each year the Tax Commissioner disallowed the deduction. By 1947 Miss Chase's lawyers became convinced that the Bureau of Internal Revenue would not allow Miss Chase or other contributors to take a tax loss for monies advanced to Ballet Theatre.* It was decided, therefore, that Ballet Theatre should seek a charter either as a non-profit, charitable foundation or, preferably, as an educational foundation.

The Ballet Theatre Foundation, Inc., was accordingly organized on May 6, 1947, as an educational foundation under the New York Membership Corporation Law, for "the primary purpose of fostering and cultivating understanding and appreciation of ballet by the general public." The tax laws in connection with charitable foundations were clear and not subject to interpretations by the Commissioner. Taxpayers could contribute up to 20 percent of their incomes to a charitable foundation (30 percent to an educational foundation) and deduct the contribution from their income in computing their taxes. This removed any uncertainty with respect to the allowance and appealed therefore to such benefactors as Dwight Deere Wiman and Lawrence Langner. To Miss Chase, however, the limitation had its disadvantage. Formerly her advisors had been able to make her excessive contributions less unpalatable by suggesting that she might as well give the money to Ballet Theatre, because if she didn't, a large share of it would go to the government in surtaxes. But under the new arrangement this argument could not be applied to sweeten contributions in excess of 30 percent of her income.

This was the position she found herself in as the spring 1948 engagement at the Metropolitan progressed. Since the year-old foundation had not yet raised substantial monies from other contributors, she herself had been forced to donate more than 30 percent of her income. When the Metropolitan engagement continued to incur a $12,000 weekly deficit, it was only a matter of simple calculation to project an annual deficit in an amount far in excess of 30 percent of her income.

---

*The court decisions that passed on the correctness of the Commissioner's rulings were not handed down until some years later. In the first case, the jury found that Miss Chase <u>had</u> loaned money with the expectation of being repaid with interest, but that when the company to which she made the loan was dissolved it was without assets and thus the loan became a bad debt. Consequently, Miss Chase was allowed the tax deduction for the season at the Majestic Theatre.

Subsequent cases were argued without a jury. The judge concluded that the law was clear: "To secure a tax deduction it is necessary that the 'taxpayer's' motive in entering the transaction was primarily profit." He ruled that no matter how worthy Miss Chase's motives in extending the loans, making a profit was not one of them. And Miss Chase was not, of course, concerned with making a profit to be taken <u>out</u> of the business (it would have been re-invested in the company), but she did continue to hope for earnings sufficient to cover operating expenses. At the beginning of each season the budgets prepared by the management indicated this would be so, provided the audience attendance was 85 to 90 percent of capacity. When it rarely rose above 50 percent, the estimates had to be recalculated, and as the season progressed, any expectation of profit became unreasonable. When Miss Chase persisted in advancing money even at such a late date, she was not—in the judge's opinion—doing so with a realistic hope of being repaid with interest.

An entire other conclusion might have been reached had the loan-making procedure been different. If Miss Chase had taken the most pessimistic view at the <u>beginning</u> of each season and

said to her budget-makers, "I hope you're right, but just in case, I'll advance a sum in excess of your projected needs so you can operate more economically from a position of being over- rather than under-financed," such a loan could not later have been characterized by the courts as "throwing good money after bad." (Putting up all the money in advance was, in fact, suggested upon occasion but Miss Chase rejected it for three valid reasons: it would discourage other contributors—"Lucia's already done it"—encourage management's natural predilection toward profligacy, and require her to take out a personal loan or sell securities, something she was loath to do unless it became unavoidable.)

Miss Chase's position was further weakened by her own repeated assertion that she exercised no control over the company's business affairs. The image she projected in court was that of a dancer who differed from other dancers in Ballet Theatre only in that she happened to be able to assist the company financially. She thus led the judges to conclude: "Her indifference to the financial management of the company and the safety of her investment is pivotal when coupled with her admitted love and devotion to ballet as an art." If her lawyers had been permitted to picture her as she more truly was—a serious businesswoman who could not only delegate authority to her managers but permit <u>them</u> to exercise discretion, all the while insisting on detailed reports concerning the disposition of her funds—the judges' conclusion might have been different.

Even when Miss Chase made advances late in the season, she did so with the full confidence that, although the company could not make a profit that year, if it survived, it would eventually become a money-maker. In 1954, when the case was heard on appeal, the judges could have found this assumption reasonable. They might have been aware that in that year the English Royal Ballet was performing for S. Hurok at the Metropolitan before capacity audiences paying inflated ticket prices (Hurok's profit motive had never been in doubt). Though this could not be mentioned at the hearing—technically it had no bearing on Miss Chase's reasons for making loans to a ballet company ten years before—judges are not required to exist in a vacuum. If given a chance they could have found a legal rationalization allowing her a tax deduction for early losses, especially since the government would lose nothing—it would make up the difference in taxes when the business became prosperous. Instead, the judges agreed with the lower court in deciding that "the taxpayer's primary purpose and perhaps her sole purpose in making these loans, was the enhancement of ballet as an art. . . . Regardless of the artistic appreciation one may have for the ballet or other arts, Congress has not seen fit to permit deductions for contributions made to support them, unless it is clear that the taxpayer had a business purpose in mind."

The Congress had enacted the law; the Executive had administered it; the Judiciary had enforced it; Miss Chase paid substantial taxes on top of her substantial contributions.

RUTH ANN KOESUN IN SHADOW OF THE WIND
DIANA ADAMS IN FALL RIVER LEGEND
JANET REED IN REHEARSAL
MARY ELLEN MOYLAN IN THE NUTCRACKER PAS DE DEUX

Her associates could find no arguments to dissuade her from her decision to suspend operations until other substantial contributors came forward.

Meanwhile, Lincoln Kirstein was having no greater success in attracting contributors to his Ballet Society, Inc. He had attended an organizational tea for the Ballet Theatre Foundation that was presided over by Mrs. Wales Latham, a semiprofessional organizer instrumental in founding Bundles for Britain and in the birth later of Common Cause. Afterward he sent her a list of publications issued by the Ballet Society, concluding his letter with:

We intend also to appeal for funds in the fall, and according to my promise to aid Miss Chase in every possible way, I would like to inform you in advance exactly what we intend to do, so that as much as possible, we aid rather than interfere with each other. I am so sensible of the great service that the Ballet Theatre has made to the real art of ballet in the United States, that it is wholly my desire to cooperate in every possible way.

A year later, while activities of Ballet Theatre were still under suspension, he wrote Miss Chase with a new proposal:

I should like to make to you a formal proposal for immediate and future collaboration between Ballet Theatre and Ballet Society. We are about to finish our first season here as the New York City Ballet Company. While it has been hard to subsist on Monday and Tuesday nights alone, the City Center is so pleased with our potential draw that they are inviting us back to do a season in the spring after the Opera season. At that time they will assume our running operational costs, and in the future are ready to assure us of two seasons a year and possible time in between. For these times we will have the whole week for the ballet.

I am convinced that the formula of the City Center as a sponsoring agent is excellent, indeed perhaps the only feasible way to work. The agreement that the Opera Company has with Chicago is a model that can be worked also with the ballet for Chicago and other large cities.

With this prospect ahead, would you consent to be president of the New York City Ballet Company? Balanchine would be Artistic Director, and I would be General Director. The New York City Ballet Company would present works from the repertories of both Ballet Theatre and Ballet Society. In the future I can imagine we would present other repertories, but always within the framework of the New York City Company. In this way the name of Ballet Theatre is kept before the public, but a step is made in a constructive direction towards a permanent group like the Sadler's Wells, which would be genuinely representative of the best that America has done for the ballet.

I am sure that there are many details upon which we would have to agree; but if you are interested in principle would you communicate with me, and we could talk to Mr. Baum.

Yours faithfully,
LINCOLN KIRSTEIN

These letters are introduced not as an indication that there was any more than what Kirstein has termed a "skittish" approach to an amalgamation, but because they reveal the difference in his and Chase's plans and hopes for ballet in America. Kirstein was interested primarily in the creation of new ballets in New York City. He once told Payne, perhaps with a degree of exaggeration, that after a ballet had been completed and given its premiere performance, he didn't care whether it was ever performed again. He was aware, of course, that dancers did not share his indifference to subsequent performances, and that his company's desire to perform was not being satisfied by scattered appearances as

the Ballet Society and in twice-weekly evenings of ballet at the City Center. Hence he approached Chase, envisioning that an organization that combined the repertory of both companies could also engage a troupe of dancers and provide them with increased, if not year-round, employment.

Chase, on the other hand, was interested in a national company that would preserve the best ballet of the past while it cautiously, perhaps less enterprisingly, added new works to the collection. The City Center, with its small stage, was not an ideal home for a company that planned to restage the classic ballets in their original elaborate productions.* Even the scenery of a number of Ballet Theatre's modern productions, such as PILLAR OF FIRE and ROMEO AND JULIET, had to be truncated and contracted in order to fit on the smaller stage with its virtually nonexistent wing space. With their eyes still hopefully on the Metropolitan, Chase and Smith declined Kirstein's offer, just as they had rejected other direct proposals from the City Center of Music and Drama that Ballet Theatre become a constituent of that organization.

LUCIA CHASE, MRS. HARRY S TRUMAN, AND BLEVINS DAVIS.

Chase's and Kirstein's ideas were not entirely incompatible, and had the point been reached at which the extinction of both groups was inevitable in the absence of an amalgamation, a union might have been consummated. However, while discussions were still in progress, dei ex machinis descended on the scene in the persons of Morton Baum and Blevins Davis, who were to enable both companies to survive as separate entities by solving their financial problems. Chase and Kirstein never again had to consider amalgamation. Like Macy's and Gimbels, they remain friendly but uncollaborative.

Kirstein's company was rescued by Morton Baum, whose political maneuvering resulted in the ballet's being promoted to a status of equality with the opera, symphony,

---

*The inadequacy of the stage presented less of a problem to Balanchine, who began to mount ballets that often as not required no scenery or costumes. His problem arose when he later moved to the New York State Theater. A sizable grant from the Ford Foundation was then required to rebuild such scenery as he had employed at the City Center to make it large enough for the new stage. Scenery, by folding, can be contracted to adapt it to a stage, but it cannot be expanded.

and drama at the New York City Center. Under the new arrangement the City Center assumed responsibility for the ballet's operating (as distinguished from its production) deficits. Ballet Theatre was saved by Blevins Davis, who had unimpeachable qualifications for the office of president of the recently formed Ballet Theatre Foundation. He had married the widow of the grandson of Jim Hill, founder of the Great Northern Railroad, and therefore had access to considerable financial reserves. The wedding, which took place in Washington, D.C., was followed by a dinner at the White House given by the incorruptible but not unaccommodating Harry S Truman. Bess Truman and Davis had been friends when he was serving as superintendent of the high school in Independence, Missouri. Before the end of 1948 he was able to assure Miss Chase that he could raise or contribute at least $100,000. By the end of 1949 he was able to assure her that his political influence would make possible Ballet Theatre's first European tour. He wrote:

I will use all my influence to get the Air Corps to fly the company over [to Europe] and furthermore ask the Cultural Relations Division of the State Department to sponsor our tour along with the U.S. Air Corps just as they did with my HAMLET [a production starring Robert Breen that played in Denmark's Elsinor Castle]. I will discuss the matter in detail with my "personal friends" in Washington so that our project will carry the proper weight in Europe. I must insist however that no one must make any statement regarding the Air Corps or the State Department until I have it all set.

Davis was unable to execute his overall plan until the summer of 1950, and so the role of immediate resuscitator of Ballet Theatre fell to Dwight Deere Wiman, whose check for $25,000 helped underwrite a three-week tour in the spring of 1949, followed by three weeks at the Metropolitan.

During the ten months between May 1948 and March 1949 that Ballet Theatre lay in a moribund state, Miss Chase could never for a moment put away from her thoughts the repertory of ballets that could be lost at least temporarily; she imagined the physical properties rotting away in the warehouse while the choreography gradually evaporated from the minds of the choreographers and dancers. The extent of the loss can be appreciated by listing only those ballets performed during the 1947–48 season: ALEKO, APOLLO, BILLY THE KID, DARK ELEGIES, FACSIMILE, FALL RIVER LEGEND, FANCY FREE, GALA PERFORMANCE, GISELLE, HELEN OF TROY, INTERPLAY, JARDIN AUX LILAS, ON STAGE!, PAS DE QUATRE, LES PATINEURS, PETER AND THE WOLF, PETROUCHKA, PILLAR OF FIRE, ROMEO AND JULIET, SHADOW OF THE WIND, LES SYLPHIDES, TALLY-HO, THEME AND VARIATIONS, and UNDERTOW. All but three of these ballets (FACSIMILE, ON STAGE!, and SHADOW OF THE WIND) have remained in the active repertory, and have been revived from time to time down through the years. These ballets would not necessarily have been lost irretrievably; they could have been staged (and several were) by existing or new companies, but this would have been cold comfort to Miss Chase.

Also continually on her mind were the dancers who had constituted the company of the past season. She could not claim all of them as hers (those who had been discovered and trained by Ballet Theatre), but there were many for whom she nursed a perhaps sentimental but nevertheless strong proprietary interest. Ironically, it was two of the dancers to whom she felt the most sentimental attachment who not only were a factor in her reaching the decision to suspend activities but who actually made it possible for her to do so. Miss Chase had followed a practice—and this was unabashedly sentimental—of entering her first contract discussions of each season with John Kriza, a favorite of hers, with whom negotiations were swift and pleasant. He served as the icebreaker to an annual task that she subconsciously dreaded and put off as long as possible. She knew she would meet with demands, some of them unreasonable, that would have to be negotiated, sometimes placing a strain on her non-business friendships with the dancers. Next in line of approach were the ballerinas, Nora Kaye and Alicia Alonso, who, in 1948, were also objects of sentiment. Here she ran into a snag. Alonso refused to sign unless she was billed ahead of Kaye, and Kaye, who had joined the company several months earlier than Alonso and had preceded her by several years in attaining ballerina status, was not about to yield her position of precedence. Neither ballerina would budge, and Chase put off signing other dancers until their dispute had been settled. She does not now recall that the squabble over billing had any effect on her decision to suspend, but it was apparent at the time that, as the engagement at the Metropolitan continued to lose in excess of $12,000 a week, the self-centered battle of the ballerinas, while it might not have served as the backbreaking straw, certainly contributed to her temporary disenchantment with the ballet. In the usual course of events, the entire company would have been signed for the 1948–49 season before the termination of the Metropolitan engagement, but by closing night only Kriza had been signed. This obviated the argument that had been brought forward on other occasions when a suspension of activities was suggested, namely that the dancers' contracts would have to be honored anyway, so it wouldn't cost that much more to go on performing. For only the second time in its history, Ballet Theatre was free of contractual obligations. It was even ruled in arbitration that the company's obligation to appear at City Center in the fall of 1948 was non-enforceable.

Had Alonso capitulated earlier during the Metropolitan engagement, Chase would doubtless have proceeded to sign a majority of the dancers to a year contract, and activities would probably have resumed in the fall on schedule. It is ironical, therefore, that the only letter of protest Chase received after notifying the dancers of the cancellation of the fall season was written by Fernando Alonso, then Alicia's husband:

We received your communication about Ballet Theatre's Fall Season being cancelled. Alicia and I are absolutely dumbfounded. It will be approximately 9 months lay-off by the time we start again! That is terrible!

The balance of the letter did not come as a surprise to those in the administration of Ballet Theatre who were aware that for some time Fernando Alonso and the assistant conductor had been urging dancers to become members of a Communist Party cell.

We have given up several opportunities to work now, and in the Fall, planning naturally to be with Ballet Theatre. But now we find ourselves with nothing to do. We cannot stay in Cuba until January without doing anything and there is no time to start anything else down here and be through by January. On the other hand we cannot fly to New York and get into just any show because of Alicia being a ballerina. It would be bad for her and bad for Ballet Theatre. I would love to take her to Europe to study there, but we cannot afford it.

Because of your position in the Ballet World, it would be comparatively easy for you to suggest something for us to do before Ballet Theatre starts operating again. We certainly would appreciate very much any advice you can give us.

What would Lucia Chase's "position in the Ballet World" enable her to do with comparative ease? Arrange for Alicia Alonso to be engaged as a ballerina by the Ballet Russe de Monte Carlo or by Balanchine and Kirstein, with whom the Alonsos had once worked? Miss Chase was unable to make any arrangements, but as it turned out, there was time to start something in Cuba. The Ballet Alicia Alonso was formed with a nucleus of a dozen dancers from Ballet Theatre and with Igor Youskevitch as premier danseur. It became a permanent company under the direction of Fernando and remained active even during periods when Alicia returned to dance with Ballet Theatre. Having performed originally under the patronage of the Batista dictatorship, the company was reorganized and renamed the Ballet de Cuba when Castro was converted to Communism (presumably not by Fernando). The suspension of Ballet Theatre activity for ten months was the best thing that ever happened to ballet in Cuba.

Happily for the dancers, most of them were able to find substitute employment when Ballet Theatre shut down; but fortunately for the future of the company, the stars and principal solists were unable to find permanent positions with the few ballet companies in existence at that time. Hence they were available to rejoin Ballet Theatre when it resumed rehearsals in March 1949. Maria Tallchief moved over temporarily from the New York City Ballet to substitute for Alonso in Tudor's JARDIN AUX LILAS (The Episode in His Past) and in her husband George Balanchine's THEME AND VARIATIONS, APOLLO, and restaged version of PRINCESS AURORA. On the other hand, the casualty list among the corps de ballet was more damaging: more than half of the dancers had to be replaced, and the replacements then rehearsed in the entire repertory. It was an arduous and expensive procedure (not perfectly accomplished) and it left Chase and Smith with the conviction, expressed on appropriate occasions in later years, that if Ballet Theatre closed down once more, it would never again be revived.

NORA KAYE, IN THE SPRING OF 1948, AS THE BLACK SWAN.

ALICIA ALONSO, THE RIVAL SWAN WHO HELD OUT FOR TOP BILLING.

Ballet Theatre was able to resume rehearsals in March 1949 because Dwight Deere Wiman's check for $25,000 and Blevins Davis' assumption of the presidency of Ballet Theatre Foundation encouraged Chase in the belief (optimistic and premature, as it turned out) that the day had arrived when others would share equally with her in the support of the company. Such a parceling of the financial burden had become even more imperative after the government ruled that she was not entitled to the tax deductions afforded other theatrical investors. Now whenever she dipped into capital to spend money in the support of Ballet Theatre, she was required to contribute an additional sum in taxes toward the support of the government. Davis assured her that this would not always be so, that the government would someday come to her aid. But in 1949 it was difficult to foresee the day when Roger Stevens (a contributor to Ballet Theatre Foundation) would preside over a government agency imposingly titled the National Foundation on the Arts and Humanities that would dispense millions in support of the ballet through its subdivision the National Endowment for the Arts.

Federal sponsorship of the arts was arrived at by a roundabout way that had little to do with the appreciation of art in governmental circles. In 1935 a group of theater men founded and obtained from Congress a charter for the American National Theatre and Academy. Despite its name, ANTA did not own or operate either a theater or a school; it acted as a service agency, passing on to regional theater groups throughout the country the know-how acquired by producers on Broadway. ANTA extended its activities abroad when Davis chose it as the sponsor of his European productions of HAMLET and PORGY AND BESS. When the time came for him to send Ballet Theatre to Europe (in August 1950), he once again chose ANTA as the sponsoring agency, for two reasons. The first was that his position as a Broadway producer was enhanced by association with ANTA's rich and distinguished theater men, like Roger Stevens, Vinton Freedley, Robert Dowling, and Joseph Verner Reed (as contrasted with the rich but commercial Shuberts). And, second, the sponsorship of Ballet Theatre by the Congress-chartered ANTA enabled his "personal friend" at the White House to officially sanction the tour, which he did in a letter printed in the souvenir program:

The enduring aspects of any civilization are rooted in its arts. May the time soon come when the free exchange of arts among all the countries of the world will be an important part of our lives.

It is with pride that we send the American National Ballet Theatre on its tour of the capitals of Europe under the sponsorship of the American National Theatre and Academy (ANTA). We look forward to welcoming an increasing number of the great dance groups and theatre companies from other nations to the United States of America.

HARRY S TRUMAN

Neither the government nor ANTA contributed more than moral support to the venture. The entire cost of the tour was borne by Davis. The same was true when the company

visited South America in 1951 and when it returned to Europe in 1953, this time with a souvenir-book letter from Dwight D. Eisenhower that concluded, "The American National Ballet Theatre sets forth on its tour abroad with our hope that it may convey through the medium of ballet some measure of understanding of America's cultural environment and inspiration." The good wishes from the White House were still unaccompanied by funds, but the last words of Eisenhower's letter gave a hint of changes to come. These changes were inspired, oddly enough, not by officials in Washington but by commissars in the Kremlin.

The thought occurred to someone in the Soviet propaganda bureau that the uncommitted nations of postwar Europe and the Middle East could be repelled from casting their lot with the capitalist United States if it was pictured as a crass, commercial country totally devoid of culture. Surely these nations would prefer to associate themselves with the Soviet Union, a country that would respect and encourage their artistic traditions, just as it honored and fostered its own. The Russians, in effect, employed culture as a weapon in the Cold War. Truman's appreciation of the arts was limited to his own piano playing and his daughter's singing. Eisenhower's knowledge of the arts was probably even less extensive, but he <u>did</u> know about weapons. In the waging of the Cold War, the Cultural Exchange Program* became an important adjunct. In the 1950s and 1960s a large share of the credit for Ballet Theatre's survival can be attributed to the periodic support it received in return for service to the Cultural Exchange Program. Later, under economic pressures, the State Department decided that its cultural offensive could be as effectively waged with small-range weapons: chamber-music ensembles, dance recital groups, and poetry readers. Symphony orchestras and ballet companies, the aircraft carriers of the culture war, were phased out. But meanwhile, the Congress (along with state and municipal governments) had grown accustomed to appropriating public funds for the support of the arts.

In the spring of 1950, however, government assistance remained a dream; the most that could be hoped for was State Department "cooperation." And on the civilian front even cooperation was withheld. Hurok presented the Ballet Russe de Monte Carlo at the Metropolitan in April and refused to release the house to Ballet Theatre in May. Consequently, the company was forced to return to the Center Theatre in Radio City, its birthplace, which had been altered in the meantime to accommodate ice shows. The alterations included a permanent ice rink, which projected over the pit and the first several rows of seats to form a no-man's land between the audience and the dancers. Nevertheless, Ballet Theatre offered a season that met with the approval of the critics and added two works to its permanent repertory, CAPRICHOS by Herbert Ross

*The Cultural Exchange Program of the State Department was established by the federal government in 1954. At first the services of ANTA were employed to administer the program, but in 1963 the State Department assumed full responsibility for managing the presentations abroad. The program is financed through appropriations by the Congress.

and DESIGNS WITH STRINGS by John Taras. William Dollar's version of Debussy's JEUX did not survive, nor did Antony Tudor's original creation NIMBUS, the last ballet Tudor created for Ballet Theatre until THE LEAVES ARE FADING, twenty-five years later.

Blevins Davis never found out whether his influence was potent enough to secure air force transportation for the company to Europe. In June 1950 the Korean War broke out, and all planes were diverted to the Pacific. On August 6 the company took off instead on a commercial airliner bound for Brussels. After a change of planes and an hour flight to Frankfurt, the company was met by army buses and transported to Wiesbaden. The cautious wartime administration of the opera there had removed all the scenery and costumes from the opera house and stored them in the deep subcellars of the adjoining concert hall, where they would be safer in the unlikely event that Allied shells or bombs should ever reach the fatherland. Then one disastrous night a firebomb penetrated through the many floors of the concert hall to the sub-basements below, and the scenery and costumes were destroyed. The opera house itself was not hit, but operas could not be performed without décor, and so the house became available for ballet.

The first ballet offered by Ballet Theatre was FANCY FREE, and John Kriza displayed an admirable sense of tact and diplomacy when he made an unauthorized alteration in Jerome Robbins' choreography, eliminating the mime sequence in which the American sailor braggingly demonstrates to his date how he shot down a marauding plane with his anti-aircraft gun. In midweek the air force flew the company to Berlin in a transport plane equipped with bucket seats suspended from the inner walls and with parachute tracks leading to the escape hatches. The pilot invited the dancers to visit the cockpit a few at a time, and at one point Nora Kaye emerged greenish-white in the face to scream, "Do you know who's flying the plane? Alicia Alonso! Do something about it!" The approach flight had to be made at an unusually low altitude to prevent spying on the Russian-controlled sector, and if the plane strayed out of the narrow corridor, it became fair game for the Russian gun emplacements. The company landed at the Templehof Airport, gave matinée and evening performances at the Neu Scala Theater, and, after a night in the air force barracks, flew back to Frankfurt.

At the conclusion of the four-month tour—which included appearances at the Edinburgh Festival and in England, Italy, Switzerland, Holland, Belgium, and France—Ballet Theatre returned to Berlin to perform for three days at the Titania Palast. Following this engagement the company got a further taste of the occupational hazards of touring abroad. Activity had been stepped up on the Korean front with the entrance of the Chinese into the war. Not only were all air force planes engaged in military activity but the unscheduled planes of every major airline had been hired to transport men and military supplies and were (continued on page 198)

THE FIFTIES

OFFENBACH IN THE UNDERWORLD
(LEFT)
NORA KAYE
HUGH LAING

(REAR LEFT)
RUTH ANN KOESUN
SCOTT DOUGLAS

(RIGHT)
LUPE SERRANO
JOHN KRIZA

MISS JULIE
(PREVIOUS PAGE)
TONI LANDER

THE VETERAN CHOREOGRAPHERS

During its first decade, thirty-two choreographers had contributed seventy-eight works to the Ballet Theatre repertory, but during the 1950s all but seven were engaged elsewhere or were temporarily devoid of choreographic inspiration. Of these seven, only de Mille, Nijinska, and Tudor created new ballets for the company, none of which survived more than one season. Of the works created for other companies and restaged for Ballet Theatre, only Taras' DESIGNS WITH STRINGS and de Mille's RODEO proved to be useful additions to the repertory, and only the latter continues to be performed by the company.

In 1950, for his first original work of the decade, Tudor offered NIMBUS, in which he eschewed his customary psychological approach and presented a simple, sentimental vignette of a working girl (Nora Kaye) and her fantasy romance with her Dream-Beau (Hugh Laing). His next contribution was not made until six years later, when he mounted a new production of OFFENBACH IN THE UNDERWORLD, staged two years previously by him for the National Ballet of Canada. It presented a dyspeptic view of the scene that Massine had examined more cheerfully in GÁITÉ PARISIENNE, and it employed the same Offenbach score (with minor alterations in the orchestration to avoid copyright infringement). The tone of the piece was set by the can-can dancers who appeared as intoxicated sluts.

NIMBUS
HUGH LAING

 RIB OF EVE
NORA KAYE

Since Ballet Theatre's inaugural season, de Mille had ineffectually urged on each successive director that he commission from her a ballet with a Civil War theme. Producers on Broadway had been more amenable to her suggestion, and the War Between the States had served as a background for dance interludes choreographed for musicals. Consequently, when Chase and Smith finally succumbed in 1952, she was able to integrate fragments from BLOOMER GIRL (and from ALLEGRO) into THE HARVEST ACCORDING, her first original work for Ballet Theatre since FALL RIVER LEGEND created more than four years earlier. Having committed herself to a score made up of selections from the compositions of Virgil Thomson, she thereafter reported to Samuel Lurie, Ballet Theatre's press agent, that she had made an unhappy discovery—she was unable to distinguish one piece of his music from another. With unaccustomed self-restraint, Lurie refrained from suggesting that Thomson might find the same to be true of her choreography.

In RIB OF EVE, created in 1956, de Mille temporarily abandoned the common folk to stage what she described in a program note as "a morality play" in which sophisticated intelligentsia reveal their shallowness at a cocktail party. The moral may well have been that dull people make for dull ballets.

At the outset of the 1950s, de Mille restaged her RODEO, created in 1942 for the Ballet Russe de Monte Carlo, and this proved to be of enduring value to Ballet Theatre. Its inclusion in the repertory of the same company that performed Loring's BILLY THE KID inevitably led to comparisons and raised such speculations as to who first conceived of horse-riding in balletic terms—who copied whom. A referee would have had to rule that de Mille was a cowgirl riding her pinto in solo recitals at the same time Loring was staging the ride of the posse in BILLY—it was a case of simultaneous though independent inspiration. But the general tone of the two ballets was in unmistakable contrast, indicative of the intellectual viewpoints of their creators. De Mille characteristically conceived of life in the West as a soap opera, in which, against all odds, the cowgirl gets her man. Loring and his co-author, Lincoln Kirstein, visualized the outlaw Billy as an allegorical figure in the progress across the continent, powerless to defy the forces of evil led by the villain, appearing in various guises under the somewhat pretentious name Nemesis.

RODEO DOROTHY SCOTT, PAULA LLOYD, RUTH ANN KOESUN, JOHN KRIZA, ALLYN McLERIE, SCOTT DOUGLAS, ERIC BRAUN, JAMES MITCHELL, CHARLYNE BAKER.

RODEO (CENTER GROUP) SCOTT DOUGLAS, JAMES MITCHELL, ERIC BRAUN, JOHN KRIZA, ENRIQUE MARTINEZ, ALLYN McLERIE, ANN BARLOW, FERNAND NAULT.

RODEO JOHN KRIZA, JENNY WORKMAN. (OPPOSITE PAGE) JACK BEABER, RALPH MC WILLIAMS, LILA POPPER, IRMA GRANT, LIANE PLANE, VERNON LUSBY, SCOTT DOUGLAS, JAN HOLLER.

Loring returned to Ballet Theatre in the 1950s in connection with a telecast of BILLY THE KID on the OMNIBUS program sponsored by the Ford Foundation over the CBS network. Fearing that the intellectual approach to the saga might be beyond the understanding of their viewers, the producers engaged Loring to deliver a commentary on the ballet as it was being performed. The response of the viewers was encouraging, and Loring was commissioned to create especially for television a new ballet, THE CAPITAL OF THE WORLD, based on Ernest Hemingway's short story. In lieu of a commentary, the producers this time presented a dramatic version of the story immediately preceding the ballet. Perhaps to avoid the double presentation of the same plot, Loring decided it must be altered in the ballet version. Over the protest of almost everyone, including A. E. Hotchner, who represented Hemingway (the author himself maintained an attitude of benign indifference to the entire venture), Loring introduced new characters and changed the locale from a seedy bullfighters' hotel to a tailor shop. The hero, Paco, still dreamed of

becoming a bullfighter but was killed not by a sword but by a pair of tailor's shears. The tailor-shop characters proved far less colorful than Hemingway's bullfighters and the viewer response was discouraging. As a consequence, the ballet world, which might have been able to look to the wealthy television companies as potential sources of funds for the production of new ballets, could no longer do so. Following the never-repeated telecast, Ballet Theatre performed the work on stage for little more than a season.

Other veteran choreographers returned to Ballet Theatre to stage works they had created for other companies. Anton Dolin offered VARIATIONS FOR FOUR, a sort of male version of PAS DE QUATRE. John Taras' DESIGNS WITH STRINGS served to introduce Erik Bruhn to American audiences. David Lichine's THE SPHINX survived for a few performances after the dress rehearsal when Nora Kaye fell from a rope ladder and landed head-first on the stage of the old Metropolitan Opera House.

THE SEARCH FOR CHOREOGRAPHERS

When Ballet Theatre found that to replenish its repertory it could no longer rely solely on choreographers who had made contributions during the early years, it enlisted others of proven skill and instituted a search for dancers with untested choreographic ambitions. From the former category, it chose William Dollar, who had created his first ballet in 1936 for Ballet Caravan and had danced in LES SYLPHIDES in Ballet Theatre's opening performance. From 1950 on, he continued to produce works for the company until a bone ailment ended his choreographic activity. In the second category, Herbert Ross proved equally prolific until he abandoned the ballet for film directing in Hollywood, where he became a millionaire—a status he would never have achieved in the world of ballet.

Dollar's choreography continued to be affected by his early association with George Balanchine, but his most enduring success, LE COMBAT, was created under the influence of Roland Petit, for whose company he choreographed a pas de deux on an incident from Tasso's "Jerusalem Delivered," in which the Christian knight Tancredi duels with the Saracen girl Clorinda. With three added Crusaders, the work was performed by the New York City Ballet under the title THE DUEL; later, when it was acquired by Ballet Theatre as a vehicle for Melissa Hayden on her return to the company in 1953, it was renamed THE COMBAT. Still later the role of Clorinda provided Lupe Serrano with one of her greatest successes.

While Herbert Ross was creating his first ballets for Ballet Theatre, he was simultaneously (and profitably) choreographing Broadway musicals and television shows. They may have affected the nature of his balletic works —he created ballets as though he were doing penance for his commercial success, employing "difficult" scores and obscure, weighty librettos. In his first and still most successful work, he animated the Goya CAPRICHOS etchings to music by Bartók. His second success, THE MAIDS, from a play by Jean Genet to Darius Milhaud's Concerto for Percussion and Small Orchestra, was presented with the program note, "Genet suggested the maids be played by two boys, hoping by this device to confuse the audience, and thereby to force upon them the effect of ambiguity which terrorizes the maids." Though Genet was probably more concerned with disguising from the censors the true nature of his study in male sado-masochism, Ross went along with his suggestion, and, as it turned out, audiences were confused.

THE COMBAT
LUPE SERRANO

CAPRICHOS JENNY WORKMAN, CHARLYNE BAKER

(TOP LEFT AND RIGHT) JOHN KRIZA, RUTH ANN KOESUN. (TOP CENTER) BAKER, MARY BURR, PETER GLADKE, WORKMAN. (BOTTOM) MELISSA HAYDEN, ERIC BRAUN, KELLY BROWN; ALICIA ALONSO.

Even when Ross employed more popular music to accompany the expression of more natural emotions, he felt compelled to intellectualize, to rise to the level of pure Art. When he was persuaded that a sensually stimulating pas de deux could be inspired by the "Liebestod" from Wagner's TRISTAN UND ISOLDE, his research led him to Thomas Mann's "Tristan." The result was not only affected but, to John Martin, repugnant: "A tuberculosis sanatorium is not exactly a happy milieu to begin with, and the sight of two dying invalids in a grotesque attempt at fulfillment of erotic passion is repellent to a degree."

TRISTAN
(TOP LEFT)
NORA KAYE
ERIK BRUHN

THE THIEF WHO LOVED A GHOST
(BOTTOM LEFT AND CENTER)
LUCIA CHASE
RUTH ANN KOESUN
JOHN KRIZA

PAEAN
(TOP CENTER)
LUPE SERRANO
MICHAEL MAULE
SHARON ENOCH

(BOTTOM RIGHT)
SALLIE WILSON
SUSAN BORREE
ELISABETH CARROLL
ENRIQUE MARTINEZ
RAY BARRA
LEO DUGGAN

THE MAIDS
(TOP RIGHT)
LOREN HIGHTOWER
PAUL OLSON

Dollar and Ross between them added thirteen ballets to the repertory during the 1950s. Another work was that of the modern choreographer Valerie Bettis, whose A STREETCAR NAMED DESIRE achieved its most newsworthy performance when Nora Kaye's flying fist accidentally knocked Igor Youskevitch unconscious. And Carmelita Maracci assembled a number of her Spanish recital pieces to form a ballet entitled CIRCO DE ESPAÑA.

Although the 1950s was not a period in which Ballet Theatre accumulated masterpieces, it was by no means devoid of choreographic activity. At the Phoenix Theatre in two workshop series and in another with the title American Ballet Theatre Previews, the company presented twenty-four works by eighteen choreographers, all of whom have gone on to exert an influence on ballet in the United States. Included in the roster were Alicia Alonso, Erik Bruhn, John Butler, Robert Joffrey, Katherine Litz, Fernand Nault, Donald Saddler, Job Sanders, George Skibine, and Anna Sokolow.

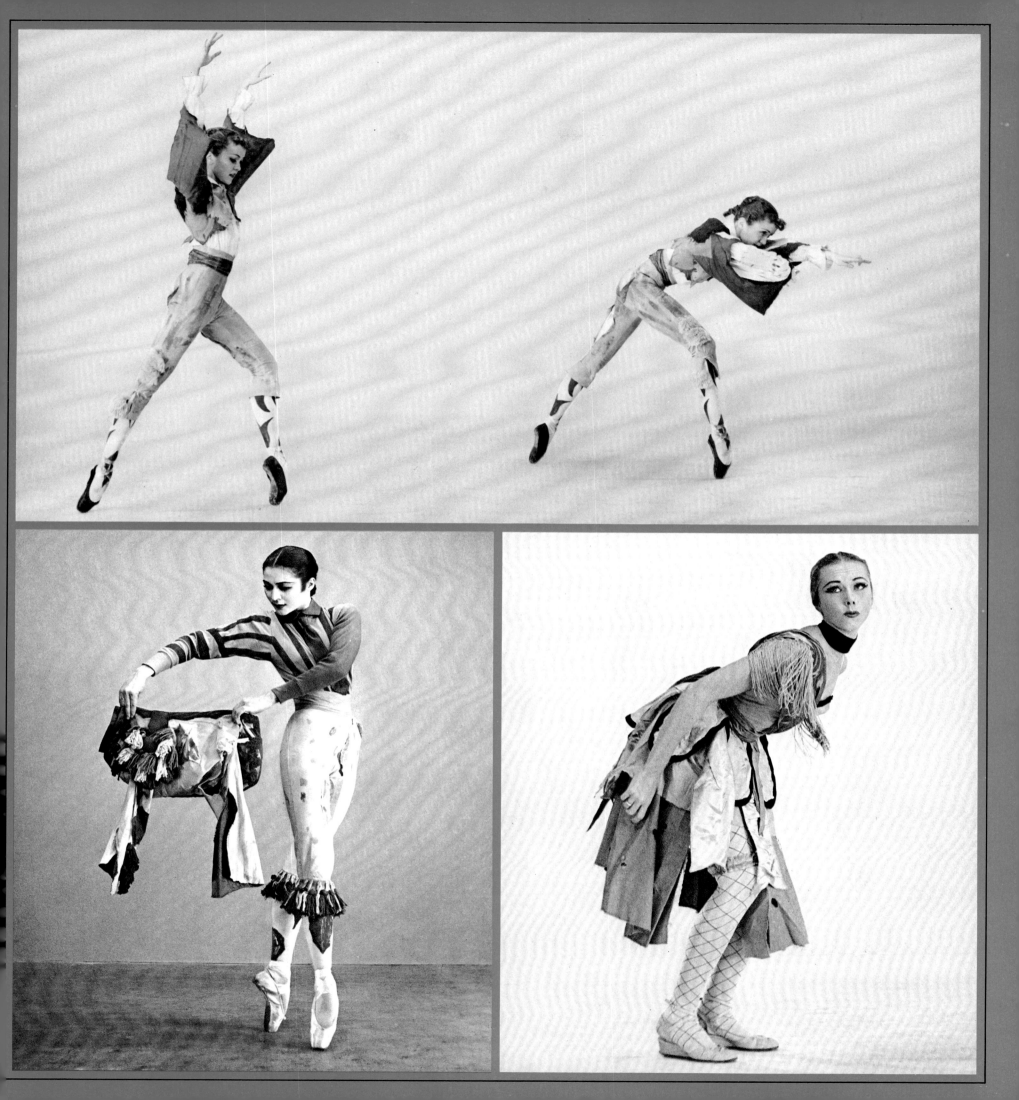

LE JEUNE HOMME ET LA MORT JEAN BABILÉE

CONTRIBUTIONS FROM ABROAD

The desperation of Ballet Theatre's search for new choreographers was alleviated to some extent when the return to normal conditions following the conclusion of the war once more permitted the free exchange of talent between continents. In the 1950s Ballet Theatre embarked on five tours abroad, during which it commissioned foreign choreographers to stage ballets and engaged foreign stars to dance in them.

Roland Petit came to New York to stage his LES DEMOISELLES DE LA NUIT, bringing with him Colette Marchand to dance the leading role with John Kriza. Jean Babilée and his wife, Nathalie Philippart, arrived to appear in Petit's LE JEUNE HOMME ET LA MORT. Babilée, who had fought with the French Underground during the German occupation of Paris, was the precursor of the image of reckless abandon (on and off stage) that Rudolf Nureyev was to project so forcefully a decade later. He remained with the company for a second season, during which he staged his own TIL EULENSPIEGEL and L'AMOUR ET SON AMOUR. No stage photographs of the latter appear to have survived, which is especially regrettable because the ballet was performed with a backdrop intriguingly designed by Jean Cocteau. However, a story concerning the setting is still told. During a performance at the Opera House in Chicago, a yellow balloon escaped from the adjacent playhouse stage on which a children's circus was being presented. It found its way through an upper areaway to the flies above the opera stage, and drifted down into view just as the curtain was about to descend on L'AMOUR ET SON AMOUR. When Babilée saw the intruder balloon, he reacted violently, suspecting sabotage. On the other hand, Emmet Dedman, critic for the Sun Times, attributed its presence to French finesse: "The settings are almost overwhelming, brilliantly modern in style, lavish in their use of color, ingeniously lighted by Peggy Clark, and saved from pretentiousness by a whimsical balloon that had its own moment of stardom."

L'AMOUR ET SON AMOUR
NATHALIE PHILIPPART
JEAN BABILÉE

MISS JULIE
VIOLETTE VERDY
ERIK BRUHN

(OPPOSITE PAGE)
GLEN TETLEY
TONI LANDER

At the conclusion of its 1950 European tour, Ballet Theatre was detained in Berlin (because commercial planes were being diverted to Korea) and was still there when the Royal Swedish Ballet followed it into the Tatania Palast. Those who attended performances of MISS JULIE recommended it to Lucia Chase and Oliver Smith, who acquired it for their repertory in 1958. Similarly, in the course of its 1956 tour, the directors became familiar in London with the work of Kenneth MacMillan, a tyro choreographer for the English Royal Ballet, and they commissioned him to create WINTER'S EVE and later JOURNEY.

The international character Ballet Theatre was acquiring evidenced itself not only in the foreign additions to its repertory but also in the procedures followed in executing the productions. MISS JULIE was rehearsed in Dublin by the Swedish Birgit Cullberg, who chose as her ballerina the French Violette Verdy and as her premier danseur the Danish Erik Bruhn, and for the premiere in New York's Metropolitan Opera House, Cullberg supplied scenery and costumes manufactured in Stockholm. WINTER'S EVE was first rehearsed in Rome by the English MacMillan while the décor was being designed in London by the Greek Nicholas Georgiadis. The scenery was then painted in Paris and the costumes executed in Monte Carlo, where the company continued rehearsals in the basement of the Casino. The world premiere took place at the Teatro Nacional de São Carlos in Lisbon.

Even the staging of works by Ballet Theatre's own choreographers was accomplished in an international milieu. The Ballet Theater production of THE COMBAT was designed by the Russian Georges Wakhevitch, a resident of Germany, and was given its first performance at London's Covent Garden; the premiere of Ballet Theatre's production of RODEO took place at the Hessisches Staatstheater in Wiesbaden; and the pas de deux from SYLVIA premiered at Rio de Janeiro's Teatro Municipal.

MISS JULIE GLEN TETLEY, TONI LANDER. (OPPOSITE PAGE TOP) ERIK BRUHN, VIOLETTE VERDY. (OPPOSITE PAGE BOTTOM) BRUCE MARKS, TONI LANDER.

WINTER'S EVE
JOHN KRIZA
NORA KAYE

unavailable for charter. Consequently, the company was stranded for a week in Berlin, surrounded by Russian-occupied territory and forever apprehensive that the Soviets might take advantage of the U.S. involvement in Korea to seize the rest of the city.

Over the years it began to appear that wherever Ballet Theatre went, there went trouble, a conclusion that can be supported by a few selected incidents:

In 1955 Ballet Theatre arrived in Buenos Aires two days before the revolution that ousted Peron. The company spent a fortnight isolated in the Hotel Claridge—one evening in the cellar when it appeared the ships in the harbor were bombarding the city (in fact, the revolutionaries were attacking the secret-police headquarters, two blocks from the hotel).

In 1956, on the day of Ballet Theatre's opening in Athens, the city was in turmoil because a group of Greek partisans were scheduled to be hanged that night on Cyprus. The authorities would not permit a change in the opening program in order to eliminate FALL RIVER LEGEND, featuring the hanging of Lizzie Borden. As it turned out, the apolitical audience accepted the stage hanging with phlegmatic calm.

On the same tour, a scheduled engagement in Israel was canceled when the British occupied Suez (a $5,000 deposit on the theater was not refunded since the Israelis denied that force majeure had prevented the appearance). A later appearance in Iran was also canceled when, after the Soviets threatened to bomb England, the American ambassador in Teheran decided that the plane carrying the company from Beirut might accidentally stray over hostile Russian territory. The company was able to continue the tour by returning to Italy, where it filled the engagements of the Moiseyev Ballet (which the Italian authorities, disapproving of the Russian stance vis-à-vis Suez, had canceled).

In 1958 Ballet Theatre's manager went to bed after the last performance at the Palm Beach Casino in Cannes and was awakened by a phone call from the driver of the truck that was transporting all the properties of the company, including the private wardrobe trunks, to Lausanne. The truck had burned, and absolutely nothing had survived except one charred souvenir program. Substitute costumes, tights, and toe shoes were rushed to Brussels by ballet companies in England and on the Continent, and five days later Ballet Theatre opened on schedule at the United States Pavilion at the World's Fair. (One last-minute hitch did threaten to delay the premiere—American-style jock straps, known in the ballet world as dance belts, had been flown in from New York but were being detained in customs. An incredulous embassy official was given an ultimatum: "You tell the ambassador that unless he arranges for the release of the straps there'll be no show.")

For the 1955 tour of South America, the State Department had agreed to supply sufficient funds to cover the costs of transportation. At the last moment it cut its contribution but insisted that all scheduled cities be visited. Ballet Theatre completed the tour only because South American governments and airlines allowed it to charter planes at illegal rates that ignored international agreements and to pay with cheaper local currency. At the conclusion of the tour, in São Paulo, Brazil, the company had run out of money and was stranded while it shopped around for an airline that would both offer a reduced charter rate and accept an American check. After several days, a midnight call was received from a Brazilian airline that would transport the company to New York at a low rate if the members could be at the airport early the following morning. The company manager got on the phone to the dancers scattered in various hotels and, at that hour, in various nightclubs, and all agreed to the rush departure, so anxious were they to get home after the four-month tour. As the chartered Constellation flew over the Brazilian jungles en route to New York, an airline representative was asked how he could accept so low a charter fee. He replied, "The plane has to go to the States anyway for major repairs and overhaul, so it isn't really costing us anything."

IN EDINBURGH, KAYE, KRIZA, ALONSO, YOUSKEVITCH, AND MOYLAN POSE FOR FESTIVAL PUBLICITY ON THE LEDGES OF THE CASTLE.

The emergencies caused by the Korean War were costly to Blevins Davis; the estimated loss on the 1950 tour of $50,000 was increased to $98,000 when the company was required to pay its own transportation costs and expenses during the idle week in Berlin. But from a long-term point of view, the tour was a productive investment: it bolstered the company's status at home, and in Europe added the approval of a second dance capital, Paris, to that of London in 1946. After the first performance at the Palais de Chaillot, Le Presse reported, "It is an absolutely remarkable company. It is impossible to imagine a troupe of fifty dancers with more poise, more distinction, and more perfect technique." Even more useful was Oliver Merlin's appreciation in Le Monde: "Jerome Robbins and the Ballet Theatre have enabled us to get to know America."

In Germany the Communist papers even aided Ballet Theatre indirectly by following the official party line: the critic

of Neue Zeit wrote of RODEO, "We left the theatre deeply disappointed because these people [the Americans], even when they dance, cannot offer anything but emptiness and canned erotica. . . . How deeply buried in these people is any form of human civilization when even dancers are like terrified children, tastelessly dressed and laughing only from a misguided sense of humor!" Who in Europe could take with any seriousness a review that deplored a romp so harmlessly gay as RODEO because its ranch characters showed less interest in fulfilling state production quotas than in rolling in the hay with jean-clad tomboys? Not surprisingly, RODEO proved a more persuasive propaganda weapon than the Soviet's equivalent, PATH OF THUNDER, which contrasted idealized collective-farm life in the U.S.S.R. with master-slave conditions on plantations abroad. The State Department and the United States Information Service became convinced that ballet, unhampered as it is by any language barriers, was an ideal medium through which American culture could challenge the boasted superiority of the Soviets. As a consequence, during the next two decades American Ballet Theatre was sent abroad to perform in forty-two countries on four continents, including, when diplomatic relations improved, seven cities in the Soviet Union. With the 1950 European tour, the company could be said to have entered the era of foreign aid.

This era was not one in which foreign countries aided Ballet Theatre financially, though in some instances they did help indirectly by making available their state-supported theaters and orchestras. They also helped Ballet Theatre to obtain aid from its own government by offering themselves as targets for America's propaganda activities. In the course of its tours, Ballet Theatre began to discover foreign dancers and choreographers—and they discovered Ballet Theatre. The dancer Erik Bruhn was a case in point. Having trained with the Royal Danish Ballet since childhood, he was anxious to broaden his sphere of activities beyond the narrow confines of Denmark. In 1947 he obtained a leave of absence to appear in the Edinburgh Festival with an English company called the Metropolitan Ballet, partnering the Bulgarian ballerina Sonia Arova in the ballet DESIGNS WITH STRINGS, which John Taras had created for the company. In 1948 Blevins Davis, who was then presenting his HAMLET in Denmark, saw Bruhn dance and recommended him enthusiastically to Miss Chase. Davis made a tentative offer, but it was necessarily vague until confirmed by Chase, and so Bruhn did not take it too seriously. Subsequently, when he and Arova received an invitation to appear for a season with the opera in Bordeaux, France, Bruhn obtained another leave of absence from the Danish Ballet. When he arrived in Bordeaux, he found that Arova had backed out of the engagement. Returning to Copenhagen, he stopped off in Paris, and when he passed the Hôtel Vendôme, where Davis customarily stayed, he dropped in on the chance Davis might be there and have further word from Miss Chase. Davis was not in residence at the time but

had left with the concierge an envelope to be delivered to Bruhn should he ever inquire after him. It contained a contract signed by Lucia Chase, who had delayed sending it until she could receive an evaluation on Bruhn from Tudor, who that season occupied the post of ballet master to the Royal Swedish Ballet. Almost literally, Bruhn was on the next plane to New York.

The addition of Bruhn to Ballet Theatre's roster was only the first of a number of personnel changes that were attributable, directly or indirectly, to the resumption of international cultural contacts following the war. Another instance was the departure from the company of Hugh Laing and Diana Adams. While preparations were under way for the 1950 European tour, it was agreed by everyone, including Laing, that a third ballerina must be engaged to back up Nora Kaye and Alicia Alonso. Even under normal circumstances four months of touring in foreign countries involves various health hazards; traveling in countries whose housing and sanitary

THE AIR FORCE PHOTOGRAPHED ALONSO IN FRANKFURT; OUTSIDE CANNES, THE COMPANY'S PROPERTIES WERE REDUCED TO ASHES.

facilities had only recently been destroyed or damaged by shells and bombs would present even greater risks. As Laing wrote in a letter to Chase, "We both realize the difficulties and responsibilities that such a tour in Europe presents and we fully understand the need for a third ballerina, if for nothing else than to safeguard the company against accidents." The "we" was significant and the understanding limited. Laing was then married to Diana Adams and was naturally concerned that with the engagement of a third ballerina, Adams' share of ballerina roles would be reduced. He therefore requested that certain commitments be made in advance, and later infused these requests with the force of an ultimatum. Included in his demands were the commitments that Adams be cast as the ballerina in every fourth performance of THEME AND VARIATIONS, that she be assigned a role in APOLLO, and that she be guaranteed "that she would have UNDERTOW in Paris, London, and Italy." On the surface these were the reasonable and selfless requests of a husband protecting his wife's interests. In reality, they were not quite as reasonable as they seemed and were far from easy to grant. The dancer chosen to be third ballerina was Mary Ellen Moylan, who had been a protégée of George Balanchine ever since, as a child, she received her ballet training at the School of American Ballet. The roles in the Ballet Theatre repertory most adaptable to her talents were in Balanchine's THEME AND VARIATIONS and APOLLO, which, in any case, she would have to share with Kaye and Alonso. If she were now told that she would have to share them with Adams as well, she would have seen little inducement to abandon the Ballet Russe de Monte Carlo, in which she was the second ballerina, even though the company was tottering close to collapse. Further, the proposal of a rigid rotation of roles was impractical, since the fourth performance of THEME AND VARIATIONS in Europe might fall on the opening night in Paris. And, finally, the demand with regard to Adams' appearances in UNDERTOW was not as selfless as it appeared. To Laing the number of performances of UNDERTOW was a matter of great <u>personal</u> concern; it was the only ballet in the repertory in which he performed the undisputed starring role, overshadowing those of participating ballerinas. Arrangements had not yet been made for UNDERTOW to be presented in Italy—and there was a strong possibility that they never would be. The ballet is susceptible to a number of interpretations, not the least credible being that it investigates the reasons why a young man should grow up to become a homosexual who murders a predatory female. In 1946 the ballet had been accepted in London, and it would doubtless be taken in stride by Paris, but could anyone <u>guarantee</u> that Italian impresarios would be permitted to show it in their theaters? Chase was advised that she could make no such binding commitment, and, not receiving it, the Laings picked up their passports, withdrew from the company, and soon joined the New York City Ballet.

The cases of Bruhn and the Laings not only exemplify the changes in Ballet Theatre's personnel during the postwar period but also point up the reasons why dancers switch companies under normal circumstances. Dancers have become and have remained dancers because they enjoy dancing; otherwise it is inconceivable that they should have chosen to pursue so arduous and short-lived a career. It follows that the company that can furnish them with the greatest number of roles—and opportunities to dance them—must automatically become the company of their choice. This is as it should be. Those who have consumed their youth in strenuous physical training in sweat-odored studios owe it to themselves to arrange their brief professional lives in such a way that they enjoy as often as possible the thrill and glamour of performing on stage to the plaudits of a hopefully packed house. To accomplish this, they must go where the roles are, and this remains the principal reason why dancers change companies. But it is too mundane and pragmatic a reason to make for

IN VIENNA, FANCY FREE WAS ONCE MORE PHOTOGRAPHED, THIS TIME BY THE EMBASSY PHOTOGRAPHER: CHRISTINE MAYER, ERIC BRAUN, JOHN KRIZA, ENRIQUE MARTINEZ.

ERIK BRUHN IN GISELLE.

interesting media accounts or provocative dinner conversation, and so other explanations are advanced. The defections of the dancers from the Soviet Union, for example, are variously accounted for: it is said that they sought more freedom of expression, that they yearned for new experiences with fresh forms of choreography, that they were covetous of the larger "capitalistic" fees, that they wished to escape from the social repressions of their motherland, et cetera. In fact, if the dancers considered these things at all, they must have regarded them as no more than fringe benefits. The decisive factor was that abroad they could dance more often. In their home opera houses (the Kirov and the Bolshoi) ballet is presented on an average of not more than twice a week, and the casting of ballets is controlled largely by a rigid system of seniority preferences. This inevitably gives rise to a situation where a young dancer with ambitions to dance the role of Prince Siegfried in SWAN LAKE, for example, can estimate the number of times he will be given the opportunity to perform it by dividing the half-dozen performances scheduled each year by the four or five senior premiers danseurs who are lined up with claims of precedence. Before defecting, Nureyev averaged little more than several performances a month at the Kirov. When he appeared with the Canadian National Ballet in New York in 1973 he danced six performances each week. He and his fellow dancers from the Kirov left Russia so they could dance more often, and in choosing a Western company with which to become affiliated they did not examine its traditions, its artistic policies, or even its credit ratings. They examined its ability and willingness to provide a steady flow of roles and performances. It was this consideration that accounted for another defection from the Ballet Theatre ranks in 1951.

During the company's 1950 European tour, Lucia Chase began negotiating contracts with the dancers for the 1951 season. Nora Kaye inexplicably withheld her signature, but assured Chase that all was well, and gave permission for her name to be printed on the company roster and for her picture to appear in the souvenir program. On the company's arrival in New York, she danced in its single performance at the Metropolitan on January 9 and in the first engagement of the tour, in Baltimore, on January 15. She then returned to New York and joined the New York City Ballet. Her action inevitably stimulated much talk and conjecture in the ballet world. William Fields, Ballet Theatre's press agent and booking manager, wrote Miss Chase, "Charlie Payne suspects, and I am inclined to agree with his belief, that the Hurok hand is evident in the Nora Kaye and other New York City Ballet Company developments." Later Miss Chase received another of Hurok's highly literate letters:

I hear from a fairly reliable source that you called a special meeting of your company to tell them that Nora Kaye left Ballet Theatre at my instigation, and that I did this because of my plans to tour the City Center Ballet . . . for your information, I have no plans whatever for booking the City Center Ballet at this moment.

There the matter rested and all remained conjecture until 1973, when Lincoln Kirstein's reminiscences were published in diary form. He recalled that in 1950 "Sol Hurok offered us a national tour, which we might take as a basic commercial accolade." But the question of Hurok's machinations becomes academic when it is recognized that Kaye's decision to join the New York City Ballet was dictated by a single, simple consideration: New York City Ballet was where her choreographers were, the choreographers who would create new roles for her.

By 1950 the New York City Ballet, Jerome Robbins, and Antony Tudor had all established residences in New York. The company was installed in the City Center and, as a matter of principle, was avoiding out-of-town tours. Robbins was working in the musical theater, and the time he could devote to the ballet had to be meshed with his Broadway schedule. Tudor remained in New York to execute Ballet Theatre's agreement with the Metropolitan to produce the ballets for operas and to operate the Ballet Theatre–Metropolitan Ballet School, a venture that proved as unproductive as the Balanchine-Metropolitan association in the 1930s, and for many of the same reasons. Balanchine in 1950 had at his disposal a company, a theater, and an almost unlimited amount of rehearsal time. Since he required only a small portion of these rehearsal periods for his own creations, he was happy to offer the excess to Robbins and Tudor, whose appetites for rehearsal hours were insatiable. They joined his company. Nora Kaye, weary of touring, had also become a New York resident and was acutely aware that in the City Center studios on West Fifty-sixth Street two of her best friends and choreographers were waiting to create new ballets for her. She needed no advice from Hurok to help her decide which of the American companies was directed with the soundest artistic policy—indeed there was no time even to think about it. She couldn't keep her choreographers waiting.

BLEVINS DAVIS SAW THIS PERFORMANCE OF BOURNONVILLEANA WITH MARGRETHE SCHANNE AND BRUHN, AND INVITED HIM TO JOIN BALLET THEATRE.

Of the other causes of personnel-shifting among companies, one of them is motherhood, either in the approaching or baby-sitting phase, which makes preferable a resident, non-touring company. It was this condition that contributed to the departures from Ballet Theatre at that time of Janet Reed, Melissa Hayden, and Barbara Fallis (Mrs. Richard Thomas, who was carrying the future John Boy when Ballet Theatre sailed for Europe). Migrations also occur when a choreographer leaves to form his own company, taking with him a nucleus of his dance disciples. This was the case with Roland Petit, who in 1944 left the Paris Opéra to form the Ballets des Champs-Elysées with his father's financial backing. He took with him a number of dancers, including Jean Babilée and Colette Marchand.

In 1947 Petit lost control of the company and of the ballets he had created for it; he then formed the Ballets de Paris de Roland Petit. During the new company's first season in 1948, he produced LES DEMOISELLES DE LA NUIT, which

immediately attracted the attention of Chase and Smith. The proprietary rights to the ballets and the contractual obligations of the dancers had become so involved that it was not until 1951 that the French contingent and their ballets could be placed under contract to Ballet Theatre. Even then all legal details were not settled, and the company was sued by Georges Wahkevitch for the unauthorized use of his scenery designs for LE JEUNE HOMME ET LA MORT, which became the first of Petit's ballets to be presented when it was given its New York premiere at the Metropolitan on April 9, 1951, with Babilée as the Young Man and his wife, Nathalie Philippart, as Death. It was followed by LES DEMOISELLES DE LA NUIT, with Colette Marchand and John Kriza in the leads, and by L'AMOUR ET SON AMOUR, Babilée's first choreographic creation, with himself as Cupid and Philippart as Psyche. The couple returned the following year, when Babilée staged his TIL EULENSPIEGEL, with himself as Til and Ruth Ann Koesun as Nell.

The French ballets provided a new experience for American dancers. They had been created in the tradition of Diaghilev's last decade, when scenarios were written for, and accepted by, the choreographer (in these instances written by Jean Anouilh and Jean Cocteau). The choreography of Petit's and Babilée's ballets offered little that was new and few challenges; its principal function was to illustrate and enact the librettos. As such, it cannot be said to have exerted any appreciable influence on choreography by Americans (nor did the works of other European choreographers who followed, among them Birgit Cullberg, Harald Lander, and Serge Lifar). Young American choreographers continued to be inspired and influenced by the works of Fokine, Tudor, Balanchine, and Robbins. But the imported ballets served a limited function: they provided vehicles for the guest stars and filled the demand for novelties.

But there were those in the press who saw in the introduction of the French stars and ballets a change in Ballet Theatre's artistic policy—one that placed less emphasis on the American nature of the company. Though this was not true, Chase and Smith had to give it serious consideration because the company could derive benefits from the State Department's Cultural Relations program only if it remained an unquestionably <u>American</u> company. Therefore by way of retort, Payne coined for the souvenir program and the Foundation Newsletter the totally meaningless epithet "American Ballet Theatre, American in Spirit—International in Scope." By 1975, when he would have thought that everyone agreed there was no such thing as American ballet but only ballet choreographed and danced by Americans, he was amazed to find the New York Times seriously recalling the epithet, as though "American in Spirit—International in Scope" was any more meaningful than "Good to the Last Drop"!

THE BABILÉES IN LE JEUNE HOMME ET LA MORT (TOP LEFT) LED THE FRENCH INVASION IN THE FIFTIES AND WERE FOLLOWED BY CLAUDE BESSEY (OPPOSITE PAGE) IN HELEN OF TROY.

The decade of the fifties in Ballet Theatre history might well be termed an era of brinkmanship or of experimentation in survival. Although the company presented a season in each of the calendar years, in some of those seasons it gave no more than a single performance in New York, and even then not always in a suitable theater. With the resumption of international cultural contacts in the postwar period, Ballet Theatre encountered increasing competition. Beginning with 1949 and the first visit of the Sadler's Wells Ballet to New York, S. Hurok had to resort only occasionally to an American-based company in order to exercise his exclusive option on the Metropolitan during the weeks that preceded and followed the regular season of opera. It was only when foreign companies (the Royal Danish Ballet, the Moiseyev, the Bolshoi, the Kirov) were not free to come to America that he filled in with Ballet Theatre or the Ballet Russe de Monte Carlo. Similarly, while the New York City Ballet's occupancy of the City Center Theatre was not maintained on an exclusive basis, the schedules of the two companies were such that the theater was never available at a time when Ballet Theatre could have used it. Thus in the twelve years preceding the opening of the New York State Theater in 1964, Ballet Theatre appeared in a proper theater (the Metropolitan) for only ninety-nine performances, an average of eight a year. Even counting performances on unsuitable stages (in Lewisohn Stadium, the Fifty-fourth Street Theatre, the Broadway Theatre, and the Delacorte Theater in Central Park), the average number of appearances in New York still did not exceed twelve a year.

As a result, a whole generation of balletgoers in New York remained virtually unaware of the continued existence of Ballet Theatre. To all but the most avid balletomanes ballet had become something that was performed by the New York City Ballet in long and regular seasons at the City Center or by foreign companies at the Metropolitan. Meanwhile, Ballet Theatre, thanks to its transcontinental tours, kept its name alive across the country, but its prestige suffered because of the traditional resistance of out-of-town audiences to any attraction that has not received the endorsement of New York critics.

Ballet Theatre's experiments were sometimes undertaken for the purpose of finding a new forum in New York, but often their only aim was to provide employment for the dancers. One of the earliest experiments fulfilled both purposes. In the 1950s the era of the great "movie palaces," where stage shows were presented in conjunction with first-run films, was drawing to a close. Movie palaces, including the Warner Brothers Theatre on Broadway, faced demolition or a division into two theaters of smaller capacity. (In 1977 only Radio City Music Hall was still operating.) In April 1952, in one of its last desperate attempts to lure New Yorkers away from their television sets, the management of the Warner's engaged Ballet Theatre to function as the complete stage show. The program chosen consisted of RODEO and exerpts from PRINCESS AURORA, a total of fifty-five minutes of dancing. This unique stage show was performed four times a day between five showings of the unmemorable low-budget film MARA MARU, starring Errol Flynn and Ruth Roman. The

entire company, including all the principals, participated, divided into two groups, each of which performed twice a day during the sixteen consecutive days of the engagement. Had the ballet been teamed with a hit picture, the combination might have drawn capacity audiences. As it was, Ballet Theatre was accorded critical approval but the experiment provided no indication that ballet's appeal was strong enough commercially to save a movie palace from extinction.

PAULA LLOYD, RUTH ANN KOESUN, ERIK BRUHN, JENNY WORKMAN, AND JOHN KRIZA STUDY WARNER THEATRE POSTER.

In another of its experiments Ballet Theatre hoped to emulate Diaghilev's early success as a shill for the Monte Carlo gambling casino. In 1952, the manager of the Last Frontier Hotel, influenced perhaps by a visit to Monaco, engaged Ballet Theatre as the star attraction of the nightclub attached to his casino. Competitors considered him, to phrase it as politely as possible, an incredible innovator. At his dinner and supper shows he presented a reduced Ballet Theatre company in FANCY FREE, a classical pas de deux, and excerpts from RODEO. To everyone's amazement, the shows sold out. His competitors began to have second thoughts. Perhaps a ballet group, considerably less expensive than a superstar, might perform as effectively the functions of a shill. But soon they noticed that though the dining tables were crowded, the gambling tables were deserted. The diners proved to be local or touring family parties who dined well, drank little, and, without stopping to try their hand at the dice, retired early to put the children to bed.

Although Ballet Theatre must be said to have failed its audition as a come-on for the crap tables of Las Vegas, nevertheless it was later invited to perform the role of séducteur to the roulette tables at Monte Carlo. Over Christmas of 1956 it performed for two weeks in La Salle Garnier, rehearsing in studios on the floor below the casino where, a quarter of a century earlier, Fokine had created LE SPECTRE DE

LA ROSE on Nijinsky. This time Kenneth MacMillan created WINTER'S EVE on Nora Kaye (back with the company) and John Kriza, and the ballet was given its premiere a few weeks later at the Teatro Nacional de São Carlos in Lisbon, Portugal. The fact that this was the first original ballet created for Ballet Theatre since the production of NIMBUS in 1950 pointed up the fallow state of the company's choreography in the last six years. Although during this period Ballet Theatre had added twenty-one works to its repertory, only three of them—Bronislava Nijinska's SCHUMANN CONCERTO and Agnes de Mille's THE HARVEST ACCORDING and RIB OF EVE—could be categorized as original creations; and none of these ballets remains in the repertory of any company. Two other works—Carmelita Maracci's CIRCO DE ESPAÑA and Edward Caton's TRIPTYCH—though performed by Ballet Theatre for the first time as entities, actually consisted of selections from the concert pieces of those choreographers. In addition, there were pas de deux by William Dollar and by Enrique Martinez, making a total of seven works that could be described loosely as new ballets. All the other works, including de Mille's RODEO and Tudor's OFFENBACH IN THE UNDERWORLD, had been staged originally by other companies. Chase and Smith were disturbed by the company's creative slump and resolved to seek out new choreographers. Accordingly, they entered into a series of workshop experiments.

The first workshop performance, at the Kaufmann Concert Hall, was in the nature of a school recital, a traditional ballet school event intended to help the students see some purpose in the past year of studio drudgery and to reassure

IN A BALLET THEATRE PREVIEW PROGRAM, JOHN KRIZA AND NORA KAYE HELPED DE MILLE EXPERIMENT WITH SEBASTIAN.

their parents that the tuition fee had been well spent. Among the original works performed by the students were William Dollar's MENDELSSOHN CONCERTO (later introduced into the Ballet Theatre repertory) and Robert Joffrey's UMPATEEDLE, his second ballet. The second workshop series, produced in cooperation with the Phoenix Theatre (a dramatic repertory group that made available to Ballet Theatre on Monday nights the theater it occupied on lower Second Avenue) used professional dancers from Ballet Theatre and other groups. During succeeding years, programs continued to be presented at various theaters, and for them a total of thirty-three works were created by eighteen choreographers, including a number who have since become established: Erik Bruhn, John Butler, Robert Joffrey, Enrique Martinez, Fernand Nault, Donald Saddler, and George Skibine.

Despite the success of the workshop experiment, it had to be abandoned after 1964 owing to a change in the ballet world's economic outlook. In earlier years a would-be choreographer brought himself to the attention of a company's directors through the cooperation of his fellow dancers, who rehearsed with him on their own time at no cost to the company. The directors could thus see at least a major portion of the ballet before committing themselves to a full and expensive production. The workshop went a step further by affording the directors the opportunity to judge audience and critical reaction before transforming the make-shift scenery and costumes into a full-scale, union-shop production. The dancers continued to work for no pay or for token salaries, and to do so enthusiastically, because not only were they helping their friend the choreographer but they could be creating new roles for themselves. The system operated to the advantage of all until two successive, socially conscious managing directors of the company decided that, to use a phrase then growing in favor, dancers should not be required to subsidize the art of ballet. With little or no urging from the dancers, they ruled that full salaries must be paid in connection with the rehearsing and performing of workshop programs. It followed inevitably that the experimenting choreographers, composers, and designers must also be paid regular fees—with the result that a workshop performance in an off-Broadway auditorium became almost as expensive as a production at the Metropolitan or the New York State Theater. A ballet by an unproved choreographer now requires as large an investment as a ballet by an experienced one. And when directors consider that an inexperienced choreographer may, in groping for expression, consume a greater number of rehearsal hours, they become hesitant and cautious about commissioning a work from a beginner.

Ballet Theatre's next experiment had to do with finding a home. By 1962 it had become so discouraged by the inhospitality of New York theater owners that it took the desperate step of establishing residency in another city. During the company's first twenty-two years it had appeared on the stages of eleven of New York City's theaters, one of its

amphitheaters, and one of its stadiums.* The point had been reached at which Ballet Theatre could appear in New York only upon the sufferance of Hurok (who controlled the Metropolitan), or of the New York City Center of Music and Drama (which controlled the City Center), or of the Shuberts (who monopolized the Broadway theaters). A Broadway theater could not be rented in advance but only after its owner had convinced himself that a short interval was forthcoming before a commercial producer would require it for a potentially long-run production. Therefore, when the Washington Ballet Guild offered a home in the nation's capital, Ballet Theatre accepted. The home, however, remained more of a dream than a reality. The one building then under construction would house rehearsal halls and a school modeled after the Royal Ballet School of England, but there was as yet no plan for a theater and thus the Ballet Theatre was no better off than it had been in New York. In those pre–Kennedy Center days the city of Washington had no suitable stage for the performance of ballet. Over the years Ballet Theatre had performed at Constitution Hall, on a totally inadequate stage intended as a platform for delegates to the conventions of the DAR, and at the National Theatre, originally designed as a playhouse. The Ballet Guild presented the company at the Capitol Theatre, a cavernous movie palace left over from the twenties, and in workshop performances at the Lisner Auditorium, the assembly hall of George Washington University. None of these theaters could lend to an evening at the ballet the sort of glamorous atmosphere that would attract new followers and, hopefully, contributors.

In the absence of such instant financial support from Washington residents, the entire responsibility for Ballet Theatre's ever-mounting deficits fell on the officers of the Ballet Guild. Though they had been warned in advance that the ballet was a voracious consumer of hard cash, the officers nevertheless underestimated its costs and overestimated the contributions the Guild would receive from its principal backer, Mrs. Merriweather Post (at that time Mrs. Herbert A. May). Mrs. May, who controlled a vast General Foods fortune, was generous within reason, but her interest in the ballet was not total and all-consuming. Understandably she did not, like Miss Chase, succumb to the temptation to devote a disproportionate percentage of her income to its support. The Guild president, Carson Frailey, and the chairman of the board, Gerson Nordlinger, Jr., gave unstintingly of their time and energies but were unable to raise sufficient funds to continue the venture. And so, in 1963, after little more than a year, Ballet Theatre left Washington (to be followed almost at once by the Washington Senators baseball team, which was driven from the capital by a similar lack of support). However, the sojourn in Washington was not without its effect on the

---

*Radio City's Center Theatre, the Majestic Theatre, the Forth-fourth Street Theatre, the old Metropolitan Opera House, the City Center, the Broadway Theatre, the Warner Brothers Theatre, the Fifty-fourth Street Theatre, the Phoenix Theatre, the Hunter College Playhouse, the Kaufmann Concert Hall, the Delacorte Theater, and Lewisohn Stadium.

future of Ballet Theatre. When Maria Tallchief suddenly withdrew from the company, the Guild engaged Margot Fonteyn as a substitute ballerina, and a short time later Rudolf Nureyev appeared with the company in Chicago. These dancers provided Chase and Smith with their first, pleasant experience with international superstars—one that helped to overcome their deep-seated prejudice against guest artists. That season, also, the Capitol Theatre became the neighborhood playhouse of the White House. For what surely must have been the first time in history, a head of state received a message from his wife to drop whatever he was doing and rush over to see a pas de deux. This precedent-setting event occurred one evening in December 1962, when President Kennedy, with a brother-in-law, drove over to watch Margot Fonteyn and Viktor Róna dance GAYANEH. It is not beyond the realm of possibility that the vision of the Kennedy Center for the Performing Arts appeared to a member of the presidential party that very evening.

From Washington, Ballet Theatre returned to New York, but most of its activities revolved around transcontinental and international tours. The one-night stands in America and the capital-hopping abroad were debilitating and diverted energies from creative work, but in retrospect they proved to have qualified the company to be a logical recipient when the bonanza of government subsidy was struck. Also, Miss Chase had a fondness for the kind of achievements that might earn Ballet Theatre entries in the GUINNESS BOOK OF RECORDS as "First American Company to Appear in Europe Following World War II," "First American Company to Dance at the New Metropolitan Opera House," and "First Ballet Company Ever to Dance on the Flight Deck of an Aircraft Carrier" (the ORISKANY for a Blood Bank benefit). One of the records she most coveted for Ballet Theatre was that of being the first company to perform in all forty-eight states. Indeed had she known in 1952 that Las Vegas was in Nevada, she probably would never have accepted the engagement at the Last Frontier, since Nevada had already been added to the list of states danced in when the company performed in Reno. However, in looking up the city on the map, she hit first upon Las Vegas, New Mexico (which would have become the forty-sixth state), and took that to be the gambling capital. In 1955 an off-the-regular-route visit to Albuquerque brought New Mexico into the fold, and the record was at last achieved at the end of that same tour by single appearances in Vermont and New Hampshire. The Ballet Theatre Foundation News reported:

The Ballet Theatre has performed in all forty-eight states of the Union. No other cultural or theatrical organization has yet come forth to challenge this record. The Ballet Theatre's booking representative can now relax until such time as Hawaii and Alaska are admitted to statehood. Then he will know no peace until he has found Miss Chase an igloo seating 2,000 people, with or without lighting equipment and dressing rooms.*

(continued on page 236)

*In 1966 Hawaii and Alaska were added to the list when the company performed in Honolulu and in four cities in Alaska.

STAGES PERFORMED ON BY BALLET THEATRE WERE MANY AND VARIED, INCLUDING THE AIRCRAFT CARRIER U.S.S. ORISKANY AND (TOP) THE OPERA HOUSE AT MONTE CARLO, WHERE DIAGHILEV SCORED MANY OF HIS GREATEST TRIUMPHS.

THE SIXTIES

SHARING CHOREOGRAPHERS
THE RETURN OF THE VETERANS

Ballet Theatre cannot regard as permanent resources the choreographic talents it has discovered and developed because of what appears to be a compulsion affecting all choreographers. With success almost inevitably comes the conviction that his (or her) choreography can best be performed by dancers of his own choosing and over whom he has complete control as they concentrate their entire efforts on performing his ballets alone. Thus it is that virtually every choreographer associated with Ballet Theatre—from Michel Fokine at one end to (at this writing) Dennis Wayne at the other—has left to form a company of his own. Since choreography is the life blood of a company and since its entire flow must almost necessarily be reserved for the choreographer's own company, Ballet Theatre has periodically suffered severe attacks of anemia. However, because the survival rate of one-choreographer companies is not high, the blood-flow is frequently reversed to the benefit of Ballet Theatre, as in 1963 when Jerome Robbins disbanded his Ballets: U.S.A. Needing a ballet company on which to create LES NOCES —a work so formidable in its logistics that three major ballet companies to which it had been offered had been frightened off—Robbins for the first time in twenty years turned to Ballet Theatre. This version was to be the first mounted in accordance with Stravinsky's original specifications, which called for the presence on stage of a singing chorus, four grand pianos, and four sets of tympany. The problem of positioning these instruments backstage while other ballets on the program were being performed could be solved only on a stage of grand-opera proportions. The cost of renting the pianos and of engaging pianists of star quality to play them could be undertaken only by a company prepared to loosen the purse strings. For both parties it was a remarriage of convenience: Ballet Theatre was so eager to obtain a new work from Robbins that it agreed to his terms; on his part, Robbins was so anxious to have the ballet produced that he was prepared to create it on dancers not of his own choosing and to generously forgo a choreographic fee. He also proposed and agreed that his royalty payments should not exceed those accepted by Stravinsky for the music rights, however low they might be. While Robbins' return provided an invigorating experience for the dancers and LES NOCES has continued to stimulate Ballet Theatre audiences, for the management it has been a mixed blessing. Though it continues to bolster the company's prestige, each performance (even when sold out) loses a considerable amount of money.

LES NOCES (CENTER ABOVE) WILLIAM GLASSMAN, ERIN MARTIN. (OPPOSITE PAGE, TOP) ERIN MARTIN, TED KIVITT (FAR LEFT), ELIOT FELD (KNEELING). (MIDDLE) WILLIAM GLASSMAN, ERIN MARTIN; MARCOS PAREDES AND SALLIE WILSON (LEFT OF TABLE), CYNTHIA GREGORY (RIGHT), (BOTTOM) ERIN MARTIN (CENTER), VERONICA MLAKAR, RICHARD GAIN, ROSANNA SERAVALLI (STANDING AT REAR).

THE WIND IN THE MOUNTAINS
JOSEPH CAROW
TED KIVITT
ELIOT FELD

Ballet Theatre was so anxious also to obtain a new ballet from Agnes de Mille that it consented to the insertion of unique provisions in her contract that would enable her to create simultaneously for Ballet Theatre and for her own company. Ballet Theatre did not receive the customary right to perform the ballet exclusively for one year, and it committed itself to executing (at no cost to the choreographer) a duplicate set of scenery and costumes that were to be delivered to de Mille to use as she wished. Whether this arrangement could provide a workable method of operation for Ballet Theatre and a choreographer with her (or his) own company was not demonstrated by de Mille's THE WIND IN THE MOUNTAINS and THE FOUR MARYS (both produced under these terms), since neither ballet was an enduring success. Another of Ballet Theatre's graduate choreographers, William Dollar, returned in the sixties to create DIVERTIMENTO-ROSSINI and his Mendelssohn CONCERTO.

214

THE FOUR MARYS
JUDITH LERNER
PAUL SUTHERLAND
CLEO QUITMAN
JUDITH JAMISON
GLORY VAN SCOTT
CARMEN DE LAVALLADE

(TOP) **DIVERTIMENTO-ROSSINI**

BRAHMS QUINTET MIMI PAUL, GAYLE YOUNG.

GARTENFEST TED KIVITT, CYNTHIA GREGORY, IVAN NAGY.

THE NEW GENERATION

With the emergence of fresh new talent in the 1960s, Ballet Theatre began to enjoy the temporary benefit of the creativity of five young American choreographers who remained with the company for a number of seasons before venturing forth to form their own groups or to assume the direction of established companies. Eliot Feld produced his first ballet, HARBINGER, for Ballet Theatre and followed it up with AT MIDNIGHT. Michael Smuin, who was to leave to direct the San Francisco Ballet, created PULCINELLA VARIATIONS and GARTENFEST, and Dennis Nahat, who later founded the Cleveland Ballet, contributed MOMENTUM and BRAHMS QUINTET. Glen Tetley danced with the company in 1960 but did not remain long enough to create a ballet before becoming a director of the Nederlands Dans Theater. He, however, returned to stage SARGASSO and RICERCARE. Dania Krupska took leave only temporarily of the modern dance school to create the ballet POINTS ON JAZZ for Ballet Theatre.

POINTS ON JAZZ SALLIE WILSON (LEFT, ARMS RAISED), SCOTT DOUGLAS (KNEELING).

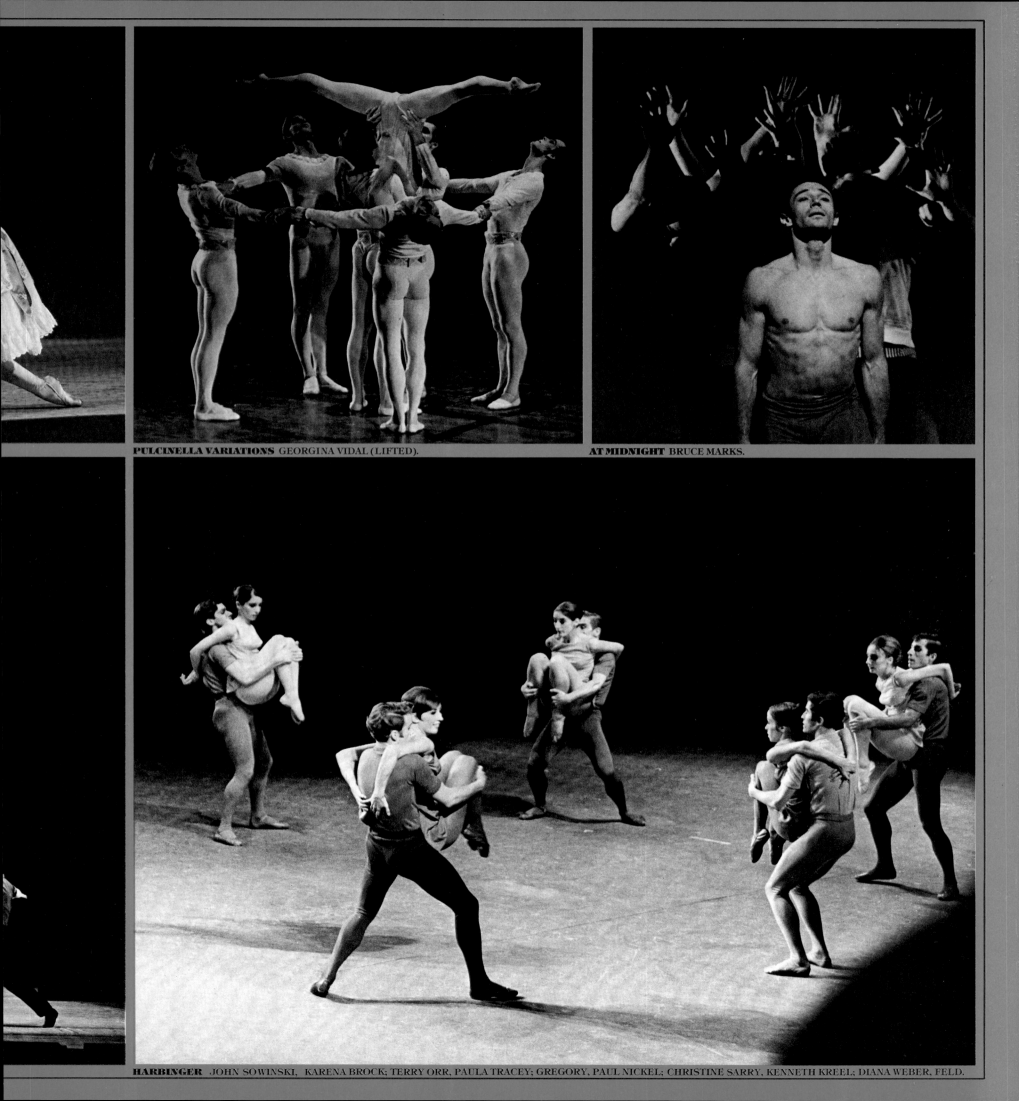

PULCINELLA VARIATIONS GEORGINA VIDAL (LIFTED).

AT MIDNIGHT BRUCE MARKS.

HARBINGER JOHN SOWINSKI, KARENA BROCK; TERRY ORR, PAULA TRACEY; GREGORY, PAUL NICKEL; CHRISTINE SARRY, KENNETH KREEL; DIANA WEBER, FELD.

ECHOING OF TRUMPETS

BALLETS FROM ABROAD

Antony Tudor and other choreographers from Europe were also less available to Ballet Theatre in the 1960s because of their engrossment with their own companies. Tudor was not only absorbed in creating for his own performing groups connected with the Metropolitan Opera and the Juilliard School, but for a time he was director of the Royal Swedish Ballet. It was for the last of these that he created ECHOING OF TRUMPETS, the only ballet he staged for Ballet Theatre during the decade. Before forming her own company and restricting her activities principally to Sweden, Birgit Cullberg added three of her works to the repertory: LADY FROM THE SEA, MOON REINDEER, and the EDEN pas de deux. Kenneth MacMillan staged three ballets, LAS HERMANAS, DANSES CONCERTANTES, and his Shostakovich CONCERTO, before his accession to the directorship of the British Royal Ballet removed him, for all practical purposes, as a contributor to Ballet Theatre.

LADY FROM THE SEA
MARIA TALLCHIEF

LADY FROM THE SEA ROYES FERNANDEZ AND LUPE SERRANO (LIFTED AT LEFT). (TOP LEFT) ROYES FERNANDEZ, LUPE SERRANO. (TOP RIGHT) MARIA TALLCHIEF.

MOON REINDEER
LUPE SERRANO
(FAR RIGHT)

**DANSES
CONCERTANTES**
(STANDING)
MARCOS PAREDES
CYNTHIA GREGORY
RICHARD GAIN

(KNEELING RIGHT)
ROYES FERNANDEZ

CONCERTO
GAYLE YOUNG
CYNTHIA GREGORY

LAS HERMANAS (CENTER PICTURE) LUPE SERRANO, ELEANOR D'ANTUONO, ALAINE HAUBERT, LUCIA CHASE, NAOMI SORKIN, ELLEN EVERETT, ROYES FERNANDEZ.

THE CLASSICS PROVIDE STABILITY

LA SYLPHIDE
TONI LANDER
ROYES FERNANDEZ

Atypically, Harald Lander's services became more readily available to Ballet Theatre because he was no longer connected with his native Royal Danish Ballet. He made a valuable contribution with his ETUDES, but perhaps the ballet which exerted the greatest influence on Ballet Theatre's future course was his staging of LA SYLPHIDE. The project, considered several times in the past when the ballet had been urged as a vehicle for Alicia Markova, had always been rejected in the belief that it was beyond the capability of the company—it required a larger roster of dancers and a home stage of opera-house size over which, for example, sylphs could be flown. Lander's demonstration that this ballet could be performed by a smaller cast and on lesser stages encouraged the directors to

mount other elaborate ballets from the repertories of the past. In rapid succession they produced complete versions of SWAN LAKE and COPPÉLIA, and in the process they made a happy discovery: Bournonville, Petipa, and Saint-Léon were not choreographers who could suddenly leave to form their own companies nor, conversely, would they return to threaten withdrawal of the works if not performed to their satisfaction. In addition, the physical productions became permanent assets, and the original choreography could always be reproduced by another ballet master. And so, as living choreographers became more demanding and as production costs rose, it was not surprising that the directors were relieved to discover that a company need not inevitably stand or fall on its ability to discover and retain new choreographers.

ACT I (TOP AND BOTTOM LEFT) TONI LANDER, ROYES FERNANDEZ. (BOTTOM RIGHT) ERIK BRUHN, CYNTHIA GREGORY, ROSANNA SERAVALLI (AS MADGE), BASIL THOMPSON (AS GURN).

ACT II CARLA FRACCI, ERIK BRUHN.

BRUCE MARKS, TONI LANDER, ROYES FERNANDEZ.

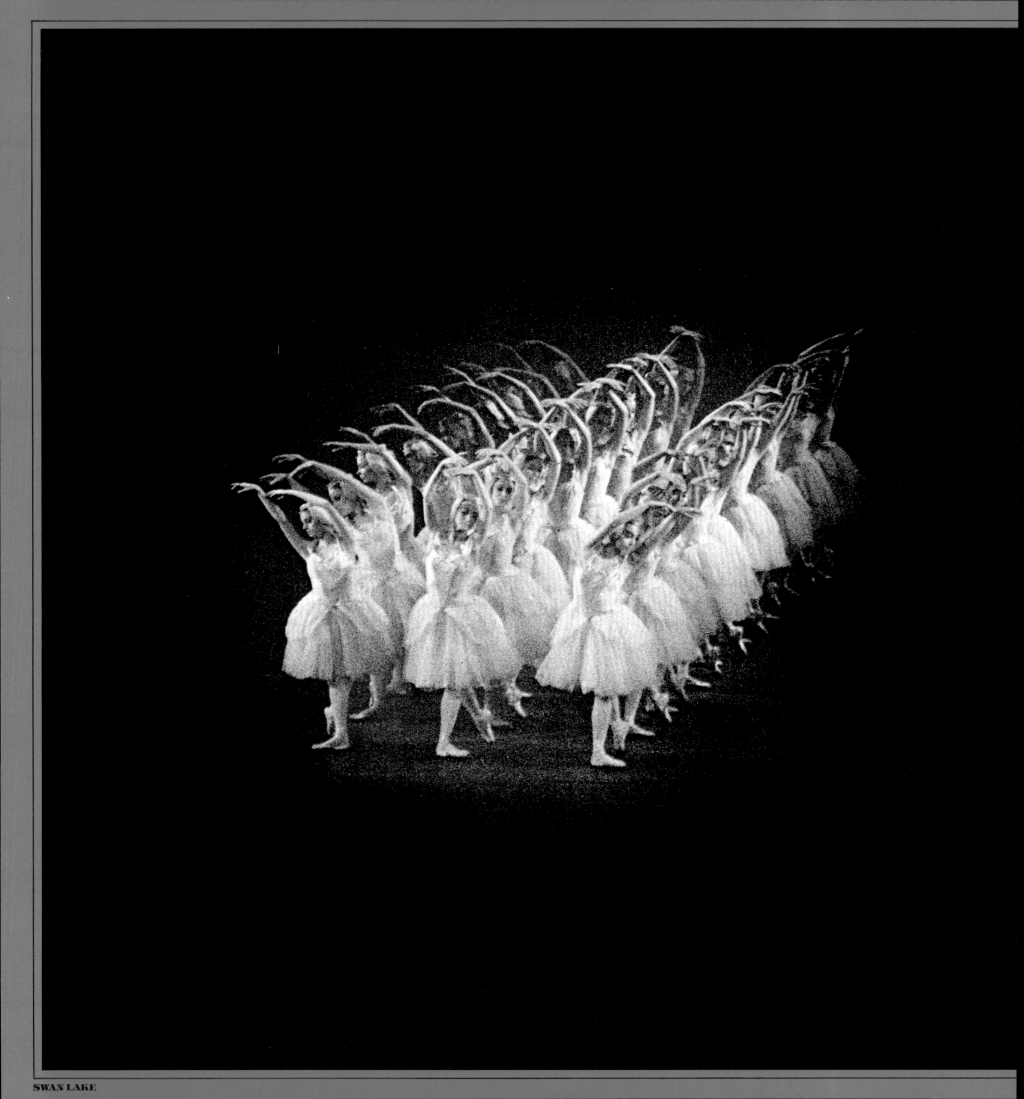

SWAN LAKE

(TOP) CYNTHIA GREGORY AS ODETTE AND ODILE. (BOTTOM) LUPE SERRANO, ROYES FERNANDEZ.

This record-setting, though frivolous in some respects, proved beneficial when the Congress got around to considering subsidization of the arts. The senators from New Mexico had the same number of votes as the senators from New York, and when they read that government funds were being awarded to Ballet Theatre, they (or more likely their wives) would note with approval that the recipient was the company that had not neglected New Mexico on its tours. And likewise when the senators from all the other states in the country consulted their grass-roots constituents, they would find that even in some of the smaller towns people were familiar with Ballet Theatre and were in favor of (or at least not opposed to) some of their tax money being earmarked for its support.* But even while the company's domestic and foreign tours were gaining it nationwide acceptance as a national institution and international recognition as a major world company, it remained without much honor in its native city.

Then in November 1963 Ballet Theatre was informed that the New York State Theater, which was about to open at Lincoln Center, would be made available to it for a four-week season beginning March 16, 1965. Chase and Smith immediately began to plan a representative program to mark the company's Twenty-fifth Anniversary. For a full-evening classical ballet they chose LA SYLPHIDE, to be staged by Harald Lander. From the workshop program they introduced Bentley Stone's L'INCONNUE into the regular repertory. As a work by a new American choreographer they selected SARGASSO by Glen Tetley, who had been a member of the company in 1960. And, finally, they solicited new ballets from the company's founding choreographers. Tudor was not creatively inspired but agreed to revive his DARK ELEGIES and to rehearse JARDIN AUX LILAS. Agnes de Mille came forward with two new works that she had been developing with a prospective company of her own, THE WIND IN THE MOUNTAINS and THE FOUR MARYS. Jerome Robbins, who had only recently completed the choreography for the hit musical FIDDLER ON THE ROOF, had not created a ballet since 1961, when he staged EVENTS for his own company, Ballets: U.S.A. Rehearsals were already in progress before he responded to Chase's and Smith's persistent requests with the startling announcement that he would undertake to create a new version of Stravinsky's LES NOCES provided he was allotted four hours of rehearsal time on each working day and it was understood that if at any point, even at the last moment before the premiere, either his creative inspiration flagged or rehearsals did not proceed well and according to schedule, the entire project would have to be canceled. He described the circumstances in an article written for the New York Times:

I am deeply grateful to Lucia Chase, head of American Ballet Theatre, for the comfort of her company out on a very high limb. I've told her over and over

*It is debatable whether their approval continued after it became apparent that the government subsidy enabled the company to abandon one-night stands and its visits to small towns and colleges.

again the tree is slippery and the height tremendous, but nothing will avail. "Forward," she cries. "Danger!" yell I. "Onward," she prods. So here we go.

The engagement was an unqualified success and restored Ballet Theatre's status in New York. The ballet historian Lillian Moore summed up the season this way:

In recent years Ballet Theatre has failed to put its best foot forward during its brief seasons in New York, and its status close to the top of the list of American dance companies has seemed in jeopardy. Now, in four weeks of magnificent dancing in the most varied and truly comprehensive repertoire of any ballet ensemble on this side of the Atlantic, it has firmly re-established its high position. The American Ballet Theatre has never been in more splendid form.

The audience's instant reaction—thunderous, delirious applause—testified to the special quality of Ballet Theatre's performances. As a company, it has always sought to entertain, arranging each program to provide something for every taste. A generation of New Yorkers had been brought up on the creations of Balanchine's genius (which Kirstein had described as "the abstracted, refined and essential material of dancing itself") and on the cerebral opaqueness of Martha Graham's modernisms. Audiences at these performances have been serious, thoughtful, sometimes grim, and often pretentious. Audiences at Ballet Theatre performances can be serious and sometimes pretentious, but principally they are in a mood to enjoy themselves, to be entertained. It is perhaps not without significance that the receipts at the bars in the New York State Theater foyer, in the Royal Opera House promenade, and in the Founder's Room of the Dorothy Chandler Pavilion increase substantially when Ballet Theatre is in residence.

ROGER STEVENS (LEFT) AND VICE-PRESIDENT HUBERT HUMPHREY DELIVER A FEDERAL CHECK TO DR. HAROLD TAYLOR.
(OPPOSITE PAGE) TONI LANDER IN FLOWER FESTIVAL IN GENZANO.

The resurgence of Ballet Theatre was given a further boost by an historic event that took place in the White House on December 20, 1965. Beneath a portrait of a doubtless astonished George Washington, Vice-President Hubert Humphrey presented a check for $100,000 to Dr. Harold Taylor, the president of the Ballet Theatre Foundation. The federal government, through the agency of the National Council on the Arts, had directly entered the ballet business. While this grant did not automatically solve all of the company's financial problems, it did enable Chase and Smith to begin to plan in advance and to abandon, at least to an extent, their former penny-pinching, last-minute, brinkmanship tactics. The time had come for them to realize one of their most cherished projects, a complete production of SWAN LAKE. The plan called for the staging of Act II in 1966, to be followed by the remaining three acts during the next or future seasons. Act II was premiered on schedule on the opening night of the second season at the New York State Theater, with Vice-President and Mrs. Humphrey, Senator and Mrs. Javits, and Mayor and Mrs. Lindsay in official attendance. After the performance the vice-president and the mayor held separate courts in different rooms of Miss Chase's apartment. The vice-president, presenting another federal check, warned Miss Chase against letting private contributors off the hook. Before the mayor was able to offer the city's advice, he was called away to a fire. As an impatient aide explained to Ballet Theatre's sympathetic press agent, Samuel Lurie, "It's sometimes very hard to keep the fire going until the mayor arrives." But there remained no doubt that Ballet Theatre had at length received recognition from official representatives of the nation, the state, and the city.

The company's newfound prosperity soon brought dissension in the ranks of its administration, and later in 1966 a palace coup was attempted with the aim of removing Lucia Chase as an administrative director. The seeds of the crisis were sown when Agnes de Mille proposed Dr. Harold Taylor for the presidency of the Ballet Theatre Foundation to succeed Byam K. Stevens, who had recently resigned. Her suggestion was enthusiastically received. The directors recognized that since government grants were to play an important role in the financing of the company, the Foundation could best be served by a president who had had experience in dealing with government-subsidy agencies. Dr. Taylor had been president of Sarah Lawrence College, and it was assumed that during his term of office he had acquired the knack of siphoning off a fair share of the billions with which government agencies and private foundations had been overwhelming educational institutions during the past decade. The trustees were convinced that this expertise could be applied to obtaining for Ballet Theatre its fair share of what was then only a token

appropriation in support of the arts. Although disclaiming any ability as a fund-raiser, Dr. Taylor advanced his first reorganization plan with the implicit assurance that its adoption would result in a flow of money to the Foundation. The plan emphasized the important role to be played by the Ballet Theatre School, which was to be provided with a building equipped to enable it to act as a nerve center for activities that would establish associations with schools and universities across the country. The Ballet Theatre School would aid these institutions in setting up dance departments, furnish dance teachers, and eventually offer employment to the participating students. In conjunction with this campaign in schools and universities, the Ballet Theatre company would continue to present ballet performances on tour at home and abroad—in effect educating the public to an appreciation of ballet, particularly native American ballet. By underlining Ballet Theatre's educational functions, the company could be represented to government agencies as a permanent educational institution, as contrasted with a run-of-the-play commercial theater venture. Government support was being sought for an educational project to be operated in all the states (local congressmen, please note). This rationalization was intended to make the Ballet Theatre Foundation eligible for educational grants as well as for grants from the new Council on the Arts, and even in approaching that agency, the trustees played down the still suspect words "ballet dancing."

The educational aspects of Dr. Taylor's reorganization plan were the fruits of his long experience in the field, and they were warmly endorsed by all of the trustees, including Miss Chase. But when it came to the reorganization of Ballet Theatre itself, Dr. Taylor was venturing into an area in which he had had no experience whatsoever. He therefore had to rely on the advice of his sponsor, Agnes de Mille. Consequently, there was appended to the plan, almost as a footnote, in small type, a recommendation for the reconstituting of artistic authority:

The artistic policy of the Company, the School, and the Workshop must take into account so many new factors and possibilities that it no longer can be dealt with by a single person [that is, Lucia Chase], no matter how gifted that person may be. . . . The first step of the Board of Trustees, acting through its Executive Committee, would be to appoint a Policy and Planning Committee composed of Lucia Chase, Oliver Smith, Agnes de Mille and Jerome Robbins.

Chase and Smith were eager to have de Mille and Robbins actively associated with the company—an eagerness demonstrated by the painstaking production of their ballets in the previous season. There was, then, no lack of good will when the committee was instituted, and the participation of these greatly admired artists was welcomed.

However, it soon developed that the admiration was not mutual. De Mille later recalled the sequence of events in a letter to John Wharton, who had for years acted as counsel for the Foundation and for Miss Chase personally. In writing, she undertook to speak also for Jerome Robbins, and it could not

be known whether her quotations were exact, but they were in keeping with opinions Robbins had expressed over the years. She reported they were prepared to create new works for Ballet Theatre and allow certain of their ballets to remain in the repertory provided a new directional staff was appointed, headed by a regisseur whom they could trust to implement their decisions and those of the artistic committee. The implementation could not be entrusted to Lucia Chase. What they intended here was that the ballet staff engaged by Chase should be dismissed and that she should be denied any part in the selection of replacements. Further, Chase should no longer supervise rehearsals and performances, this function to be taken over by Nora Kaye, who had been appointed assistant director by Chase and Smith in 1965. With respect to the company roster, she reported that Robbins wanted dancers of his choice to be added and suggested that in the future selections should be made more carefully. Similar privileges of choosing dancers would, of course, be accorded Miss de Mille. In other words, Chase should no longer, as she had in the past, select the dancers of the company with the advice of her staff and the choreographers. The selection of at least a portion of the company would be the exclusive privilege of Robbins and de Mille, who could also decide which of the dancers previously selected by Chase should be dismissed.

Finally, de Mille recalled that both she and Robbins had recommended that the production of the four-act SWAN LAKE be shelved considering the company's financial condition. The money, they thought, might better be spent on three new works of theatric interest.

The "new works of theatric interest" would doubtless be choreographed by Robbins and de Mille, and possibly by Tudor if inspiration struck. Ballet Theatre's original policy of presenting the classics along with new creations was to be put on the back burner to simmer. The implementation of the committee's demands would have effectively stripped Chase of all her functions in the company. And it was further decided, as reported by Taylor, that Chase should not be permitted to speak directly with the dancers but that all communication should be carried on through Kaye (a proposal that did not meet with Kaye's approval). Presumably Chase would be allowed to continue performing the two stage roles that remained for her in the repertory, the Stepmother in FALL RIVER LEGEND and the Narrator in PETER AND THE WOLF. And she would, of course, retain the privilege of making substantial contributions to the financial support of the company, support still required because Taylor had not yet obtained grants from any source other than the federal government.

Chase continued to press for the production of SWAN LAKE, and in early January 1967 the committee replied in effect, "If you insist on producing it, you must take full responsibility; Foundation funds must not be diverted to the project." The committee announced further that should SWAN LAKE be produced, not enough time would remain in which to prepare new American works for the season at the New York

State Theater, scheduled to open May 9. It therefore recommended, with the backing of the president, that the engagement be canceled and in any case not be financed with Foundation funds.

Chase and Smith consulted Wharton, who replied in a memorandum. Recalling the experience of 1949, he agreed with Miss Chase that if the New York State Theater engagement was canceled and the company laid off for an extended period, it might prove to be the end of Ballet Theatre. With the advent of government subsidy, he urged that the company be kept going at all cost, even if the cost involved Miss Chase's assumption of responsibility for the season. He expressed no opinion in regard to the production of SWAN LAKE, but instead posed the question whether the committee's statements did not suggest that it was intent on usurping the authority of the administrative directors. To put it bluntly, was the committee planning a take-over? The situation, he advised, should be clarified. The memorandum was brought to the attention of Taylor, who then showed it to Robbins and de Mille. All three believed they had been insulted by its implications and submitted hurt letters of resignation—De Mille, as a member, and Robbins, as an advisor, to the Policy and Planning Committee. Once again, as in 1946, artistic direction-by-committee had miscarried, and for much the same reason.

When Lucia Chase chose to take full responsibility for the completion of SWAN LAKE, she was not wholly aware of the momentousness of her decision, for in doing so, she determined the nature of the company's activities and the nature of the company itself during the next decade. She was, in the first place, opting for a super-size company. Ballet Theatre had started its career, in 1940, with a multi-group company of some sixty-odd dancers, but had reduced to more practical proportions immediately following its debut engagement at the Rockefeller Center Theatre. The size of the corps was determined by the number of women (eighteen) required to perform LES SYLPHIDES and Dolin's version of SWAN LAKE, and by the number of men (ten) who appeared in BILLY THE KID. Two or three dancers were added as emergency substitutes, making a total corps of approximately thirty dancers, which was topped off with soloists and stars to round out the roster at forty-odd dancers. Over the years this number was exceeded on occasion, for instance when Fokine cast all available dancers in a new ballet with the result that for the following season additional dancers were required to act as standby-substitutes. However, as late as 1964 the company's roster still did not carry more than fifty dancers, broken down approximately into eight stars, twelve soloists, and twenty-five corps de ballet. A troupe of this size could perform the French classics (GISELLE, LA FILLE MAL GARDÉE), which had been created on moderate-size opera ballet companies, and it could stage the Diaghilev adaptations of the Russian classics (PRINCESS AURORA and SWAN LAKE, ACT II). In 1964 Ballet Theatre even mounted a production of the Bournonville

ROYES FERNANDEZ (IAGO) AND BRUCE MARKS (OTHELLO) IN THE MOOR'S PAVANE.

classic LA SYLPHIDE with a company of only forty-five dancers. But for such a small company there was no possibility of duplicating the ballets created for the Russian Imperial Theaters, and Ballet Theatre could only look on with envy as visiting foreign companies presented the complete SLEEPING BEAUTY and SWAN LAKE. Then in 1966 the first step in Ballet Theatre's expansion was taken when the company staged SWAN LAKE, ACT II in the form in which it had first been presented at the Maryinsky Theater. This version called for twenty-six female dancers: six soloists and twenty corps. Automatically the company's roster rose to fifty-some dancers. The other three acts could be performed with a minimum of fifty dancers, but to this number must be added the standbys and the alternate stars and soloists who could not appear in every performance. Consequently, when the complete SWAN LAKE went into production, the roster had swollen to more than sixty dancers.

The predictions made by the committee and Dr. Taylor—that no private foundation would make a grant to a company which was directed artistically and administratively by Chase and Smith alone; that no new American ballets could be created simultaneously with the preparation of SWAN LAKE; and that SWAN LAKE could not be performed without a foreign ballerina—all proved to be inaccurate. The company not only continued to receive government grants after the departure of Dr. Taylor but before the end of the year it was awarded a grant from the Rockefeller Foundation for a choreographer-in-residence project. And not only was SWAN LAKE completed on schedule, but the season was also distinguished by the discovery of a new American choreographer, Eliot Feld, who had created for it his first ballet, HARBINGER. Finally, it was simply not true that Ballet Theatre had "no proper Swan Queen," though it did prove to be convenient to import a foreign star for the out-of-town tryout. With the departure on maternity leave of Lupe Serrano, on whom David Blair had set the Odette role in his staging of Act II, there still remained available to him Toni Lander and Sallie Wilson, who had shared the role with Serrano. However, Blair persuaded Chase that he could more quickly set the other three acts if he could employ as his first-cast Swan Queen Nadia Nerina, with whom he had worked in the Royal Ballet. Accordingly, the first performance in Chicago was danced by Nerina and Royes Fernandez, the second by Toni Lander and Bruce Marks, and the third by Sallie Wilson and Gayle Young. Lander and Marks danced the premiere at the New York State Theater, and later in that season Cynthia Gregory graduated to full ballerina status with her first performance of the Odette-Odile role.

Though the importation of Nerina had no influence on the direction the company was to take in the future, the production of the complete SWAN LAKE did have a lasting effect on the company's relationship with world stars. When, shortly after his defection, Rudolf Nureyev appeared with the company in Chicago in 1962, he brought with him the

CORSAIRE pas de deux, danced in the Dimitri Romanoff version of LA FILLE MAL GARDÉE (which closely resembled the one performed at Nureyev's old company, the Kirov), and learned Balanchine's THEME AND VARIATIONS.* At that time Nureyev was looking for a company he could adopt as his home and from which he could branch out on his world conquests. Though he was sincerely in search of fresh dance experiences with new forms of choreography, he was not prepared to totally and immediately abandon the classics, in the performance of which he had acquired his technique and attained such great prowess. In Ballet Theatre he found a pleasant but antiquated production of LA FILLE MAL GARDÉE, a controversial version of GISELLE, and only truncated portions of SWAN LAKE and THE SLEEPING BEAUTY. There is no way of evaluating the various considerations that went into Nureyev's choice of a home company. Not the least of them may have been the company's stability and promise of permanence, and here he was aware that the British government's support of the Royal Ballet could offer him unmatched security for the future. But he must also have been influenced by the fact that the Royal Ballet's repertory contained complete and seemingly authentic versions of the classics, which would serve as vehicles for the instant display of his technical and dramatic skills. If Nureyev, on his part, entertained doubts that Ballet Theatre could supply him with satisfactory roles, Lucia Chase, on her part, was still leery of foreign stars, who might become a disruptive influence in the Ballet Theatre family. And so Nureyev joined the Royal Ballet, where he exercised not a disruptive but certainly a very definite influence on the dancing, particularly that of the men.†

The production of SWAN LAKE did not so much change the direction of Ballet Theatre as it did the force of that direction. Although the classics had been an integral part of the company's repertory since its debut in 1940, previous activities in that "wing" had been restricted to mini-productions. But with the mounting of the complete SWAN LAKE, Ballet Theatre acquired the confident assurance that it could now rank itself among the half-dozen major ballet companies of the world. The rise in Ballet Theatre's status was strikingly affirmed when it appeared in 1968 for a three-week engagement at the new Metropolitan Opera House, the stage of which had hitherto been exclusively reserved for visits by foreign companies whose enormous rosters and spectacular productions enticed the general public as well as balletomanes into buying tickets at inflated prices. The stature of

---

*When Ballet Theatre arrived in Leningrad in 1960, Nureyev was sent off with a group to dance in East Germany. As he could not see the American repertory in person, he asked a friend to photograph as much of it as possible. The friend filmed THEME AND VARIATIONS, but since film was in short supply and hard to come by, he did not waste it on unnecessary duplications. Thus when Erik Bruhn executed the six successive double air-turns, he photographed only the first two—and that was the number Nureyev performed when he stopped in Australia en route to Chicago to be coached by Bruhn. "Sorry," said Bruhn, "but in Chicago you'll have to do all six." This was the first Nureyev had known there were six, and though the news came as a shock, he of course had no difficulty in executing them.

†Incidentally, as a state-supported institution, the Royal Ballet could engage him only as a "guest"; none but British citizens can be regular members of the company.

a ballet company is similar to that of a ballet star. The direction may award stardom and note it in the company's official roster, the press may bestow confirming accolades, but no dancer becomes a star in fact until the public so wills it. In 1968 the public willed with its acclaim that Ballet Theatre should be recognized as the equal of the world's greatest companies—and this recognition was made possible because that public had been provided with a standard, SWAN LAKE, against which it could make its more considered judgment.

THE FOUR-ACT SWAN LAKE IN 1967 ALTERED THE COURSE OF BALLET THEATRE.

Ballet Theatre's new productions of SWAN LAKE, GISELLE, and COPPÉLIA greatly enhanced the company's reputation, and its stature was even further increased by presentation of the star performers those ballets require. For, once a company has opted to perform the classics in full, it automatically commits itself to the acceptance and the fostering of star dancers. It is possible to create a new ballet in which the choreographer is the star, that is, one in which no individual dancer dominates the action or colors the choreography with special techniques or distinctive personality traits. It is even possible to create a ballet starring the corps de ballet, one in which all the dancers are expected to dance alike and any intrusion of individual style or personality is regarded as discordant. But the classics were created as vehicles for stars, and only stars can perform them as their creators conceived them. The roles of Giselle and Albrecht, for example, cannot be performed by promising dancers. They can be interpreted effectively only by mature artists with secure techniques and a thorough understanding of the art of projecting to the audience. Even when the roles are performed by merely promising dancers, the audience assumes that they regard themselves as stars and judges them accordingly.

Consequently, a company that continuously maintains the classics in its repertory must also maintain a stable of mature ballerinas and premiers danseurs and provide for frequent replacements. Ideally, as vacancies occur, they should be filled with dancers who have been trained and promoted through the ranks within the company. But the direction cannot rely on a dancer of the company to reach maturity at the precise moment when the need for a new Giselle becomes desperate. Circumstances alter too rapidly, and the direction, despite careful planning, may suddenly find that the ranks of veterans have become depleted before their replacements are ready. In the spring of 1960, for example, the direction was confident it had an ample supply of Giselles—Alonso, Kaye, and Serrano—and of Albrechts—Youskevitch, Bruhn, and Fernandez—yet within a few months the supply was drastically reduced. The first loss was Alonso, who chose to remain temporarily with her own company in Cuba while Ballet Theatre undertook a tour of Europe that was to wind up with its first visit to the Soviet Union. She could not have foreseen that political developments would prevent her from rejoining Ballet Theatre during the ensuing fifteen years. The second Giselle was lost when Nora Kaye danced her last performance with the company in Lisbon, Portugal, before departing for the European debut of her own company, the Ballet of Two Worlds. The first casualty in the ranks of the Albrechts was Igor Youskevitch, who in a few short weeks lost muscular control over his superb technique, a rapid deterioration that culminated in a dramatic incident in Moscow.

One of the provisions of the Cultural Exchange Treaty between the United States and the Soviet Union stated that exchange visits should be made by performing companies of equal stature. If the Soviet Union sent a major ballet company to the United States, the United States was required to, and could insist on its right to, send a major company to the Soviet Union. In the case of Ballet Theatre's proposed visit in 1960, the Soviet Ambassador in Washington had certified to the fact that Ballet Theatre was a major company, but the signing of the official contract was nevertheless delayed. This delay was caused by a policy recently promulgated by the Kremlin decreeing that artistic organizations would no longer automatically receive open-ended support from the state; they must prove that the people needed and wanted them—a need that could be demonstrated only by the number of tickets sold, not by the number issued free to deserving workers. The new policy was made applicable to foreign organizations, whose tours were underwritten by the state. Therefore, the Soviet Concert Bureau, which managed such tours, was charged with the responsibility of importing only those attractions that would be certain to sell tickets. Accordingly, a Bolshoi ballet master, Alexander Tchintchinadze, was dispatched to Holland to attend performances there by Ballet Theatre. He reported back to the Bureau that Ballet Theatre was indeed a major company, that there was reason to believe it would sell tickets, and that he had seen a superlative performance of the Black Swan pas de deux by a Ukrainian-born dancer named Igor Youskevitch. The Bureau consequently insisted that

Youskevitch dance the Black Swan pas de deux at the opening performance, replacing Erik Bruhn, who was to have danced the pas de deux from DON QUIXOTE. Upon arriving in Moscow, Miss Chase, conscious of Youskevitch's lessening technical security, urged the Bureau to revert to her original schedule, reserving him for the second-night performance. It refused. Even Anatole Heller, the Paris agent who had negotiated the contract with the Soviet Union for the State Department and who had also attended the performances in Holland, was convinced that Miss Chase was acting from some devious motive that had nothing to do with Youskevitch's ability to perform. Only at the dress rehearsal was the drastic change in the dancer's condition revealed to all—and it remained for Miss Chase to perform the painful duty of informing her favorite dancer that Bruhn must replace him, and for Bruhn to perform the equally painful task of supplanting his idol.

Such a rapid loss of technical skill is not uncommon, but it always takes the dancer and the direction by surprise. Only a few months earlier Miss Chase had been confident that Youskevitch would be available to perform Albrecht for at least several more years. Suddenly her stable of Giselles and Albrechts was reduced from six to three: Bruhn and the neophytes Serrano and Fernandez, who had danced the roles for the first time only a few months before. When Bruhn took a leave of absence following the Soviet tour to protect his pension rights with the Royal Danish Ballet, the stable was further reduced. There remained only Serrano and Fernandez, and shortly thereafter Serrano succumbed to the nonoccupational hazard of pregnancy. All of this occurred before Ruth Ann Koesun and Scott Douglas had reached the point where they could step into the roles.

It is, of course, impossible to present GISELLE without dancers capable of performing the roles of Giselle and Albrecht. It is also impossible to perform PILLAR OF FIRE without a dancer capable of excelling in the role of Hagar. But whereas the dance public accepts the explanation that the dance world is temporarily devoid of a Hagar, it cannot accept casting problems as an excuse for failure to present GISELLE. The dance world can always provide a Giselle, if not from within the company, then from another American company, or from Europe, South America, or even Japan. Hence any company that pretends to be a preserver of classic ballets must <u>find</u> a Giselle if it is to validate its claim. In 1967, as Ballet Theatre was preparing for its second engagement at the New York State Theater, this search for a Giselle became urgent.

After Lupe Serrano once more departed on maternity leave, Ballet Theatre was left with only Ruth Ann Koesun, whose Giselle had not yet come up to the standards set by New York critics and by the increasingly discriminating and demanding public. Clearly another Giselle must be found and signed to a contract, even if on terms that violated Miss

SCOTT DOUGLAS AS BILLY THE KID
AND LUPE SERRANO AS GISELLE.

Chase's directorial principles—one of the most determined of which was that there should be no "guest artists." Miss Chase was able to assert consistent adherence to this principle by explaining away apparent exceptions in the past. Some guests, for instance, had been engaged not by her but by outside management: Toumanova by Hurok, Fonteyn and Nureyev by the Washington Ballet Guild. Others had come as part of a package deal for the importation of their ballets: Babilée, Argentinita, Maracci. Still others were not really guests at all, but rather alumni, returning to take part in anniversary celebrations. And, finally, there were those like Toni Lander who, although they danced with Ballet Theatre while still committed to another company, were not tainted with the designation "guest" because they had expressed the intention of becoming permanent members. But when the 1967 search for a Giselle concluded with the engagement of Italy's Carla Fracci, there was a change, at first imperceptible, in Miss Chase's thinking. Only an unrealistic stretch of rationalization allowed her temporarily to ignore Fracci's status as a guest. Fracci was the prima ballerina of La Scala, in her native Milan. The opera house had been her home since she graduated from its ballet school in 1944, and she now reigned supreme on its stage. It was inconceivable that she would sacrifice all this to become a permanent member of Ballet Theatre. However, Fracci was not fettered by the restrictions of American semantics. She went along with the fiction that she now belonged to Ballet Theatre and allowed the fact to be publicized in America and in Europe—even in Italy, where, of course, no one was fooled. But in time even Miss Chase was forced to face the realities of the situation. The more mundane considerations of contract negotiations —and Miss Chase negotiated and signed all the dancers contracts*—made it inescapably apparent that there was something different about Fracci's relationship with Ballet Theatre.

The contract signed by the regular members of the company is a standard form published by the dancers' union, AGMA. All the conditions of the dancer's employment are spelled out in print, and it only remains to insert in the blanks provided for the purpose the dancer's weekly salary and the date on which the performing year will start. The company is obligated to pay the salary for services performed in thirty-six weeks over a fifty-two-week period, and the dancer agrees to

be available to rehearse or perform whenever called upon to do so during that period. Since becoming director in 1945 Miss Chase had signed thousands of these contracts following annual face-to-face discussions with all the dancers.* However, in the late sixties a new element entered these discussions.

Until that time Miss Chase had not been required to specify in advance the dates of the thirty-six weeks in which the dancer's services would be required. Often the bookings for the latter half of the year had not yet been made when the contract was being signed. But if the dancer inquired about these dates, it was more out of casual curiosity than for any practical purpose. Then in the late sixties a change swept over the entire ballet world with the revived interest in the classics, the proliferation of companies, and the introduction of jet travel. Whereas previously there had been no more than half a dozen classical ballet companies of major status, by the mid-sixties there were several dozen, some of them in countries like Germany and Japan in which ballet had only recently been virtually unknown. In the process of establishing themselves these new companies sought to bolster their public appeal by presenting international stars as guests in leading roles. And as jet planes could transport the stars halfway around the world in a matter of hours, it became feasible to sign them for a short engagement of only a few performances. But if the stars were to be free to accept such engagements, they would have to inform themselves well in advance concerning the dates when their services would be required by their home companies. Consequently, during contract discussions dancers began to ask such precise questions as "Can I be free to dance THE NUTCRACKER in Atlanta on January 4th?" "The Munich Opera wants me to do SWAN LAKE and GISELLE from March 12th through the 22nd. What can I tell them?" As Miss Chase was acutely aware that dancers were underpaid in comparison with other performers and that their active dancing careers must be short, she not only approved of their making as much money as possible outside the company but urged them not to miss an opportunity. And with her own dancers flying off to appear as guests in Seattle, Miami, London, Tokyo, Brisbane, and Buenos Aires, it occurred to Miss Chase that perhaps the time had come for Ballet Theatre to frankly adapt itself to the use of guests from abroad.

That the first step had already been taken with the engagement of Fracci was made clear by the nature of her contract. She was not, like the regular members of the company, engaged for the year or by the week. She was signed for specific performances to dance specific roles. Miss Chase soon resigned herself to the reality that Fracci was in fact a guest star, and as other dancers sought the same status, she began to reshape the company's policy and to visualize Ballet Theatre as a company that could function in much the same manner as the Metropolitan Opera. From its earliest days the Metropolitan had acknowledged that grand opera required grand star singers, and that since such singers were

---

*As union regulations became more specific and restrictive and as company policies changed, the area of negotiation between Miss Chase and the dancer narrowed. Previously the salaries of all the dancers from the latest entrant to the top star were open to negotiation, provided they were not set below the single specified minimum. Later the union set separate minimums for first-year corps de ballet dancers and first-year soloists, in both cases with automatic minimum increases in each subsequent year. Once these minimums were established, negotiations became superfluous and no dancer was paid more than the specified minimum. Previously, too, the starting dates had differed for individual dancers. If a dancer was not needed for the early rehearsal weeks he was not called or paid. Later the union decreed that all dancers must begin work on and be paid from the same day. Earlier all dancers, down to the last corps de ballet member, were listed not in alphabetical order but in an order determined by a combination of talent and seniority. The dancer's position on the roster was often the subject of the most prolonged discussions at contract-signing time. Most of this was eliminated when the company adopted the policy of listing dancers in alphabetical order in the three categories of principal dancer, soloist, and corps de ballet—leaving only the category to which the dancer would be assigned as a point for debate. Otherwise contract negotiations were limited to reaching agreements on opportunities the dancer would be given to perform new roles. Only with the principal dancers does the question of salary still arise, because the union has set no minimum for stars.

always in short supply, they must be shared with other companies. Accordingly the Metropolitan trained and maintained its own chorus, its contingent of soloists, and its ballet corps, but it imported stars from abroad for limited engagements. And when the Met developed its own American stars, it shared these too with foreign companies. Ballet Theatre's unannounced but realistic adoption of a similar modus operandi came at a time when dancers were emerging from behind iron curtains and when West European dancers were seeking a showcase in New York, the new capital of the dance world. Just as, earlier in the century, a singer could not be said to have reached the pinnacle of international fame until he or she had sung at the Metropolitan, so it had now become necessary for a dancer to win the approval of New York critics and audiences. Foreign stars were anxious to become associated with an American company, and Ballet Theatre was ready to receive them.

With the gratifying artistic and financial success of SWAN LAKE, Chase and Smith had increased their concentration on the classic wing of the repertory. In rapid succession they added to SWAN LAKE and LA SYLPHIDE fresh productions of GISELLE, COPPÉLIA, LA FILLE MAL GARDÉE, and PETROUCHKA—works that constituted a ready-made repertory for the visiting stars, all of whom had become familiar with at least similar versions in their home companies. Thus the visitors could step into the leading roles with a minimum of preparation (something they could not do with the contemporary ballets of, say, Tudor, Balanchine, and Robbins, which required extended rehearsals before the dancers could not only learn the choreography but also adjust themselves to the choreographers' unique mental and stylistic approaches to ballet). By 1970, then, Ballet Theatre had a supply of classical vehicles in which the guests could star, and its directors' distaste for the designation "guest star" had all but vanished.

Natalia Makarova was the first of the stars to arrive from the Soviet Union. In the summer of 1970 Ballet Theatre was performing at Covent Garden during the same weeks in which the Kirov Ballet was appearing across the river in Festival Hall. Konstantin Sergeyev and his wife, Natalia Dudinskaya, the artistic director and ballet mistress of the Kirov Ballet, attended a performance at Covent Garden and were spotted by Payne. He reminded Miss Chase that they had entertained Ballet Theatre in 1960 with a banquet at the Artists Club in Leningrad, and he suggested it would be appropriate for her to greet them. During a cordial exchange the Sergeyevs introduced Miss Chase to what appeared to be a shy, schoolgirlish youngster who accompanied them. Afterward, back in the Crush Bar, Miss Chase breathlessly announced to an uninformed and therefore unimpressed Payne, "That was Makarova with them!" A few weeks later, after Makarova was accorded political asylum in England, the Sergeyevs returned to Leningrad fully expecting to be declared "non-persons." And when, after some months, Marakova joined Ballet Theatre their nights may well have been disturbed by night-

mares in which they once more inadvisedly introduced her to Lucia Chase. The introduction, in fact, played no part in the engagement of the ballerina, who did not defect until after Ballet Theatre had left London.

As soon as the defection was announced, Miss Chase dispatched offers by mail, but a contract might never have been signed had not Sherwin Goldman, the president of the Ballet Theatre Foundation, flown to London to meet with Makarova's lawyer, her English advisors, and her English-speaking Russian fiancé. The agreement contained a guarantee that she would receive a minimum of $35,000 in salaries from Ballet Theatre and in fees from guest appearances outside the company. Though her earnings during the first year exceeded the guarantee, she later denounced the agreement as unfair. This is perhaps not so much a commentary on the shrewdness of American managers as on the speed with which Soviet defectors master the workings of American capitalism. It is true that her presence brought added money to the box office, but it is questionable whether Ballet Theatre made money on her. More accurately, she lowered the deficit incurred by Ballet Theatre in maintaining a company that would serve as a fine setting for her brilliance.

Makarova was scheduled to make her American debut at City Center on December 22, 1970, dancing GISELLE with Erik Bruhn, who became ill and was replaced by Ivan Nagy.* Subsequently during the three-week engagement she danced COPPÉLIA with Ted Kivitt, LES SYLPHIDES with Erik Bruhn, and JARDIN AUX LILAS with John Prinz. This was the first of what have become known as Ballet Theatre's superstar-studded seasons, and it broke all existing box-office records at the City Center. The public rushed to see Makarova, but it also filled the house to compare her Swanilda with those of Fracci, Gregory, and D'Antuono. A section of the vast balcony that had customarily been curtained off was opened up and all the seats were sold, many of them to people who must have been making their first acquaintances with Ballet Theatre. Attracted to the theater by the appearances of the foreign guests, they remained to applaud debut performances by regulars Cynthia Gregory, in MISS JULIE, and John Prinz, as the lead in LES PATINEURS. And those with discriminating eyes may have taken note of a young Dutch soloist who had come to Ballet Theatre via the National Ballet of Canada and who substituted for Gregory in the premiere of Dennis Nahat's ONTOGENY. Her name was Martine van Hamel and four years earlier she had won a gold medal at the International Competition in Varna, Bulgaria (the male winner that year was a young Russian named Mikhail Baryshnikov). (continued on page 276)

---

*The seeds of a new myth similar to that which grew out of Markova and Bruhn's first performance of GISELLE in 1955 (see page 324) were sown in a report printed in the official Ballet Theatre Friends Newsletter of March 1971: "Erik Bruhn was to have been Miss Makarova's partner; however, he unfortunately fell ill and was hospitalized during the last week of rehearsals. Ivan Nagy, who had been making guest appearances with the Boston Ballet, quickly returned to New York and replaced Mr. Bruhn, having time only to rehearse some of the lifts and some of the mime passages with Miss Makarova before they went on." Bruhn was ill and Nagy did return from Boston, but he returned the day before the performance in time to rehearse for two hours with Makarova and dance with her in a full dress rehearsal with the entire company on stage.

THE SEVENTIES

Ballet Theatre entered the 1970s with its repertory problems largely solved. In addition to its production of enduring classics, it had a storehouse of successful modern works that could be brought forth as required. Whenever it appeared advisable to retire a ballet for a rest—either because the dancers were bored with performing it or because audiences were tired of repeated viewings—it was possible for the directors to revive a work then in hibernation. If, for example, THE RIVER were due for a well-earned sabbatical, its function as a closing ballet with roles for young soloists could be fulfilled by a revived GRADUATION BALL or RODEO. While the search for new choreographers continued, it became less desperate because established choreographers in almost every category produced successful ballets.

From among the veterans, Antony Tudor contributed two works: SHADOWPLAY, which he had previously choreographed for the British Royal Ballet and which provided a challenging exposure to the Tudor style for Mikhail Baryshnikov, Fernando Bujones, and Charles Ward. Tudor's THE LEAVES ARE FADING was the first ballet he had created especially for Ballet Theatre since NIMBUS in 1950. OTHER DANCES entered the repertory by fortuitous circumstance: Jerome Robbins had created it for Natalia Makarova and Baryshnikov to dance at a benefit for the Lincoln Center Library of the Performing Arts. It is now being performed by both Ballet Theatre and the New York City Ballet, a distinction for modern works duplicated at this time only by Balanchine's THEME AND VARIATIONS. Frederick Ashton's WALTZES IN THE MANNER OF ISADORA [Duncan] also reached the Ballet Theatre stage via a gala benefit. A ROSE FOR MISS EMILY and TEXAS FOURTH were created by Agnes de Mille for pupils in North Carolina but were given professional performances by Ballet Theatre.

THE LEAVES ARE FADING GELSEY KIRKLAND, JONAS KAGE, KIM HIGHTON.

WALTZES IN THE MANNER OF ISADORA LYNN SEYMOUR.   **A ROSE FOR MISS EMILY** (CENTER TOP) SALLIE WILSON.   **THE MOOR'S PAVANE** BRUCE MARKS, R

NANDEZ, SALLIE WILSON, CYNTHIA GREGORY.   **GAÎTÉ PARISIENNE** MIMI PAUL, BRUCE MARKS; (TOP) CYNTHIA GREGORY, IVAN NAGY.

MENDELSSOHN SYMPHONY MARTINE VAN HAMEL.

SOME TIMES DENNIS NAHAT.

The revival of ballets by the Russian choreographers Fokine (FIREBIRD) and Massine (GAÎTÉ PARISIENNE) did not live up to expectations. It had long been thought that GAÎTÉ would prove ideal for the spirited personalities of successive Ballet Theatre companies, but present-day dancers could not take seriously Massine's 1930s approach to comedy. It had been hoped that FIREBIRD would provide an ideal ballerina role, but its revival proved only that Fokine's 1910 choreography was old-fashioned, not yet to be accepted with the tolerance accorded to unchallenged classics. José Limon's masterpiece, THE MOOR'S PAVANE, and his THE TRAITOR were revived, and the final contribution from a veteran was supplied by the Ballet Theatre graduate Alberto Alonso, who staged his version of CARMEN, which he had created for his sister-in-law Alicia in 1967. Soloists of the Cuban Ballet and Ballet Theatre, which had interchanged dancers in the fifties, danced together in 1976 for the first time since their governments had broken off relations fifteen years before — once more indicating that art is, or should be, above politics.

MEDEA CARLA FRACCI, MIKHAIL BARYSHNIKOV.

The young American talent that had blossomed in the sixties continued to flourish in the seventies. Dennis Nahat created three works, ONTOGENY, MENDELSSOHN SYMPHONY, and SOME TIMES. With the production of MEDEA, which was previewed at the Festival of Two Worlds in Spoleto, John Butler became the first American with whom Baryshnikov worked in the choreographic style of the West. In 1971 Eliot Feld created two works for Ballet Theatre, A SOLDIER'S TALE and ECCENTRIQUE, and the next year contributed two more ballets, THEATRE and INTERMEZZO, which he had choreographed originally for his own company. Of the four, INTERMEZZO gives promise of enduring. During the first half of the 1970s, Glen Tetley's creative activities were concentrated in Europe, and it was not until 1975 that he returned to stage for the company works he had created abroad: GEMINI, LE SACRE DU PRINTEMPS, and VOLUNTARIES. Before departing to become a director of the San Francisco Ballet, Michael Smuin staged his SCHUBERTIADE for Ballet Theatre.

THEATRE
ELIOT FELD

ECCENTRIQUE CHRISTINE SARRY, JOHN SOWINSKI.

INTERMEZZO CYNTHIA GREGORY, IVAN NAGY.

INTERMEZZO CHRISTINE SARRY, ELIOT FELD.

A SOLDIER'S TALE DANIEL LEVANS, SALLIE WILSON.

GEMINI CYNTHIA GREGORY, JONAS KAGE; (TOP) CLARK TIPPET, MARTINE VAN HAMEL, KAGE, GREGORY. **VOLUNTARIES** (TOP)

LE SACRE DU PRINTEMPS (CENTER BOTTOM) MIKHAIL BARYSHNIKOV; (TOP RIGHT) BARYSHNIKOV; (BOTTOM RIGHT) CLARK TIPPET, MARTINE VAN HAMEL.

HAMLET CONNOTATIONS ERIK BRUHN, MIKHAIL BARYSHNIKOV, MARCIA HAYDÉE, WILLIAM CARTER.

SCHERZO FOR MASSAH JACK BONNIE MATHIS, WILLIAM CARTER.

LE BAISER DE LA FÉE JONAS KAGE, IVAN NAGY, CYNTHIA GREGORY.

THREE ESSAYS IAN HORVATH, CLARK TIPPET, CHRISTINE SARRY, WARREN CONOVER.

EPILOGUE NATALIA MAKAROVA, ERIK BRUHN.

Four Americans whose talent had already been revealed elsewhere made their first contributions to the Ballet Theatre repertory during the decade. John Neumeier had attained international recognition as a choreographer through his work as ballet master with European companies. To Ballet Theatre he brought his version of LE BAISER DE LA FÉE, and he devised for Natalia Makarova and Erik Bruhn the EPILOGUE pas de deux. HAMLET CONNOTATIONS was created for the star-studded cast of Mikhail Baryshnikov, Erik Bruhn, William Carter, Marcia Haydée, and Gelsey Kirkland. Lar Lubovitch worked with the company for two seasons to produce two unconventional works, SCHERZO FOR MASSAH JACK and THREE ESSAYS, that were meant to be experimental but proved to be no more than incomprehensible. Alvin Ailey took time off from his own company to create THE RIVER and SEA-CHANGE. With a score by Duke Ellington and numerous solo roles that could exploit the talents of young dancers, THE RIVER became a most useful component in the fashioning of programs. PAS DE "DUKE," created originally as a vehicle for Judith Jamison and Baryshnikov in a benefit performance for Ailey's own company, was later included in the Ballet Theatre season. Twyla Tharp was also an accomplished choreographer before Baryshnikov's presence in the company inspired her to create PUSH COMES TO SHOVE. It was a hit of such proportions as is apt to occur only once in a decade, and went on to become the triumph of Ballet Theatre's 1977 European tour. For a Ballet Theatre benefit, she created ONCE MORE, FRANK for Baryshnikov and herself.

SEA-CHANGE
SALLIE WILSON

PAS DE "DUKE" (TOP)
MIKHAIL BARYSHNIKOV
JUDITH JAMISON

THE RIVER
WILLIAM CARTER

(CENTER TOP)
CYNTHIA GREGORY, GAYLE YOUNG

(CENTER BOTTOM)
KEITH LEE, MARIANNA TCHERKASSKY

PUSH COMES TO SHOVE MIKHAIL BARYSHNIKOV, MARIANNA TCHERKASSKY; (OPPOSITE PAGE) RICHARD SCHAFER, MARTINE VAN HAMEL, CLARK TIPPET.

ONCE MORE, FRANK MIKHAIL BARYSHNIKOV, TWYLA THARP.

TALES OF HOFFMANN ELEANOR D'ANTUONO, TED KIVITT; (TOP) CYNTHIA GREGORY; (TOP CENTER) DENNIS NAHAT, D'ANTUONO, FERNANDO BUJONES, IVAN NAGY; (TOP RIGHT) KIVITT, D'ANTUONO

Three imports were of Russian origin. GRAND PAS CLASSIQUE was created by the Saint Petersburg expatriate Victor Gsovsky; VESTRIS had been choreographed for Baryshnikov by Leonid Jacobson; and the pas de deux from FLAMES OF PARIS, staged by David and Anna-Marie Holmes, was originally the work of the Soviet choreographer Vasily

MONUMENT FOR A DEAD BOY NAGY, MARCOS PAREDES, FRANK SMITH, CHARLES WARD.

VESTRIS MIKHAIL BARYSHNIKOV.

Vainonen. From Scotland came Peter Darrell's full-evening TALES OF HOFFMANN; from the Netherlands, Rudi van Dantzig's MONUMENT FOR A DEAD BOY. Sweden contributed THE MIRACULOUS MANDARIN, Ulf Gadd's interpretation of Bartók's score, which was no more successful than all previous versions.

THE NUTCRACKER
MIKHAIL BARYSHNIKOV
MARIANNA TCHERKASSKY

Not since the early days of the company had the dancers of Ballet Theatre been afforded the opportunity of working under the direction of dancer-choreographers whose experiences in the Maryinsky Theater (now the Kirov) were still fresh in their minds. Like Fokine, Nijinska, and Bolm in the 1940s, Makarova, Baryshnikov, and Nureyev in the 1970s not only staged their versions of the Russian classics but conveyed to the American dancers an aura of the old Russian style which, despite the Revolution, must still survive in the classrooms and stages of Leningrad. Makarova's staging of the Kingdom of the Shades scene from LA BAYADÈRE was designed to reproduce the original choreography, and although Baryshnikov's THE NUTCRACKER and Nureyev's RAYMONDA were revised ver-

sions, they remained stylistically Russian. Dimitri Romanoff, in staging the new production of LA FILLE MAL GARDÉE, reproduced the choreography that Mikhail Mordkin had brought with him from the Bolshoi in 1910. With the new complete SLEEPING BEAUTY, it appeared unnecessary for Ballet Theatre to add further to its repertory of great nineteenth-century classics, but this production did in fact additionally stimulate the appetite of the directors and the dancers. The vast public that viewed on television the live performances of SWAN LAKE and GISELLE from Lincoln Center — an audience of millions, larger than the combined audience at all previous performances of GISELLE — was also eager for more. So it was that thought was immediately given to other classics: a complete BAYADÈRE to be staged by Makarova and a full production of DON QUIXOTE by Baryshnikov.

LA FILLE MAL GARDÉE NATALIA MAKAROVA WITH IVAN NAGY, MARCOS PAREDES, FRANK SMITH; (OPPOSITE PAGE) HELYN DOUGLAS, MICHAEL SMUIN, JAN FISHER.

LA BAYADÈRE
GELSEY KIRKLAND
MIKHAIL BARYSHNIKOV

(OPPOSITE PAGE, TOP)
MARTINE VAN HAMEL
VLADIMIR GELVAN

(MIDDLE)
IVAN NAGY
CYNTHIA GREGORY

(BOTTOM)
NATALIA MAKAROVA
FERNANDO BUJONES

RAYMONDA CYNTHIA GREGORY, RUDOLF NUREYEV.

NUREYEV, ERIK BRUHN; (TOP) KARENA BROCK, NUREYEV, CHARLES WARD, GREGORY, BRUHN, CLARK TIPPET, MARTINE VAN HAMEL.

WITH ITS PERFORMANCES IN LA BAYADÈRE, THE BALLET THEATRE DANCERS EARNED ACCLAIM AS A CORPS DE BALLET SECOND TO NONE.

Makarova's supreme art greatly enhanced Ballet Theatre's stature during the ensuing years (not to mention the bolstering of its box office), but it was not until 1974 that the ballerina made her greatest contribution to the company. In that season she staged the Shades scene from the fourth act of Marius Petipa's LA BAYADÈRE. The ballet had been one of the favorite vehicles of the Imperial Russian ballerinas, but the true star of this act was the corps de ballet of twenty-four girls who portray the spirits in the Kingdom of the Shades. The spirits enter one by one down a ramp to the continual repetition of a single phrase of music. They proceed in an attenuated line to trace a serpentine pattern back and forth across the stage as they execute in unison a series of cantilever arabesques. For Ballet Theatre this was a daring undertaking. There were those who feared that this complete harmony of movement could not be attained by the disparate elements that made up the company's corps de ballet. Payne, for example, protested that the ballet should be attempted only by a corps de ballet like that of the Kirov, whose individual dancers had all been trained at the same school, or by a company like the Royal Ballet, whose dancers had all

been born in the same English village; the Entrance of the Spirits was not for the American girls, who were of all sizes, from all schools of dance education, and of every racial and ethnic background. Happily, this prediction only proved how wrong one can be after thirty-four years of intimate association with a ballet company. The American corps danced as though they had all been born and trained in Makarova's hometown, Leningrad. And this finesse was almost entirely the result of Makarova's stern discipline, careful attention to detail, and inspiring enthusiasm. The corps emerged from the experience with new confidence, a confidence they carried over into the performances of other ballets. Thereafter at the conclusion of such corps passages as the Dance of the Wilis in GISELLE, they received ovations as prolonged as those usually reserved for the stars. At about the same time, Goldman obtained a grant from the Rockefeller Foundation to expand the artistic staff. Ballet Theatre graduates Scott Douglas and Michael Lland returned and, with others, rehearsed, coached, and oversaw performances to assure the maintenance of high standards of ensemble work.

NATALIA MAKAROVA IN SWAN LAKE AND IN THE DON QUIXOTE PAS DE DEUX.

ELEANOR D'ANTUONO IN DIANA AND ACTAEON.

SALLIE WILSON IN FALL RIVER LEGEND.

MARTINE VAN HAMEL IN SWAN LAKE.

GELSEY KIRKLAND IN THE DON QUIXOTE PAS DE DEUX.

CHARLES WARD IN ETUDES.

IVAN NAGY IN APOLLO.

TED KIVITT IN LE CORSAIRE PAS DE DEUX.

FERNANDO BUJONES IN THEME AND VARIATIONS.

In 1974, when Mikhail Baryshnikov was making a decision as to the company with which he would become associated, Ballet Theatre was in a favorable position. It was not the only company equipped with a superior corps de ballet and headed by stars of international repute against whom he could continue to prove his mettle. Neither was it unique in having accumulated a strong repertory of classic ballets in which he could appear when he so wished, or in having won favor with a large and enthusiastic audience. But Ballet Theatre could offer other attractions that Baryshnikov found irresistible. Its diversified collection of contemporary ballets by many choreographers was as strong as its classic repertory, and this served as a powerful magnet to Baryshnikov in view of his expressed determination to explore the new fields of choreography that had been opened up in the West. This appeal was further strengthened by Ballet Theatre's proven commitment to searching out and employing new choreographers, making it probable that he would find opportunities to collaborate with one or more of them in the creation of new roles and ballets. Further, Ballet Theatre had commissioned Makarova and Nureyev to stage ballets from the Kirov repertory. If Baryshnikov, too, were so commissioned, it would enable him to try his hand at staging—which might lead to experiments in original choreography.

The desire for free access to progressive choreography had been suggested before as a prime motivation for defection,

MIKHAIL BARYSHNIKOV AS ALBRECHT IN GISELLE AND ON OPPOSITE PAGE (TOP) AS JAMES IN LA SYLPHIDE AND (BOTTOM) AS HAMLET WITH GELSEY KIRKLAND, AS THE BOY WITH MATTED HAIR IN SHADOWPLAY, AND AS FRANZ WITH KIRKLAND IN COPPÉLIA.

but among previous defectors the search for new choreographic experiences had been barely distinguishable from the search for new roles common to all dancers. Baryshnikov, however, very quickly demonstrated his indisputable sincerity. He proved to be not only an unsurpassed classical dancer, a sensitive actor, and a complete and dedicated artist but also an ardent and receptive student. Choreographers, who, as might be expected, were eager to work with him, were amazed not so much by his fantastic virtuosity as by his serious and cooperative attitude. His concentration was at all times intense, his dancing at rehearsals always "full out," and he clearly never even considered the possibility that he might know more about choreography than the choreographer. His instinctive movements during rehearsals might inspire choreography, but in performance he executed the steps exactly as taught to him by the choreographer. Within a year, in the role of the Boy with Matted Hair in SHADOWPLAY, he was dancing in total harmony with Tudor's unique style and psychological approach. He captured the subtleties of Bruhn's conception of James in LA SYLPHIDE long before they were understood by other less attentive stars. And, finally, he had adjusted his classic technique unerringly to the grotesqueries of Twyla Tharp's far-out PUSH COMES TO SHOVE, which could be regarded as the ultimate in the exploration of new fields of choreography. Like Makarova, he boosted the reputation of Ballet Theatre, but as great premiers danseurs sell even more tickets than great ballerinas,* his contribution to the company's financial well-being was more noteworthy. All of his performances were sold out.

While Baryshnikov was considering how best to conduct his career in the West, he was confronted with the problem that faces all performing artists in this jet age, namely, how to satisfy the demands for appearances around the world and take advantage of the future financial security the fees will make possible, while at the same time maintaining artistic integrity and continuing to grow as an artist. Baryshnikov's advisors recognized the danger, already discovered by the violinist Yehudi Menuhin, that a superstar might find himself wasting a disproportionate number of life's hours on board jet planes. After analyzing the experiences of other superstars of ballet, they came to the conclusion that Baryshnikov must choose a company that would serve not simply as a base from which he could embark on globe-circling guest appearances but as a "home" to which he could return for protracted periods of artistic and creative rejuvenation. Ballet Theatre gave promise of providing such a home. Only time will tell whether the company will satisfactorily fulfill this promise or whether other fields may someday appear greener to Baryshnikov.

---

*Only male stars of the magnitude of Nureyev and Baryshnikov will invariably sell out every performance—and when they appear together with such ballerinas as Makarova and Fonteyn, the box office may even be forced to turn away potential ticket buyers. So far there has never been a ballerina who could sell out every performance on her own—not even Pavlova, whose box-office appeal was weaker than Nijinsky's. This difference is perhaps explained by the nature of classic choreography. The steps assigned to male dancers are physically exhibitionistic, appear difficult to execute, involve an element of danger, and would seem to defy the laws of gravity. On the other hand, the steps assigned to the ballerina (with the exception of the thirty-two fouettés) are executed most properly and aesthetically when performed with restraint and understatement. Consequently, to the average viewer, who is not a connoisseur, the performance of a premier danseur generates more excitement than that of a ballerina.

BALLET THEATRE 1977: (TOP ROW) GEORGE DE LA PENA, MARTINE VAN HAMEL, CLARK TIPPET, MARIANNA TCHERKASSKY, ENRIQUE MARTINEZ, NANETTE GLUSHAK, MICHAEL OWEN; (BOTTOM) KARENA BROCK, KIRK PETERSON, FERNANDO BUJONES.

Baryshnikov joined Ballet Theatre in time to participate in its Thirty-fifth Anniversary celebrations, appearing in the Gala Performance at the City Center on January 11, 1975. On the same date in 1940, Ballet Theatre had given its debut performance at the Rockefeller Center Theatre—since demolished—only a few blocks away. The 1940 program had opened with LES SYLPHIDES, and when that ballet was repeated in 1975, the original dancers of the Mazurka and the Prelude, Karen Conrad and Lucia Chase, were in the audience to verify that the company had remained steadfast to the lyrical style impressed upon it in its early years by Fokine. He had instilled the same style in the ballet of Saint Petersburg–Leningrad while serving after the Revolution as ballet master of the State Ballet (the transitional company between the Maryinsky and the Kirov), and eventually it was inherited by Baryshnikov and Makarova.

The Rose Adagio from THE SLEEPING BEAUTY was presented with Igor Youskevitch and André Eglevsky dancing two of the leading male roles, and Irina Baronova and Anton Dolin, who had performed in Ballet Theatre's original version, were there to testify that the company had always staged the classic ballet and had welcomed foreign stars as guests.

Makarova's appearance in an excerpt from Kenneth MacMillan's CONCERTO was reminiscent of Alicia Markova's earlier appearances in the modern works of the young Englishman Antony Tudor, who, along with Hugh Laing, was present to recall that Ballet Theatre had always sought to enrich its repertory by including works by European choreographers.

Excerpts from PILLAR OF FIRE, FANCY FREE, and THREE VIRGINS AND A DEVIL were witness to the fact that Ballet Theatre had in the past devoted a large proportion of its energies to creativity and had succeeded in producing its share of durable masterpieces. The presence on stage of Jerome Robbins, Agnes de Mille, and Antony Tudor was ample proof of the diversity of the company's choreographic contributors. And Nora Kaye, John Kriza, and Sono Osato also came forward to demonstrate that there had always been dancers who, when given the opportunity to choose, had chosen Ballet Theatre over other companies because of its repertory, just as the same choice had been made more recently by Cynthia Gregory, Gelsey Kirkland, and Fernando Bujones.

When the corps de ballet danced a section from Alvin Ailey's THE RIVER, the evening's artists and audience could indulge in at least the illusion of stability and permanence. For in 1940, when Ballet Theatre gave its first performance, Ailey had been only nine years old and not one of the participating dancers had yet been born.

Out front in the audience and in the lobbies during intermission there was a reminder of the excitement and glamour that had played so important a role in the success of Diaghilev's premieres in Paris and in the introduction of ballet to New York at the old Metropolitan Opera House. The equivalent of what used to be known as "tout Paris"—translated into "all New York"—was present that night, as it was, in even greater numbers, at subsequent performances. This sort of audience excitement had not been seen in ballet theaters for a good many years.

The whole evening was, of course, a source of renewed satisfaction to Lucia Chase, a convincing confirmation that thirty-five years had been well spent. She would continue to resist any suggestion that she was solely responsible for the success and survival of Ballet Theatre, and certainly there were hundreds of other contributors. But of Lucia Chase alone could it be said that had she not been there, Ballet Theatre would never have been alive to celebrate its Thirty-fifth Anniversary.

(CLOCKWISE FROM LOWER LEFT) GELSEY KIRKLAND, MARTINE VAN HAMEL, CYNTHIA GREGORY, MARIANNA TCHERKASSKY, NATALIA MAKAROVA.

IN THE REPERTORY

(TOP) **THEME AND VARIATIONS** KIRKLAND, BARYSHNIKOV. **APOLLO** GREGORY, MICHAEL DENARD, DEBORAH DOBSON, VAN HAMEL. **JARDIN AUX LILAS** MAKAROVA, BUJONES. **ROMEO AND JU**

JOHN PRINZ, MAKAROVA. (BOTTOM) **GALA PERFORMANCE** SALLIE WILSON, GREGORY, D'ANTUONO. **PILLAR OF FIRE** GAYLE YOUNG, WILSON. **ROMEO AND JULIET** LYNN SEYMOUR, BUJONES.

288   (TOP LEFT) **SHADOW OF THE WIND** JOHN KRIZA.   (BOTTOM LEFT) **UNDERTOW** STEVEN-JAN HOFF.   (ABOVE) **ROMEO AND JULIET** NORA KAYE, DIMITRI ROMANOFF, HUGH LAING.

290 (TOP LEFT) **RODEO** CHRISTINE SARRY, TERRY ORR. (BOTTOM LEFT) ***THREE VIRGINS AND A DEVIL*** DENNIS NAHAT, WILSON. (ABOVE) ***FANCY FREE*** BUJONES, ORR, BUDDY BALOUGH.

ILY THE KID ORR, TCHERKASSKY.

FALL RIVER LEGEND CHASE, YOUNG, WILSON.

ADUATION BALL ORR, BALOUGH, SARRY, SOWINSKI, BUJONES, RICHARD CAMMACK, CONOVER, KENNETH HUGHES, (REAR) RORY FOSTER, TIPPET, DENNIS MARSHALL, RICHARD SCHAFER, WARD.

292 (LEFT) **LA SYLPHIDE** MIKHAIL BARYSHNIKOV, MAKAROVA. **GISELLE** (TOP CENTER) MAKAROVA, ERIK BRUHN; (BOTTOM CENTER) NANETTE GLUSHAK, VAN HAMEL, JOLINDA MENENDEZ.

294 **GISELLE** (TOP LEFT) KIRKLAND; (BOTTOM LEFT) MAKAROVA, BARYSHNIKOV; (ABOVE) GREGORY, KIVITT.

(TOP) **GISELLE** MAKAROVA, RUTH MAYER, IVAN NAGY. **COPPÉLIA** (BOTTOM LEFT) KIVITT, MAKAROVA; (BOTTOM RIGHT) KIRKLAND, BARYSHNIKOV. 295

(TOP LEFT) **LA BAYADÈRE** BARYSHNIKOV. (TOP RIGHT) **DON QUIXOTE PAS DE DEUX** KIRKLAND. (BOTTOM) **LES SYLPHIDES** LUPE SERRANO, NAGY, NAOMI SORKIN, GREGORY.

FIREBIRD (TOP LEFT) KARENA BROCK, BRUHN; (TOP RIGHT) BRUHN, MAKAROVA. (BOTTOM) **SWAN LAKE** YOUNG, LUCIA CHASE. 297

298   (TOP ROW) **LA SYLPHIDE** (LEFT) THE REEL;   (CENTER) BRUHN, NAGY, KIRKLAND;   (RIGHT) MAKAROVA, BARYSHNIKOV.

(BOTTOM ROW) **SWAN LAKE** MAKAROVA, NAGY; GREGORY, NAGY; GREGORY, NAGY. (RIGHT) **THE SLEEPING BEAUTY** FERNANDO BUJONES, YOKO MORISHITA. 299

THE SLEEPING BEAUTY (TOP LEFT) MARCOS PAREDES, YOUNG, WILSON; (TOP RIGHT) NAGY, MAKAROVA; (BOTTOM) VAN HAMEL WITH (KNEELING, CLOCKWISE) REBECCA WRIGHT, LESLIE BROWN

302 (TOP LEFT) **SPECTRE DE LA ROSE** TCHERKASSKY, BARYSHNIKOV. (TOP RIGHT) **THE MAIDS** DANIEL LEVANS, YOUNG. (BOTTOM) *LES SYLPHIDES* MAKAROVA.

(TOP LEFT) **CONCERTO** NAGY, MAKAROVA **ETUDES** (TOP RIGHT) D'ANTUONO, BUJONES; (BOTTOM) THE CORPS. **303**

(TOP LEFT) **SHADOWPLAY** KIRKLAND, BARYSHNIKOV. (TOP RIGHT) *LE JEUNE HOMME ET LA MORT* BARYSHNIKOV, BONNIE MATHIS. (BOTTOM) **PUSH COMES TO SHOVE** BARYSHNIK

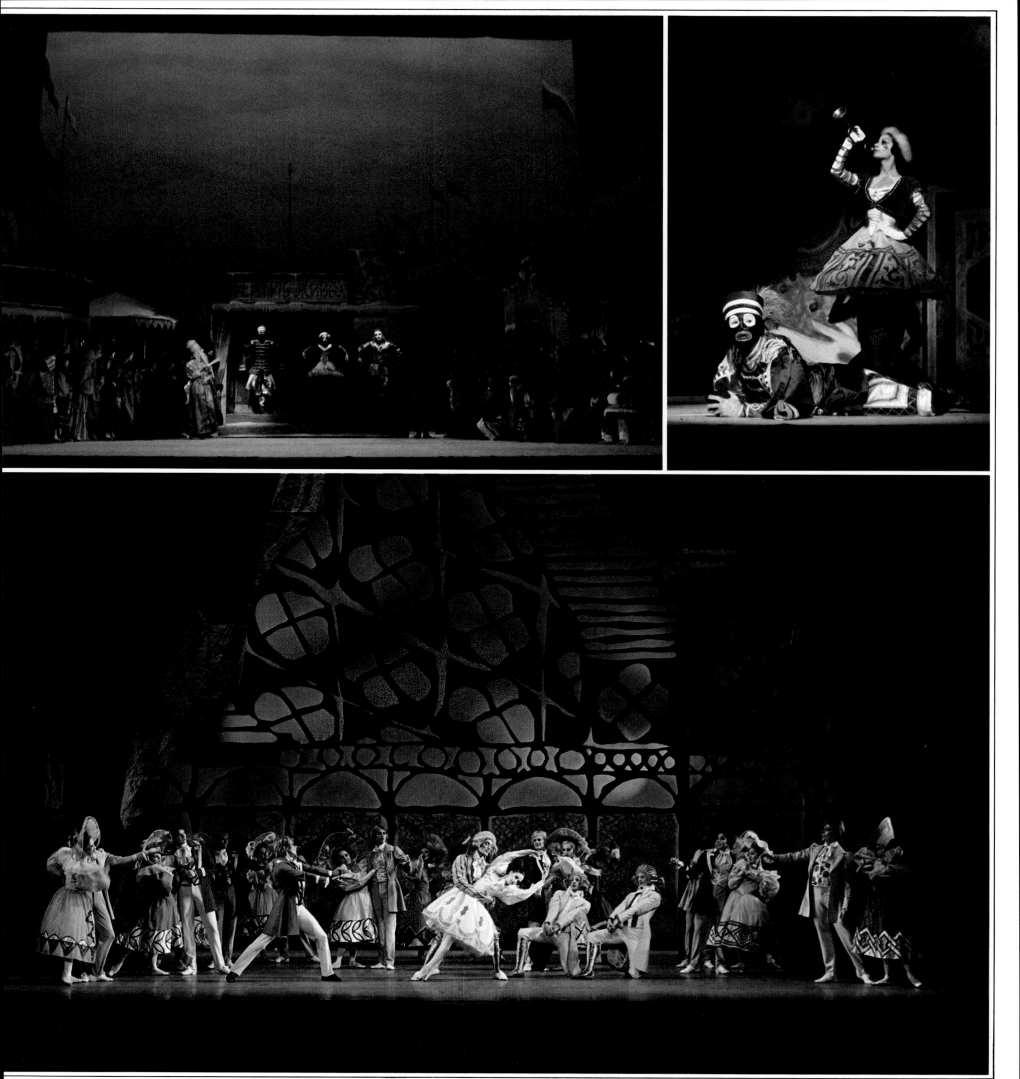

ET, VAN HAMEL. **PETROUCHKA** (TOP LEFT) FAIR SCENE; (TOP RIGHT) KIVITT, D'ANTUONO. (BOTTOM) **TALES OF HOFFMANN** NAGY, D'ANTUONO.

FIREBIRD CYNTHIA GREGORY.

THE LURE OF
BALLET THEATRE
NORA KAYE

There is a bond between Ballet Theatre and former company members. Even those of us who have left it occasionally to pursue other challenges have never really felt completely separated from it. I was especially aware of this during the Thirty-fifth Anniversary celebrations and the 1975 Gala when Alicia Alonso returned to New York for the first time in fifteen years.

The lure of the company is as strong as ever. Its primary attraction for all of us has been the range of its repertory, and yet for each of us it has had its own unique appeal. For me that appeal was specifically the Tudor ballets, in addition to the classics. For Alicia Alonso it was GISELLE, plus the contemporary works. Erik Bruhn, who had little prior knowledge of the company when he joined it, soon found that the variety of its repertory strengthened his performing skills. We were all professional dancers when we joined, already destined for ballet careers, but we needed to extend ourselves, to have our individual talents used by choreographers who recognized them.

Ballet Theatre was from the start a multi-choreographer company. There were eleven in 1940 who helped us discover our own potential; for the Thirty-fifth Anniversary season an even larger internationally famous group was on hand to create and rehearse their works and to spot fresh dancing talent. The choreographers present (listed alphabetically) were Alvin Ailey (THE RIVER), Erik Bruhn (LA SYLPHIDE), Peter Darrell (TALES OF HOFFMANN), Agnes de Mille (THREE VIRGINS AND A DEVIL), Natalia Makarova (LA BAYADÈRE), Enrique Martinez (COPPÉLIA), Dennis Nahat (SOME TIMES), John Neumeier (LE BAISER DE LA FÉE), Rudolf Nureyev (RAYMONDA), Roland Petit (LE JEUNE HOMME ET LA MORT), Dimitri Romanoff (LA FILLE MAL GARDÉE), Herbert Ross (THE MAIDS), and Antony Tudor (THE LEAVES ARE FADING). Others whose ballets were rehearsed by proxies were Frederick Ashton, George Balanchine, David Blair, Eliot Feld, Harald Lander, and Jerome Robbins. Dancers can thrive only in an atmosphere charged with creativity, so it was not surprising that several soloists found themselves directed onto the way to stardom.

Ballet entered my life at a very early age. When I was five my mother enrolled me in a class conducted by Alexis Kosloff, a graduate of the Russian Imperial Ballet School in Moscow. But after a year I had to stop because of a mild diabetic condition attributed to a vegetarian diet. A year later, fully recovered, I resumed my training in Margaret Curtis' children's classes at the Metropolitan Opera Ballet School. Luckily, I had suffered no permanent damage from the illness, so when it became apparent that I could become a dancer, my mother decided I should be taught by the best. To her the best was Michel Fokine, who had been the ballet master at the Maryinsky Theater in Saint Petersburg while my parents were still in Russia. And so, at the age of eight, I was taken to his house on the corner of Seventy-second Street and Riverside Drive in New York City for an audition. He agreed to accept me as a pupil, but when my mother told him I had to have a

scholarship because there was no money for my tuition, he made it a condition that I study only with him; I would thus be a product exclusively of his teaching and would dance only in the style he had developed in his reform of pure classicism.

I soon discovered that as a coach Fokine was certainly the best but as a teacher he left something to be desired. He was too concerned with matters of style to give much thought to technique or to try to improve his pupils' technical skills. I was immediately aware of this lack because both my earlier teachers had stressed the importance of physical discipline. Kosloff had remained faithful to Russian classicism, and Miss Curtis was a teacher of the Cecchetti method, developed by Enrico Cecchetti, an Italian who had become an instructor at the Imperial Theater in Saint Petersburg in the 1890s and had taught the Russians the more spectacular technical feats accomplished by the Milanese dancers, including the thirty-two fouettés. These were sometimes referred to as vulgar, flashy tricks, particularly by those who were unable to execute them, and they were not much admired by Fokine.

Fokine started each session in a small room at the top of the house where his pupils were put through a number of random exercises, more in the nature of a muscle warm-up than a real class. It was as if he couldn't wait to get downstairs to the larger studio on the parlor floor where he could illustrate his theories and impart his own style of dancing. He did this by teaching us passages from his ballets: LES SYLPHIDES, CARNAVAL, and so on. From them he had eliminated those features that he found objectionable in the technique employed by Marius Petipa and other choreographers of the so-called classical ballets. The arms were not held "au couronne" above the head, and the hips were not held rigid to support a straight back. His was a freer, a liberated style. His dancers moved naturally, as though walking or running. Patricia Bowman recalls that when she auditioned for Fokine's classes she showed him all the technical skills she had learned from Lisa Gardiner in Washington. He was only casually interested in them. To her surprise, he asked her to run. She ran self-consciously. It was not until he himself demonstrated how to run properly and beautifully that she understood what he was driving at. He taught his dancers to hold their arms loosely, with limpid wrists and soft elbows, to stand with one hip thrust out to present a curved line, and to move slightly off balance to attain fluidity. As Annabelle Lyon discovered, it is impossible to execute the fast bourrées backward across the stage in the Mazurka from LES SYLPHIDES if the body is kept straight and the back rigid.

While teaching his freer style, Fokine theorized a great deal, stressing the importance of beauty of line and movement. But at the same time, he employed some of the difficult technical steps from the classical ballet that I had not yet mastered. And so, without his knowledge, I returned to the Metropolitan Opera Ballet School, where on Monday, Wednesday, and Friday I was trained in the classical technique—on Tuesday, Thursday, and Saturday I was told by Fokine not to use it, or at least only in his reformed version.

BOLM'S PETER AND THE WOLF

FOKINE'S PETROUCHKA (WITH LAING)

MASSINE'S MADEMOISELLE ANGOT (WITH MASSINE)

TARAS' GRAZIANA (ALONSO AND EGLEVSKY)

ROBBINS' FACSIMILE (WITH KRIZA AND LA

DE MILLE'S FALL RIVER LEGEND (WITH JAMES MITCHELL)

MACMILLAN'S JOURNEY

ANCHINE'S WALTZ ACADEMY

KIDD'S ON STAGE! (WITH KIDD)

SEMENOFF'S GIFT OF THE MAGI (WITH KRIZA AND SEMENOFF)

LAR'S JEUX (WITH YOUSKEVITCH AND VANCE)

LICHINE'S THE SPHINX

S'S CONCERTO (WITH BRUHN)

BETTIS' A STREETCAR NAMED DESIRE

Later I learned that my experience with Fokine was not unique. At about the same time, Dimitri Romanoff was discovering that Mikhail Mordkin was less concerned with technique than with inspiring his students to become extroverted, emotional, and demonstrative dancers. Like Fokine he was an inspirational teacher, and his students had to go elsewhere to supplement their training in ballet technique. Romanoff, as it happened, had received a basic training in California from Theodore Kosloff, Alexis' older brother, but there were many Fokine and Mordkin students who did not go elsewhere. Consequently, a surprising number of dancers in the early days of Ballet Theatre could boast of only limited skills, and it was often difficult to cast roles created originally for European-trained dancers. For example, in AURORA'S WEDDING (the last act of THE SLEEPING BEAUTY) it sometimes proved impossible to provide each of the six fairies with a male cavalier who was capable of executing the required double air-turns, nor could two girls always be found who could successfully whip off the fouettés called for in the Competition in GRADUATION BALL.

But difficult as it was at that time for an American dancer to acquire the proper ballet training, finding a job was almost impossible. I was luckier than most because from the age of eight I had been given the opportunity to appear on stage. In WILLIAM TELL, THE SUNKEN BELL, and other operas in which children appeared, Rosina Galli, the ballet mistress of the Metropolitan Opera, would use the pupils from the school. She was thus the first choreographer I worked with as a professional, that is if what she gave us to do—running about, tossing flowers, and so forth—could be called choreography and if the 50¢ or $1 that I was paid could be said to have qualified me as a professional. This childhood experience remained with me throughout my career. I cannot remember ever not being on the stage; I felt at home there and was never nervous till the day I stopped dancing. In 1934, when I was fourteen, I signed my first official contract as a dancer. (I am told it is still on file in the archives of the Met.) I was engaged to dance with the Metropolitan Opera Ballet for the fourteen-week season at a salary of $12 per week.

The following year the Kirstein-Balanchine company, which was called the American Ballet, became the resident ballet of the Met, and I was one of the few dancers retained from Galli's group. It was in the course of that year that I became disenchanted with ballet—not with the American Ballet company but with opera ballet in general. As dancers we were definitely ranked as second-class citizens. We performed a superfluous, often unwanted role in the opera. The space allotted us to dance on was often too restricted, the attention of the audience was frequently distracted from our dancing by the singing chorus (naturally we were never permitted to dance while the prima donna was singing), and the stage and orchestra were rarely made available to us for rehearsals. We served as a sort of moving scenery whose principal function was to give the audience something to look at while the singers rested their voices. I could see no happy or

productive future as a dancer at the opera, and so, for the second time, I retired from ballet. As it turned out, my disenchantment was matched by that of Balanchine. After another year of acting as fifth wheel, with all his attempted innovations being resented and resisted, he too gave up trying to improve the lot of opera ballet.

While I was still with the Metropolitan, I appeared occasionally during the summer in ballet programs that Michel Fokine staged at Lewisohn Stadium, performing in SCHÉHÉRAZADE, LES ELFES, and CLEOPATRA and in a number of lesser-known works, including THE ADVENTURES OF HARLEQUIN (to the music of Beethoven), the Venusberg Scenes from TANNHÄUSER, and BOLERO, to Ravel's score. In PRINCE IGOR, I performed as one of the boy adolescents because of the scarcity of male dancers. But otherwise there was no ballet company in which I, as an American dancer, could appear on a regular, year-round basis. And so when I left the opera ballet I turned to Broadway. My first show, GREAT LADY, starring Irene Bordoni, featured a classical ballet choreographed by William Dollar and performed by ballet dancers, a number of whom later joined Ballet Theatre: Alicia Alonso, Annabelle Lyon, Albia Kavan, André Eglevsky, Fernando Alonso, Paul Godkin, and Jerome Robbins. The show survived for only three weeks but this did not discourage the producer, Dwight Deere Wiman, from employing the same group of dancers (this time adding Maria Karnilova) for his production of STARS IN YOUR EYES, which starred Ethel Merman and Jimmy Durante and featured the Russian ballerina Tamara Toumanova. I felt then that I had a foothold in the theater and could build myself a theatrical career. As a result, I refused to attend the auditions held by the Ballet Russe de Monte Carlo when it needed American dancers to substitute for the Russians stranded by the war in Europe. I also had no interest in the first auditions of Ballet Theatre; I attended them only at the persistent urging of Maria Karnilova and Donald Saddler. When we arrived we found they were being conducted by Michel Fokine and Alexander Gavrilov. All of us were engaged to begin rehearsals on October 1, 1939.

To me, the first weeks of Ballet Theatre were just more of the same thing that I had learned as a child. Fokine, as before, accompanied rehearsals of SYLPHIDES and CARNAVAL with much discussion and theorizing about the beauty of line and the glories of Greece, which he claimed as his inspiration. He believed that the finest examples of beauty in motion were to be found in the friezes of Greek temples. When, for example, he was teaching the male role in LES SYLPHIDES to Dimitri Romanoff, he sent him to the Metropolitan Museum to study the Greek statuary, which would suggest how he should pose in the ballet. In his concept of beauty Fokine was completely confident and firm. When he first saw me perform the role of Hagar in PILLAR OF FIRE, he came backstage and complained, "Nora, all those years I taught you about beauty, and now you've had a great success in something I find has ugly movements." He spoke reproachfully and I was taken aback. I replied, "Perhaps what you think is ugly some may find to be

beautiful." "No," he insisted, "there is only one way of seeing beauty."

Had Fokine been the only choreographer engaged by Ballet Theatre or had he been its artistic director, his theories on beauty would have determined the company's style and repertory. The style would have been one that eliminated the stiffness, artificiality, and absurdities of classical technique while retaining its more pliant aspects and combining them with the natural movements of modern dance (never with the excessive muscular contractions of Martha Graham, which he considered not dance but gymnastics). Had he wielded despotic control over the style and content of the works presented by Ballet Theatre, there would never have been a PILLAR OF FIRE, a LES NOCES, or a FALL RIVER LEGEND. And had he been Ballet Theatre's only choreographer, I soon would have become disillusioned and looked for inspiration elsewhere. Happily, after a few weeks Antony Tudor arrived from England, and I began working with the choreographer who gave life to all my as yet unformed aspirations.

Tudor's first rehearsals were for JARDIN AUX LILAS. I was one of the corps de ballet, playing the spiteful girl who is always spying on Caroline. I thought it was the most beautiful ballet I had ever seen. Tudor's approach to creation was entirely different from that of any other choreographer. He had his own special method of probing a character's emotions and displaying them in dance form. He had me indicate Hagar's frustrated emotional state in the opening scene of PILLAR OF FIRE with the simple gesture of raising my hand to my cheek. This gesture, however, was arrived at only after hours of probing. Tudor would say, "You live in such-and-such a town, you eat such-and-such food, you dress so-and-so, you have this sort of a family, you live in this sort of a house." Only after he (with me) had determined just what sort of a person Hagar was, did he begin to think how Hagar would move.

Perhaps Tudor's approach to ballet had special relevance to me because I had been guided by Fokine and also by my father, who had worked with Stanislavsky in Russia. All my life I had heard talk of method acting. When I began to work with Tudor, I learned that it could be applied also to the dance. Fokine's whole approach had been through the proper use of the body. Tudor worked through the mind. Mental events dictated what the character would be like as a person and how she would move. This opened to me a whole new concept of the dance. I realized for the first time that I could become an actress through the dance, through movement without the use of the spoken word, and that acting in a ballet could be as valid as in a play. Everything fell into place for me and my attitude toward ballet became positive. I once more enjoyed and was excited by what I was doing. Soon I discovered that what I had learned from Tudor I could apply to the choreography of others. Sometimes it worked and sometimes it did not, but in Ballet Theatre there were always a number of choreographers on whose ballets it could be tried.

Tudor's method did <u>not</u> work with Balanchine ballets. When Balanchine created ballets, at least the ones I was in, he was not at all interested in what the dancer was thinking. All she was required to do was to execute the steps he set for her and to perform them in the manner he indicated. In THEME AND VARIATIONS, for example, the Ballerina has no thoughts or emotions; she is simply a dancer dancing the glorious choreography Balanchine has created for her.

Tudor was the principal Ballet Theatre choreographer who sustained my interest in ballet, but there were others. Dolin, for example, with his flamboyant style taught me a great deal about how to project to the audience—how to convey my thoughts and emotions across the footlights or, to use an old show-business expression, how to "sell" myself.

I probably would not have stayed long with Ballet Theatre had Fokine been its only choreographer; it might be that even with Tudor I would have looked for other inspirations. But the continuous arrival of fresh choreographic talents kept my enthusiasm at a high level. There was Agnes de Mille, the American extension of the English Tudor. There was Jerome Robbins, who gave me characters to perform that were fascinating in their originality of movement and content. There were John Taras and Kenneth MacMillan—and Herbert Ross, who married me and called a halt to my professional ballet career.

During the Thirty-fifth Anniversary season I saw my own experience with choreographers repeated with today's dancers. I saw Varna Gold Medal winner Martine van Hamel gain renewed confidence through working with Dennis Nahat and Glen Tetley, a confidence she carried over into superb performances as Odette-Odile in SWAN LAKE and as Myrtha in GISELLE. I saw Gelsey Kirkland, still magnificent in Balanchine's THEME AND VARIATIONS, move on to even bigger triumphs in the classics and in a role created for her by Tudor in THE LEAVES ARE FADING. And then there was Charles Ward, a promising soloist who was thrust into greater prominence and soon became a principal dancer because Tetley found in him special qualities that he could use in GEMINI. Dancers have always needed choreographers to inspire them and to bring out <u>their</u> unique best. At Ballet Theatre today they can find their choreographer, just as I found Tudor, and the choreographer can shape their talents as he shaped mine.

Looking back at Ballet Theatre, I can recognize Fokine's contribution in its general style: the soft arms, the dropped wrists, the pliant bodies, and the more natural movements. I can also see the effects of the Dolin tradition of individuality and personality-projection. And, of course, there remains the strong Tudor influence, which continues to make it the "thinking" company. Beyond that, it is a versatile company, one that feels equally at home in the French romantic GISELLE, the PETROUCHKA of Fokine's reform era, or the most recent modernisms of Glen Tetley or John Neumeier. And, as in the past, Ballet Theatre still plays frequent host to internationally known choreographers. Ultimately that may be its greatest lure for the dancers and the public.

RESTAGING
THE CLASSICS
ERIK BRUHN

When discussing the preservation of the classics, it is necessary to define carefully both "classic" and "preservation." The purists maintain that classic ballet should be termed more accurately "academic ballet," that is, ballet whose choreography is based on the five absolute positions of the danse d'école, employing those expressions, gestures, and steps that form the traditional ballet vocabulary. In selecting from the Ballet Theatre repertory an example of a classic ballet, the choice falls first on THE SLEEPING BEAUTY, which contains all the accumulations of the centuries—the dancing on toe, the turn-out, elevation, beats, turns, mime—but the choice might fall as well and as properly on Balanchine's THEME AND VARIATIONS or Robbins' INTERPLAY, both of which adhere strictly to the rules and traditions of the danse d'école. Romanticism was introduced into the classic ballet in 1832, when Filippo Taglioni created LA SYLPHIDE for his daughter Maria. The romantic movement in ballet followed the same form as in other arts; it dramatized the conflict between the real and the ethereal, the material and the spiritual. In ballet the unearthly was usually represented by good or evil sylphs and creatures of the spirit world. These brought with them an appropriate style of dancing—light, airy, and floating—and they were clothed in appropriate costumes of misty, soft tulle. The more obvious examples of the romantic ballet in the Ballet Theatre repertory are GISELLE and the Bournonville LA SYLPHIDE, but the designation is equally applicable to Fokine's SPECTRE DE LA ROSE or to John Neumeier's LE BAISER DE LA FÉE. This is the technical definition of the classic ballet, which covers also that branch or division known as romantic ballet. But there remains a looser, commonly used definition of classic ballet, one which is extended to include those works that have survived the lifetime of their creators and are destined to earn for themselves a permanent place in ballet literature. In this enlarged category would fall Fokine's LES SYLPHIDES and PETROUCHKA, Nijinska's LES BICHES, and even Lichine's lightweight GRADUATION BALL and HELEN OF TROY. In terms of this broader definition, the question to be answered is, "How is Ballet Theatre keeping alive those ballets that can no longer be reproduced, restaged, or revised with authority and accuracy by the choreographers who created them?"

With respect to the word "preservation," there would appear to be at least three definitions: the process of embalming, that of keeping alive, and that of instilling new life into a ballet. Early in my career with the Danish Ballet, my experiences with the first two processes were discouraging. The ballets of August Bournonville, which made up by far the greater portion of the Danish repertory, were maintained according to strict traditions. We dancers were taught from our early school days that we must execute each of the expressions, gestures, or steps exactly as originally conceived by Bournonville. This was impressed on us even more sternly when we began to perform on stage, for then the slightest deviation was noted and reprimanded by the critics and objected to by the public. Those who criticized gave no consideration to the fact that succeeding generations had developed different bodies and stronger techniques: contemporary dancers were taller, their muscles were less bulky and more elastic, they jumped higher, turned faster. The critics also ignored a whole new school of dramatic acting that had evolved in the theater since the days of Bournonville and that had inspired new approaches to the interpretation of old roles. Further, in comparing performances, they were seemingly unaware of the fact that the last dancer they had seen in the role had been a veteran, who in his mature years was very probably not performing technically as perfectly as he had when he first learned the role from his predecessor.*

When, after years of waiting, I was finally given an opportunity to dance a solo role, I was taught to dance it "precisely" as it had been—presumably—conceived by Bournonville one hundred and ten years earlier. I was instructed that I could accomplish this seemingly impossible feat by copying in every detail the performance of my predecessor, to whom all the expressions and movements had descended through each generation of dancers who had faithfully reproduced them. I was asked to believe this even after witnessing an incident that occurred during the rehearsals for the revival of NAPOLI. When no one could recall the detailed choreography of a passage danced by a pair of girls, two dancers were called out of retirement to refresh the regisseur's memory. The first dancer remembered it all, and reproduced the steps with great facility and speed. The second dancer admitted she remembered only some of it, but she was absolutely certain that the steps were nothing like those reproduced by her contemporary. Obviously the human element had intruded itself. The regisseur had to ask himself whether the first dancer was pretending to an accurate memory, or whether she was correct and the second dancer was challenging her because she was embarrassed by her own lapse of memory. Even a reference to the file of choreographic notes did not resolve the questions, for over the years successive regisseurs, in making these notes, had used their individual brands of shorthand and had employed the dance slang of their day, much of which could no longer be understood. In the end, the current regisseur had to reconstruct the dance as he thought it might have or must have been originally choreographed to fit the musical score and libretto, which had survived in unambiguous language.

As a result of this and similar incidents, I was left with no great confidence that I was always being taught the original choreography. And yet when I wanted to use a new expression or a novel gesture that I thought would be in keeping with the character I was portraying, I was refused permission to do so on the ground that I would be departing from the original conception. I was not only dubious but resentful. I lost my enthusiasm for performing in this mummifying fashion, as it did not seem to me that the true spirit of Bournonville was being reproduced.

(PREVIOUS PAGE) ERIK BRUHN AS PARIS IN ROMEO AND JULIET.

*As an artist matures, he often modifies his dramatic interpretation to match his changing personality. A young dancer cannot, and should not attempt to, imitate this maturity. [E.B.]

My first experience with the classic ballet that was merely being kept alive occurred in connection with Alexander Volinine's 1946 revival of GISELLE, in which I danced one of the peasant boys. Volinine had performed in the ballet when he was a member of the Imperial Ballet at the Bolshoi Theater at the beginning of the century and later with the Mordkin-Pavlova company during its first visits to America. The version he taught to the Danish Ballet was the one presented by Pavlova during the world tours of her own company. In the process of adapting the ballet to the dictates of circumstances, a great deal had been lost. The structure of the production had been modified to make it adaptable to one-night stands in theaters around the world; the choreography had been adjusted to the limited techniques of the dancers picked up by Pavlova in transit; and finally, so it was said, the solo passages of the other dancers were restyled to assure that no one's performance could outshine Madame's. This GISELLE had been kept alive solely to serve as a vehicle for Pavlova. It was a poor man's edition of the ballet that had been passed on to us in a half-dead condition. It aroused no enthusiasm among the Danish dancers—though Margot Lander enjoyed a personal triumph as Giselle—and it certainly did not inspire me with any ambition to dance the role of Albrecht. Two years later, when I attended performances by Markova and Dolin with the Sadler's Wells Ballet in London, I began to appreciate the virtues of the ballet, but the role of Albrecht did not become one I wished to add to my repertoire until I saw it danced by Igor Youskevitch with Ballet Theatre in New York in 1949.

Youskevitch became my ideal at first sight. Handsome and virile, he was possessed of the perfect physique and manner for a danseur noble, and at the same time he was equipped with a flawless technique. Though Dolin's technique was less brilliant, he, too, had these qualities to a degree, but his attitude toward the character Giselle was very different, influenced perhaps by his personal feelings for the ballerina who performed the role. He appeared to regard Markova as his protégée; he was the Svengali who had instructed her and was now presenting her to the public. Throughout the ballet he was her protective mentor, a relationship that was made even more evident during the final curtain calls, when with his arms about her he seemed to say to the audience, "Isn't this a lovely Giselle I have created?" By contrast, Youskevitch was always the noble lover in full control of his dalliance with the peasant girl in the first act. In today's terms he might be called a male chauvinist pig, but when he performed the role, he proved the falseness of the commonly held belief that GISELLE is a ballet that belongs completely to the ballerina.

In the second act Youskevitch maintained the character of the true nobleman in his restrained grief at the loss of Giselle. In his confrontation with Myrtha, he retained his dignity while submitting to her will. And in obeying her command that he continue to dance until he dies of exhaustion, he performed one of the most difficult passages in romantic ballet, perfectly balancing technique with characterization. Albrecht must grow progressively weaker as he is prodded on by the Queen of the Wilis, while at the same time executing classical steps requiring technical virtuosity. A lesser artist will indicate Albrecht's weakening by staggering between the choreographed leaps and turns, which he will execute with full strength and virtuosity. Youskevitch, on the other hand, was able to make it appear that as Albrecht lost strength, he executed the choreographed steps less brilliantly. Albrecht, the character, seemed to be dancing less well, but it was always clear that Youskevitch, the dancer, had lost none of his technical capability. He was intentionally subjecting his technique to the demands of the dramatic characterization.

I modeled my early performances on Youskevitch and have never departed radically from his conception, although I introduced individual changes in later years. I was fortunate that at the time I was preparing myself for the role of Albrecht I was able to observe Youskevitch, one of the great Albrechts of all time. And I was doubly fortunate that my first Giselle was Alicia Markova, who almost instantly instilled in me a feeling for the romantic tradition. Of our first performance, on May 1, 1955, John Martin wrote: "Alicia Markova made her second appearance [that season] in GISELLE and Erik Bruhn appeared opposite her in his very first Albrecht. It may well be a date to write down in history books, for it was as if the greatest Giselle of today were handing over a sacred trust to what is probably the greatest Albrecht of tomorrow."

The handing over of the sacred trust was accomplished in only a few hours, owing to circumstances that Markova recalls in her book, GISELLE AND I:

Our season was due to end on Sunday, May 1st, and an extra performance of GISELLE had been put in as a matinée. The management felt this would give a fair chance to children, theatre-people and week-end visitors to New York who wanted to see me in the ballet. But complications arose on the subject of an Albrecht for this May Day performance.

Youskevitch, who was due for an evening appearance that day, felt it physically impossible to dance in GISELLE in the afternoon. So blond young Erik Bruhn, on leave of absence from the Royal Danish Ballet, was mentioned to me as a possibility. He had never danced Albrecht, but he had partnered me that season in LES SYLPHIDES. I am always alert for new talent, and I had noticed how well he caught the romantic mood of this Fokine ballet. Would I, asked Lucia Chase, Director of Ballet Theatre, accept him as a partner for GISELLE? I was very glad to try this; and poor Bruhn, though inwardly petrified, as he afterwards told me, attempted no retreat!

About two days remained in which to coach my new Albrecht, and this meant concentrated work, though his sure fluency in the language of Romantic Ballet made things much simpler. By a lucky chance, Anton Dolin, who was passing through New York,* was able to call in and spend about an hour instructing Bruhn in some of the finer points of partnering in the second act. But otherwise, we had to "go it alone," almost oblivious of time. . . .

Markova's recollection corresponds pretty much to mine. I, too, recall that when we were informed that I was to dance the role of Albrecht, only a few days remained before the performance. Since then I have been bragging that we rehearsed the entire ballet in about three hours because that was all the time allotted to us. However, when I came to examine the records, I discovered the facts to be somewhat different.

I have been impressed with the important role that chance and exceptional circumstances have played in the careers of dancers or, for that matter, in the creation of ballets. When, for example, Marius Petipa was choreographing the ballet CINDERELLA in 1893, it happened that the Italian ballerina Pierina Legnani was appearing that year as a guest artist at the Maryinsky. He cast her in the title role and soon discovered that she had brought with her from Italy an extraordinary balletic trick that no Russian ballerina was able to perform: she could execute thirty-two fouettés in rapid succession. He incorporated the trick into his choreography and it caused a sensation with the public. Two years later, when Petipa was staging the second version of SWAN LAKE, he cast Legnani as Odette-Odile, and obligingly found a place in the third act where she could do what she did best—whip out these thirty-two fouettés. The resulting Black Swan pas de deux not only contributed greatly to the success of the ballet but has served ever since as a showpiece for qualifying ballerinas. Had Legnani not remained at the Maryinsky beyond the one-year period for which she had been invited as a guest, there would have been no memorable Black Swan. Similarly, had the Maryinsky not imported French and Italian ballerinas to dance the role of Giselle, there would be no "peasant pas de deux" in today's versions. The pas de deux

---

JOINING BALLET THEATRE IN 1949, BRUHN STUDIED YOUSKEVITCH'S ALBRECHT AND MADE IT HIS MODEL. HE LEARNED MORE ABOUT THE SUBTLETIES OF ROMANTIC STYLE WHILE DANCING IN LES SYLPHIDES WITH MARKOVA.

*Dolin was in New York to dance his original role in BLUEBEARD and to stage his PAS DE QUATRE, which Markova rehearsed and danced. [C. P.]

BRUHN REHEARSED WITH MARKOVA IN THE STUDIO ATOP THE OLD MET, AND (OPPOSITE PAGE) MADE HIS DEBUT IN GISELLE ON MAY 1, 1955.

was inserted to accommodate the resident Russian ballerinas, who wished to appear in as many as possible of the comparatively few (two a week) ballet evenings at the Maryinsky. Later when the Russian ballerinas began to assume the role of Giselle, they insisted that the "peasant pas de deux" be eliminated as a superfluous distraction. In all these instances the ballet was affected by circumstances that had little to do with artistic worth or integrity. In the same way, it must be recorded that my first performance as Albrecht was owing to chance and exceptional circumstances rather than to any recognition of my talent as a dancer. And, as at the Maryinsky, the exceptional circumstances might not have arisen had not a foreign ballerina, this time an English one, been invited to appear as a guest artist.

In 1955 Ballet Theatre celebrated its Fifteenth Anniversary by inviting twenty-three dancers to return to perform roles they had created with the company. Alicia Markova was engaged to appear six times: twice as Juliet, with Hugh Laing as Romeo, in Tudor's ROMEO AND JULIET; twice as Giselle, with Youskevitch; once in LES SYLPHIDES, partnered by me; and once as Taglioni in PAS DE QUATRE. The GISELLE performances were scheduled for Wednesday evening of the second week and for the matinée on the last Sunday, May 1; the first performance on Thursday of the first week was reserved for the resident ballerina, Alicia Alonso, partnered by Youskevitch. All appeared to be feasible until Lucia Chase began to check with the prospective partners. When she approached Youskevitch, he agreed to

(ABOVE) MARKOVA AND BRUHN IN THE FAREWELL SCENE FROM ACT II.

dance the first GISELLE with Alonso and the second with Markova, but he pointed out that his assignment to the third performance was in violation of a provision in his contract which specified that he would not be required to dance in matinée performances. Miss Chase returned to Markova to inquire whether she would dance with Dolin in the final matinée. She said no; they were currently engaged in a public controversy concerning her failure to appear on tour with his Festival Ballet company. It was then that Miss Chase offered me as a partner. Markova delayed her acceptance until after we had danced together in LES SYLPHIDES on the opening night. Meanwhile the casting had been announced for every performance of the season except that of the third GISELLE, and letters from potential ticket buyers demanding the information had begun to pile up at the Ballet Theatre office. On April 15 these letters were answered with the announcement that Markova would dance in the final matinée and Bruhn would be her partner. Copies of answers to these letters remain in the Ballet Theatre archives and have been shown to me as convincing evidence that not later than April 15th Markova and I knew that we were to dance the final GISELLE.*

*The evidence was convincing because Miss Chase has always been most careful to preserve her prerogative of being the first to inform dancers of casting assignments, before they could learn of them from other sources. No one in the office staff would have leaked the information to outsiders without first making sure that Miss Chase had already spoken to both Markova and Bruhn.

Although it was only a matter of time before the rapidly advancing Bruhn would be cast as Albrecht—a role then danced exclusively by Youskevitch—neither the public nor Bruhn himself was aware of the many special circumstances that so suddenly propelled him into superstar status on the afternoon of May 1, 1955. When Yousekevitch bowed out of the matinée with Markova, Miss Chase contemplated a number of alternate program changes, but there were serious objections to all of them. She considered a complete cast change, substituting Nora Kaye and Dolin for Markova and Youskevitch, but this move would have been vetoed by Hurok, who was underwriting the season. He would have contended that the public wanted to see only Markova. That he was right in rating her as the biggest box-office draw of that engagement is indicated by a review of the receipts. The number of tickets sold for each performance of GISELLE were: with Alonso and Youskevitch, 1,409; with Markova and Youskevitch, 2,835; with Markova and Bruhn, 2,763. [C.P.]

But although, contrary to our recollections, Markova and I were notified two weeks in advance of our performance, we did, in fact, rehearse together for only a few hours, and I received a minimum of coaching in the role of Albrecht. The limited amount of rehearsing could only have been a matter of choice on Markova's part. Had she demanded additional hours, they would have been made available to her. She devoted so little time to GISELLE over the two-week period because she was preoccupied with relearning the role of Juliet and because she was not, in general, a believer in prolonged, in-depth rehearsals. The lack of coaching provided to me was also attributable to Markova. Dimitri Romanoff, the ballet master in charge of GISELLE, worked with me on the solo passages, but when the time came for me to rehearse with Markova, he sent in his place Fernand Nault, who was to dance Hilarion and who was at that time an unofficial apprentice-regisseur. Romanoff was annoyed with Markova because she had taken liberties with the choreography of LES SYLPHIDES and had insisted upon dancing the Prelude along with the Waltz pas de deux. Fokine had specified that the same ballerina who danced the Mazurka should also perform the pas de deux, and he had so advised Romanoff shortly before his death. Romanoff regarded these instructions as a sacred trust.* Dolin did, as Markova says in her account, attend one rehearsal, but instead of coaching me, he criticized Markova so indelicately that he was asked not to return. Youskevitch also stayed away from rehearsals. His difference of opinion with Markova as to how certain passages should be performed had resulted in an onstage clash of wills that had been apparent even to the audience. He doubtless felt he could offer no helpful contribution to the development of this new Giselle-Albrecht partnership.

Thus Markova and I were left to work things out by ourselves. As we proceeded, I made a discovery that astonished, even somewhat shocked me. Often I would ask Markova, "What does Albrecht do here?" And she would reply, "I don't really know, but I am doing this, so if I am doing this, he must be doing such and such." It was as if she were asking herself for the first time what her partner had been doing and asking only because I was asking her! It reminded me of Tamara Karsavina's first GISELLE rehearsal with Nijinsky, which she described in her THEATRE STREET: "I was sadly taken aback when I found that I danced, mimed, went off my head and died of [a] broken heart without any response from Nijinsky. He stood pensive and bit his nails. 'Now you have to come across towards me,' I suggested. 'I know myself what to do,' he said moodily." I had been trained to relate my dancing to what others in the ballet were doing. This required

*Romanoff had forgotten that during the last year of his life Fokine had made an exception in the case of Markova, permitting her to dance both the Prelude and the pas de deux while Ballet Theatre was performing in Mexico. He and Miss Chase apparently had again forgotten this exception in 1976, for only with the greatest reluctance did they allow Natalia Makarova to dance the pas de deux along with the Prelude. [C.P.]

knowing not only what they were doing but what they were thinking. It astounded me that with two roles so closely interdependent as those of Giselle and Albrecht, Markova could dance Giselle without knowing what Albrecht was doing. However, we were able to coordinate our parts because Markova was helpful and I was not completely unprepared. At that time, more so than now, if a dancer wanted to be cast in a particular role, he would watch from the wings while it was being performed on stage. In this way he would get to know the choreography long before he could reasonably entertain hopes of being allowed to dance the role. I had been doing this for some time whenever Youskevitch was dancing Albrecht, even though I was resigned to the fact that the role would remain exclusively his as long as he continued with the company. What Markova and I worked out must have been convincing, because John Martin wrote in his review, "The two artists saw eye to eye, played together with a beautiful rapport and developed the dramatic theme with power and irresistible poignance."

At these rehearsals I made another discovery that also astonished me. It was not the realization that there was no such thing as an "authentic" GISELLE, or the recognition that Ballet Theatre had adopted no "official" version. These things I already knew. But I was surprised to discover that in two consecutive weeks a ballerina could easily and unconcernedly dance in two different versions offering seemingly opposite interpretations. I became aware of this when Markova and I began to discuss the closing scene of Act I. When Youskevitch had performed it with her on April 20, I had been looking on from the wings. I noted that as Giselle died in her mother's arms, Youskevitch, as Albrecht, was remorseful but allowed himself to be led away by his equerry to follow the hunting party of the Duke of Courland and presumably to rejoin his fiancée, Bathilde. This indicated that he regarded his affair with Giselle, however passionate, to have been no more than the dalliance of a noble with a peasant, a dalliance that according to the social dictates of the day could never lead to marriage. Moreover, his action appeared consistent with the original termination of Act II, in which Bathilde seeks out Albrecht at Giselle's graveside and, as the librettist Théophile Gautier describes it, leads him away, "his head resting on the shoulder of the beautiful Bathilde, who forgives and consoles him." But when we came to the rehearsal of the death scene, Markova said she preferred to have me play it as Dolin had, that is, for me to continue holding her in my arms until the curtain fell. This action would seem to indicate that Albrecht's love had been a genuine and enduring one, that it had been his intention to abandon Bathilde completely.

Either interpretation is valid, but the Albrecht who runs back to his royal fiancée is a very different character from the Albrecht who chooses to remain faithful to Giselle even after her death; and as such, he would behave differently toward her, if not from their first meeting, at least as their love ma-

tured. At the time, I asked myself how Markova could react dramatically in almost the same way toward one Albrecht who was essentially a cad as she did toward another, ten days later, whose love was to prove genuine and eternal. To find the answer, perhaps we should not inquire into the acting theories of the dancers but rather determine who holds the power of decision. When Markova danced as a guest of Ballet Theatre with her contemporary Youskevitch, he was in control. She did it his way. When she danced with me, her junior and newfound protégé, <u>she</u> was in control. We did it her way. I was still asking the question in 1976 when I saw Natalia Makarova readily accept two such contrasting interpretations. When she danced with Baryshnikov, she died in the arms of her faithful Albrecht. Two days later, when she appeared with Ivan Nagy, she died in the arms of her mother while Albrecht was dragged away by the Duke's hunting party. If there was a difference in her own reaction throughout the ballet to these basically different Albrechts, it was not discernible to me.

Since 1955 I have come to suspect that the ballerina's preference for dying in Albrecht's arms has little to do with authenticity, tradition, or dramatic verity. Subconsciously, or perhaps even consciously, she is aware that once she has died in her mother's arms, the attention of the audience shifts from her to the confrontation between Albrecht and Hilarion and to the fracas caused when Albrecht is wrestled off in the wake of the ducal party. If, however, he returns to clasp Giselle in his arms as the curtain falls, the attention of the audience is once more focused on the ballerina, where it belongs. To others this may not be dramatically authentic, but there is no doubt in her mind that it is <u>theatrically</u> sound.

No one pretends that GISELLE as danced today duplicates exactly the first performance at the Paris Opéra in 1841, or even the performances at the Russian Imperial theaters before the Revolution. For one thing, there are now too many physical limitations. Touring companies cannot be assured of performing in theaters with trapdoors and flying equipment. Thus, no longer can the Wilis fly above the stage as Giselle emerges (through a trapdoor) from her grave and later, at the end of the act, as she sinks out of sight (again through a trapdoor) into a bank of flowers. Even when performances are given in opera houses, the trapdoors are sealed over with the linoleum flooring that is now laid down to provide a smooth dancing surface. As late as my debut performance in 1955, Eugene Berman's set retained the bough of a tree that protruded on stage. Originally the bough had been mounted on a mechanism with a cantilever device by which it could be raised and lowered, and on which Giselle could make her first appearance above Albrecht as he knelt at her grave. The machinery was soon discarded as being impractical for touring and only the stationary bough remained. It must be said that without all these magical effects, the ballet loses a great deal of its romantic atmosphere.

Another alteration over the years has been the elimination of a large proportion of the mime. Modern audiences will not accept extended passages of conventional mime, which they cannot understand. But when it is reduced or eliminated, blank spaces are left in the action. The music plays on but there is no prescribed choreography, and long moments must be filled in with natural movement or gesture. Originally, for example, Giselle's mother was assigned an elaborate mime passage in which she explained to Giselle, and incidentally to the audience, that she has visions of the Wilis waiting for her daughter to join their band if she should die before her wedding day. An easy substitute for the mime was found when the ballet was filmed in Spain with Ballet Theatre: the dancing Wilis were simply superimposed on the film. But on stage, when Giselle's mother is deprived of mime in a performance, she can only communicate the nature of her vision by staring into space above her daughter's head and registering horror for what seems like an inordinately long interruption of the action.

From time to time choreographers and dancers have introduced arbitrary changes into the choreography. Alterations by choreographers began very early in the ballet's history and have continued down to today. To cite a few examples, during its first decade Jules Perrot modified his choreography when, as the new ballet master at the Maryinsky in Saint Petersburg, he staged the ballet for the guest artist Fanny Elssler. At the same theater at the end of the last century, as has been noted, Marius Petipa inserted what has become known as the "peasant pas de deux" in order to pacify the resident ballerinas in the days when only guest artists such as Grimaldi danced the role of Giselle. In 1940, when Anton Dolin staged the ballet for Ballet Theatre, he introduced peasant boys into several first-act dance passages that had formerly been danced exclusively by girls. For instance, when the peasants return from picking grapes (after the scene in which Hilarion finds Albrecht's sword), he had them make their first entrance dancing in groups of four, three girls and a boy together.

We cannot know how many more such choreographers' alterations have been introduced in the past and how many of them have become a permanent part of the choreography. We can only know that in recent years the changes have come and gone. For example, the "peasant pas de deux," which was cut from the Dolin version, has been restored in the Blair staging. There are valid aesthetic arguments for its removal. Dramatically, it contributes nothing toward the advancement of the story. Choreographically, Petipa's formal classical pas de deux is alien to the romantic choreography. During Blair's rehearsals, it was Carla Fracci who made the suggestion as to how the pas de deux could be made relevant. She suggested that after Giselle has received a necklace from Bathilde, she offers a return gift in the form of a performance by her friends of a pas de deux with which they had won a prize in a recent

dance festival. While agreeing to the restoration of the pas de deux, Blair insisted on the elimination of the boys introduced by Dolin into the hitherto all-girl passages. However, his insistence was met by an equally strong determination on the part of Lucia Chase that the boys should appear and dance in the scene. As a compromise, Blair allowed the boys to tag along, but not to make their entrance dancing with the girls, who reverted to entering in groups of three. For the boys he created new choreography, which they danced alone. In the above instances the direction was aware that the choreographers were tampering with what was accepted as the original choreography. But this awareness did not survive when graduates of Ballet Theatre began to stage the ballet for regional companies. The graduates mounted the version they had last been taught, with those who left the company before 1968 reproducing the Dolin version, later graduates the Blair version. Each regional company very likely made the reasonable assumption that the ballet it was adding to its repertory was the original, <u>authentic</u> version of GISELLE.

Intentional or inadvertent alterations can also be introduced by individual dancers. The inadvertent changes can be monitored and corrected by the direction, and control can be maintained through constant supervision. In Ballet Theatre, Miss Chase is in the audience for virtually all performances, and at least four of her staff of seven ballet masters and assistants are also watching. This concentrated vigilance makes it unlikely that even the slightest alteration can go unnoticed and become permanent.

Intentional alterations by dancers are also quickly noted, but they are sometimes tolerated, sometimes approved, and sometimes even welcomed. An example of the last category is the comic inventions both Jerome Robbins and John Kriza added to the role of Hermes in HELEN OF TROY, which improved on Lichine's choreography, received his enthusiastic acceptance, and became officially permanent. Typical of alterations that will meet with approval are those introduced because of an individual dancer's special skills or limitations. Approval is accorded, for instance, when on a good day Ted Kivitt attempts and successfully executes a series of four double air-turns in rapid succession in the finale of ETUDES, or when Stuttgart's Richard Cragun introduces triple air-turns into THE TAMING OF THE SHREW. These alterations add excitement to the performance without doing violence to the choreographer's conception. Conversely, when a dancer has not been able to master the trick of the double air-turn, it is not only acceptable but preferable that he substitute steps he can execute with confidence and assurance.

Tolerance can be shown by the direction in those areas in which it is debatable whether the alteration is at variance with the dramatic and atmospheric structure of the ballet. In the virtuoso passages of purely classical ballet almost any liberty can be taken. In the Black Swan pas de deux, for example, the dramatic line is unimportant. Odile is flirting with Siegfried,

who thinks she is Odette. It matters little whether Odile in her flirtation employs brisés, fouettés, or even the entrechats that are usually reserved for males. In the romantic second act of GISELLE, on the other hand, the dramatic line and mood are most important. The grieving Albrecht visits Giselle's grave and is entrapped by the vengeful Wilis. He must submit to Myrtha's command that he perform a dance of death, and is released only by the coming of dawn. The general atmosphere is one of sorrow and terror. Inasmuch as it cannot be known what steps were originally performed, the introduction of new steps by a modern Albrecht is permissible, provided they permit him to remain in character as a sorrowing nobleman under the spell of a hostile Queen of the Wilis. In this respect, the rapid brisés with which Mikhail Baryshnikov approached Myrtha fall into the category of alterations that must be accepted with caution. To me they are the steps of an exuberant, confident youth who appears to be defying the Queen of the Wilis. However, to others they are an expression of desperation and terror. Certainly Baryshnikov, himself a great artist and trained by Alexander Pushkin, one of the greatest dramatic coaches in the ballet world, must have been inspired by a valid dramatic motivation. But what is right for Baryshnikov may not be right for a dancer with less technical skill and dramatic force. The direction, therefore, must be cautious lest other dancers attempt to imitate Baryshnikov and perform his version ineffectively in the belief that it is the authentic one.

The purist will protest, "How can the direction permit a flagrant violation of the choreographer's integrity? It must be an ineffectual direction indeed that cannot prevent an individual dancer from tampering with the official choreography!" The direction is more likely being pragmatic than ineffectual. It may be facing the fact that sometimes it is better to make concessions than to engage in a counterproductive confrontation, one that might endanger the healthy and cooperative relationship between the principal dancer and the company, and impede his development as an artist. And there is always the outside chance that the dancer may be right! I have worked under the direction of Harald Lander in the Royal Danish Ballet, under Ninette de Valois in the English Royal Ballet, under George Balanchine in the New York City Ballet, and under Lucia Chase in Ballet Theatre, and I can personally certify that none of them harbors delusions of omnipotence. Even the most militant martinet, Ninette de Valois, when she invited me in 1975 to give classes to the boys of the Royal Ballet, said, "They need them because they are all imitating Nureyev even when he does things which might not appear to be academically correct, and because he is a success they won't listen to me, but if you tell them. . . ." No competent director attempts to maintain an absolute dictatorship. As in business and politics, compromise is the name of the game in ballet, and eventually more can be accomplished through persuasion than through dictation.

In spite of the many alterations, all GISELLES being performed today by companies around the world are more or less similar because they all derive from the version that was being performed at the Maryinsky Theater in Saint Petersburg when Nicholas Sergeyev was its ballet master. In 1917 he defected to the West, taking with him his choreographic notes on ballets, including GISELLE. Thereafter he staged the ballet for a number of companies: in 1924 for the Paris Opéra with Spessivtseva; in 1934 for the Vic-Wells (subsequently the Sadler's Wells and then the Royal Ballet) with Alicia Markova; in 1935 for the Markova-Dolin company; in 1938 for the Ballet Russe de Monte Carlo; and in 1948 for the Ballet International with Moira Shearer. Dancers who appeared in these productions have passed the choreography on to other companies: Dolin and Blair to Ballet Theatre; Celia Franca to the National Ballet of Canada; Peggy van Praagh to the Australian Ballet. For this reason, when I began rehearsing with each new ballerina, I found that in general she performed the same steps as Markova had during our first rehearsal in 1955. Just as Sergeyev's staging became the choreographic prototype, so Markova's image became the model on which all her successors based their interpretation of Giselle. Her own interpretation derived from the poses illustrated in nineteenth-century lithographs. She consciously adopted some of the same poses and styled her movement to conform with what she imagined would have occurred had the ballerinas depicted in those prints suddenly come to life.

The Sergeyev choreography and the Markova image were so universally accepted that it is possible for a premier danseur to partner a new Giselle for the first time with virtually no rehearsal. A brief run-through will determine whether either dancer has introduced any individual choreographic alterations and will disclose which of the alternate dramatic interactions are to be followed. Does she, for example, execute two or three pirouettes at a certain point, and does he prefer to remain on stage or to rush off during the mad scene? After having partnered Markova in several performances, I found it was an easy transition to subsequent Giselles—Kaye and Hightower, for example. They did not unexpectedly introduce unfamiliar steps or change the dramatic conception of Giselle. That would have been as though a soprano had capriciously introduced an aria from another opera or had begun to perform the role of Violetta as though she had suddenly turned into Carmen. But as I moved from one ballerina to another, I found myself in the position of a tenor who must adjust his singing to blend with the various kinds of soprano voice, from light lyrical to heavily dramatic. There was a similar difference between my first and my subsequent Giselles. Compared to Markova, with her delicate lyricism, Kaye and Hightower were heavily dramatic. Not that Markova was physically more frail and light; she could easily have crushed my hand in her powerful grip, and she was harder to

BRUHN WITH THREE OF HIS EARLY
BALLET THEATRE GISELLES:
NORA KAYE (LEFT),
ALICIA MARKOVA (ABOVE),
ROSELLA HIGHTOWER (OPPOSITE PAGE).

lift than the two Americans, who were more cooperative in elevating themselves at the right moment. But Markova looked fragile, while the Americans gave the impression of sturdiness. To maintain the image of a strong Albrecht, I had to move and perform differently with the more robust Americans than with the feathery-appearing Markova. Kaye and Hightower had surer techniques than remained to Markova at that time; their extensions were higher, they could do more turns, traverse the stage in more hops, and so on. But Markova had learned how to employ her technique to create an image faithful to the romantic tradition—above all, she had mastered the indispensable secret of floating.

I first recognized this quality when, as a young boy at the Danish Academy, I was performing at the opera house as one of the children in LA SYLPHIDE. The ballerina was a beautiful lady but she was almost huge for a dancer, and one would have thought her totally unsuited to the role of the Sylph. And yet she was convincing as a supernatural spirit. Although she had little elevation, when she jumped she seemed to soar up and then float in suspension. It is difficult to describe and even more difficult to explain how floating is achieved. Perhaps the secret lies in the arms or the back, as well as in strong feet, but the effect is that no one notices when the dancer takes off or lands; the only impression is of her gliding above the stage. Markova had the secret. Also, in patterning her performance after Taglioni, she modified her technique to conform to the poses in old prints. An illustration of how she sought to attain the effect can be found in the passage in which Giselle begins her solo after emerging from her grave and bowing to Myrtha. When Alicia Alonso performed the role, she stretched her extension to the utmost, raising her foot so high that her legs formed an angle close to 180 degrees. This stirred the admiration of the audience, but not of Markova, who in her performances raised her leg to an angle of less than 45 degrees. There were those—no doubt including Alonso—who maintained that Markova raised her leg as high as she could. For myself, although aware of the limitation of Markova's technique at the time, I believe she considered the exaggerated arabesque a deviation from the romantic style, and that even had she been able to raise her leg higher, she would have refrained from doing so.

These differences between Markova and the American ballerinas had nothing to do with their qualifications for the role of Giselle. The role can be danced by any competent ballerina, regardless of whether she is tall or short, frail or sturdy (but not too solid), long- or short-legged. Her success as Giselle is determined by a mental attitude that enables her to use her body and technique to project convincingly the right image. But the differences in physique and technique do result in different timing, phrasing, and spacing. It is with these differences that the Albrecht must become acquainted if he is to adjust his own dancing to the ballerina's so that as a couple they can move in easy harmony. The attainment of this physical and mental harmony takes time and much conscious

study. And so it is that while young dancers can dance the roles of Giselle and Albrecht, and should be given the opportunity, they should not be expected to give great performances until they have reached full maturity as artists. A ballerina must first of all be in complete control of her muscles. She must have the absolute assurance that they will perform as she commands. Nothing destroys illusion more surely than for a dancer to appear tentative in her movements, uncertain whether she can accomplish what she is attempting. She must therefore become aware of her limitations and adapt her performance to them. If she cannot confidently execute three pirouettes, she should be content with two. In a purely classic ballet, she could perhaps bring added excitement to a performance by attempting the three pirouettes. If she failed, the loss would be personal only. But if she failed in GISELLE, she could shatter the whole romantic aura for at least a moment.

A ballerina must also learn to be in full control of her legs and feet, her arms and hands. I remember Markova demonstrating the piqué ballonné during our rehearsal at the Metropolitan. "It's a nineteenth-century effect—more delicate than the more open ballonné customarily used in its place today. In the romantic era, the feet were literally supposed to 'twinkle,' and the neat flick of the toe on the floor in the piqué ballonné helps to give just that effect." The ballerina must have

CARLA FRACCI AND BRUHN REACHED GREAT HEIGHTS IN THEIR PROTRACTED PARTNERSHIP AS GISELLE AND ALBRECHT.

so conditioned herself that she will instinctively employ the piqué balloné and not inadvertently lapse into the open balloné she employs in other ballets. This is a difficult achievement for a dancer whose training and experience have been in classical purism. It requires a radical adjustment, mentally and technically, to transform a classical dancer into a free-floating spirit, as in the second act of GISELLE, where the dancer must be more concerned with symmetry of line and movement than with the strict observation of the rules of the danse d'école. Gelsey Kirkland had to make this adjustment when she moved from the classicism of Balanchine to the romanticism of GISELLE. She made the transition gradually and only with conscious effort.

Finally, a ballerina must be able to control all her gestures and facial expressions so that they express exactly the meanings she intends them to convey and are consistent with the character of Giselle as she conceives it.

Reaching an ultimate decision as to how to portray a character in a romantic ballet (and to a lesser extent in a purely classical ballet) is the most time-consuming process in the development of a role. I am often asked whether the determination is made by the direction or arrived at independently by each dancer. I remember Lupe Serrano at a party in Leningrad explaining why she had left the Ballet Russe de Monte Carlo to join Ballet Theatre. "Everyone told me that Ballet Theatre had no artistic direction, and no artistic direction was just what I was looking for." I could understand what she meant. From my own experience I have found that once the specifics of a role have been taught to me, I then do a lot of performances, in the course of which people come back to offer criticisms and suggestions. Whether or not I concentrate on what they are saying, something stays with me and becomes a part of my subconscious thought. After a while I have taken in all I can absorb, and the time has come to work out my own conception of the character, the one that is right for me and that I can accept as being believable and real. With GISELLE this process has to be gone through twice. Once I have established my own conception of Albrecht, and the ballerina, through the same process, has fixed on her conception of Giselle, we must then work together to determine how the characters we have created will feel and act toward each other. This process is less important in preparing for a purely classic ballet. It matters little how the Swan Queen feels toward Prince Siegfried or Princess Aurora toward Prince Florimund. All Siegfried has to know is that Odette is sad because she has been turned into a swan, and Florimund has only to be aware that Aurora has been asleep for a hundred years because she pricked her finger with a needle. But for Giselle and Albrecht to perform convincingly together, they must know much more about each other's thoughts and feelings.

During the ten years following my debut as Albrecht I danced with half a dozen Giselles without establishing a perfect union. Nora Kaye's approach was in the Tudor method. Her mad scene, for example, was the product of the analyst's couch. It was cerebral and realistic but it projected little of romantic madness to me or to the audience. By contrast, Alonso's performance was completely extroverted; her mad scene was stark and raving. I could appreciate John Martin's observation after her performance with Youskevitch in 1955 that she was "utterly and completely Latin." Yvette Chauviré brought a still different flavor to Giselle with a thrust and accent that was peculiar to the French school of dancing. And so it went. My performances with all these different though excellent ballerinas met with the approval of the critics and public, and were satisfying—some of them even exciting—to dance. It was not, however, until I met the Italian Carla Fracci that I began to sense what the affair between Giselle and Albrecht was all about. And even this awareness developed gradually. When Carla first came with me to Ballet Theatre in 1967, we did not arrive as a team; we had danced

together only a few times at La Scala and elsewhere. At first we did GISELLE with Berman's old, tired sets and worn and faded costumes, but almost immediately it became apparent to Lucia Chase that we had something going between us and she gave us our head, allowing us to concentrate on our partnership. Later we began to perform in the new David Blair–Oliver Smith production, and the partnership grew from season to season until we reached the point where Carla could not do Giselle without me and I could not do Albrecht without her. This came about despite the fact that Lucia Chase, in principle, is opposed to the formation of so-called teams. She believes that all the Giselles in the company should dance with all the Albrechts, provided there are no overwhelming differences of height. I agree with this policy, particularly in regard to dancers who are still in search of their ideal partner. But once they have found each other, nothing can stand in their way. They belong together, and together they perform such miracles that no one would consider separating them.

In 1975 Ballet Theatre was well-supplied with dancers available to perform the roles of Giselle and Albrecht either as resident stars or as guests: Eleanor D'Antuono, Carla Fracci, Cynthia Gregory, Gelsey Kirkland, and Natalia Makarova; and Mikhail Baryshnikov, Paolo Bortoluzzi, Michael Denard, Ted Kivitt, and Ivan Nagy. All of them were still going through the process of working with different partners, pressed into it by Lucia Chase. None of them had yet formed a perfect union in which it could be said they were offering their definitive characterizations of Giselle and Albrecht. When Makarova joined Ballet Theatre, she was exposed to a GISELLE different from the one in which she had performed at the Kirov, and her conception and execution of the role thereafter underwent a fantastic change. She retained something that was Kirov and added something that was Ballet Theatre. Eventually her interpretation was neither Russian nor American, but because it had been developed in the environment of Ballet Theatre, it clearly bore the stamp of that company. Today Makarova ranks as one of the great Giselles of our generation. In 1974 she was joined by Mikhail Baryshnikov, who is not only a very great dancer but a dedicated artist. They made their debut as a partnership in the Ballet Theatre production on July 27, 1974, at the New York State Theater. During the next two years their individual engagements on the international circuit allowed them to dance together in the company's GISELLE only twice more—scarcely often enough for them to have reached final, in-depth interpretations of the roles. In January 1976 they danced GISELLE together for the fourth time with Ballet Theatre. If this performance can be taken as a portent, there can be no doubt that this will prove to be a partnership of unsurpassed excellence.

The partnership of Kirkland and Baryshnikov was also in development in 1976. In their initial interpretation they seemed to be playing the roles as teen-agers, as a very much "of-now" couple. This is a valid conception, but no one can know, least of all themselves, what characterization they will arrive at after they have worked it all out together. Nor, indeed, can it be known whether they will _ever_ become as one. There is no doubt, however, that the potential is there for a most fabulous Giselle-Albrecht team.

All of my experiences since my student days at the Royal Danish Ballet School have convinced me that the following minimal requirements must be fulfilled by any company that proposes to preserve the classics.

The company must maintain a corps de ballet and a cadre of soloists whose members are conscious of the difference between various dance styles and can employ the style that is correct for classical and romantic ballets. They must also be given sufficient dramatic coaching so they can participate convincingly in the unreal, other-day dramatic action.

It must acknowledge the existence of what the public recognizes as stars and encourage them to perform as stars. The classics were conceived as vehicles for ballerinas and premiers danseurs, and to pretend they can be performed by dancers of less than star quality is to do violence to the choreographers' conceptions. Jerome Robbins' LES NOCES can be performed with or without stars, but Petipa's THE SLEEPING BEAUTY cannot.

It must mount productions with décor that is rich, even though perhaps not as opulent and spectacular as the original scenery and costumes. Classical ballet is grand ballet and cannot be presented in velvet curtains and leotards.

Even when these requirements are met, the preservation process may become one of merely embalming unless the director can instill new life into the classics by facing up to the fact that people change, tastes change, and life itself changes. A ballerina may, for example, validly base her Giselle on the Taglioni image. This interpretation may at first be fresh and alive, but gradually it can become mannered and eventually end up as a cold stereotype, which should not be imitated by succeeding Giselles. But even had the interpretation remained vital and unmannered, it probably should still not be accepted as a model. I have watched movies of myself taken fifteen years ago and have said, "If I performed that role today I would not dance it as I danced it then." As time moves on, changes are effected in dance techniques, acting styles, social mores, and philosophical concepts. All of these must be taken into consideration when a classic is restaged. Even if a film existed that recorded _exactly_ a previous production, it should not be enshrined as a sacrosanct model. Each production and each performance must be re-examined with a view to eliminating undesirable embellishments and to restoring subtleties that have been lost. And if the ballet is to retain meaningful life, periodically it must be completely restudied and freshly conceived to bring it into conformity with the changing conditions of life.

PERFORMING GISELLE
ALICIA ALONSO

I received my early training in traditional ballet in Cuba at the school of the Pro Arte Musical and in New York with several teachers. I went most often to the seventy-five-year-old Enrico Zanfretta, a graduate of the ballet school of La Scala, Milan, who taught the Cecchetti method in the basement of a West Side church, charging only 50¢ a lesson. From his training I acquired the ability to move my feet with great rapidity. I also studied with Alexandra Fedorova, the wife of Alexander Fokine (brother of Michel), whose fee of $1 per lesson I could not always afford, but she allowed me to take class on credit. Michel Fokine himself was beyond my means; his fee for a lesson was $5. Eventually my financial problems were solved when I was awarded a scholarship to the School of American Ballet, where I first came in contact with George Balanchine's neo-classic style of dancing.

My first professional stage performances were in musical comedies—GREAT LADY and STARS IN YOUR EYES—rather than the ballet. Not until Ballet Caravan was organized as an adjunct to the School of American Ballet was I able to perform exclusively as a ballet dancer. Even then the ballets in which I danced, Eugene Loring's BILLY THE KID and CITY PORTRAIT, were not in the purest tradition of classical ballet. I believe Loring drew his inspiration from two sources: from one of his teachers, Michel Fokine, who had brought about a reform in the rigid restraints of academic classical ballet; and from Lincoln Kirstein, who had become convinced that his School of American Ballet could so train dancers that they would bring to classical dancing a distinctly American style, and that it could develop American choreographers who would create ballets that were American both in style and subject matter, using librettos he wrote for them. One such ballet was BILLY THE KID. Kirstein wrote the story of the American outlaw, and Loring devised the choreography in accordance with Fokine's theory that the dancers should move naturally and should perform in costumes appropriate to the period they were depicting. The execution was not totally consistent. Although the cowboys wore Stetsons and boots, they also wore the traditional tights, and although their legs and feet were not "turned out" and they walked with underslung, swaying hips, they did execute such classical steps as double air-turns. Of all the women—dance-hall entertainers, pioneer wives, cowgirls—I alone in the role of the Mother/Sweetheart danced on pointe. This unnaturalness was permissible only because the Sweetheart was a dream, a figment of Billy's imagination. In the same company, I danced also in William Dollar's AIR AND VARIATIONS and Lew Christensen's CHARADE, works created under the influence of Balanchine's neo-classicism. I had no opportunity to dance in authentic classical ballets because there were none in the repertory.

On April 11, 1940, I attended my first performance of GISELLE at the Metropolitan Opera House, danced by Alicia Markova and Anton Dolin.* It was immediately clear to me that though the classics might be old, they could be very much alive. For me, Markova's dancing—so different from the sharp, strong style we were accustomed to in Ballet Caravan—brought a whole new dimension to the art of ballet. I resolved at once that I must find a company in which I could dance the classics such as GISELLE and also continue performing in modern ballets. I soon found such a company.

While I had been on tour with Ballet Caravan in 1939, Ballet Theatre was founded. In its repertory were GISELLE, SWAN LAKE, ACT II, and LA FILLE MAL GARDÉE. I attended one of its auditions and was accepted. Within a few weeks I was rehearsing GISELLE under the direction of Anton Dolin. My first two performances in the ballet took place that August in Lewisohn Stadium. I danced one of Giselle's friends in the first act, and in the second I was one of the two soloists, nameless in Dolin's version but usually identified as the Wilis Moyna and Zulma. I was Moyna, the one who executes the renversés, and Nora Kaye was Zulma. Nana Gollner was Giselle. Thereafter we gave eight performances at the Civic Opera House in Chicago and the Majestic Theatre in New York, with Annabelle Lyon and Nana sharing the title role.

The last performance of GISELLE at the Majestic on March 7, 1941, might well have been my last ever. My vision had been troubling me and I was told I must have an operation for a detached retina. After surgery and a three-month rest, I was able to join a group from Ballet Theatre, including John Kriza, who were invited to perform with Ballet Caravan on a tour of South America. I had already begun to rehearse Balanchine's THE BAT (DIE FLEDERMAUS) when I suffered a relapse and underwent a second operation, following which I returned to Cuba to recuperate. Not long after I again resumed dancing, I was injured in an automobile accident and required a third operation. This time the doctor ordered that I remain in bed, flat on my back, with my head held motionless. To retain my sanity, I continued to dance in my mind, and one of the ballets I performed was GISELLE. As I was in charge of the casting of these performances, I naturally did not assign myself the role of Moyna. Instead I danced Giselle herself, and found that I not only remembered all the steps as I had seen them performed by others but that I could re-create the actions of all the other characters, including those of Albrecht. My mental dancing became so real that I could watch my own performances and criticize them severely. Sometimes I danced particularly well; at other times I made mistakes—which in true ballerina tradition I'm sure I blamed on my partner. This bedridden season lasted a year.

When I was once more able to dance, I hurried back to New York to rejoin Ballet Theatre and was soon rehearsing GISELLE in reality, no longer as Giselle herself but again in the role of Moyna. Dancing Zulma was

---

*Anton Dolin was free to appear for a single performance with the Ballet Russe de Monte Carlo because Ballet Theatre's season at the Center Theatre had concluded on February 3. [C.P.]

Janet Reed, Nora Kaye having been promoted to the Queen of the Wilis during my absence. Also in my absence, Alicia Markova had joined the company, and for the past year she had danced all the Giselles, with Dolin as her Albrecht.* Now that Nana and Annabelle were no longer with Ballet Theatre, the company was in a precarious position, particularly as Markova's health was unpredictable; twice during the previous season she had fainted on stage. Nevertheless, Markova was to dance both performances scheduled for the Metropolitan (one in the first week and the other in the fourth), and no understudy was prepared. But no one was concerned about this when the season opened on October 10, 1943. I danced CAPRICCIO ESPAGNOL with Jerome Robbins, and Markova and Dolin performed PRINCESS AURORA. On the second night, Markova danced SWAN LAKE, ACT II with Dolin, and on the third night she joined Rosella Hightower, Janet Reed, and myself in PAS DE QUATRE. For the fourth performance she was scheduled to dance Zemphira in ALEKO. This was the ballet in which she had twice fainted and she panicked at the thought of doing it again. At the last minute Nora Kaye substituted for her.

Meanwhile Markova went to a doctor, who told her that what she had regarded as an occasional cramp was in fact a hernia that had been aggravated by one of the steps or lifts Massine had devised for ALEKO. The doctor ordered an immediate operation. Emergency rehearsals were then scheduled so that we juniors—Kaye, Hightower, and myself—could replace Markova in roles that had been exclu-

*There was one exception. On February 9, 1942, the company arrived in Toronto, Canada, to discover that Markova and Dolin had been assigned rooms on the thirteenth floor. They refused to remain on a floor with so ominous a number. Payne, who was then the executive director, shamed Markova out of her subservience to superstition, but the Irish Dolin was adamant. Eventually another room was found for him, but Markova remained on the thirteenth floor. That evening in PAS DE QUATRE she sprained her ankle. In the emergency, Annabelle Lyon replaced her as Giselle on the 11th, dancing the role for the first time in more than a year. She never danced it again while she remained with Ballet Theatre. [C. P.]

THE FIRST SEASON'S GISELLE WITH ANTON DOLIN AS ALBRECHT, NORA KAYE AS MOYNA, AND ALONSO AS ZULMA.

sively or principally hers. Nora took over Princess Aurora and Juliet in Tudor's ROMEO AND JULIET; I replaced her as Elora in Dolin's ROMANTIC AGE and danced her role in LES SYLPHIDES; and Rosella became Taglioni in PAS DE QUATRE. As a consequence, only two changes had to be made in the scheduled performances: PILLAR OF FIRE was substituted for GISELLE on the sixth night and JARDIN AUX LILAS for ROMEO AND JULIET on the seventh.

Everyone was so busy learning Markova's roles, while at the same time rehearsing for the premiere of Tudor's DIM LUSTRE, that little thought was given to the second performance of GISELLE, scheduled for November 2. And so it was not until a week before the performance date that Dolin came to our dressing room and announced to Nora, Rosella, and me that since Markova could not return, one of us would have to dance Giselle. We all laughed. Dolin often made outrageous remarks with a straight face and we had learned not to take him too seriously. And even if he was serious, none of us was about to expose herself to New York critics and the discriminating Metropolitan audience in an ill-prepared, under-rehearsed debut performance of one of the most challenging roles in the ballet repertory. The others remained adamant,

but it took only a little more pressure from Dolin to make me succumb to the temptation. After all, why should I waste my year of bedridden rehearsals! I had my first rehearsal with Dolin from five to six on October 28, and that evening danced the Fairy of the Pine Woods in PRINCESS AURORA. My schedule for the next five days was as follows:

October 29	5–6	Rehearsal with Dolin. Evening Performance: LES SYLPHIDES
October 30	1–2	Rehearsal with Dolin. Matinée Performance: PRINCESS AURORA
October 31	11–12	Run-through of Act I. Matinée Performance: PRINCESS AURORA Evening Performance: ROMANTIC AGE
November 1	3–5	Run-through of Acts I and II. Alonso not in Evening Performance
November 2	11–1	Run-through of Act II. Evening Performance: GISELLE, Alonso debut

On the call board that evening there appeared the notice, "After the performance of GISELLE is over, all remain on stage for pictures." The pictures were presumably being taken for future publicity. That fact, together with congratulations from everyone and favorable critical reviews the next morning, gave me ample reason to believe I had succeeded in breaking the

Markova monopoly. I was confident not only that I would substitute for Markova as long as she was ill, but that even after her recovery we would share the role of Giselle. But I might as well have returned to Cuba, lain flat on my back, and gone on dancing Giselle in my mind, for it was exactly one year, two months, and twenty-six days before I was once more cast as Giselle in a Ballet Theatre performance. Following my debut in November, the ballet was withdrawn from the touring repertory, and it was not performed again until the following summer, when Markova returned to resume her monopoly during the engagements in California.

However, while we were in Hollywood, my hopes were once more raised. I learned that Markova and Dolin had signed a contract with Billy Rose to appear in a musical revue titled THE SEVEN LIVELY ARTS, scheduled to open sometime in December. I also discovered that the contract contained a provision that Markova could not dance in New York prior to the opening. From Rose's layman's point of view, only the ballerina was important. He offered no objections to Dolin's appearing at the Metropolitan in October. Nothing, therefore, stood in the way of repeats of the Alonso-Dolin performance of GISELLE of November 1943. Nothing, that is, except Hurok's conviction that all ballerinas must have Russian parentage or at least a Russian name. Tamara Toumanova had both, so Hurok insisted she be engaged as a replacement for Markova. While Ballet Theatre was appearing at the Hollywood Bowl, she rehearsed daily with Dolin, and then in the fall joined the company in Montreal, where they danced their first GISELLE and all subsequent ones until Dolin left to join the Rose show. Hugh Laing was chosen as the substitute Albrecht, and he began rehearsing with Toumanova when the company re-sumed its tour of one-night stands.

It was only an element in Toumanova's personal life that eventually brought me back into the GISELLE picture. She was married to Casey Robinson, a prominent screenwriter, who insisted that she spend at least some time at home in Hollywood. Consequently, she took leave of the company in St. Louis with the understanding that she would rejoin it on the Coast. Meanwhile Laing was left without a Giselle with whom to rehearse, and I was assigned to stand in for Toumanova. I don't know whether she was supposed to dance the first performance, scheduled for Seattle, but she did not show up, and so I performed my second Giselle, with Laing as my partner, at the Moore Theatre on January 27, 1945. Toumanova rejoined the company in Oakland and remained to dance all the Giselles in San Francisco and Los Angeles. I was given two further performances in Long Beach and San Diego when the company was forced to perform in neighboring towns on the days the Los Angeles Symphony displaced it from Philharmonic Hall. My performances of Giselle on the Coast reminded me of a story dancers used to tell about Alexandra Danilova. At an after-ballet party in Texas, a balletomane was somewhat tactlessly assuring Danilova that Nathalie Krassovska was very popular in Houston. Danilova agreed and generously went further explaining, "We all have our special towns in which we are particularly popular. Nathalie not only has Houston, she has Portland, Milwaukee, and Boston." As an afterthought she added, "My towns are Los Angeles, San Francisco, Chicago, New York, London, Paris. . . ." In 1945 my towns were Seattle, Long Beach, and San Diego. Toumanova's were San Francisco, Los Angeles, and New York.

ALONSO REPLACED THE AILING MARKOVA AS GISELLE AND WAS IN TURN REPLACED BY TAMARA TOUMANOVA (BELOW WITH HUGH LAING).

When THE SEVEN LIVELY ARTS closed on May 12, 1945, Markova and Dolin rejoined Ballet Theatre, and Toumanova returned to Hollywood. Markova and Dolin might have continued to monopolize GISELLE but for a number of extraneous circumstances. At that time Hurok was receiving from local concert managers more requests for ballet than he could fill. He therefore persuaded Markova and Dolin to form a small dance group, which they would head but leave occasionally to appear as guests with Ballet Theatre in key cities. André Eglevsky then became the regular premier danseur of Ballet Theatre, and, like me, he wanted to appear in GISELLE. But when he told the management he wanted to appear as Albrecht it was quite a different thing from my request to once more be allowed to dance Giselle. I was still ranked only as the fourth soloist; as first male dancer he had to be listened to and had to be given performances in major cities. Thus the Alonso-Eglevsky partnership came into existence, and we danced our first GISELLE at the Metropolitan Opera House on October 23, 1945. The critics were enthusiastic, and I have always treasured the encouragement given me by John Martin in the opening paragraph of his review for the New York Times:

Alicia Alonso received a real ovation at the Metropolitan Opera House last night for her performance of GISELLE with the Ballet Theatre, and, what is perhaps more to the point, she deserved it. The extraordinarily brilliant ballerina from Cuba will one day be one of the great Giselles, if only she is allowed to dance the role often enough. Her last appearance in it was two years ago, and that is definitely not enough.

I most certainly agreed with him that twice in two years was "definitely not enough," but within another year I was dancing the role twice in one day, which was definitely too much. Events of that year brought this about. Lucia Chase and Oliver Smith became co-directors of the company; I was promoted to the rank of ballerina; Chase and Smith broke with Hurok; Markova and Dolin left the company; and Ballet Theatre was engaged for a season at the Royal Opera House, Covent Garden, in the summer of 1946. The management of the opera house scheduled performances for the benefit of subscribers. In the same week one program of ballets was performed on Monday evening, Wednesday matinée, Wednesday evening, and Friday evening; a second program was presented Tuesday evening, Thursday evening, Saturday matinée, and Saturday evening. As a result, Eglevsky and I performed during the week of July 15 in accordance with the following schedule:

July 15 GISELLE: Alonso and Eglevsky
July 16 PETROUCHKA: Eglevsky (Blackamoor)
BLACK SWAN PAS DE DEUX: Eglevsky and Nora Kaye
GALA PERFORMANCE: Alonso (Italian Ballerina)
July 17 Matinée GISELLE: Alonso and Eglevsky
Evening GISELLE: Alonso and Eglevsky
July 18 APOLLO: Alonso and Eglevsky
July 19 GISELLE: Alonso and Eglevsky
July 20 Matinée APOLLO: Alonso and Eglevsky
Evening APOLLO: Alonso and Eglevsky

WHILE AWAITING BALLERINA STATUS, ALONSO PERFORMED SOLOIST ROLES WITH TUDOR IN JARDIN AUX LILAS; WITH LAING IN UNDERTOW; WITH DOLIN AND MARKOVA IN LES SYLPHIDES; WITH KRIZA IN ALEKO; AND WITH RICHARD REED IN GRADUATION BALL.

All of the stars of the company were asked to follow the same pattern, performing eight times a week and twice in the same ballet on Wednesdays and Saturdays. Nora Kaye danced PILLAR OF FIRE twice in the same day, and John Kriza performed LES SYLPHIDES, the DON QUIXOTE PAS DE DEUX, and HELEN OF TROY in the matinée and again in the evening. I often think back to that season in London when today's young dancers express reluctance to perform leading roles twice in one day and protest if they are asked to dance major roles more than three times in the same week. They have been warned (not by me!) that the physical strain will shorten their careers.

AFTER ANDRÉ EGLEVSKY BECAME ALONSO'S PARTNER (AS ABOVE IN APOLLO), THEY WERE CAST TOGETHER REGULARLY IN GISELLE.

Although André and I danced a dozen performances of GISELLE, we devoted little effort to developing our characterizations. In the first place, we were given little opportunity to work together between performances, and, in the second, we knew that he was to leave the company after the London season, to be replaced by Igor Youskevitch. In the absence of Dolin, rehearsals were conducted by Dimitri Romanoff, who reproduced Dolin's choreography. As a result, my performances with André were in the Markova-Dolin tradition. Not until I began dancing with Igor in the new production designed by Eugene Berman did I start to build toward my final characterization of Giselle in cooperation with a partner who brought intelligence and integrity to his dramatic interpretations. And it was then that I appreciated the coaching I had received while rehearsing with Hugh Laing as Toumanova's standby. Ordinarily Antony Tudor took little interest in the company's staging of classical ballets, but this case was an exception because Laing, with whom his own career had been so closely intertwined, was attempting his first romantic role in classical ballet. Tudor was on hand primarily to assist Laing, but I, too, was a beneficiary. I found that he applied to classical ballet the same method he used in developing characterizations in his

BEGINNING IN 1946, ALONSO AND YOUSKEVITCH DEVELOPED THEIR
CHARACTERIZATIONS OF THE ROLES OF GISELLE AND
ALBRECHT FOR MORE THAN A DECADE.

own works, a unique method that Nora Kaye has described on page 316. It forced me to get to know Giselle as a real-life person, to ask myself how she had come to be the kind of a girl she was and to imagine how that girl would react to the people and events in her life.

Igor had danced with Markova but in a Sergeyev version that had been tampered with by Serge Lifar. He had never worked under Tudor, but his approach to the study of a role was similar. From the start we had to make adjustments and a choice of elements from the two versions—his by Sergeyev and mine by Dolin. We had to decide, for example, which treatment of the daisy-plucking (she loves me, she loves me not) scene to use. From there we moved on to more subtle characterizations and bits of dramatic action. During all the years we danced together Igor and I continued to develop our conceptions of the characters of Giselle and Albrecht. Each time we danced we re-examined our roles, searching for new ways to illuminate their personalities and their relationship to each other. By the time I left Ballet Theatre to devote full time to my own company, my characterization of Giselle had crystallized. I knew her intimately as a naïve girl in the first act and as a disembodied spirit in the second. Consequently, I did not alter this characterization later when I danced with the Bolshoi and the Kirov ballets. Nor was I required to. One of the principal reasons for engaging a guest star is to afford the public an opportunity to experience the special interpretation offered by the visiting dancer, and thus for the occasion the Soviet artists modified their interpretations to match mine. However, I did observe new aspects in the interpretation of other roles (particularly that of Giselle's mother), and I remembered these when I was asked to stage the ballet for a film in Cuba.

For that film, produced by the Cuban Institute of Artistic and Industrial Films (ICAIC) in 1963, I made a completely fresh study of GISELLE. Aware that the film would be seen by many who had never attended a live performance of GISELLE and were not familiar with the traditions of ballet, I looked at the work through their eyes and realized that many sequences whose meaning we took for granted would appear puzzling and unclear to them. For example, in the first few moments of the ballet, Giselle emerges from her cottage in response to a knock on the door. Obviously she hopes to find Loys (Albrecht in disguise), the boy from next door with whom she has fallen in love. And yet when he comes out of hiding and confronts her, she repeatedly attempts to elude him and return to her cottage. Why does she behave so irrationally? She appears to be acting the role of a kittenish tease rather than that of a naïve country girl experiencing her first love. To explain her behavior, I inserted an additional bit of action. By holding up the edge of her skirt and miming the stitching of a hem, she tells Loys she must leave him because there is sewing to do inside the cottage.*

*In 1976 ballerinas preparing for their debuts as Giselle in Ballet Theatre performances studied the Alonso film at Lincoln Center's Library and Museum of the Performing Arts and incorporated the new action in their own interpretations. [C.P.]

In the same way, I reviewed all the action of the ballet and proceeded on the theory that even in an unearthly, romantic story the characters could act rationally and with comprehensible motivation. The early identification of Giselle as a seamstress led to the elimination of other seeming inconsistencies. For one thing, it explained plausibly how Albrecht could have discovered Giselle without his own identity being revealed to her friends and neighbors: he had first observed her when she was delivering a finished piece of needlework to the town or to a neighboring castle. Fixing on her as a target for seduction, he had disguised himself as an itinerant laborer named Loys, and it was then an easy matter for him to rent a cottage and make the acquaintance of the girl across the way. To continue the logical sequence of events, I have Giselle introduce Loys to her friends when they return from the vineyard. They readily accept him as a worker like themselves and have no reason to suspect that he is a nobleman in disguise. It remains for Hilarion to first entertain doubts as to the true identity of Loys. Here again I reworked the scene. In traditional versions Hilarion employs conventional mime to say to Giselle, "Do you think he loves you? He does not. I am the one who loves you." Few in present-day audiences are schooled in the language of mime, and to those who would be watching the film it would be incomprehensible. And so I replaced the mime with dance movement. Giselle is dancing with Loys when Hilarion cuts in and tries to make her dance with him instead. The imperious manner in which Loys orders him to leave makes Hilarion suspect that he is dealing with more than an ordinary peasant.

By making these and other revisions, I hoped to tell the story more clearly and, where possible, to tell it with dancing rather than with mime or dramatic action. My concern that the character of each role be delineated through a combination of acting, mime, and dancing extended to every member of the corps de ballet. As a director I took care that each dancer in the corps understood the role she was playing and expressed the individuality of the person she represented. Giselle's friends were not all alike, and neither were the Duke's courtiers meant to be stereotyped characters. Their individual personalities should be conveyed to the audience by the distinctive ways in which the dancers portraying them move, mime, and act.

When the time came to stage the so-called "peasant pas de deux," I decided it must be eliminated. A classical duet, with bows taken between each variation, was completely out of place in the setting of a vineyard community. However, while abandoning the pas de deux, I kept the music. It is now danced to by ten of Giselle's friends, who perform as trios, quartets, or as an entire group. Many of the original steps were retained but they are integrated with the dancing of the corps de ballet as a whole.

I have never felt that any of my revisions did violence to the choreographer's original conception. If anything, they

may perhaps have restored the ballet to its pristine form. My introduction of a Master Huntsman is an example. In the Dolin version it always bothered me that Wilfred, Albrecht's equerry, accompanied Albrecht to Giselle's cottage—leaving him there with full knowledge that he is about to attempt seduction—and then, a very short time later, leads the Duke of Courland's hunting party to the same cottage in search of refreshment. Wilfred must be aware that Albrecht's fiancée, Bathilde, is a member of the party and might surprise him in his dalliance. In my version I added a Master Huntsman, who unwittingly leads the ducal party to the scene of Albrecht's rendezvous with Giselle. It might almost be said that if Coralli and Perrot did not, in fact, include such a huntsman in their cast of characters, they should have.*

In general, I believe it is impossible to maintain a ballet over the years exactly in its original version. Even if changes should not be made, they inevitably are made. Change in itself is not bad as long as the style of the original is preserved. If the changes add strength to a role or contribute to deeper expressiveness in the dancing, they are permissible. Thus my alterations in the second act were intended to enhance the role of the Queen of the Wilis, who should be danced by a ballerina with a very strong technique. I have given her more difficult steps to perform than in other versions. I have also altered somewhat the choreography for the corps of Wilis. Whereas formerly they appeared at one time in straight lines and at another gathered in circles, I have combined the two formations in a single scene in accordance with what I discovered through a study of nineteenth-century engravings. At the same time, I have emphasized the supreme importance of maintaining the soft, romantic style. I stressed to the dancers the care that must be taken in assuming the romantic attitudes—in the position of the body, in the port de bras free of all angularity, and in the movements of purest romanticism.

When approached in this manner, I believe GISELLE, of all the classical ballets, can come the closest to retaining its original form. The music and the libretto are so controlling that if they are followed, the ballet emerges pretty much the same under any ballet master's direction. However, GISELLE is also a ballet that requires constant restudy because it is susceptible to varied dramatic interpretations. Decades have passed since I first danced as one of Giselle's friends and since I first assumed the role of Giselle herself, but I still find myself inspired with fresh insights as to how a role or a certain dramatic passage should be performed. It is for this reason that GISELLE has remained for the dancer and the director the most intriguing of all the ballets in the classical repertory.

---

*The Master Huntsman has appeared in other versions, including the one with which Diaghilev re-introduced GISELLE to Paris in 1910 and the one currently performed by American Ballet Theatre. The character is not listed in the program of the original production, but if the role was then performed by a member of the corps de ballet—as it might well have been—it would have been included anonymously under the heading "Courtiers, Ladies-in-Waiting, Huntsmen, etc." The roles of Wilfred and the Master Huntsman may have been consolidated by Dolin into a single character because the Markova-Dolin company was short of boys. [C. P.]

DIRECTING A
BALLET COMPANY
LUCIA CHASE

When I am asked what it is I do with Ballet Theatre, I usually reply that I am in charge of the company. I realize this can lead to confusion unless the term "the company" is clearly defined and understood. When I speak of the company I do not mean the corporate entity that administers the business affairs. These are conducted by the officers of the Ballet Theatre Foundation in accordance with policies set by the Board of Governing Trustees. The company of which I am in charge is the performing unit known as American Ballet Theatre, whose members create, rehearse, and perform the ballets of its repertory. My principal concern is with the dancers, with whom I first come in contact during the selection process.

The procedure for selecting dancers has varied considerably over the years. There was a time when we could hold "open" auditions which any dancer could attend without a special invitation. Because of the tremendous increase in the number of ballet-school graduates, this is no longer feasible. (More than three hundred dancers appear for the annual auditions to the American Ballet Theatre School alone.) Today, a limited number of recommended dancers are invited to apply in smaller groups, or from time to time individuals are asked to take a company class where they can be seen by myself, the ballet masters, and the choreographers and be judged in comparison with the dancers of the company.* These applicants are recommended by sources all over the country. (They used to come to us from all over the world, but new government and dancers' union regulations now require that only American citizens be chosen for the corps de ballet and that foreigners be engaged as soloists or principal dancers only under special circumstances.) We have never seriously considered restricting the applicants to graduates of our own school because we are aware that there are many talented dancers throughout the country who cannot afford to come to New York for study. As it is our aim to employ the most promising talent available, we take it where we can find it.†

What is looked for in a dancer and by what criteria are selections made? Standards and the procedure for examination have altered enormously since the days when, as a dancer myself, I first observed the selection process. In the 1940s it was necessary to begin by determining the extent of the applicant's mastery of the ballet technique, which often

proved to be scarcely adequate. In that first decade of Ballet Theatre, it was not unusual for a dancer to be taken into the company even though she was unable to execute a series of fouettés or he could not perform a double air-turn. Today, we can assume that dancers will not be put forward for our consideration, or will not offer themselves, unless they have mastered these and other technical feats. It is no longer a question of <u>can</u> they perform. The questions now asked are can they perform with ease, with authority, and with beauty of line? We do, of course, first check the dancer's physical qualifications—the proportions and placement of the body and limbs. Today, with the company performing LA BAYADÈRE, for example, in which the dancers must move uniformly, it is essential that they all be able to extend the leg in high arabesque (made possible only by the proper "turn-out" at the hips). And with the addition of so many classic ballets to the repertory the possession of "good feet" has assumed even greater importance.

Poor feet and faulty turn-out are physical defects that would be deplored by the auditioners for any classic ballet company. But there are also stylistic variants that are regarded as defects at a Ballet Theatre audition. Take, for example, the matter of the arms, wrists, and hands. Through the company's and Dimitri Romanoff's early association with Michel Fokine, we acquired a taste for the rounded arm and wrist, with the fingers held in a soft, natural position. This is a matter of preference. Other companies may prefer straight, thrusting arms, with "broken" wrists and fingers extended at sharp angles. There is, of course, no "right" or "wrong" style for the classic ballets; it is, as I say, a matter of preference. But our teachers, ballet masters, and choreographers devote endless hours to inculcating our preferred style into our dancers.

These physical and stylistic attributes, together with the proportions of the body, are apparent to the eye and can be observed objectively. Other attributes are less obvious and require a certain amount of guesswork in their detection. Is the dancer attractive, does she have charm, is she alert, does she project an interesting personality, is she friendly, amiable, and good-natured? Some of these qualities, particularly the last, appear to be irrelevant, but they assume importance in a touring repertory company where the dancer must remain in close contact with her fellow dancers over protracted periods and where she must accept the vicissitudes of a constantly changing repertory that may suddenly deprive her of one of her most treasured roles. To remain a contented dancer in such a company, one must necessarily be good-natured. It would seem impossible to detect these intangible qualities during a brief audition, and yet experience has proved that a great deal can be learned from apparently casual observation at a time when the dancer is not aware of being observed—as she walks to the barre, or puts on her toe shoe, or talks with her fellow dancers, or listens to the instructions of the ballet master conducting the audition.

---

*On every rehearsal or performance day, separate women's and men's classes (or a combined class) are given. A class serves the double purpose of warming up the muscles and of enabling the dancer to practice combinations of steps. The dancer begins at the barre with exercises designed to stretch and strengthen the muscles and continues on the studio floor with the performance of dancing exercises. Classes are conducted by a ballet master, who points out any bad habits the dancer may have acquired and suggests how they may be corrected. Thus these are not classes in the usual sense of the word; they are not sessions in which one is taught to dance. [C.P.]

†It is to be hoped that the time may come when funds are sufficiently available to enable us to search out young talent throughout the country and to provide scholarships to our School for the most promising. At such time we will doubtless accept more School graduates into the company. In the meantime we audition those who are recommended to us by the School faculty, by our ballet masters and choreographers, by regional teachers and companies with whom we come in contact on tour, and by our own dancers. [L.C.]

LUCIA CHASE APPEARS ON THE PREVIOUS PAGE AS QUEEN CLEMENTINE IN BLUEBEARD.

Chance also sometimes plays a role in the selection of a dancer. She may by good fortune have applied at just the right moment. As we prepare for each season we review the roster of dancers and determine our requirements for replacements. Our dance dramas require performers of varying sizes. The role of Lizzie Borden as a child in FALL RIVER LEGEND or of the Youngest Sister in PILLAR OF FIRE must necessarily be performed by a short dancer, as must the boys' roles of the Grooms in PETROUCHKA or of the Satyrisci in UNDERTOW. When these shorter dancers are cast in the classic ballets, from SWAN LAKE down through ETUDES, they cannot be dispersed haphazardly among the taller dancers. To present an aesthetically pleasing line of the corps de ballet it is imperative, as with a string of pearls, that the dancers be placed in graduated order with respect to size. Since I keep this continually in mind, I find myself approaching an audition with reminders such as, "We need two more short boys," or "If so-and-so leaves to get married we'll need another tall girl to replace her." Thus it is that chance and the right moment may improve the fortunes of a girl of five feet six inches who comes to our attention just at the time when we must engage a tall dancer.

And finally, in a company that presents the ballets of so many different choreographers, the quality of adaptability must be sought for in its dancer applicants. Each particular choreographer would be very happy if we engaged every dancer whose qualities appealed to him and who he thought would be "just right" for a role in one of his ballets. However, the roster of a repertory company cannot be enrolled on this basis. Every dancer selected must appear to be capable of performing roles created by a dozen other choreographers and, even more important, be equipped with the technique demanded in the performance of the company's increasingly dominant classic repertory.

A review of our selection actions over the years reveals that more often than not dancers, particularly those with previous ballet experience, have chosen to join Ballet Theatre rather than have been selected by us. A case in point is that of John Kriza, who came back from a tour of South America with one of Ruth Page's companies during Ballet Theatre's first year. Unless he could find dance employment in New York he was faced with the prospect of returning to Chicago to assist in running his father's meat market. With only enough money in his pocket to pay for a last meal, he attended three auditions in the same day: for the Ballet Russe de Monte Carlo, a Broadway musical, and Ballet Theatre. He was offered employment by all three companies and chose us, where he remained to become known as "Mr. Ballet Theatre" until his retirement a quarter of a century later. For me, Johnny occupied a very special and unique position in the company—one similar to that occupied today by Mikhail Baryshnikov. Although the technical skills of these two dancers are not to be compared, as warm human beings they are twin spirits—understanding, cooperative, generous of their time and talent, blessed with a humor sometimes sly but

always good, and, above all, totally dedicated to the integrity of their art. Thus, at the other end of Ballet Theatre's thirty-five years, it was not significant that we chose to engage Mikhail Baryshnikov. Who in his right mind would not have? The significant decision was the one Mischa made when he chose American Ballet Theatre as his home company.

LUCIA CHASE IN THE ROLE OF THE PRELUDE IN LES SYLPHIDES.

Along with the selection of the dancing company, accomplished in consultation with the ballet masters and the resident choreographers, I also collaborate with Oliver Smith in the selection of the repertory. Here again, the elements of chance and of the "right moment" inevitably play an important role both for the choreographer and the direction. When reviewing the repertory to determine what ballets will be presented during the forthcoming season, the directors may decide, for example, that the opening ballets in the active repertory have been seen too often by the public—that a new opening ballet is required. If by chance a choreographer comes forward at that right moment with an idea for a new work suitable for use as an opening ballet, he and his idea may be accepted, whereas at another time they might have been rejected. Or the directors may conclude that a new ballet must be created for one of our principal dancers. In 1975, for instance, it was agreed that we must acquire a modern ballet that would afford Mikhail Baryshnikov an opportunity to display his unique comic talent. Previously we had been discussing the commissioning of a new work with Twyla Tharp, and when coincidentally she and Baryshnikov came together, PUSH COMES TO SHOVE was created. If they had not met at that particular time, Ballet Theatre would still have added a Tharp ballet to its repertory and would eventually have produced a comic ballet for

MIKHAIL BARYSHNIKOV

JOHN KRIZA

Baryshnikov by another choreographer, but in neither case would the result have resembled PUSH COMES TO SHOVE.

More than in any other branch of the performing arts, the directors of a ballet company are, for the most part, forced to embark on a new production in blind faith. Opera and symphony scores or scripts of dramatic works can be played or read before rehearsals are undertaken. The producers cannot know whether the production will be a success but at least they know what they are producing. Ballet producers can know in advance only what is in the choreographer's head, and that is often vague or incommunicable. Much must be taken on faith. Fortunately, Richard Pleasant performed such an act of faith in 1940 when a choreographer approached him with an idea he had been mulling over for some time. The choreographer had in mind a ballet, to be called I DEDICATE, that would trace the traumatic psychological experiences of a frustrated female who lived in terror of remaining a spinster like her older sister and yet was not willing to adopt the predatory flirtation tactics employed by her younger sister in getting her man. On the basis of this brief synopsis—and the choreographer offered little more—Dick accepted the ballet, but the sketch for the scenery he commissioned from Peter Piening indicates that the choreographer's conception had not been made clear to him. When Gerry Sevastianov took over the direction of the company, he hesitated to proceed with rehearsals of the ballet and was particularly dubious that a classical ballet could be danced on pointe to Schönberg's "Verklärte Nacht." However, he crossed his fingers and went through with the production, which by that time the choreographer, Antony Tudor, had renamed PILLAR OF FIRE.

The "crossing of fingers" has become the customary course of action when the direction embarks on the production of a new ballet by an established choreographer, and the risk it runs is even greater when it commissions a work from a novice. These risks must be taken into consideration when Oliver Smith and I are deciding whether to entrust the creation of a ballet to an untried choreographer. We are aware that it will not be until the rehearsals are virtually completed, and perhaps not until after the scenery and costumes have been executed, that we will be able to tell whether we have in fact discovered a choreographer with talent or have merely found one capable of flashes of choreographic brilliance but not of creating a complete, well-constructed work. During these final rehearsals we must also determine whether further investments should be made in the new choreographer regardless of the success or failure of his first ballet. For it is then that we learn the answers to such questions as, can he communicate his thoughts and wishes to the dancers, does he understand how to use their bodies (their potentialities and limitations), and, perhaps most important, can he organize

his own thinking and his use of rehearsal time? If he can do these things, he is a good risk for a second ballet even if his first has been a failure. If he cannot, his chances of being given another opportunity are diminished even if his first work is an unquestioned success. In these days when rehearsal time is severely restricted by union regulations and overtime rates are so high, a company can no longer permit a dancer to be called for rehearsal only to sit by idly, unused by the choreographer. With established choreographers, the directors must tolerate "slow periods" and those sessions in which inspiration fails, but they cannot permit the same luxury to a novice. Impatience is forced on the directors by the economics of present-day production of ballets.

Having performed the function of selecting choreographers, ballets, and dancers, I am then called upon to operate what I have come to refer to as the "complaint department." Complaints of every nature, most of them understandable and many of them justified, are directed to me not only by the choreographers and dancers but also by our subscriber-patrons, the general public, and the press. The complaints from choreographers begin with the early rehearsals, when they feel not enough rehearsal time is allotted them, and continue through the performing season, when their ballets are not scheduled often enough or in the right order. (They will protest, "My ballet should never be on the same program as such-and-such ballet," or "My ballet should always be placed in the middle of the program and should be immediately preceded only by the undramatic, neutral LES SYLPHIDES.") The dancers' complaints begin at the same time as the choreographers', when during rehearsals they have not been cast in the roles of their choice, and they continue throughout the season, when they are not scheduled to perform as often as they wish the roles for which they have been chosen.

It will be asked how one could find fault with a choreographer's eagerness to rehearse an infinite number of hours to attain perfection. No one does find fault, but eventually facts must be faced: the number of rehearsal hours and of studios is limited, and a dancer can be made available to only one choreographer in one studio at one time. To arrange for the right dancer to be in the right studio for the right choreographer at the right time presents a formidable problem of logistics that could never be easily solved even by a computer. It is solved daily in a time-consuming juggling act performed by Enrique Martinez. To give some indication of the complexity of these schedules, we have reproduced here one of the rehearsal call sheets, picked at random from among those on file from the rehearsal period preceding our 1976 season at the Metropolitan Opera House.

(PREVIOUS PAGES) OVER THE YEARS LUCIA CHASE HAS REGARDED AS TWIN SPIRITS MIKHAIL BARYSHNIKOV (IN COPPÉLIA) AND JOHN KRIZA (IN FANCY FREE).

REHEARSAL SCHEDULES SUCH AS THE ONE REPRODUCED ON THE OPPOSITE PAGE ARE SOMETIMES FURTHER COMPLICATED WHEN REHEARSALS ARE HELD AT BOTH THE SCHOOL AND THE THEATER. THE NAMES IN THE FAR RIGHT COLUMN ARE THOSE OF THE PIANISTS WHO PLAY FOR THE REHEARSALS.

A. B. T. SCHOOL	AMERICAN BALLET THEATRE	WEDNESDAY, NOV. 24, 1976		
	REHEARSAL SCHEDULE			
10:00 - 11:15	COMPANY CLASS - LADIES	Mr. Schneider	Kay	
10:00 - 11:15	COMPANY CLASS - GENTLEMEN	Mr. Minz		Irving
11:30 - 12:30	NUTCRACKER ACT II -FULL w/ Principals	Mr. Baryshnikov	Rosenthal	
		Mr. Douglas		
		Mr. Schneider/Mr. Holden		
11:30 - 12:30	CONCERTO - van Hamel, Young	Mr. Lland		Barr
11:30 - 12:30	PATINEURS - Prinz, Orr	Mr. Orr		Johnson
~~11:30 - 12:30~~	~~GISELLE - Gregory~~	~~Mr. Romanoff~~	~~Staplin~~	
12:30 - 1:30	VOLUNTARIES-Menendez, Orborne, Nesbitt,Johansson,Owen, Browne, Schafer, Barbee, Shibata, Maple, Rhodes, Gustafson, Whitaker, Cuevas, Elliott, Peterson, Glushak, Smith, Wallach, Wright, Conover, Serrano, Harvey, Fonseca, Spizzo, delaPena, Maule, Sanchez, Hammerli	Mr. Tetley	Staplin	
		Mr. Douglas		
12:30 - 2:30	NUTCRACKER - Claras, Prince, Drosselmeyer	Mr. Baryshnikov	Rosenthal	
		Mr. Schneider		
		Mr. Holden		
12:30 - 1:30	SWAN -Czardas - Barth, Benash, (Collier) Gordon, Jasinski, KUPO Sanchez, ~~Serrano~~, ~~Wallach~~	Mr. Martinez	Kaufman	
12:30 - 1:30	~~GISELLE~~ - van Hamel, Tippet SWAN	Mr.Romanoff	Johnson	
12:30 - 1:30	FITTING - Ashton, Wesche, Soleri			
1:30 - 2:30	SWAN - Neapolitan - Yeager(Hammerli), (Kovak), Benash,Warner,Lockwood, Conover, Peterson,de la Pena, Fonseca	Mr. Orr	Kaufman	
1:30 - 2:30	JARDIN - Browne,de la Pena,Glushak, Young	Mr. Tudor	Johnson	
1:30 - 2:30	PUSH - Schafer,Ashton,Barbee,Soleri, Rinehart	Miss Jones	TAPE	
		Mr. Conover		
1:30 - 2:30	SWAN - Spanish - Whitaker (Prieto, Hernandez), Carter, Owen PAREDES	Mr. Martinez	Barr	
1:30 - 2:15	FITTING - Johansson, Menendez			
2:30 - 3:30	SWAN - Gregory, Nagy	Mr.Martinez	Kaufman	
2:30 - 3:30	BEAUTY - van Hamel, Tippet	Mr. Helpmann	Barr	
		Mr. Lland		
2:30 - 3:30	JARDIN - Glushak, Young	Mr. Tudor	Staplin	
2:30 - 3:30	PUSH - de la Pena	Mr.Orr	TAPE	
		Mr.Conover		
2:30 - 3:15	FITTING - Collier, Gordon			
3:30 - 4:30	BEAUTY - Gregory, Ward	Mr. Lland	Johnson	
3:30 - 4:30	NUTCRACKER - Spanish, Chinese, Russian, Shepherds	Mr.Baryshnikov	Rosenthal	
		Mr.Douglas/Schneider/Holde		
3:30 - 4:30	SWAN - Shibata, Wesche, Maule, Whitaker (Glushak, when free of "Beauty")	Mr.Helpmann	Staplin	
		Mr.Martinez		
3:30 - 4:00	CONCERTO - III Movement -Menendez (when out of "Nutcracker")	Mr.Orr	Barr	
4:30 - 6:30	VOLUNTARIES - Gregory, Ward,Barbee, van Hamel, Tippet, Schafer, Osborne,.Menendez, Maple,Morales, Peterson,~~Conover~~,Browne,Owen, CONOVER Smith, Tcherkassky, Nagy	Mr. Tetley	Staplin	
		Mr.Douglas		
4:30 - 5:30	PUSH - Groups A and B - All Girls w/ Understudies	~~Mr.Orr~~	TAPE	
		Miss Jones		
		Mr. Holden		
4:30 - 5:30	NUTCRACKER Baryshnikov	Mr.Schneider	Rosenthal	
5:30 - 6:30	SWAN- Mazurka - Maule(Rosal,Whitaker) (Cordell,Rinehart) (Wesche,Soleri) (~~Barbee~~,Gustafson) (Nesbitt,~~Osborne~~)(Cuevas,~~Owen~~)	Mr.Martinez	Johnson	
5:30 - 6:30	LEAVES - Shibata, Barth	Miss Hynninen	Barr	
6:30 - 7:30	BEAUTY - PROLOGUE	Mr. Helpmann	Barr	
		Mr. Lland		

The compiling of the season's performing schedules is equally complex, as ballets are constantly shifted until they are formed into a series of programs for the season that will satisfy the demands of the dancers, the choreographers, and the public. The manipulation is generally performed by Enrique Martinez and me with suggestions and advice from Antony Tudor and from Daryl Dodson, who contributes the stage expertise he acquired while serving as production stage manager. When the final arrangement of ballets has been arrived at, we separate, usually in a state of mental fatigue, and await the receipt of typed copies. It is then, the following day, that our refreshed minds begin to make unwelcome discoveries. The phones begin to ring. Daryl, as former stage manager, calls to point out that Ballet X cannot possibly follow Ballet Y on the second Friday because the scene-shifting involved would require an intermission of not less than thirty-five minutes even if there were no hitches. Enrique is on the phone to report that the second week's schedule contains only one ballet in which Martine van Hamel performs. This means she will have only one performance that week unless we insert an additional ballet or she learns an additional role. My secretary, Florence Pettan, calls to remind me that I had agreed to let Ivan Nagy dance with Margot Fonteyn on the 17th in Montreal, the day on which I have scheduled Ballet X for the Met. "Is this a mistake or is someone else learning Ivan's role?" Daryl rings again, this time in his capacity as general manager, to report that the subscription department has discovered an error. PETROUCHKA cannot be scheduled for the third Thursday because it was seen only last season by the Thursday-night subscribers. At about that time, I notice that we have programmed Ballet Y to precede LES NOCES, which I had promised Jerry Robbins never to do. While I am still puzzling over the solution to this problem, Nancy Zeckendorf, of the American Ballet Theatre Friends, phones to tactfully protest that the new pas de deux for dancers A and B has been scheduled for the 18th, two days before the Gala. It should be reserved for the Gala alone, but if there must be additional performances they should follow the Gala and not be announced until she has sold more of the $100 tickets.

After countless adjustments have been made and, it is hoped, all the problems have been solved, I am almost immediately pressured by the publicity department to furnish it with a list of the casting of the principal roles in all of the scheduled performances. This I cannot do until I have gone through a routine I customarily follow after the programs have been set. I review with each of the principal dancers in turn the proposed casting. I frequently find that their thought processes have differed from mine and that they are able to offer valid reasons for changes. Dancer A, for example, is scheduled to dance Giselle for the first time with Dancer B. So that she can devote more time to preparation, she would prefer that the performance of GISELLE be scheduled <u>after</u> the

premiere of the new ballet on which she is now concentrating her complete attention. Even when all adjustments have been made, the casting list as published must sometimes require change due to illness or injury. And then there are always special circumstances and unknown factors that make it impossible to state with certainty who will dance which roles weeks or months hence.

These "unknowns" differ from season to season, but those which preceded the 1976 Met season are illustrative of their general nature. Erik Bruhn had been injured during the previous season and was still recuperating in Denmark when the casting lists, announcing that he would dance Petrouchka, were issued. He had never danced the role, and not until he had returned to New York would he be able to find out whether he had recovered sufficiently to dance or whether the movements devised by Fokine could be executed without causing a recurrence of his injury. Also during the previous season, Gelsey Kirkland had fallen victim to a dietary deficiency, and she was still under a doctor's care when her performances were announced. Her recovery depended to a large extent on her own determination to get well, and there appeared to be no better way of bolstering her will power than by including her name in the published casting lists as an expression of our confidence in her rapid recovery. The third unknown was perhaps unique in the annals of ballet. Arrangements had been made for Alicia Alonso to appear in the Cuban Ballet version of CARMEN, but at the time the programs and castings were to be released it could not be ascertained whether the Cuban and American governments would issue the necessary visas. A spate of hard words directed at each other by Fidel Castro and Gerald Ford might upset all plans. And even should Alicia arrive on schedule in this country, it was deemed inadvisable for security reasons to announce her appearances in advance. Consequently, four performances of Tudor's SHADOWPLAY were scheduled. If all went well, CARMEN would be substituted for them. If not, SHADOWPLAY would be performed as announced. The castings of Bruhn and Kirkland and the scheduling of SHADOWPLAY were made with honest intentions but also with the knowledge that they might not materialize. However, I did not feel they justified a protest that was registered at my complaint department by a balletomane who should have been better acquainted with the exigencies of casting predictions. "Your list," he said accusingly, "is nothing but a tissue of unmitigated lies!" Was he one of those who had, in the first place, demanded casting information so far in advance?

THE ARTISTIC STAFF FOR
LUCIA CHASE AND OLIVER SMITH
HAVE ALL GONE THROUGH THE RANKS
AS DANCERS IN BALLET THEATRE.
THE STAFF OF BALLET MASTERS IS HEADED BY
ASSOCIATE DIRECTORS NORA KAYE AND ANTONY TUDOR.
TUDOR IS SHOWN IN THE ROLE OF TYBALT IN ROMEO AND JULIET.

The complaints that come to my department from the dancers fall on more sympathetic ears because they echo my own experiences as a dancer. When they ask for roles that cannot be assigned to them, I recall that I, too, coveted roles for which I had to wait. In 1941 Anton Dolin staged PAS DE QUATRE, and although I rehearsed the role of Cerrito perhaps even from the start, it was not until 1943, when the role fell vacant because its originators, Katharine Sergava and Annabelle Lyon, were no longer with the company, that it was assigned to me. When a dancer complains about having to share a role with another dancer, I remember how I felt about LES SYLPHIDES. During the first season, I happily shared the Prelude with Annabelle, but when in the following year Dick Pleasant required us to share the role with a third dancer, I resented it. It meant that Annabelle and I would be given fewer performances, being replaced, if even only occasionally, by a dancer whom neither of us recognized as her equal. Like every dancer, I had my moments of greed. Later, when Alicia Markova joined the company and replaced me in most of the important performances of LES SYLPHIDES, I accepted it because she was a dancer of international reputation. I don't mean to suggest that I felt <u>no</u> resentment, I can only repeat that I <u>accepted</u> it. In still another instance, in 1965 Antony Tudor was reviving PILLAR OF FIRE after it had been out of the active repertory for six years. In Lisbon, Portugal, Nora Kaye had given her last performance as Hagar, a role she had danced for eighteen years, and at the same time I had decided to hang up my toe slippers and restrict future appearances to acting roles. Consequently, Tudor had to find not only a new Hagar but a new Eldest Sister. Watching another perform the role which had been mine for so many years was not without emotional complications. Most dancers retain proprietary feelings about a role that was created on them, one they rehearsed while the choreographer was originally devising it, and one that they danced at the premiere performance–they are reluctant to share it or give it up entirely. This claim to ownership continues in varying degrees of intensity as long as the dancer performs the role and even for some time afterward.*

My personal experiences as a dancer will not allow me as a director to take casually the emotional factors—or even quirks—which motivate the dancers and drive them to register complaints and demands. But an understanding of their problems does not simplify my solutions. When a dancer covets a new role, I cannot always grant her request. Aside from the obvious reason that she might not be suited to the role, there is the possibility that she might not be ready for it—that the demands of the role exceed her technical and emotional maturity. Many a career has been adversely affected because the dancer was pushed prematurely into a role

requiring advanced technical and dramatic skills. The first reaction of the critics and public may be one of surprised delight, but thereafter they begin to apply more stringent criteria to the dancer, judging her by too-high standards, and causing her to lose confidence in herself. For this reason a dancer must be brought along slowly and carefully nurtured, even if it means temporarily curbing her eagerness and enthusiasm.

When a dancer (or more often an ardent fan in her behalf) complains that she is being forced too often to share a role in which she has been acclaimed by the public (especially by her own sector of the public), I can only reply that Ballet Theatre policy dictates that for every role there must be alternates and understudies. This policy is required principally because the occupational hazards of ballet dancing make it imperative that substitutes be prepared at all times to take the place of the injured. But there is an additional justification of the policy. In a repertory company it is important to provide each dancer with as many roles in as many ballets as possible. Otherwise a dancer may find herself with no role to perform in a series of performances, and for a dancer to remain idle is debilitating both to her morale and her physical well-being.

There are, of course, exceptions, dictated by the choreographer and the demands of the public. For instance, a choreographer may ask that a certain role be reserved exclusively to one dancer over an extended period. Thus for eighteen years no one but Nora Kaye danced the role of Hagar. This was Tudor's wish. But during that time it was also clear that anyone who bought tickets to see PILLAR OF FIRE expected to see Nora as Hagar and would accept no substitute. The same situation sometimes occurs on Broadway when a particular star is as important as the play in which she is appearing. When such a star becomes ill, performances are suspended. In the ballet, rather than substitute another dancer in the role so closely associated with the indisposed star, the program is changed and the ballet replaced with another. More recently this has been true of the ballet PUSH COMES TO SHOVE and the dancer Mikhail Baryshnikov. Those who bought tickets to the ballet demanded to see Mischa in the leading role. We prepared an understudy, and he danced admirably, but it became apparent that in the foreseeable future the role should be performed exclusively by Baryshnikov.

In allowing ourselves to make an exception in the case of a role particularly identified with one dancer, we have sometimes run into trouble. There have been occasions when another ballet could not be substituted at the last moment, and because we had not expected the lead to be danced by anyone but the original star, the choreographer had been indifferent to preparing an understudy and I had been negligent in not insisting that he do so. This was the case with THEME AND VARIATIONS. Everyone who bought tickets during its early years demanded that Igor Youskevitch dance the lead role created for him by George Balanchine. When he was

*Recently in Los Angeles, Nora Kaye was asked by Lynn Seymour whether she hated to have her old roles of Hagar and Lizzie Borden danced by others. "Not at all," she insisted. "It doesn't bother me a bit. I enjoy watching different interpretations. The more the better." I doubt if she meant a word of it. [C.P.]

(OPPOSITE PAGE TOP LEFT)
ASSISTANT DIRECTOR
ENRIQUE MARTINEZ
IN LA FILLE MAL GARDÉE.

(OPPOSITE PAGE BOTTOM LEFT)
BALLET MASTER
SCOTT DOUGLAS
IN FANCY FREE.

(CENTER)
BALLET MASTER
MICHAEL LLAND
IN JARDIN AUX LILAS.

(LEFT)
REGISSEUR
DIMITRI ROMANOFF
IN TALLY-HO.

353

unavailable, performances were canceled. For the Paris season of 1950, THEME was on the program for the first three performances. Igor danced on the opening night with Mary Ellen Moylan and woke up the next morning too ill to perform; he was unable to dance for the next ten days. We had no choice but to substitute another ballet for the remaining two scheduled performances, and so advised the French impresario, who sternly informed us that this could not be done. Programs were not capriciously changed in France; there was, in fact, a law against it, and the impresario spoke with a touch of hysteria about the possibility of police intervention. Surely, he protested, a company calling itself the American National Ballet Theatre (as we did on that tour) must be of such magnitude that it could provide at least one other premier danseur capable of replacing Youskevitch! We did have Johnny Kriza (Erik Bruhn was on leave), but his enormous talents did not include a facility for performing double air-turns—and THEME called for eight of them to be executed in rapid succession. With reluctance I telephoned him. It was unfair to ask him to make his debut in the ballet at such short notice and doubly unfair to require him to do so before a hypercritical Paris audience. However, he arrived before noon at the Palais du Chaillot, where he rehearsed with Alicia Alonso and danced the next two performances. Alicia was not surprised. She had often danced the DON QUIXOTE PAS DE DEUX with him and was aware that he worried little about technical limitations. In the wings he would say, "Let's get out there and enjoy ourselves." I'm afraid this daring and "joy of dancing" is sometimes missing from much of today's performing as dancers concentrate over-much on their techniques.

Not infrequently dancers approach my complaint department with certain illusions concerning my powers in regard to casting. They will assert confidently, "Lucia, if you really wanted to, you could give me a performance of such-and-such a role." And then they refuse to believe or prefer to ignore the fact that I am not omnipotent, that I am subject, if not to the dictates, at least to the pressures applied to me by the choreographers, my business associates, and the public. The degree of control exercised by choreographers varies according to the provisions in their contracts. The standard choreographer's agreement provides that he will have the right to choose the first cast from among the members of the company. On his part, he agrees to rehearse a second, understudy cast, to be chosen jointly by himself and the directors. He retains no control over castings in future years. This does not, however, represent the complete picture. Not all contracts are in the standard form and not all casting decisions are made in strict accordance with the contract provisions. In the interest of maintaining cordial relationships, concessions to which the choreographer is not entitled contractually are often made. And each choreographer must be dealt with as an individual. With Antony Tudor, who in his capacity as associate director is almost

continually at hand to make casting decisions with respect to his own ballets, I acknowledge his authority as absolute. I make no attempt to influence his casting choices and even refrain from offering casual suggestions, which he might interpret as a pressure tactic that he must discourage by making a contrary decision. With Jerry Robbins, I can presume to discuss alternative castings, and we usually arrive at a mutually satisfactory solution—which is sometimes disrupted later when an emergency decision has to be made and he is not available.*

With Agnes de Mille, I have always felt free to offer suggestions, and we have reached impasses only on the casting of the Cowgirl in RODEO, a role Agnes danced in the original production by the Ballet Russe de Monte Carlo. She maintains that it can be danced only by an accomplished comedienne, and on this point there is no disagreement. However, I am constantly surprised when she is unable to find such a comedienne within the ranks of American Ballet Theatre, a company noted for its actor-dancers. Over the years, at her behest, we have allowed ourselves to be persuaded to engage a series of charming and talented comediennes from the Broadway musical stage, without whom, in Agnes' view, "RODEO could not possibly be performed." There were times when we were able to persuade Agnes to permit a regular member of the company to dance the role, principally on tour in smaller cities. We and the critics, along with the public, found these to be admirable Cowgirls, and in time Agnes was won over to them—so much so that when they left the company, she insisted they be brought back as guest artists, "as there was no one in the company capable of performing the role."†

Even when I inform a dancer that I cannot cast her in a role because the choreographer is withholding his permission, she will still insist, "You could do it if you wanted to." Technically, she may be right, particularly in cases where the choreographer was not in a strong bargaining position when negotiating his contract and thus not able to reserve all casting rights to himself. But as a practical matter, I can act in

---

*In one notable instance Miss Chase and Robbins were unable to reach a satisfactory agreement. Robbins retained complete control of his ballet INTERPLAY (which Billy Rose had commissioned for his revue CONCERT VARIETIES after seeing Ballet Theatre's production of FANCY FREE). When it was first performed by Ballet Theatre in 1945, it was danced by a member of the corps de ballet (Melissa Hayden), by five soloists, and by Janet Reed and John Kriza, who had that season been raised to the rank of principal dancers by Lucia Chase as one of her first acts as the new director. In later years, Robbins' memory told him that all, or the majority, of the roles had been danced originally by principal dancers and he insisted that it continue to be performed only by stars. When this proved impractical, he withdrew the ballet from the repertory. But since then he has allowed it to be danced by a company that designates none of its dancers as stars and by another whose principal dancers would rank only as soloists in Ballet Theatre. [C.P.]

†Allyn McLerie was imported from Broadway for the Ballet Theatre production that premiered in Wiesbaden, Germany, in 1950. Jenny Workman, a company member, succeeded her but was replaced by Broadway's Joan McCracken when the company toured South America. The role was again Workman's until she was replaced by Broadway's Annabelle Gold for the 1957 European tour. Workman then left the company and the role was taken over by regular members Leslie Franzos and Ady Addor. But in 1960 de Mille refused to permit the company to perform RODEO in the Soviet Union without Workman, and she was engaged as a guest artist. When Workman retired permanently, de Mille came under persuasive pressure from Miss Chase and reluctantly permitted Christine Sarry to learn the role. Most recently, after Sarry had joined the Eliot Feld company, de Mille advised Chase that "RODEO could not possibly be performed without the return of Sarry as a guest artist." [C.P.]

THE GREATEST THRILLS EXPERIENCED BY A DIRECTOR OCCUR ON NIGHTS WHEN A NEW BALLET, SUCH AS PUSH COMES TO SHOVE, SCORES A TRIUMPH.

defiance of a choreographer's wishes only if I am prepared to have him decline to choreograph future works for the company or refuse to continue to rehearse those already in the repertory. With the scarcity of choreographers, this is a risk I am seldom willing to take.

Another pressure to which I must respond is exerted by my business associates, whose paramount concern is the sale of tickets and box-office receipts, and it is a fact of theater life that some star performers attract more patrons to the ticket window than do others. Consequently, I am continually being urged to schedule more performances for the more popular principal dancers, and I can do so only by conversely scheduling fewer performances for the less popular dancers. There are a number of systems and procedures for determining who will dance what role in which performance, but none of them can operate with complete fairness to all the dancers, and all of them inevitably give rise to instances of anger and unhappiness. The first of these systems, the so-called "seniority system," functions in most state-supported ballet companies, including those in the Soviet Union. In what is virtually a civil-service organization, the junior members must wait until their seniors relinquish roles or magnanimously permit them an occasional performance. Although this system assures contentment to the senior principals, it leaves the juniors with depressing and discouraging frustrations. A second system is employed in companies where the director operates with the assurance that he (and it is sometimes a "she") knows who should dance which roles and when—with the wishes of the dancer or the public regarded as immaterial. This system can succeed only so long as the dancers and the public concede that the director has earned the right to make such decisions on the basis of his or her experience, accomplishments, and, sometimes, genius. I, for one, would never adopt it.

In Ballet Theatre we have adopted a third system, which though apparently more benevolent in its intentions, in practice, I'm afraid, does not guarantee a greater degree of fairness or any fewer incidents of unhappiness. We try for a more equal distribution of roles, apportioned on the basis of merit, with a concession to the wishes of the public. The inclusion of the factor of public popularity, as indicated by ticket sales, may be said to add a taint of commercialism, yet in the end it may produce what is perhaps the most democratic system. The purchase of tickets can be looked upon as the public's exercise of its franchise. Of course, this policy can be followed only by a company which considers its principal function to be that of entertaining its audiences and providing them with moments of excitement, inspiration, and sheer beauty. And while such a company recognizes the importance of continual exploration and experimentation in order to

expand the art of ballet, it must not pay too great attention to those who would nag its conscience by insisting that its primary duty is to educate the public—to give it not necessarily what it likes, but what it should like. We seek the happy medium: to maintain our integrity while giving the public what it wants. And my business associates assure me that what the public wants, indeed demands, is performances by star dancers. As it happens, the preponderance of our repertory, particularly the classics, also demands performances by dancers of star quality. To the impresarios who pay us fees and assume the costs of performances, there is no doubt as to which stars are of the greatest magnitude—and they insist that these performers must shine in their theaters. But there is sometimes doubt in the minds of stars of lesser magnitude, those whom connoisseurs appreciate but who shine less brilliantly in the eyes of the general public. Their best friends and ardent fans do not tell them about the empty seats (which cannot be seen from the stage), and they feel that my failure to schedule them for more performances is arbitrary and misguided. However, my associates and I cannot ignore the box-office figures. We do not enjoy the total support of the government, and therefore cannot, even if we wished, operate on the basis of "the public be damned." The sources that contributed funds to make up the deficits that are admitted to be inevitable would be discouraged if we played consistently to only partly filled houses. And so it is that I am frequently frustrated when protests concerning casting and performance scheduling are lodged at my complaint department and I find myself able to do little about them.

I do not, however, mean to overstress the importance of my function as the head of the complaint department. To do so would be to indulge in a negative attitude, which I take such pains to discourage in others. The frustrations I feel when I am forced to refuse dancers' requests are insignificant when compared to the positive joy I derive from delighting and sometimes surprising them with affirmative replies. One of my first satisfying experiences after becoming director occurred in 1945, when I was able to inform the American soloists, whom Hurok had refused to recognize or publicize as stars, that they would henceforth be accorded full status as principal dancers.* The ability to bring pleasure to the dancers

---

*The soloists were Alicia Alonso, John Kriza, Janet Reed, Maria Karnilova, Rosella Hightower, Jerome Robbins, and Michael Kidd. [C. P.]

carries with it greater satisfaction because they are so deserving. They are the hardest workers in the field of entertainment and are the least rewarded. The opportunities for increasing these rewards, with a boost not in salary but rather in morale, usually occur during the rehearsal sessions, the most exciting weeks during the ballet year. It is then that the choreographers are creating and new talents are being discovered in the dancers as they seize the opportunity to learn new roles either at the suggestion of the direction or on their own initiative. We are always encouraging dancers to aim higher, to aspire to new and more difficult roles, and this often results in happy surprises for both the direction and the dancer. It is important that the dancers be made aware of the direction's positive interest in their careers. Otherwise they become discouraged and disgruntled, and individual discontent can spread rapidly and infect the entire company.

Over the years the thrills of discovery and the joys of making deserved awards have been innumerable. To cite a few examples from recent seasons only, there were the times when I could announce to Charles Ward and Clark Tippet that they had been promoted to the rank of principal dancer; when I could tell Marianna Tcherkassky that she would be given performances of the role of Giselle. The excitement of moments like these is exceeded only by the ultimate exhilaration experienced when the curtain falls on the first performance of a new ballet and the roars of applause from the audience bolster my own personal assurance that this time I don't have to wait until I have read the critics' reviews to be convinced that Ballet Theatre has produced another hit. The satisfaction I experienced on the opening nights of, for example, PILLAR OF FIRE, FANCY FREE, and THEME AND VARIATIONS, was doubled recently following the premiere of PUSH COMES TO SHOVE. For on that occasion Ballet Theatre had not only produced another hit but had been instrumental in enabling Mischa Baryshnikov to realize a cherished ambition—that of exploring the new territories being opened up by American choreographers. That evening alone would have convinced me that my thirty years as co-director of Ballet Theatre, with all the headaches, had been well worthwhile, and it encouraged me to continue in the position that I first accepted in 1945 with the understanding that it would be temporary.

BALLET THEATRE PRODUCTIONS,
1940-1977

AWAKENING MIKHAIL BARYSHNIKOV, GELSEY KIRKLAND.

AFTERNOON OF A FAUN JEANETTE LAURET, HUGH LAING.

BARN DANCE NANA GOLLNER, (SEATED) JOHN KRIZA, PAUL PETROFF.

BY HENRY WISNESKI

Compiled from the archives of American Ballet Theatre and of the Dance Collection, the Library and Museum of the Performing Arts, the New York Public Library.

Key: Names of the ballets are as they first appeared in American Ballet Theatre programs (CARNAVAL not LE CARNAVAL; FIREBIRD not THE FIREBIRD). After a choreographer has died and his choreography is reproduced by another, it is not possible to determine with certainty how much of the original has been retained, and so the phrase "from the original by" is used here throughout if the current choreographer intended to reproduce exactly or approximately the original choreography (as did Blair with GISELLE and Martinez with COPPÉLIA.). The statistics of the original production are appended. If, however, the current choreographer intended that his choreography should be entirely or predominantly new (as did Tetley with LE SACRE DU PRINTEMPS and Baryshnikov with THE NUTCRACKER), reference to previous productions is omitted.

All changes in scenery, costume, and lighting designs between the first and latest stagings have not been recorded. In recent years the lighting has been designed by Nicholas Cernovitch, Gilbert Hemsley, Jr., Tom Lingwood, Nananne Porcher, John B. Read, Jean Rosenthal, Tom Skelton, and Jennifer Tipton.

Personnel associated with the company have arbitrarily altered the spelling of their names from time to time or changed them completely. Михаил Мордкин used Mikhail Mordkin (My-kill Mordkin) as his name in English; Михаил Фокин (My-kill Fo-kin) preferred the French Michel Fokin (Mish-shell Fo-kin), which he later further Gallicized to Fokine (Fo-keen). To complicate matters still further, Mordkin's son chose to call himself Michael Mordkin, Jr. With the outbreak of World War II and for obvious reasons, German Sevastianov changed his name to Gerald (when Stalin signed a pact with Adolf Hitler, he changed the Sevastianov to Severn), and Adolf Bolm changed the spelling of his name to Adolph. The translation of names from Polish to Russian to English led to other complications. Yurek Lazowski successively called himself Yurek Lazovsky and Yura Lazovsky. Yura Skibin became first the French Georges Skibine and later the American George Skibine. Americans contributed to the confusion when, in mid-career, Nora Koreff became Nora Kaye; Jimmie Hicks, Scott Douglas; Mildred Herman, Melissa Hayden; and Holland Stoudenmire (known as Nat) ended as Michael Lland. During her first transition year, Nora Kaye sometimes appeared in an evening's program as Kaye in one ballet and Koreff in another. In this book one name (presumably the last-chosen) is used throughout to denote one person.

In recording the cast, the character name in parentheses is not repeated when listing the cast of a previous production, unless necessary for clarity. Where the choreographer intended that the ballet should be divided into separate movements, the listing of the dancers that appeared in the movement is preceded by a Roman numeral. Lists of names grouped for other reasons (such as to separate males from females or to denote their rank as stars, soloists, or corps de ballet) are separated by semicolons.

Charles Payne's notes are appended to supply information not appearing elsewhere in the book and to give a précis of the libretto where it is significant or unfamiliar.

AFTERNOON OF A FAUN

Choreography: Yura Lazovsky, from the original by Vaslav Nijinsky. Music: Claude Debussy. Scenery and costumes: Léon Bakst. Libretto: Stephane Mallarmé.

Premiere: Palacio de Bellas Artes, Mexico City, November 4, 1941.

Dancers: Jeanette Lauret (Nymph), George Skibine (Faun).

First U.S. performance by Ballet Theatre (with additional Nymphs as in original) Metropolitan Opera House, New York City, November 1, 1942.

Dancers: Jeanette Lauret, Hugh Laing; Rosella Hightower, Barbara Fallis, Nina Popova, Jean Davidson, Galina Razoumova, Roszika Sabo.

World premiere (under the title L'APRÈS-MIDI D'UN FAUNE): Les Ballets Russes de Diaghilev, Théâtre du Châtelet, May 29, 1912.

Dancers: Lydia Nelidova, Vaslav Nijinsky; Bronislava Nijinska, Olga Khokhlova, Leocadia Klementovicz, and Mmes Maicherska, Tcherepanova, and Kopyshinska.

ALEKO

Choreography: Leonide Massine. Music: Peter Ilyich Tchaikovsky (Trio in A Minor), arranged by Erno Rapee. Scenery and costumes: Marc Chagall.

World premiere: Palacio de Bellas Artes, Mexico City, September 8, 1942.

Principal dancers: Alicia Markova (Zemphira), George Skibine (Aleko), Hugh Laing (A Young Gypsy), Antony Tudor (Zemphira's Father), Lucia Chase (Fortuneteller).

New York premiere: Metropolitan Opera House, October 6, 1942.

An aristocrat kills Zemphira and her gypsy lover and is banished from the encampment by the chieftain.

L'AMOUR ET SON AMOUR

Choreography: Jean Babilée. Music: César Franck (symphonic poem "Psyché"). Scenery and costumes: Jean Cocteau.

U.S. premiere: Metropolitan Opera House, New York City, April 17, 1951.

Cast: Jean Babilée (Cupid), Nathalie Philippart (His Love), William Burdick and Ralph McWilliams (The Men); Rochelle Balzer, Irma Grant, Jan Hollar, Barbara Lloyd, Lucinda Macy, Lila Popper, Jenny Workman.

World premiere: Les Ballets des Champs-Elysées, Théâtre des Champs-Elysées, Paris, December 13, 1948.

Principal dancers: Jean Babilée and Nathalie Philippart.

The story of Psyche and Cupid.

ANGRISMENE
(THE ANGRY MAIDEN)

Choreography: William Dollar. Music: Igor Stravinsky (Octet for Wind Instruments).

World premiere: Ballet Theatre Workshop, Phoenix Theatre, New York City, April 21, 1958.

Principal dancers: Lupe Serrano and Royes Fernandez.

ANNABEL LEE

Choreography: George Skibine. Music: Byron Schiffman. Libretto suggested by the poem by Edgar Allan Poe.

Premiere: Ballet Theatre Previews, Phoenix Theatre, New York City, May 6, 1957.

Cast: Ruth Ann Koesun (Annabel Lee), John Kriza (Her Lover); Richard Beaty, Jim Clouser, William Guske (Her Highborn Kinsmen).

World premiere: Théâtre du Casino, Deauville, France, August 26, 1951. Scenery and costumes: André Delfau.

Cast: Marjorie Tallchief, George Skibine; Michel Resnikoff Roland Lorrain, Donald Spotswood.

The Edgar Allan Poe tale of the girl who died in a kingdom by the sea.

APOLLO

Choreography: George Balanchine. Music: Igor Stravinsky. Scenery: Dunkel Studios. Costumes: Barbara Karinska.

Premiere: Metropolitan Opera House, New York City, April 25, 1943.

Cast: André Eglevsky (Apollo), Vera Zorina (Terpsichore), Nora Kaye (Polyhymnia), Rosella Hightower (Calliope), Miriam Golden and Shirley Eckl (Nymphs), June Morris (Leto).

World premiere (under the title APOLLON MUSAGÈTE): Les Ballets Russes de Diaghilev, Théâtre Sarah Bernhardt, Paris, June 12, 1928. Scenery and costumes: André Bauchant.

Cast: Serge Lifar, Alice Nikitina, Lubov Tchernicheva, Felia Doubrovska, Dora Vadimova and Henriette Maicherska ("Déesses"), Sophie Orlova.

Apollo is born and assumes his duties as the tutor of the muses.

AT MIDNIGHT

Choreography: Eliot Feld. Music: Gustav Mahler ("Sieben Lieder aus letzter Zeit"). Scenery: Leonard Baskin. Costumes: Stanley Simmons.

World premiere: City Center, New York City, December 1, 1967.

Principal dancers: Cynthia Gregory, Christine Sarry; Eliot Feld, Bruce Marks, Terry Orr.

AWAKENING
(PAS DE DEUX)

Choreography: Robert Weiss. Music: Craig Steven Shuler ("Sinfonietta"). Costumes: Susan Tammany.

World premiere: Uris Theatre, New York City, December 30, 1975.

Dancers: Gelsey Kirkland and Mikhail Baryshnikov.

LE BAISER DE LA FÉE

Choreography: John Neumeier. Music: Igor Stravinsky and Peter Ilyich Tchaikovsky ("Feuillet d'album," op. 19, no. 3, and "Nur wer die Sehnsucht kennt," op. 6, no. 6). Scenery and costumes: Jürgen Rose. Libretto: John Neumeier, adapted from the original 1928 libretto by Stravinsky.

U.S. premiere: New York State Theater, New York City, July 18, 1974.

Principal dancers: Ivan Nagy (Rudi), Jonas Kage (Rudi's Sehnsucht), Zhandra Rodriguez (Babette), Cynthia Gregory (The Fairy).

World premiere: Frankfurt Opera Ballet, Städtische Bühnen, Frankfurt am Main, January 2, 1972.

Principal dancers: Maximo Barra, Stephen Maurer, Marianne Kruuse, Persephone Samaropoulo.

As a child Rudi dreamed of being kissed by a beautiful Fairy. When he is about to marry Babette, his Sehnsucht (his subconscious alter ego) draws him away from the premarital celebrations and compels him to continue his search for the beautiful Fairy.

LE BAL

Choreography: Robert Joffrey. Music: Emmanuel Chabrier.

World premiere: Ballet Theatre Workshop, Phoenix Theatre, New York City, May 20, 1957.

Principal Dancers: Dianne Consoer, Françoise Martinet, Brunilda Ruiz, Beatrice Tompkins; Gerald Arpino, Glen Tetley, Jonathan Watts, John Wilson.

BALLADEN DER LIEBE

Choreography: Enrique Martinez. Music: Max Bruch (Violin Concerto No. 1 in G Minor). Costumes: Robert Davison.

World premiere (under the title CONCERTO ROMANTIQUE): West High School, Anchorage, Alaska, September 23, 1965.

Principal dancers: Eleanor D'Antuono, Bruce Marks, Jeanne Armin, Gayle Young; Karen Krych, Janet Mitchell, Diana Weber, Ted Kivitt; Karena Brock, Ellen Everett, Cynthia Gregory; Eliot Feld, Terry Orr, Burton Taylor.

New York premiere: New York State Theater, February 3, 1966.

Same principal dancers as above.

BARN DANCE

Choreography: Catherine Littlefield. Music: David Guion, John Powell, and Louis Gottschalk. Scenery and costumes: Salvatore Pinto.

Premiere: Metropolitan Opera House, New York City, May 9, 1944.

Principal dancers: Dorothie Littlefield (Light Maiden); Thomas Cannon (City Slicker); John Taras (Deacon); Simon Semenoff (Banjo Player); Rosella Hightower, Alicia Alonso, Mary Heater (Mothers).

World premiere: Littlefield Ballet, Fox Theatre, Philadelphia, April 23, 1937.

Principal dancers: Dorothie Littlefield, Thomas Cannon, Edward Hedges.

The Deacon disapproves of the country dancing, and a young city couple is disdainful of it, but finally all join in the barn dance.

LA BAYADÈRE
(KINGDOM OF THE SHADES, ACT IV)

Choreography: Natalia Makarova, from the original by Marius Petipa. Music: Ludwig Minkus. Costumes: Marcos Paredes. Libretto: Sergei Khudekov.

Premiere: New York State Theater, New York City, July 3, 1974.

Principal dancers: Cynthia Gregory (Nikiya); Ivan Nagy (Solor); Karena Brock, Deborah Dobson, Martine van Hamel (Shadows).

World premiere of the complete ballet: Imperial Ballet, Maryinsky Theater, Saint Petersburg, February 4, 1877.

Principal dancers: Ekaterina Vazem, Lev Ivanov.

In what is now the closing scene of the Soviet version of Petipa's four-act ballet, the warrior Solor visits the Kingdom of the Shades in search of the Indian Temple dancer Nikiya, who has been poisoned by a jealous rival.

BEATRICE

Choreography: Richard Wagner. Music: Ralph Vaughan Williams (Fantasia on a Theme of Thomas Tallis). Libretto suggested by Maurice Maeterlinck's play SOEUR BÉATRICE.

World premiere: Ballet Theatre Workshop, Hunter College Playhouse, New York City, May 11, 1964.

Cast: Hester Fitzgerald (Beatrice), Joseph Carow (Prince Pellidor), Mary Stone (Abbess), Karena Brock (Statue of the Virgin), Peter Saul (Priest), Karen Krych (Sister Eglantine), Gilian Orpin (Sister Clemency), Victoria Leigh (Sister Regina), Rosanna Seravalli (Sister Balbine).

A novice in a convent prays to a statue of the Virgin for permission to leave with a prince. When she has left, the statue comes to life and takes her place as a novice.

THE BELOVED

Choreography: Bronislava Nijinska. Music: Franz Schubert and Franz Liszt, arranged by Darius Milhaud. Scenery and costumes: Nicholas de Molas. Libretto: Alexandre Benois.

Premiere: Palacio de Bellas Artes, Mexico City, October 24, 1941.

Principal dancers: Alicia Markova (The Beloved), Anton Dolin (The Musician), Lucia Chase and Sono Osato (Grisettes), Yura Lazovsky and Dimitri Romanoff (Students), Jeanette Lauret (The Lioness), George Skibine (Evil).

U.S. premiere: Forty-fourth Street Theatre, New York City, November 9, 1941.

Same principal dancers as above except Miriam Golden (The Lioness).

World premiere (under the title LA BIEN-AIMÉE): Ida Rubinstein Ballet, Théâtre National de l'Opéra, Paris, November 22, 1928. Scenery and costumes: Alexandre Benois.

Principal dancers: Ida Rubinstein and Anatole Vilzak.

A musician is inspired by dreams of past romances.

BILLY THE KID

Choreography: Eugene Loring. Music: Aaron Copland. Scenery and costumes: Jared French. Libretto: Lincoln Kirstein.

Premiere: Civic Opera House, Chicago, December 8, 1940.

LE CORSAIRE LUPE SERRANO, RUDOLF NUREYEV.

CONCERTO (ROSS) LUPE SERRANO, SCOTT DOUGLAS.

DEATH AND THE MAIDEN ANDRÉE HOWARD, KARI KARNAKOSKI.

Principal dancers: Eugene Loring (Billy), Alicia Alonso (Mother / Sweetheart), David Nillo (Alias), Richard Reed (Pat Garrett).

New York premiere: Majestic Theatre, February 13, 1941.
Same principal dancers as above.

World premiere: Ballet Caravan, Civic Opera House, Chicago, October 16, 1938.

Principal dancers: Eugene Loring, Marie Jeanne, Todd Bolender, Lew Christensen.

The ballet depicts in eleven episodes the pioneering of the West as illustrated by incidents in the life of Billy the Kid, the famous outlaw, born William Bonney in New York City at the close of the Civil War.

BITTER RAINBOW

Choreography: Fernand Nault. Music: Nelson Keyes. Costumes: Ming Tyler Dick.

World premiere: Ballet Theatre Workshop, Hunter College Playhouse, New York City, May 11, 1964.

Principal dancers: Karen Krych, Robert Powell, Karena Brock, Robert Holloway.

BLACK RITUAL
(OBEAH)

Choreography: Agnes de Mille. Music: Darius Milhaud ("La Création du monde"). Scenery and costumes: Nicholas de Molas.

World premiere: Center Theatre, New York City, January 22, 1940.

Dancers: Carole Ash, Maudelle Bass, Valerie Black, Clementina Collingwood, Muriel Cook, Azelean Cox, Mable Hart, Edith Hurd, Anne Jones, Evelyn Pilcher, Edith Roth, Elizabeth Thompson, Dorothy Williams, Lavinia Williams, Bernice Willis.

BLOOD WEDDING

Choreography: Alfred Rodrigues. Music: Denis Aplvor. Libretto: Denis Aplvor and Alfred Rodrigues, based on Federico García Lorca's play BODAS DE SANGRE.

Premiere: Ballet Theatre Previews, Phoenix Theatre, New York City, May 6, 1957.

Principal dancers: Nora Kaye (Bride), Erik Bruhn (Bridegroom), Lucia Chase (His Mother), John Kriza (Leonardo), Nadine Revene (Leonardo's Wife), Scott Douglas (The Moon), Jillana Williams (Death).

World premiere: Sadler's Wells Theatre Ballet, Sadler's Wells Theatre, London, June 5, 1953. Scenery and costumes: Isabel Lambert.

Principal dancers: Elaine Fifield, Pirmin Trecu, Margaret Hill, David Poole, Doreen Tempest, Kenneth MacMillan, Sheilah O'Reilly.

Leonardo is killed when he attempts to elope with another man's wife.

BLUEBEARD

Choreography: Michel Fokine. Music: Jacques Offenbach, arranged by Antal Dorati. Scenery and costumes: Marcel Vertès. Libretto: Fokine, based on Meilhac and Halévy's libretto for Offenbach's opéra bouffe BARBE-BLEU.

World premiere: Palacio de Bellas Artes, Mexico City, October 27, 1941.

Principal dancers: Vania Psota (King Bobiche); Borislav Runanine (Count Oscar); Anton Dolin (Baron Bluebeard); Simon Semenoff (Alchemist Popolani); Miriam Golden, Jeanette Lauret, Maria Karnilova, Nora Kaye, Rosella Hightower (Wives of Bluebeard); Lucia Chase (Queen Clementine); The Queen's Lovers: Dimitri Romanoff (Alvarez), Donald Saddler (Armando), Annabelle Lyon (Angelo, a page), Jerome Robbins (Alfonso), and Yura Lazovsky (Orlando); Alicia Markova (Fioretta); George Skibine (Prince Sapphire); Irina Baronova (Boulotte).

U.S. premiere: Forty-fourth Street Theatre, New York City, November 12, 1941.
Same principal dancers as above except Antony Tudor (King) and Ian Gibson (Prince Sapphire).

The alchemist Popolini puts Bluebeard's wives to sleep instead of killing them. They are revived and married to Queen Clementine's ex-lovers, with whom they live happily ever after.

BOLERO
(Solo)

Choreography: Anton Dolin. Music: Maurice Ravel.

Premiere: Robin Hood Dell, Philadelphia, June 25, 1940.

Dancer: Anton Dolin.

World premiere: Vic-Wells Ballet, Sadler's Wells Theatre, London, December 6, 1932.

BRAHMS QUINTET

Choreography: Dennis Nahat. Music: Johannes Brahms (Quintet No. 2 in G, op. 111). Costumes: Willa Kim.

World premiere: Academy of Music, Brooklyn, December 10, 1969.

Principal dancers: Eleanor D'Antuono, Cynthia Gregory, Mimi Paul, Naomi Sorkin; Ian Horvath, Ivan Nagy, Terry Orr, Gayle Young.

THE BULL DANCERS

Choreography: Lawrence Gradus. Music: Jacques Ibert ("A Louisville Concerto").

World premiere: Ballet Theatre Workshop, Hunter College Playhouse, New York City, December 17, 1963.

Principal dancers: Ted Kivitt (Minotaur), William Glassman (Theseus); Judith Lerner, Antony DeVecchi (Lovers).

Events leading up to the slaying of the Minotaur by Theseus in the bull arena of ancient Crete.

THE CAPITAL OF THE WORLD

Choreography: Eugene Loring. Music: George Antheil. Scenery and costumes: Esteban Francés. Libretto based on Ernest Hemingway's short story, adapted by Eugene Loring and A. E. Hotchner.

World stage premiere: Metropolitan Opera House, New York City, December 27, 1953.

Principal dancers: Roy Fitzell (Paco), Lupe Serrano (Elena), Scott Douglas (Enrique), Vernon Wendorf (Cowardly Matador), Leo Duggan (Sick Matador), Job Sanders (Proud Matador), Fernand Nault (Tailor Shop Proprietor).

World premiere: "Omnibus" (Ford Foundation TV Workshop), CBS Television, New York City, December 6, 1953. Scenery: Henry May.

Same principal dancers as above.

Paco, an apprentice in a tailor's shop, dreams of becoming a matador but is killed when he plays the part of the bull in a practice fight with his friend Enrique.

CAPRICCIO ESPAGNOL

Choreography: Leonide Massine in collaboration with Argentinita. Music: Nikolai Rimsky-Korsakov. Scenery and costumes: Mariano Andreu (same as those originally designed for Fokine's 1937 ballet JOTA ARAGONESA. Libretto: Massine.

Premiere: War Memorial Opera House, San Francisco, January 28, 1943.

Principal dancers: Miriam Golden and Donald Saddler (Variation); Margaret Banks and Galina Razoumova (Alborado); Nora Kaye and Leonide Massine (Gypsy scene and songs); Lucia Chase, Yura Lazovsky, Nora Kaye, Leonide Massine (Asturian Fandango).

New York premiere: Metropolitan Opera House, April 6, 1943.
Same principal dancers as above.

World premiere: Ballet Russe de Monte Carlo, Théâtre de Monte Carlo, Monaco, May 4, 1939.

Principal dancers: Argentinita, Alexandra Danilova, Leonide Massine, Michel Panaieff.

CAPRICCIOSO

Choreography: Anton Dolin. Music: Domenico Cimarosa, orchestrated by Gian Francesco Malipiero and Vittorio Rieti. Scenery and costumes: Nicholas de Molas. (A completely new version of what was originally Dolin's ITALIAN SUITE.)

World premiere: Civic Opera House, Chicago, November 3, 1940.

Principal dancers: Lucia Chase, Karen Conrad, Annabelle Lyon, Nina Stroganova; Leon Danielian, Anton Dolin, Dimitri Romanoff.

New York premiere: Majestic Theatre, February 14, 1941.
Same principal dancers as above.

CAPRICHOS

Choreography: Herbert Ross. Music: Béla Bartók (Contrasts for Piano, Clarinet and Violin). Costumes: John Ward. Libretto based on Goya's commentaries to his series of etchings "Caprichos."

Premiere: Center Theatre, New York City, April 26, 1950.

Cast: I. Charlyne Baker, Jenny Workman; II. Nana Gollner, Eric Braun, Peter Gladke; III. John Kriza, Ruth Ann Koesun; IV. Mary Burr, Jack Beaber, Scott Douglas, Vernon Lusby, Ralph McWilliams.

World premiere: Choreographer's Workshop, Hunter College Playhouse, New York City, January 29, 1950.

Dancers included Herbert Ross, Gina Snyder, Alice Temkin, Dorothy Hill, Ilona Murai, and Emy St. Just.

THE CARELESS BURGHERS

Choreography: Job Sanders. Music: Donald Marsh.

World premiere: Ballet Theatre Previews, Phoenix Theatre, New York City, May 27, 1957.

Principal dancers: Erik Bruhn (Troubadour), Fernand Nault (Mayor), Nadine Revene (Mayoress).

The battle of the sexes in medieval Flanders. After the workshop performance it was placed in the company's regular repertory.

CARMEN

Choreography: Alberto Alonso. Music: Georges Bizet, arranged by Rodion Schedrin. Scenery: Boris Messerer. Costumes: Salvador Fernández.

Premiere: Metropolitan Opera House, New York City, July 11, 1976.

Principal dancers: Alicia Alonso (Carmen); Orlando Salgado (Don Jose); Jorge Esquivel (Escamillo); Martine van Hamel (Destino); Clark Tippet (Zuñiga).

World premiere: Bolshoi Ballet, Bolshoi Theater, Moscow, April 20, 1967.

Principal dancers: Maya Plisetskaya, Nicolai Fadeyechev, Sergei Radchenko.

CARNAVAL

Choreography: Michel Fokine. Music: Robert Schumann, orchestrated by K. Konstantinov. Scenery and costumes: Léon Bakst.

Premiere: Center Theatre, New York City, January 13, 1940.

Principal dancers: Patricia Bowman (Columbine), Annabelle Lyon (Chiarina), Viola Essen (Estrella), Nina Stroganova (Butterfly), William Dollar (Harlequin), Adolph Bolm (Pierrot), Yurek Shabelevski (Eusebius), Eugene Loring (Pantalon), Hugh Laing (Florestan).

World premiere: Pavlova Hall, Saint Petersburg, March 5, 1910, for a charity ball. Music: Schumann, orchestrated by Alexander Glazunov, Nicholai Rimsky-Korsakov, Anatole Liadov, and Alexander Tcherepnine. Scenery and costumes: Léon Bakst.

Principal dancers: Tamara Karsavina, Vera Fokina, Ludmila Shollar, Bronislava Nijinska; Leonide Leontiev, Vsevolod Meyerhold, Alexander Chiriaiev, Alfred Bekefi, Vaslav Nijinsky.

(First performance in Western Europe: Les Ballets Russes de Diaghilev, Theater des Westens, Berlin, May 20, 1910.)

THE CATHERINE WHEEL

Choreography: Michael Smuin. Music: Timothy Thompson. Scenery: Oliver Smith. Costumes: Stanley Simmons.

World premiere: Wisconsin Union Theater, Madison, Wisconsin, November 9, 1967.

Cast: Veronika Mlakar (Wife), Paul Nickel (Husband), Michael Smuin (Soldier), Susan Casey (His Fiancée), Edward Verso (Playboy), Paula Tracy (The Woman).

New York premiere: City Center, December 7, 1967.
Same cast as above.

Based on the film LA RONDE (itself based on a play by Arthur Schnitzler), in which a venereal disease was transmitted from person to person until it returned to the original infector.

CIRCO DE ESPAÑA

Choreography: Carmelita Maracci. Music: Turina, Granados, de Falla, Albéniz. Scenery and costumes: Rico Lebrun.

World premiere: Metropolitan Opera House, New York City, April 18, 1951.

Dancers: I. Entrada—Liane Plane, Barbara Lloyd, Jenny Workman. II. Oracion del Torero—Charlyne Baker, Irma Grant, Angela Velez; Lillian Lanese, Paula Lloyd, Lila Popper, Dorothy Scott. III. La Maja y el Ruiseñor—Carmelita Maracci. IV. Fire Dance—Paul Godkin, Virginia Barnes, Jan Hollar, Carmelita Maracci. V. Portrait in Raw España—Maracci and ensemble.

THE COMBAT

Choreography: William Dollar. Music: Raffaello de Banfield. Scenery and costumes: Georges Wakhevitch. Libretto: Roland Petit, based on Tasso's poem "Gerusalemme liberata."

Premiere: Royal Opera House, Covent Garden, London, July 23, 1953.

Cast: Melissa Hayden and John Kriza; Scott Douglas, Eugene Tanner, Eric Kristen.

U.S. premiere by Ballet Theatre: Metropolitan Opera House, New York City, December 27, 1953.
Same cast as above except Ivan Allen for Eric Kristen.

World premiere (as a pas de deux, under the title LE COMBAT): Les Ballets de Paris de Roland Petit, Prince's Theatre, London, February 24, 1949. Scenery and costumes: Marie Laure.

Dancers: Janine Charrat and Vladimir Skouratoff.

The helmeted Clorinda is not recognized by her lover, the Christian knight Tancredi, who kills her in a duel on horseback.

CONCERTO

Choreography: William Dollar. Music: Frédéric Chopin (Piano Concerto in F Minor, arranged by Adolf Schmid). Scenery and costumes: Robert Davison.

Premiere: Metropolitan Opera House, New York City, April 9, 1951. Performed also under the title CONSTANTIA.

Principal dancers: Alicia Alonso, Igor Youskevitch, Norma Vance; Lillian Lanese, Paula Lloyd, Liane Plane, Dorothy Scott.

World premiere: Ballet International, International Theatre, New York City, October 31, 1944. Scenery: Horace Armistead. Costumes: Grace Houston.

Principal dancers: Marie Jeanne, William Dollar, Yvonne Patterson.

CONCERTO

Choreography: William Dollar. Music: Felix Mendelssohn (Piano Concerto No. 1 in G Minor).

World premiere: Ballet Theatre Workshop, Lisner Auditorium, Washington, D.C., February 20, 1963.

Principal dancers: Susan Borree, Gayle Young, Diana Weber.

New York premiere: Delacorte Theater, Central Park, September 5, 1963.
Same principal dancers as above.

CONCERTO

Choreography: Kenneth MacMillan. Music: Dimitri Shostakovich (Piano Concerto No. 2, op. 102). Scenery and costumes: Jürgen Rose.

U.S. premiere: Jacksonville, Florida, March 28, 1967.

Principal dancers: I. Eleanor D'Antuono and Scott Douglas; II. Toni Lander and Bruce Marks; III. Cynthia Gregory.

New York premiere: New York State Theater, May 18, 1967.
Same principal dancers as above.

World premiere: Deutsch Oper Ballet, Städtische Oper, West Berlin, November 30, 1966.

Principal dancers: I. Didi Carli and Falco Kapuste; II. Lynn Seymour and Rudolf Holz; III. Silvia Kesselheim.

ENSAYO SINFÓNICA BRAUN, LLAND, VELEZ, SCOTT, LANESE, LLOYD, MARTINEZ, BROWN.

THE ENCHANTED WILLIAM WESLOW, GEMZE DE LAPPE, JAMES MITCHELL.

THE ETERNAL IDOL CYNTHIA GREGORY, IVAN NAGY.

CONCERTO

Choreography: Herbert Ross. Music: Peter Ilyich Tchaikovsky (Violin Concerto in D). Scenery and costumes: Roger Bezombes.

World premiere: Metropolitan Opera House, New York City, September 16, 1958.

Principal dancers: I. Lupe Serrano, Scott Douglas, Royes Fernandez, Michael Maule; II. Ruth Ann Koesun and John Kriza; III. Nora Kaye and Erik Bruhn.

CONFLICT

Choreography: David Shields. Music: Eva Wainless.

World premiere: Ballet Theatre Workshop, Hunter College Playhouse, New York City, May 11, 1964.

Principal dancers: Ted Kivitt (The Innocent); Basil Thompson (Hate and Prejudice); Marion Choma, Victoria Shick, Richard Colton (Children).

An examination of hate and prejudice between majorities and minorities.

CONTINUUM

Choreography: Harry Asmus. Music: Wolfgang Amadeus Mozart ("Eine kleine Nachtmusik").

World premiere: Ballet Theatre Workshop, Phoenix Theatre, New York City, May 7, 1956.

Dancers: Nana Prudente and Thatcher Clarke; Carole Asnin, Anne Boley, Ann Etgen, June Evans, Beth Fisher, Janet Greschler, Mary Jackson, Sandra Sims; Bill Atkinson, Richard Beaty, Paul Hangauer, Herb Kummel.

COPPÉLIA

Choreography: Enrique Martinez, from the original by Arthur Saint-Léon. Music: Léo Delibes. Scenery and costumes: William Pitkin. Libretto: Charles Truinet and Arthur Saint-Léon.

Premiere: Academy of Music, Brooklyn, December 24, 1968.

Principal dancers: Carla Fracci (Swanilda), Erik Bruhn (Franz), Enrique Martinez (Coppélius), Robert Gladstein (Harlequin), Ian Horvath (Chinese), Dennis Nahat (Arabian / Priest), Zhandra Rodriguez and Steven-Jan Hoff (Spanish Couple), Christine Sarry (Dawn), Susan Casey (Prayer).

World premiere: L'Académie Nationale de Musique (Salle Le Peletier), May 25, 1870.

Principal dancers: Giuseppina Bozzacchi, Eugénie Fiocre, François Dauty, Louis Petit (Chinese), Angelo Ganforini (Persian), Laure Fonta (Dawn), Annette Mérante (Prayer).

Previous production by Ballet Theatre:

Premiere: Palacio de Bellas Artes, Mexico City, September 1, 1942.

Choreography: Simon Semenoff, in one act and three scenes, from original by Saint-Léon. Scenery and costumes: Roberto Montenegro.

Principal dancers: Irina Baronova, Anton Dolin, Simon Semenoff; John Kriza (Harlequin), Ian Gibson (Chinese), John Duane (Turk), Hubert Bland (Death), Virginia Wilcox (Colombine), Alpheus Koon (Pierrot / Priest).

New York premiere: Metropolitan Opera House, October 22, 1942.

LE CORSAIRE
(PAS DE DEUX)

Choreography: Rudolf Nureyev, from the original by Joseph Mazilier, revised by Marius Petipa. Music: Cesare Pugni, Riccardo Drigo, and others, orchestrated by John Lanchbery.

Premiere: Civic Opera House, Chicago, December 25, 1962.

Dancers: Lupe Serrano and Rudolf Nureyev.

World premiere of Nureyev's staging: Covent Garden, London, November 3, 1962.

Dancers: Margot Fonteyn and Rudolf Nureyev.

DANSES CONCERTANTES

Choreography: Kenneth MacMillan. Music: Igor Stravinsky. Scenery and costumes: Nicholas Georgiadis.

U.S. premiere: Syria Mosque, Pittsburgh, October 10, 1967.

Principal dancers: Toni Lander, Bruce Marks, Royes Fernandez; Karen Krych, Burton Taylor, Ellen Everett.

New York premiere: City Center, November 29, 1967.

Principal dancers: Eleanor D'Antuono, Bruce Marks, Michael Smuin; Karen Krych, Burton Taylor, Janet Mitchell.

World premiere: Sadler's Wells Theatre Ballet, Sadler's Wells Theatre, London, January 18, 1955.

Principal dancers: Maryon Lane, David Poole, Donald Britton; Sara Neil, Gilbert Vernon, Annette Page.

DARK ELEGIES

Choreography: Antony Tudor. Music: Gustav Mahler ("Kindertotenlieder"). Scenery and costumes: Nadia Benois.

Premiere: Center Theatre, New York City, January 24, 1940.

Principal dancers: Nina Stroganova (first song), Miriam Golden and Antony Tudor (second song), Hugh Laing (third song), Lucia Chase (fourth song), Dimitri Romanoff (fifth song).

World premiere: Ballet Rambert, Duchess Theatre, London, February 19, 1937.

Principal dancers: Peggy van Praagh, Maude Lloyd and Antony Tudor, Walter Gore, Agnes de Mille, Hugh Laing.

DEATH AND THE MAIDEN

Choreography and costumes: Andrée Howard. Music: Franz Schubert ("Andante cantabile" from the String Quartet in D Minor).

Premiere: Center Theatre, New York City, January 18, 1940.

Principal dancers: Andrée Howard (The Maiden), Kari Karnakoski (Death).

World premiere: Ballet Rambert, Duchess Theatre, London, February 23, 1937.

Principal dancers: Andrée Howard and John Byron.

Death and his attendants come for the Maiden.

LES DEMOISELLES DE LA NUIT

Choreography: Roland Petit. Music: Jean Françaix. Scenery and costumes: Léonor Fini. Libretto: Jean Anouilh.

U.S. premiere: Metropolitan Opera House, New York City, April 13, 1951.

Principal dancers: Colette Marchand (Agatha, the White Kitten), John Kriza (Young Musician), Eric Braun (Cat Baron de Grotius), Angela Velez (Black Cat).

World premiere: Les Ballets de Paris de Roland Petit, Théâtre Marigny, Paris, May 21, 1948.

Principal dancers: Margot Fonteyn, Roland Petit, Gordon Hamilton, Joan Sheldon.

The White Kitten falls in love with a Young Musician but is lured away from him by her cat companions.

DESIGNS WITH STRINGS

Choreography: John Taras. Music: Peter Ilyich Tchaikovsky (Piano Trio in A Minor, second movement). Scenery and costumes: Irene Sharaff.

Premiere: Center Theatre, New York City, April 25, 1950.

Dancers: Diana Adams, Norma Vance, Lillian Lanese, Dorothy Scott; Erik Bruhn, Michael Lland.

World premiere: Metropolitan Ballet, Edinburgh, February 6, 1948. Scenery and costumes: George Kirsta.

Dancers: Svetlana Beriosova, Sonia Arova, Celia Franca, Delysia Blake; Paul Gnatt, David Adams.

DIALOGUES

Choreography: Herbert Ross. Music: Leonard Bernstein (Serenade for Violin Solo, Strings and Percussion). Scenery: Jean Rosenthal. Costumes: Florence Klotz. Libretto: Leonard Bernstein, based on Plato's dialogue "The Symposium."

U.S. premiere: Metropolitan Opera House, New York City, April 26, 1960.

Dancers: Ady Addor, Nora Kaye, Christine Mayer; Scott Douglas, Royes Fernandez, Tommy Rall, Glen Tetley.

World premiere (under the title SERENADE FOR SEVEN): American Ballet, Teatro Nuovo, Spoleto, Italy (Festival of Two Worlds), June 13, 1959. Scenery and costumes: Gian Carlo Isola.

Dancers included Nora Kaye, Bambi Linn, Scott Douglas, and Glen Tetley.

DIANA AND ACTAEON
(PAS DE DEUX)

Choreography: Rudolf Nureyev, from the original by Agrippina Vaganova. Music: Cesare Pugni, arranged by John Lanchbery. Costumes: Marcos Paredes.

Premiere: New York State Theater, New York City, July 3, 1973.

Dancers: Eleanor D'Antuono and Ted Kivitt.

World premiere of Nureyev's staging (taping for television): NBC color studios, Brooklyn, July 10, 1963.

Dancers: Svetlana Beriosova and Rudolf Nureyev.

DIM LUSTRE

Choreography: Antony Tudor. Music: Richard Strauss (Burleske in D for Piano and Orchestra). Scenery and costumes: Motley.

World premiere: Metropolitan Opera House, New York City, October 20, 1943.

Principal dancers: Nora Kaye (The Lady with Him), Hugh Laing (The Gentleman with Her), Muriel Bentley (A Reflection), Michael Kidd (Another Reflection), John Kriza (It Was Spring), Rosella Hightower (She Wore a Perfume), Antony Tudor (He Wore a White Tie).

The Lady and her Gentleman recall individual past love affairs as they waltz together.

DIVERTIMENTO–ROSSINI

Choreography: William Dollar. Music: Gioacchino Rossini–Benjamin Britten (from Britten's "Soirees musicales" and "Matinées musicales" suites).

Premiere: Fifty-fourth Street Theatre, New York City, October 11, 1961.

Principal dancers: Ruth Ann Koesun, Ivan Allen, Eleanor D'Antuono.

DIVERTISSEMENT D'AUBER

Choreography: Lew Christensen. Music: François Auber. Costumes: Marcos Paredes.

Premiere: Ballet Theatre Players, Fine Arts Center, Castleton State College, Castleton, Vermont, September 27, 1969.

Dancers: Alexandra Radius, Terry Orr, Diana Weber.

New York premiere: Academy of Music, Brooklyn, December 2, 1969.

Dancers: Cynthia Gregory, Ted Kivitt, Roni Mahler.

World premiere: San Francisco Ballet, Alcazar Theatre, San Francisco, February 19, 1960. Designer: Tony Duquette.

Dancers: Jocelyn Vollmar, Roderick Drew, Fiona Fuerstner.

DON DOMINGO DE DON BLAS

Choreography: Leonide Massine. Music: Silvestre Revueltas (six piano pieces arranged for orchestra). Scenery and costumes: Julio Castillanos. Libretto: Massine, based on a story by Juan Ruiz de Alarcón.

World premiere: Palacio de Bellas Artes, Mexico City, September 16, 1942.

Principal dancers: Anton Dolin (Don Domingo), Alicia Markova (Leonor), Lucia Chase (Constanza), Antony Tudor (Viceroy), Dimitri Romanoff (Don Juan), Simon Semënoff (Don Ramiro), Yura Lazovsky (Nuno), Ian Gibson (Beltran).

U.S. premiere: Metropolitan Opera House, New York City, October 9, 1942. Principal dancers same as above.

Don Domingo and Don Juan, rivals for the hand of Leonor, present her with gifts, the bearers of which perform Mexican-Indian dances. The world premiere was given on Mexico's Independence Day.

DON QUIXOTE
(PAS DE DEUX)

Choreography: Anatole Oboukhoff, from the original by Marius Petipa. Music: Leon Minkus. Costumes: Barbara Karinska.

Premiere: Metropolitan Opera House, New York City, October 25, 1944.

Dancers: Tamara Toumanova and Anton Dolin.

World premiere of complete ballet: Imperial Ballet, Bolshoi Theater, Moscow, December 14, 1869.

ECCENTRIQUE

Choreography: Eliot Feld. Music: Igor Stravinsky (Four Etudes for Orchestra and Suites Nos. 1 and 2 for Small Orchestra). Scenery: Oliver Smith. Costumes: Frank Thompson.

World premiere: Kennedy Center, Washington, D.C., December 30, 1971.

Principal dancers: Elizabeth Lee, Christine Sarry, John Sowinski; Karena Brock, Zola Dishong, Ellen Everett, Marianna Tcherkassky; David Coll, Warren Conover, Daniel Levans, Frank Smith.

New York premiere: City Center, January 18, 1972. Same principal dancers as above.

ECHOING OF TRUMPETS

Choreography: Antony Tudor. Music: Bohuslav Martinů ("Fantaisies symphoniques"). Scenery and costumes: Birger Bergling. Created to the memory of the Czech village of Lidice, which was destroyed in 1942.

Premiere: University Auditorium, East Lansing, Michigan, November 15, 1967.

Dancers: Sally Brayley, Cynthia Gregory, Alaine Haubert, Karen Krych, Elizabeth Lee, Veronika Mlakar, Paula Tracy; Thatcher Clarke, Richard Gain, Reese Haworth, Steven-Jan Hoff, Paul Nickel, Terry Orr, Marco Paredes, Burton Taylor.

New York premiere: City Center, November 30, 1967. Same dancers as above.

World premiere (under the title EKON AV TRUMPETER): Royal Swedish Ballet, Royal Theater, Stockholm, September 28, 1963.

Principal dancers: Gerd Andersson, Annette Wiedersheim-Paul; Svante Lindberg, Mario Mengarelli.

Enemy soldiers brutally attack the inhabitants of an undefended village.

EDEN
(PAS DE DEUX)

Choreography: Birgit Cullberg. Music: Hilding Rosenberg (Concerto for String Orchestra). Scenery and costumes: Per Falk.

World premiere: Fifty-fourth Street Theatre, New York City, October 4, 1961.

Dancers: Caj Selling (Adam), Mariane Orlando (Eve).

ELECTRA

Choreography: Enrique Martinez. Music: Béla Bartók (Music for Strings, Percussion and Celesta). Libretto based on Euripides' tragedy.

World premiere: Ballet Theatre Workshop, Lisner Auditorium, Washington, D.C., February 20, 1963.

Principal dancers: Eleanor D'Antuono (Electra), Bruce Marks (Orestes), Arnott Mader (Agamemnon), Sallie Wilson (Clytemnestra), Gayle Young (Aegisthus).

New York premiere: American Ballet Theatre Workshop, Hunter College Playhouse, December 17, 1963. Same principal dancers as above except Ted Kivitt (Aegisthus), Gayle Young (Orestes), Joseph Carow (Agamemnon).

THE ENCHANTED

Choreography: Katherine Litz. Music: Richard Banks. Libretto based on the play by Jean Giraudoux.

World premiere: Ballet Theatre Workshop, Phoenix Theatre, New York City, May 7, 1956.

Principal dancers: Gemze de Lappe (Isabel), James Mitchell (Doctor), Ray Barra (Arthur, a Ghost), William

FIVE SKETCHES ALEXANDRA RADIUS, HAN EBBELAAR.

FLAMES OF PARIS ELEANOR D'ANTUONO, FERNANDO BUJONES.

FLOWER FESTIVAL IN GENZANO CARLA FRACCI, ERIK BRUHN.

Weslow (Robert, the Lover), Louis Johnson and Kenn Duncan (Executioners).

In a detective-story fantasy, Isabel falls in love with a ghost.

THE ENCOUNTER

Choreography: Fernand Nault. Music: César Franck.

World premiere: Ballet Theatre Workshop, Phoenix Theatre, New York City, May 13, 1957.

Cast: Ruth Ann Koesun (The Girl); Nana Prudente (Her Sister); Rae Brown, Nancy Charles, Gail Church, Marilyn Poudrier (Their Friends); Scott Douglas (A Passerby).

A young girl learns about life and grows up.

ENSAYO SINFÓNICA

Choreography: Alicia Alonso. Music: Johannes Brahms (Variations on a Theme by Haydn). Scenery and costumes: Irene Sharaff.

U.S. premiere: Metropolitan Opera House, New York City, April 19, 1951.

Dancers: Dorothy Scott and Eric Braun, Angela Velez and Kelly Brown, Lillian Lanese and Enrique Martinez, Paula Lloyd and Michael Lland.

World premiere: Ballet Alicia Alonso, Havana, 1950.

EPILOGUE
(PAS DE DEUX)

Choreography: John Neumeier. Music: Gustav Mahler (Symphony No. 5, "Adagietto"). Costumes: Michel.

World premiere: New York State Theater, New York City, July 8, 1975.

Dancers: Natalia Makarova and Erik Bruhn.

LA ESMERALDA
(PAS DE DEUX)

Choreography: John Gilpin, from the original of Jules Perrot as revived by Nicholas Beriosoff. Music: Cesare Pugni.

Premiere: New York State Theater, New York City, March 19, 1965.

Dancers: Lupe Serrano and John Gilpin.

World premiere of Nicholas Beriosoff's full-length production: Festival Ballet, Royal Festival Hall, London, July 15, 1954.

Principal dancers: Natalie Krassovska and John Gilpin; Anton Dolin, Oleg Briansky, Belinda Wright.

ESPAÑA

Choreography: Valentina Pereyaslavec. Music: Alexis Chabrier.

World premiere: Ballet Theatre Players, Don Watters Theater, State University of New York at Binghamton, Binghamton, New York, September 29, 1969.

Dancers: Karena Brock, Gail Israel, Robert Gladstein, Keith Lee.

THE ETERNAL IDOL
(PAS DE DEUX)

Choreography: Michael Smuin. Music: Frédéric Chopin (Piano Concerto No. 2 in F minor). Costumes: Marcos Paredes.

World premiere: Academy of Music, Brooklyn, December 4, 1969.

Dancers: Cynthia Gregory and Ivan Nagy.

The statuary of Auguste Rodin comes to life.

ETUDES

Choreography: Harald Lander. Music: Karl Czerny (piano studies, arranged by Knudaage Riisager). Scenery and costumes: Rolf Gerard.

U.S. premiere: Fifty-fourth Street Theatre, New York City, October 5, 1961.

Principal dancers: Toni Lander, Royes Fernandez, Bruce Marks; Eleanor D'Antuono, Elisabeth Carroll.

World premiere: Royal Danish Ballet, Royal Theater, Copenhagen, January 15, 1948. Designer: Erik Nordgreen.

Principal dancers: Margot Lander, Hans Brenaa, Svend Erik Jensen; Inge Sand, Inge Goth.

FACSIMILE

Choreography: Jerome Robbins. Music: Leonard Bernstein. Scenery: Oliver Smith. Costumes: Irene Sharaff.

World premiere: Broadway Theatre, New York City, October 24, 1946.

Cast: Nora Kaye (A Woman), Jerome Robbins (A Man), John Kriza (Another Man).

Inspired by the quotation, "Small inward treasure does he possess who, to feel alive, needs every hour the tumult of the street, the emotion of the theater, and the small talk of Society."

FAIR AT SOROCHINSK

Choreography: David Lichine. Music: Modest Mussorgsky (selections from the opera of the same name, and from "A Night on Bald Mountain," arranged by Antal Dorati). Scenery and costumes: Nicholas Remisoff. Libretto: Lichine, adapted from Nikolai Gogol's stories.

World premiere: Metropolitan Opera House, New York City, October 14, 1943.

Principal dancers: Anton Dolin (Red Coat); Lucia Chase (Khivria); Margaret Banks (Parassia); André Eglevsky (Gritzko); Rex Cooper (Father); John Taras (Friend); Dimitri Romanoff (Mayor); Simon Semenoff (Sexton); Michael Kidd (Peddler); Janet Reed (Candy Girl / The Cat); Jerome Robbins, John Kriza, and Richard Reed (Gypsies); Nicholas Orloff (Hopak Leader); Rosella Hightower (White Witch).

A witch, Khivria, and the Devil of the Ukraine try to secure the souls of the inhabitants of Sorochinsk, but they are defeated by the purity of two young lovers.

FALL RIVER LEGEND

Choreography: Agnes de Mille. Music: Morton Gould. Scenery: Oliver Smith. Costumes: Miles White.

World premiere: Metropolitan Opera House, New York City, April 22, 1948.

Principal dancers: Alicia Alonso (Accused), Diana Adams (Mother), Muriel Bentley (Stepmother), Peter Gladke (Father), Ruth Ann Koesun (Accused as a Child), John Kriza (Pastor).

An adaptation of the famous case of Lizzie Borden, who was accused of murdering her father and stepmother with an ax in Fall River, Massachusetts. In fact she was acquitted, but in the ballet she is hanged. The role of Lizzie was choreographed on Nora Kaye, who danced the great majority of the performances after the premiere, when, because of her illness, Alicia Alonso substituted for her.

FANCY FREE

Choreography: Jerome Robbins. Music: Leonard Bernstein. Scenery: Oliver Smith. Costumes: Kermit Love.

World premiere: Metropolitan Opera House, New York City, April 18, 1944.

Cast: Jerome Robbins, Harold Lang, John Kriza (Sailors); Muriel Bentley, Janet Reed, Shirley Eckl (Passersby); Rex Cooper (Bartender).

Three sailors on shore leave vie for the attentions of two girls.

THE FANTASTIC TOY SHOP

Choreography: Leonide Massine. Music: Gioacchino Rossini (selections from "Les Riens," arranged and orchestrated by Ottorino Respighi). Curtain, scenery, and costumes: André Derain.

Premiere: Central High School Auditorium, Omaha, January 4, 1943.

Principal dancers: Simon Semenoff (Shopkeeper), Nicholas Orloff (Assistant), Hubert Bland (Thief), Muriel Bentley (English Old Maid), Antony Tudor (American), Shirley Eckl (Wife), Jerome Robbins (Son), Nora Kaye and Yura Lazovsky (Tarantella Dancers), Richard Reed (The Snob), John Taras (Melon Hawker), André Eglevsky (Cossack Chief), Karen Conrad and John Kriza (Dancing Poodles), Irina Baronova and Leonide Massine (Can-Can Dancers).

New York premiere of Ballet Theatre's production: Metropolitan Opera House, April 14, 1943.

World premiere (under the title LA BOUTIQUE FANTASQUE): Les Ballets Russes de Diaghilev, Alhambra Theatre, London, June 5, 1919.

Principal dancers: Enrico Cecchetti (Shopkeeper), Alexander Gavrilov (Assistant), Lydia Sokolova and Leon Woizikowski (Tarantella Dancers), Stanislas Idzikowski (The Snob), Nicholas Zverev (Cossack Chief), Vera Clark and Nicholas Kremniev (Dancing Poodles), Lydia Lopokova and Leonide Massine (Can-Can Dancers).

An American couple with their children visit a toy shop in which the dolls come to life.

FESTA

Choreography: Erik Bruhn. Music: Gioacchino Rossini, orchestrated by Joseph Levine.

World premiere: Ballet Theatre Previews, Phoenix Theatre, New York City, May 6, 1957.

Dancers: Lupe Serrano and Scott Douglas; Sallie Wilson, Susan Borree, Elisabeth Carroll, Fredda Maurice; Ray Barra, Leo Duggan, Enrique Martinez, George Tomal.

FEST POLONAISE
(PAS DE DEUX)

Choreography: Harald Lander. Music: Johanne Svenson.

U.S. premiere: Constitution Hall, Washington, D.C., November 26, 1963.

Dancers: Toni Lander and Royes Fernandez.

World premiere: Royal Danish Ballet, Royal Theater, Copenhagen, May 15, 1942.

Principal dancers: Margot Lander and Borge Ralov.

LA FILLE MAL GARDÉE

Choreography: Dimitri Romanoff, from the original by Jean Dauberval. Music: Peter Hartel. Scenery and costumes: Rolf Gerard. Libretto: Jean Dauberval.

Premiere: City Center, New York City, January 13, 1972.

Principal dancers: Natalia Makarova (Lise), Ivan Nagy (Colin), Enrique Martinez (Mme Simone), Michael Smuin (Alain), Vane Vest (Thomas).

World premiere: Grand Théâtre, Bordeaux, France, July 1, 1789. Music: various composers.

Previous production by Ballet Theatre:

Premiere: Center Theatre, New York City, January 19, 1940.

Choreography: Bronislava Nijinska. Scenery and costumes: Serge Soudeikine.

Principal dancers: Patricia Bowman, Yurek Shabelevski, Edward Caton, Alexis Kosloff, Charles Ewing.

Revived by Ballet Theatre in 1941 as THE WAYWARD DAUGHTER and in 1942 as NAUGHTY LISETTE. Revived under the original title in April 1949, with choreography by Dimitri Romanoff.

Lise's mother has arranged for her to marry the doltish son of a wealthy farmer, but in the end she is permitted to marry the love of her choice.

FIREBIRD

Choreography: Christopher Newton, from the original by Michel Fokine. Music: Igor Stravinsky. Scenery and costumes after designs by Nathalie Gontcharova. Libretto: Michel Fokine.

Premiere: Dorothy Chandler Pavilion, Los Angeles, February 21, 1977.

Principal dancers: Natalia Makarova (Firebird), Clark Tippet (Ivan Tsarevitch), Marcos Paredes (Kostchei), Marie Johansson (Tsarevna).

New York premiere: Metropolitan Opera House, April 26, 1977.

Same principal dancers as above except Ivan Nagy (Ivan Tsarevitch), Karena Brock (Tsarevna).

World premiere (under the title L'OISEAU DE FEU): Les Ballets Russes de Diaghilev, Théâtre National de l'Opéra, Paris, June 25, 1910 Scenery and costumes: Alexander Golovine and Léon Bakst.

Principal dancers: Tamara Karsavina, Michel Fokine, Enrico Cecchetti, Vera Fokina.

Previous production by Ballet Theatre:

Choreography: Adolph Bolm. Scenery and costumes: Marc Chagall.

Premiere: Metropolitan Opera House, New York City, October 24, 1945.

Principal dancers: Alicia Markova, Anton Dolin, John Taras, Diana Adams.

The Tsarevitch, aided by the Firebird's magic feather, rescues the Princess from the evil Kostchei.

FIVE SKETCHES
(PAS DE DEUX)

Choreography: Hans van Manen. Music: Paul Hindemith (Five Pieces for String Orchestra, op. 44).

Premiere: Ballet Theatre Players, Fine Arts Center, Castleton State College, Castleton, Vermont, September 27, 1969.

Dancers: Alexandra Radius and Han Ebbelaar.

World premiere: Nederlands Dans Theater, Royal Theater, The Hague, October 19, 1966. Designer: Jan van der Wal.

FLAMES OF PARIS
(PAS DE DEUX)

Choreography: David and Anna-Marie Holmes, from the original by Vasily Vainonen. Music: Boris Asafiev. Costumes: Marcos Paredes.

Premiere: Kennedy Center, Washington, D.C., December 31, 1972.

Dancers: Eleanor D'Antuono and John Prinz.

World premiere of complete four-act ballet: Kirov Ballet, Kirov Theater, Leningrad, November 6, 1932.

Principal dancers: Galina Ulanova (Mireille de Poitiers) and Vakhtang Chabukiani (Jerome).

FLOWER FESTIVAL IN GENZANO
(PAS DE DEUX)

Choreography: Harald Lander, from the original by August Bournonville. Music: Edvard Helsted and Holger Paulli.

Premiere: Ballet Theatre Workshop, Lisner Auditorium, Washington, D.C., February 20, 1963.

Dancers: Toni Lander and Royes Fernandez.

World premiere of the complete ballet (under the title BLOMSTERFESTEN I GENZANO): Royal Danish Ballet, Royal Theater, Copenhagen, December 19, 1858.

THE FOUR MARYS

Choreography: Agnes de Mille. Music: Trude Rittman. Scenery: Oliver Smith. Costumes: Stanley Simmons. Libretto based "The Ballad of Mary Hamilton."

World premiere: New York State Theater, New York City, March 23, 1965.

Dancers: Judith Jamison (Mary Seaton), Carmen de Lavallade (Mary Hamilton), Cleo Quitman (Mary Beaton), Glory Van Scott (Mary Carmichael), Judith Lerner (Mistress), Paul Sutherland (Her Suitor).

The old Scottish ballad relates an episode at court during the reign of Mary Queen of Scots in which a mistress had the power of life and death over her subjects. The locale has been transposed to a plantation in the American South where the mistress has a similar power over her slaves.

GAÎTÉ PARISIENNE

Choreography: Leonide Massine. Music: Jacques Offenbach, orchestrated by Manuel Rosenthal. Scenery, costumes, and libretto: Comte Etienne de Beaumont.

Premiere: Popejoy Hall, Albuquerque, New Mexico, January 12, 1970.

Principal dancers: Toni Lander (Glove Seller), Roni Mahler (Flower Girl), Betsy Erickson (La Lionne), Michael Smuin (Peruvian), Royes Fernandez (Baron), Han Ebbelaar (Officer), Dennis Nahat (Tortoni).

New York premiere by American Ballet Theatre: New York State Theater, June 17, 1970.

Same principal dancers as above except Mimi Paul (Glove Seller), Bruce Marks (Baron).

World premiere: Ballet Russe de Monte Carlo, Théâtre de Monte Carlo, Monaco, April 5, 1938.

Principal dancers: Nina Tarakanova, Eugenia Delarova, Jeanette Lauret, Leonide Massine, Frederic Franklin, Igor Youskevitch, Robert Irwin.

The adventures of a rich Peruvian in a French casino-in-the-park of the 1890s.

GRAND PAS CLASSIQUE
CYNTHIA GREGORY, TED KIVITT.

GRAND PAS–GLAZUNOV GROHMAN, YOUNG, CARLTON, ALLEN, DOUGLAS, LANDER, SMITH, BORREE, GRADUS, CARROLL.

L'INCONNUE CHRISTINE SARRY, RUTH ANN KOESUN, WILLIAM GLASSMAN.

GALA PERFORMANCE

Choreography: Antony Tudor. Music: Serge Prokofiev (first movement of his Piano Concerto No. 3, and his "Classical Symphony." Scenery and costumes: Nicholas de Molas.

Premiere: Majestic Theatre, New York City, February 11, 1941.

Principal dancers: Nora Kaye ("La Reine de la Danse"—from Moscow), Nana Gollner ("La Déesse de la Danse"—from Milan), Antony Tudor (Her Cavalier), Karen Conrad ("La Fille de Terpsichore"—from Paris), Hugh Laing (Her Cavalier), Edward Caton (Maître de Ballet), Tania Dokoudovska (A Dresser).

World premiere: London Ballet, Toynbee Hall Theatre, London, December 5, 1938. Scenery and costumes: Hugh Stevenson.

Principal dancers: Peggy van Praagh, Maude Lloyd, Antony Tudor, Gerd Larsen, Hugh Laing, Richard Paul, Thérèse Langfield.

At a gala performance, three ballerinas—Russian, Italian, and French—vie for the attention of the audience.

GARTENFEST

Choreography: Michael Smuin. Music: Wolfgang Amadeus Mozart (Cassation No. 1 in G, K. 63). Scenery: Jack Brown. Costumes: Marcos Paredes.

World premiere: Academy of Music, Brooklyn, December 18, 1968.

Principal dancers: Cynthia Gregory, Sallie Wilson; Ted Kivitt, Ivan Nagy, Paul Nickel.

GAYANEH
(PAS DE DEUX)

Choreography: Viktor Róna, from the original by Nina Anisimova. Music: Aram Khachaturian.

Premiere: Capitol Theatre, Washington, D.C., December 10, 1962.

Dancers: Margot Fonteyn and Viktor Róna.

World premiere of Róna's staging: Royal Academy of Dancing Gala, Drury Lane Theatre, London, December 6, 1962.
Same dancers as above.

GEMINI

Choreography: Glen Tetley. Music: Hans Werner Henze (Symphony No. 3). Scenery and costumes: Nadine Baylis.

U.S. premiere: New York State Theater, New York City, July 9, 1975.

Dancers: Cynthia Gregory, Martine van Hamel; Jonas Kage, Charles Ward.

World premiere: Australian Ballet, 1973.

GIFT OF THE MAGI

Choreography: Simon Semenoff. Music: Lukas Foss. Scenery and costumes: Raoul Pène DuBois. Libretto based on the story by William Sydney Porter (O. Henry).

World premiere: Boston Opera House, Boston, October 5, 1945.

Principal dancers: Nora Kaye (Dela), John Kriza (Jim), Diana Adams (Rich Lady), Marjorie Tallchief (Hairdresser / Christmas Shopper), Alpheus Koon (Rich Man), Stanley Herbertt (Pawnshop Keeper / Christmas Tree Peddler), Muriel Bentley (Spanish Lady).

New York premiere: Metropolitan Opera House, October 15, 1945.
Same cast as above.

The girl sells her hair for the money with which to buy a watch chain for her fiancé; he sells his watch to buy her a comb.

GISELLE

Choreography: David Blair, from the original by Jean Coralli and Jules Perrot. Music: Adolphe Adam. Scenery: Oliver Smith. Costumes: Peter Hall. Libretto: Vernoy de Saint-Georges and Théophile Gautier, based on a theme by Heinrich Heine.

Premiere by Ballet Theatre: Carter Barron Amphitheatre, Washington, D.C., July 4, 1968.

Principal dancers: Lupe Serrano (Giselle), Royes Fernandez (Albrecht), Paul Nickel (Hilarion), Eleanor D'Antuono and Ted Kivitt ("peasant pas de deux"), Cynthia Gregory (Myrtha), Diana Weber (Moyna), Karen Krych (Zulma).

New York premiere: Metropolitan Opera House, July 10, 1968.
Same principal dancers as above.

World premiere: Théâtre de l'Académie Royale de Musique, Paris, June 28, 1841. Choreography: Jean Coralli and Jules Perrot.

Principal dancers: Carlotta Grisi (Giselle), Lucien Petipa (Albrecht), Adèle Dumilâtre (Myrtha).

Previous productions by Ballet Theatre:

Premiere: Center Theatre, New York City, January 12, 1940.

Choreography: Anton Dolin. Scenery and costumes: Lucinda Ballard.

Principal dancers: Annabelle Lyon, Anton Dolin, Harold Haskin, Nina Stroganova.

Premiere: Broadway Theatre, New York City, October 15, 1946.

Choreography: Dimitri Romanoff, with contributions from George Balanchine and Antony Tudor. Scenery and costumes: Eugene Berman.

Principal dancers: Alicia Alonso, Igor Youskevitch, Stanley Herbertt, Nora Kaye.

GOYA PASTORAL

Choreography: Antony Tudor. Music: Enrique Granados, orchestrated by Harold Byrns. Scenery and costumes: Nicholas de Molas.

World premiere: Lewisohn Stadium, New York City, August 1, 1940.

Principal dancers: Alicia Alonso and Nora Kaye (Majas), Jerome Robbins and Donald Saddler (Escorts), Lucia Chase (Marchesa), Hugh Laing (Young Man), Eugene Loring (His Excellency the Ass), Antony Tudor (Nobleman), Tilly Losch (Maiden).

(GOYA PASTORAL was performed during the 1940–41 season under the title GOYESCAS.)

An aging marchesa tries to buy a young man with her gambling winnings.

GOYESCAS

Choreography: José Fernandez. Music: Enrique Granados. Scenery and costumes: Nicholas de Molas. Libretto: Alder Jenkins.

World premiere: Center Theatre, New York City, January 15, 1940.

Principal dancers: Iolas (Conde de Azagra), Ada Verova (La Condesa), Leon Danielian (Count Azagra), José Fernandez (Don Pedro de Torres), Monna Montes (Maria de Azagra), Alexis Kosloff (Lackey in Rust and Brown).

GRADUATION BALL

Choreography and libretto: David Lichine. Music: Johann Strauss (various pieces arranged and orchestrated by Antal Dorati). Scenery and costumes: Mstislav Dobujinsky.

Premiere: St.-Denis Théâtre, Montreal, September 26, 1944.

Principal dancers: Alpheus Koon (Headmistress), Tatiana Riabouchinska (A Junior Girl), David Lichine (A Junior Cadet), John Taras (Old General). Divertissement: Tatiana Riabouchinska (Mistress of Ceremonies), John Kriza (Drummer), Alicia Alonso and Richard Reed (pas de deux), Rosella Hightower (Dance Impromptu), Margaret Banks and Marjorie Tallchief (Competition), Harold Lang (Tyrolian Boy).

New York premiere: Metropolitan Opera House, October 8, 1944.
Same cast as above.

World premiere: Original Ballet Russe, Theatre Royal, Sydney, Australia, February 28, 1940. Scenery and costumes: Alexandre Benois.

Principal dancers: Borislav Runanine, Tatiana Riabouchinska, David Lichine, Igor Schwezoff. Divertissement: Tatiana Riabouchinska, Nicholas Orloff, Natasha Sobinova and Paul Petroff (Sylphide and the Scotsman pas de deux), Tatiana Leskova, Alexandra Denisova and Geneviève Moulin.

The cadets from a neighboring military academy attend the graduation ball at a girls' school.

GRAND PAS CLASSIQUE
(PAS DE DEUX)

Choreography: Victor Gsovsky. Music: Daniel François Auber. Costumes: Marcos Paredes.

Premiere: New York State Theater, New York City, July 11, 1972.

Dancers: Cynthia Gregory and Ted Kivitt.

World premiere: Les Ballets des Champs-Elysées, Théâtre des Champs-Elysées, Paris, November 12, 1949.

Dancers: Yvette Chauviré and Vladimir Skouratoff.

GRAND PAS–GLAZUNOV
(PAS DE DIX)

Choreography: George Balanchine. Music: Alexander Glazunov (from RAYMONDA, Act III). Costumes: Barbara Karinska and Tom Lingwood.

Premiere: Music Hall, Cleveland, January 28, 1961.

Dancers: Maria Tallchief and Royes Fernandez; Ady Addor, Susan Borree, Elisabeth Carroll, Christine Mayer; Ivan Allen, Leo Duggan, Lawrence Gradus, Felix Smith.

New York premiere: Broadway Theatre, April 25, 1961.

World premiere of the three-act version of RAYMONDA from which GRAND PAS was excerpted: Ballet Russe de Monte Carlo, City Center, New York City, March 12, 1946. Choreography: George Balanchine and Alexandra Danilova, from the original by Marius Petipa. Scenery and costumes: Alexandre Benois.

Dancers: Alexandra Danilova and Nicholas Magallanes; Ruthanna Boris, Yvonne Chouteau, Marie Jeanne, Maria Tallchief; Herbert Bliss, Ivan Ivanov, Robert Lindgren, Nikita Talin.

LE GRAND SPECTACLE

Choreography: Anna Sokolow. Music: Teo Macero.

World premiere: Ballet Theatre Workshop, Phoenix Theatre, New York City, May 13, 1957.

Dancers: Paul Taylor, Jeff Duncan, Eve Beck, Anita Dencks, Kate Friedlich, David Gold, Dorothy Krooks, Jack Moore.

A satirical view of old-time French vaudeville.

GRAZIANA

Choreography: John Taras. Music: Wolfgang Amadeus Mozart (Violin Concerto No. 3, K. 216). Costumes: Alvin Colt.

World premiere: Metropolitan Opera House, New York City, October 25, 1945.

Principal dancers: (I) Nora Kaye, André Eglevsky, Alicia Alonso; (II) Diana Adams.

THE GREAT AMERICAN GOOF

Choreography: Eugene Loring. Music: Henry Brant. Scenery and costumes: Boris Aronson. Libretto: William Saroyan.

World premiere: Center Theatre, New York City, January 11, 1940.

Principal dancers: Eugene Loring (title role), Miriam Golden (The Woman), Antony Tudor (The Dummy), Dimitri Romanoff (Old Man in Prison), Lucia Chase (A Little Girl), Vladimir Dokoudovsky (Priest), Annabelle Lyon (Girl Dancing).

The native white hope of the human race encounters a cross-section of the characters who make up American society.

HAMLET CONNOTATIONS

Choreography: John Neumeier. Music: Aaron Copland (Piano Variations, Connotations for Orchestra, and selections from the Piano Fantasy). Scenery: Robin Wagner. Costumes: Theoni Aldredge.

World premiere: Uris Theatre, New York City, January 6, 1976.

Cast: Mikhail Baryshnikov (Hamlet), Marcia Haydée (Gertrude), Gelsey Kirkland (Ophelia), Erik Bruhn (Claudius), William Carter (Ghost of Hamlet's Father).

HARBINGER

Choreography: Eliot Feld. Music: Serge Prokofiev (Piano Concerto in G, op. 55). Scenery: Oliver Smith. Costumes: Stanley Simmons.

World premiere: Dade County Auditorium, Miami, Florida, March 31, 1967.

Principal dancers: Cynthia Gregory, Janet Mitchell, Christine Sarry; Eliot Feld, Marcos Paredes, Edward Verso.

New York premiere: New York State Theater, May 11, 1967.
Same principal dancers as above except Paula Tracy for Janet Mitchell.

THE HARVEST ACCORDING

Choreography: Agnes de Mille. Music: Virgil Thomson (various passages from his Cello Concerto, Symphony on a Hymn Tune, and "The Mother of Us All"). Scenery and costumes: Lemuel Ayres.

World premiere: Metropolitan Opera House, New York City, October 1, 1952.

Principal dancers: I. Birth—Liane Plane (Girl), Gemze de Lappe (Mother). II. Games—Ruth Ann Koesun (Child), Kelly Brown (Boy). III. The Harvest—Gemze de Lappe (Woman), Liane Plane (Friend), Jenny Workman (Child Grown Up), Kelly Brown (Young Man).

A study of the cycle of birth and death as epitomized in Walt Whitman's lines, "Life, life is the tillage / And death is the harvest according."

HARVEST TIME

Choreography: Bronislava Nijinska. Music: Henri Wieniawski, arranged by Antal Dorati. Costumes: Enid Gilbert.

World premiere: Metropolitan Opera House, New York City, April 5, 1945.

Cast: Tamara Toumanova (Girl); John Kriza (Shepherd); Barbara Fallis and Margaret Banks (Friends of the Girl); Marjorie Tallchief, Shirley Eckl, June Morris, Fern Whitney (Peasant Girls); Fernand Nault, Robert De Voye, Stanley Herbertt, Alpheus Koon (Peasant Boys).

Shepherd meets shepherdess to no great purpose, unfortunately.

HELEN OF TROY

Choreography: David Lichine. Music: Jacques Offenbach (for "La belle Hélène," arranged by Antal Dorati). Scenery and costumes: Marcel Vertès. Libretto: Lichine and Antal Dorati.

World premiere: Masonic Auditorium, Detroit, November 29, 1942.

Principal dancers: Anton Dolin (Paris), Irina Baronova (Aphrodite / Helen), Jerome Robbins (Hermes), Lucia Chase (Athena / Bacchis), Jean Hunt (Lamb), Rosella Hightower (Hera), Simon Semenoff (Menelaus), Donald Saddler (Calchas), Yura Lazovsky (Orestes), Annabelle Lyon (Chrisothemis).

New York premiere: Metropolitan Opera House, April 3, 1943.

Previous production by Ballet Theatre:

World premiere: Palacio de Bellas Artes, Mexico City, September 10, 1942. Choreography and libretto: Michel Fokine.

Principal dancers: Irina Baronova (Helen), Anton Dolin (Paris), Donald Saddler (Menelaus / Zeus), Simon Semenoff (Calchas), Nora Kaye (Aphrodite), Lucia Chase (Athena), Rosella Hightower (Hera), Ian Gibson (Hermes), Jerome Robbins (Hymen).

A comic version of the Trojan Wars, using the score and décor employed in the Fokine version, but with entirely different choreography and treatment of the story.

LAS HERMANAS

Choreography: Kenneth MacMillan. Music: Frank Martin (Concerto for Harpsichord and Small Orchestra). Scenery and costumes: Nicholas Georgiadis. Libretto based on Federico García Lorca's THE HOUSE OF BERNARDA ALBA.

U.S. premiere: City Center, New York City, November 29, 1967.

KONTRASTE (FRONT ROW) TERRY ORR, ROSALIN RICCI, PAUL SUTHERLAND.

LADY INTO FOX DAVID NILLO, WILLIAM DOLLAR, LEON DANIELIAN.

THE MIRACULOUS MANDARIN NATALIA MAKAROVA, ERIK BRUHN.

Cast: Lucia Chase (Mother), Lupe Serrano (Eldest Sister), Eleanor D'Antuono (Jealous Sister), Ellen Everett (Youngest Sister), Naomi Sorkin and Alaine Haubert (Other Sisters), Royes Fernandez (The Man).

World premiere: Stuttgart Ballet, Württembergische Staatstheater, Stuttgart, July 13, 1963.

Principal dancers: Ruth Papendick (Mother), Marcia Haydée (Eldest Sister), Birgit Keil (Jealous Sister), Ray Barra (The Man).

The eldest sister in a family of five, dominated by their tyrannical widowed mother, discovers that the man who is courting her is attempting to seduce her youngest sister.

HUAPANGO

Choreography: Enrique Martinez. Music: José Pablo Moncayo.

World premiere: Ballet Theatre Players, Fine Arts Center, Castleton State College, Castleton, Vermont, September 27, 1969.

Principal dancers: Roni Mahler, Gail Israel, Han Ebbelaar.

L'INCONNUE

Choreography: Bentley Stone. Music: Francis Poulenc. Scenery: Ann Folke. Costumes: Joseph Kaminski. Libretto based on a newspaper account.

Premiere: American Ballet Theatre Workshop, Hunter College Playhouse, New York City, May 11, 1964.

Principal dancers: Ruth Ann Koesun (The Unknown), Karen Krych (River Girl), Charles Schick (River Boy), John Kriza (First Intruder), George Mamales (Second Intruder), Paul Nickel (Third Intruder).

First performance of version with music by Hershy Kay: New York State Theater, New York City, April 6, 1965. Scenery: Jack Owen Brown. Costumes: Ann Roth.

World premiere: Stone-Camryn Ballet, St. Alphosus Athenaeum Theatre, Chicago, May 17, 1963.
Same principals as above except Steve Primus (Second Intruder), John Spina (Third Intruder).

The discovery of the body of an unknown girl drowned in the Seine in the 1950s captures the imagination of Paris.

INTERMEZZO

Choreography: Eliot Feld. Music: Johannes Brahms (Intermezzi, op. 117 and 118, and some of the Waltzes, op. 39). Costumes: Stanley Simmons.

Premiere: New York State Theater, New York City, July 6, 1972.

Dancers: Cynthia Gregory, Christine Sarry, Mimi Paul; Ivan Nagy, Eliot Feld, Jonas Kage.

World premiere: American Ballet Company [Feld's], Teatro Nuovo, Spoleto, Italy (Festival of Two Worlds), June 29, 1969.

Dancers: Christine Sarry, Elizabeth Lee, Cristina Stirling; David Coll, John Sowinski, Alfonso Figueroa.

INTERPLAY

Choreography: Jerome Robbins. Music: Morton Gould ("American Concertette"). Scenery: Oliver Smith. Costumes: Irene Sharaff.

Premiere: Metropolitan Opera House, New York City, October 17, 1945.

Dancers: John Kriza, Harold Lang, Tommy Rall, Fernando Alonso, Janet Reed, Melissa Hayden, Muriel Bentley, Roszika Sabo (Ensemble); Harold Lang (Solo); Janet Reed and John Kriza (Pas de Deux).

World premiere: Ziegfeld Theatre, New York City, June 1, 1945, part of Billy Rose's "Concert Varieties." Scenery and costumes: Carl Kent.

Dancers: Jerome Robbins, Janet Reed, John Kriza, Muriel Bentley, Michael Kidd, Roszika Sabo, Erik Kristen, Bettina Rosay.

JARDIN AUX LILAS

Choreography: Antony Tudor. Music: Ernest Chausson (Poème). Scenery and costumes: Hugh Stevenson.

Premiere: Center Theatre, New York City, January 15, 1940.

Principal dancers: Viola Essen (Caroline), Hugh Laing (Her Lover), Antony Tudor (The Man She Must Marry), Karen Conrad (An Episode in His Past).

World premiere: Ballet Rambert, Mercury Theatre, London, January 26, 1936.

Principal dancers: Maude Lloyd, Hugh Laing, Antony Tudor, Peggy van Praagh.

Caroline is about to enter upon a marriage of convenience and attends a party with her fiancé. Among the guests are the man she really loves and the woman who has been her fiancé's mistress.

LE JEUNE HOMME ET LA MORT
(PAS DE DEUX)

Choreography: Roland Petit. Music: Johann Sebastian Bach (Passacaglia in C Minor, orchestrated by Ottorino Respighi). Scenery: Georges Wakhevitch. Costumes: Christian Bérard. Libretto: Jean Cocteau.

U.S. premiere: Metropolitan Opera House, New York City, April 9, 1951.

Dancers: Jean Babilée and Nathalie Philippart.

World premiere: Les Ballets des Champs-Elysées, Théâtre des Champs-Elysées, Paris, June 25, 1946.
Same dancers as above.

Death, masquerading as a young girl, drives her lover to suicide by hanging. The ballet was presented in 1951 without the complete sets, which were restored when the ballet was performed at the City Center, New York, in 1975 by Mikhail Baryshnikov and Bonnie Mathis as the lovers.

JEUX

Choreography: William Dollar. Music: Claude Debussy. Scenery and costumes: David Ffolkes.

World premiere: Center Theatre, New York City, April 23, 1950.

Dancers: Igor Youskevitch, Nora Kaye, Norma Vance.

A new and different version of the erotic tennis match first envisioned by Vaslav Nijinsky.

JOURNEY

Choreography: Kenneth MacMillan. Music: Béla Bartók, orchestrated by Joseph Levine. Scenery and costumes: Nicholas Georgiadis.

World premiere: Ballet Theatre Previews, Phoenix Theatre, New York City, May 6, 1957.

Principal dancers: Nora Kaye, John Kriza, Erik Bruhn, Scott Douglas; Susan Borree, Andrina Miller, Nadine Revene.

The Three Messengers accompany a woman on her last journey to death. After the workshop performance, the ballet was placed in the regular repertory.

JUDGMENT OF PARIS

Choreography: Antony Tudor. Music: Kurt Weill (selections from "Die Dreigroschenoper"). Scenery, costumes, and libretto: Hugh Laing.

Premiere: Center Theatre, New York City, January 23, 1940.

Cast: Viola Essen (Juno), Agnes de Mille (Venus), Lucia Chase (Minerva), Antony Tudor (Client), Hugh Laing (Waiter).

World premiere: London Ballet, Westminster Theatre, London, June 1938. Costumes: Hugh Laing. (Given as a curtain-raiser to Gogol's MARRIAGE.)

Cast: Thérèse Langfield, Agnes de Mille, Charlotte Bidmead, Antony Tudor, Hugh Laing.

The ancient tale of Paris' choice as re-enacted by three Victorian whores.

KONTRASTE

Choreography: Todd Bolender. Music: Bernd Alois Zimmermann.

U.S. premiere: New York State Theater, New York City, February 3, 1966.

Dancers: Jeanne Armin, Cynthia Gregory, Erin Martin, Janet Mitchell, Veronika Mlakar, Eliot Feld, Ted Kivitt, Ray Morgan, Paul Nickel, Terry Orr, Paul Sutherland, Edward Verso.

World premiere: Cologne Ballet, Bühnen der Stadt Köln, Cologne, Germany, July 9, 1964. Scenery: Ed Wittstein.

Principal female dancer: Helga Held.

LADY FROM THE SEA

Choreography: Birgit Cullberg. Music: Knudaage Riisager. Scenery and costumes: Kerstin Hedeby. Libretto based on Henrik Ibsen's play.

World premiere: Metropolitan Opera House, New York City, April 20, 1960.

Principal dancers: Lupe Serrano (Ellida), Royes Fernandez (Sailor), Glen Tetley (Wangel, a widower), Elisabeth Carroll and Janie Barrow (His Daughters).

Ibsen's lady learns that a conventional marriage is preferable to life with a footloose sailor.

LADY INTO FOX

Choreography: Andrée Howard. Music: Arthur Honegger, selected by Charles Lynch. Scenery and costumes: Nadia Benois. Libretto based on the novel by David Garnett.

Premiere: Center Theatre, New York City, January 26, 1940.

Principal dancers: Andrée Howard (Sylvia Telrick), William Dollar (Mr. Telrick), Miriam Golden (Nurse), Leon Danielian (Huntsman).

World premiere: Ballet Rambert, Mercury Theatre, London, May 15, 1939.

Principal dancers: Sally Gilmour, Charles Boyd, Veronica Iverson, Leo Kersley.

A lady inexplicably turns into a fox to the bafflement of her husband.

THE LEAF AND THE WIND
(PAS DE DEUX)

Choreography: William Dollar. Music: Paul Ramseier.

World premiere: State Fair Auditorium, Dallas, Texas, February 3, 1954.

Dancers: Melissa Hayden and Eugene Tanner.

THE LEAVES ARE FADING

Choreography: Antony Tudor. Music: Antonin Dvořák ("Cypresses," for string quartet, together with other chamber music for strings). Scenery: Ming Cho Lee. Costumes: Patricia Zipprodt.

World premiere: New York State Theater, New York City, July 17, 1975.

Principal dancers: Gelsey Kirkland, Jonas Kage; Kristine Elliott, Nanette Glushak, Marianna Tcherkassky; Clark Tippet, Charles Ward.

LILTING FATE

Choreography: Steven-Jan Hoff. Music: Harold Farberman. Costumes: Ann Roth. Projections by Jim Housley.

World premiere: Oakland University Auditorium, Rochester, Michigan, August 8, 1969.

Principal dancers: Amy Blaisdell, Karena Brock, Alexandra Radius, Naomi Sorkin; Han Ebbelaar, Steven-Jan Hoff, Dennis Nahat, Terry Orr.

THE LOVE SONG

Choreography: Adeline Genée. Music: Dora Bright, orchestrated by Vittorio Rieti. Costumes: Lucinda Ballard.

Premiere: Civic Opera House, Chicago, November 3, 1940.

Dancers: Nina Stroganova, Anton Dolin; Tania Dokoudovska, Kirsten Valbor, Billie Wynn.

World premiere: Drury Lane Theatre, London, June 7, 1932 (gala charity matinée in aid of the Hertford Hospital in Paris).

Principal dancers: Adeline Genée and Anton Dolin.

MADEMOISELLE ANGOT

Choreography: Leonide Massine. Music: Charles Lecocq, arranged by Efrem Kurtz and orchestrated by Richard Mohaupt. Scenery and costumes: Mstislav Dobujinsky. Libretto based on Lecocq's operetta LA FILLE DE MADAME ANGOT.

World premiere: Metropolitan Opera House, New York City, October 10, 1943.

Principal dancers: Nora Kaye (Soubrette), Leonide Massine (Barber), Rosella Hightower (Aristocrat), André Eglevsky (Artist), Simon Semenoff (Old Official), John Kriza (His Confidant), Nicholas Orloff (Officer), Michael Kidd (Vagabond). At the Masquerade: Simon Semenoff (The Pear), John Kriza (The Knife), Jean Davidson and John Taras (Troubadors).

The Soubrette, betrothed to the Barber, falls in love with the Artist, who loves the Aristocrat.

THE MAIDS

Choreography: Herbert Ross. Music: Darius Milhaud (Concerto for Percussion and Small Orchestra). Scenery: William Pitkin. Libretto based on the play by Jean Genet.

World premiere: Ballet Theatre Workshop, Phoenix Theatre, New York City, May 13, 1957.

Cast: Loren Hightower (Claire), Paul Olson (Solange), Ilona Murai (Madame), Ralph Beaumont (Monsieur).

Solange smothers her fellow maid, Claire, as the climax to a psychologically murky sexual involvement.

MECHANICAL BALLET

Choreography: Adolph Bolm. Music: Alexander Mossolov ("Music of the Machines"). Costumes: John Hambleton.

Premiere: Center Theatre, New York City, January 18, 1940.

Principal dancers: Viola Essen and Dimitri Romanoff (principal Dynamos).

World premiere (under the title THE IRON FOUNDRY): Hollywood Bowl, Los Angeles, July 28, 1931. Costumes: Nicholas Remisoff.

Principal dancers: Elise Reiman and Robert Bell (with a company of 60 dancers).

MEDEA
(PAS DE DEUX)

Choreography: John Butler. Music: Samuel Barber ("Medea," op. 23). Scenery and costumes: Rouben Ter-Arutunian.

U.S. premiere: Uris Theatre, New York City, January 13, 1976.

Dancers: Carla Fracci (Medea), Mikhail Baryshnikov (Jason).

World premiere: Teatro Nuovo, Spoleto, Italy (Festival of Two Worlds), June 28, 1975. Costumes: Martin Kamer.
Same dancers as above.

MENDELSSOHN SYMPHONY

Choreography: Dennis Nahat. Music: Felix Mendelssohn (Symphony No. 4, op. 90). Costumes: Robert O'Hearn.

World premiere: New York State Theater, New York City, July 15, 1971.

Principal dancers: Cynthia Gregory, Royes Fernandez, Ian Horvath; Karena Brock, Ellen Everett, Zhandra Rodriguez, Marianna Tcherkassky; David Coll, Warren Conover, Terry Orr, John Prinz.

MINKUS PAS DE TROIS

Choreography: George Balanchine. Music: Ludwig Minkus.

Premiere: Municipal Auditorium, Austin, Texas, February 3, 1971.

Dancers: Roni Mahler, Han Ebbelaar, Diana Weber.

World premiere: Opera House, Monte Carlo, Monaco, 1948.

Dancers: Rosella Hightower, Nina Vycoubova, Serge Golovine.

THE MIRACULOUS MANDARIN

Choreography: Ulf Gadd. Music: Béla Bartók. Scenery and costumes: Hermann Sichter.

U.S. premiere: New York State Theater, New York City, July 29, 1971.

Cast: Natalia Makarova (The Girl); Erik Bruhn (Mandarin); Alexander Filipov, Ian Horvath, Gaudio Vacacio (Three Gangsters); David Coll (Sailor); Warren Conover (Young Boy).

World premiere: The New Swedish Ballet, The Place, London, September 9, 1970.

NAPOLI DIVERTISSEMENTS RICHARD BEATY, SUSAN BORREE, GAIL ISRAEL, GAYLE YOUNG.

OTHER DANCES MIKHAIL BARYSHNIKOV, NATALIA MAKAROVA.

ONTOGONY HELYN DOUGLAS, ZOLA DISHONG, IAN HORVATH, KARENA BROCK, TERRY ORR.

Principal dancers: Marie Johansson; Tadeusz Zlamal.

The Mandarin, who has attacked the Girl, miraculously refuses to die when beaten and hanged by the Three Gangsters.

THE MIRROR

Choreography: Enrique Martinez. Music: Kenneth Schermerhorn.

World premiere: Ballet Theatre Workshop, Phoenix Theatre, New York City, April 21, 1958.

Principal dancers: Nora Kaye (The Woman), Fredda Maurice (Her Reflection); Her Longings: Scott Douglas (Force), Ray Barra and Leo Duggan (Lust), Michael Lland (Love).

The mirror performs the functions of a woman's psychoanalyst.

MISS JULIE

Choreography: Birgit Cullberg. Music: Ture Rangström, arranged by Hans Grossman. Scenery and costumes: Sven Erixon. Libretto: Allan Fridericia, based on August Strindberg's play FRÖKEN JULIE.

U.S. premiere: Metropolitan Opera House, New York City, September 18, 1958.

Principal dancers: Violette Verdy (Miss Julie), Erik Bruhn (Jean, the butler), Scott Douglas (Julie's fiancé), Sallie Wilson (Kristine, the cook), Susan Borree (Clara, a peasant), Ray Barra (Anders, a peasant).

World premiere: Swedish Ballet, Riksteatern, Västerås, Sweden, March 1, 1950. Scenery and costumes: Allan Fridericia.

Principal dancers: Elsa-Marianne von Rosen (Miss Julie), Julius Mengarelli (Jean), Birgit Cullberg (Kristine).

The ancestors of a count's daughter, in a vision, make her so ashamed of her love affair with the butler that she commits suicide.

MOMENTUM

Choreography: Dennis Nahat. Music: Peter Ilyich Tchaikovsky ("Souvenirs de Florence").

World premiere: Brooklyn College Auditorium, Brooklyn, March 15, 1969.

Dancers: Karena Brock, Eleanor D'Antuono, Mimi Paul, Naomi Sorkin; Ian Horvath, Dennis Nahat.

MONUMENT FOR A DEAD BOY

Choreography: Rudi van Dantzig. Electronic music: Jan Boerman. Scenery and costumes: Toer van Schayk.

Premiere: Kennedy Center, Washington, D.C., January 2, 1973.

Principal dancers: Ivan Nagy (Boy), Warren Conover (His Youth), Bonnie Mathis and William Carter (His Parents), Marianna Tcherkassky (The White Girl), Deborah Dobson (The Blue Girl), Marcos Paredes (The School Friend).

New York premiere by Ballet Theatre: City Center, January 11, 1973.

Same principal dancers as above.

World premiere: Het National Ballet, Stadsschowburg, Amsterdam, June 19, 1965.

Principal dancers: Toer van Schayk (Boy), Yvonne Vendrig (The White Girl).

Traumatic experiences in his youth propel a young man to homosexuality and death.

MOONLIGHT SONATA

Choreography: Leonide Massine. Music: Ludwig van Beethoven (Piano Sonata in C Sharp Minor, op. 27, no. 2, arranged by Antal Dorati). Scenery and costumes: Serge Soudeikine.

World premiere: Civic Opera House, Chicago, November 24, 1944.

Cast: Tamara Toumanova (Young Girl), Leonide Massine (Poet), Albia Kavan (Cupid), Richard Reed (The Dark Lover).

New York premiere: Metropolitan Opera House, April 7, 1945.

Same cast as above except Paul Petroff (The Dark Lover).

MOON REINDEER

Choreography: Birgit Cullberg. Music: Knudaage Riisager. Scenery and costumes: Per Falk. Libretto: Birgit Cullberg, based on a Lapp folk tale.

U.S. premiere: Fifty-fourth Street Theatre, New York City, October 2, 1961.

Principal dancers: Lupe Serrano (Aili, the Moon Reindeer); Royes Fernandez (Nilas); Martin Scheepers (Uno); Basil Thompson (Naaiden, the Sorcerer); Felix Smith (Antti); Ted Kivitt, Gayle Young, Joseph Carow (Lapp Boys).

World premiere: Royal Danish Ballet, Royal Theater, Copenhagen, November 22, 1957.

Principal dancers: Mona Vangsaa (Aili), Henning Kronstam (Nilas), Fredbjørn Bjørnsson (Naaiden).

The magician Naaiden gives the girl Aili the power to attract the boy Nilas, in return for which on moonlit nights she must transform herself into a white reindeer and lure young hunters over an abyss to die as human sacrifices to the evil spirits.

THE MOOR'S PAVANE

Choreography: José Limón. Music: Henry Purcell, arranged by Simon Sadoff (from "Abdelazer," "The Gordian Knot Untied," and the pavane from "Pavane and Chaconne for Strings"). Costumes: Pauline Lawrence. Libretto based on a theme of Shakespeare's OTHELLO.

Premiere: New York State Theater, New York City, June 27, 1970.

Dancers: Bruce Marks (The Moor), Royes Fernandez (His Friend), Sallie Wilson (His Friend's Wife), Toni Lander (The Moor's Wife).

World premiere: Palmer Auditorium, Connecticut College, New London, Second American Dance Festival, August 17, 1949.

Dancers: José Limón, Lucas Hoving, Pauline Koner, Betty Jones.

LA MUERTE ENAMORADA

Choreography: Enrique Martinez. Music: Joaquin Turina.

World premiere: Ballet Theatre Workshop, Phoenix Theatre, New York City, May 20, 1957.

Principal dancers: Erik Bruhn (The Youth), Annabelle Gold (Gypsy Girl), Enrique Martinez (Gypsy Boy), Jillana Williams (Death).

Once again Death comes in search of a victim, but this time love and life win out.

NAPOLI DIVERTISSEMENTS

Choreography: Toni Lander, from the original by August Bournonville. Music: Holger Paulli, Edvard Helsted, and Niels Gade.

Premiere: Ballet Theatre Workshop, Lisner Auditorium, Washington, D.C., February 20, 1963.

Dancers: Susan Borree, Eleanor D'Antuono, Gail Israel, Fern MacLarnon, Melina Plank; Bruce Marks, Richard Beaty, Ted Kivitt, Richard Wagner, Gayle Young.

World premiere of complete ballet: Royal Danish Ballet, Royal Theater, Copenhagen, March 29, 1842.

Principal dancers: Caroline Fjeldsted and August Bournonville.

NIMBUS

Choreography: Antony Tudor. Music: Louis Gruenberg (Concerto for Violin and Orchestra). Scenery: Oliver Smith. Costumes: Saul Bolaski.

World premiere: Center Theatre, New York City, May 3, 1950.

Principal dancers: Nora Kaye (The Dreamer), Diana Adams (The Dream), Hugh Laing (Dream-Beau).

A working-girl dreams of herself as an ethereal creature of grace and beauty who irresistibly charms her "dream-beau."

LES NOCES

Choreography: Jerome Robbins. Music: Igor Stravinsky. Scenery: Oliver Smith. Costumes: Patricia Zipprodt.

World premiere: New York State Theater, New York City, March 30, 1965.

Principal dancers: Erin Martin (Bride), Veronika Mlakar and Joseph Carow (Her Parents), William Glassman (Groom), Sallie Wilson and Bruce Marks (His Parents), Rosanna Seravalli and Ted Kivitt (Matchmakers).

The engagement and marriage of a couple in Old Russia.

THE NUTCRACKER

Choreography: Mikhail Baryshnikov. Choreography for "Snowflake" dance from the original by Vassily Vainonen. Music: Peter Ilyich Tchaikovsky. Scenery: Boris Aronson. Costumes: Frank Thompson.

World premiere: Kennedy Center, Washington, D.C., December 21, 1976.

Principal dancers: Marianna Tcherkassky (Clara), Mikhail Baryshnikov (Nutcracker-Prince), Alexander Minz (Drosselmeyer), Warren Conover (Fritz), Gayle Young (Mr. Stahlbaum), Sallie Wilson (Mrs. Stahlbaum), Marcos Paredes (King of Mice).

New York premiere: Metropolitan Opera House, May 18, 1977.

Same principal dancers as above.

THE NUTCRACKER
(PAS DE DEUX)

Choreography: Anton Dolin, from the original by Lev Ivanov.

Premiere: Metropolitan Opera House, New York City, October 27, 1943.

Dancers: Rosella Hightower and André Eglevsky.

ODE TO GLORY
(PAS DE DEUX)

Choreography: Yurek Shabelevski. Music: Frédéric Chopin ("Polonaise militaire"). Scenery and costumes: Michel Baronov.

Premiere: Center Theatre, New York City, January 25, 1940.

Dancers: Sonia Woizikowska and Yurek Shabelevski.

World premiere: Hartford, Connecticut, 1939.

OFFENBACH IN THE UNDERWORLD

Choreography: Antony Tudor. Music: Jacques Offenbach ("Gaîté parisienne" score, arranged by David Simon). Scenery and costumes: René Bouché.

Premiere: Metropolitan Opera House, New York City, April 18, 1956.

Principal dancers: Ruth Ann Koesun (Debutante), Nora Kaye (Operetta Star), Lupe Serrano (Queen of the Carriage Trade), Hugh Laing (Painter), John Kriza (His Imperial Excellency), Scott Douglas (Young Officer).

World premiere: Philadelphia Ballet Guild, Convention Hall, Philadelphia, May 8, 1954.

Principal dancers: Sylvia Kim, Viola Essen, Elaine Wilson; Michael Lland, Michael Lopuszanski, Maurice Phillips.

An evening with an assorted group of characters at a fashionable Paris café in the 1870s.

ONCE MORE, FRANK
(PAS DE DEUX)

Choreography: Twyla Tharp. Music: songs recorded by Frank Sinatra ("Something Stupid," "One for My Baby," and "That's Life"). Costumes: Santo Loquasto.

World premiere: New York State Theater, New York City, July 12, 1976.

Dancers: Twyla Tharp and Mikhail Baryshnikov.

ON STAGE!

Choreography: Michael Kidd. Music: Norman Dello Joio. Scenery: Oliver Smith. Costumes: Alvin Colt. Libretto: Michael and Mary Kidd.

World premiere: Boston Opera House, Boston, October 4, 1945.

Principal dancers: Michael Kidd (Handyman), Nora Kaye (Ballerina), John Kriza (Her Partner), John Taras (Ballet Master), Janet Reed (Girl in Pink), Shirley Eckl (Girl in Blue), Roy Tobias (Piano Player).

New York premiere: Metropolitan Opera House, October 9, 1945.

Same cast as above.

A shy ballet student aspires to become a ballerina and is befriended and aided by a sympathetic stagehand who permits her to attend rehearsals.

ONTOGENY

Choreography: Dennis Nahat. Music: Karel Husa (Quartet No. 3). Scenery and costumes: Willa Kim.

Premiere: City Center, New York City, January 6, 1971.

Dancers: Karena Brock, Zola Dishong, Helyn Douglas, Naomi Sorkin, Martine van Hamel; Robert Brassel, William Carter, Ian Horvath, Terry Orr, Gaudio Vacacio.

World premiere: Royal Swedish Ballet, Royal Theater, Stockholm, 1970.

OTHER DANCES
(PAS DE DEUX)

Choreography: Jerome Robbins. Music: Frédéric Chopin (a waltz and four mazurkas). Costumes: Santo Loquasto.

Premiere by Ballet Theatre: Metropolitan Opera House, New York City, June 22, 1976.

Dancers: Natalia Makarova and Mikhail Baryshnikov.

World premiere: Gala Evening for the Library of Performing Arts at Lincoln Center, Metropolitan Opera House, New York City, May 9, 1976.

Same dancers as above.

OVID METAMORPHOSES

Choreography: Herbert Ross. Music: Arnold Schönberg (Sonata for Violin and Piano, op. 16).

World premiere: Ballet Theatre Workshop, Phoenix Theatre, New York City, April 21, 1958.

Principal dancers: Sallie Wilson (Io and the Cloud); Loren Hightower, Paul Olson, Ruth Ann Koesun (Narcissus and Echo), Lupe Serrano and Michael Lland (Daphne and Apollo), Jillana Williams (Calpurnia), Leo Duggan (Caesar), Nadine Revene (Venus).

PAEAN

Choreography: Herbert Ross. Music: Ernest Chausson (Concerto for Violin, Piano, and Strings). Costumes: John Ward. Libretto derived from verses of Sappho.

World premiere: Ballet Theatre Previews, Phoenix Theatre, New York City, May 27, 1957.

Principal dancers: Nora Kaye, Ruth Ann Koesun, Lupe Serrano, Jillana Williams, Sallie Wilson; Ray Barra, Scott Douglas, Leo Duggan, John Kriza, Michael Lland.

PAQUITA

Choreography: Rudolf Nureyev, from original by Mazilier as staged by Marius Petipa. Music: Ludwig Minkus, orchestrated by John Lanchbery. Costumes: Freddy Wittop.

Premiere: New York State Theater, New York City, July 6, 1971.

Principal dancers: Cynthia Gregory and Michael Denard; Karena Brock, Ellen Everett, Zhandra Rodriguez, Diana Weber; Gail Israel, Betty Chamberlin, Naomi Sorkin, Marianna Tcherkassky.

World premiere of Nureyev version: Royal Academy of Dancing Gala, Drury Lane Theatre, London, November 17, 1964. Costumes: Philip Prouse.

Principal dancers: Margot Fonteyn and Rudolf Nureyev; Deanne Bergsma, Vyvyan Lorrayne, Monica Mason, Georgina Parkinson.

PAQUITA
(PAS DE DEUX)

Choreography: Alexandra Fedorova.

World premiere: Carter Barron Amphitheatre, Washington, D.C., August 6, 1957.

Dancers: Nora Kaye and Erik Bruhn.

THE PARLIAMENT OF THE BIRDS

Choreography: William Dollar. Music: Ottorino Respighi ("Gli uccelli" suite for small orchestra). Libretto based on

OVID METAMORPHOSES LUPE SERRANO, MICHAEL LLAND.

ROMEO AND JULIET (PAS DE DEUX) ERIK BRUHN, CARLA FRACCI.

QUINTET ANTON DOLIN, LUCIA CHASE.

themes from Farid ud-Din Attar's poem "The Conference of the Birds."

World premiere: Ballet Theatre Workshop, Phoenix Theatre, New York City, April 21, 1958.

Danced by students from the Ballet Theatre School.

The Persian poem by Farid ud-Din Attar provides the excuse for some humorous bird-watching.

PAS DE DÉESSES

Choreography: Robert Joffrey. Music: John Field, arranged by John Wilson. Costumes adapted from an 1846 English dance print.

Premiere: Ballet Theatre Workshop, Phoenix Theatre, New York City, May 7, 1956.

Cast: Lupe Serrano (Taglioni), Ruth Ann Koesun (Grahn), Sonia Arova (Cerrito), Erik Bruhn (Saint-Léon).

World premiere: Robert Joffrey Ballet, Kaufmann Concert Hall, New York City, May 29, 1954.

Cast: Lillian Wellein, Barbara Ann Gray, Jacquetta Kieth, Michael Lland.

PAS DE DEUX

Choreography: Anatole Oboukhoff. Music: Nicholas Tcherepnine, orchestrated by Eugene Fuerst. Costumes: Barbara Karinska.

World premiere: Metropolitan Opera House, New York City, April 9, 1946.

Dancers: Alicia Alonso and André Eglevsky.

PAS DE "DUKE"
(PAS DE DEUX)

Choreography: Alvin Ailey. Music: Duke Ellington ("Such Sweet Thunder," "Sonnet to Caesar," "Hank Cinq," "Clothed Woman"). Scenery and costumes: Rouben Ter-Arutunian.

Premiere by Ballet Theatre: New York State Theater, New York City, July 29, 1976.

Dancers: Judith Jamison and Mikhail Baryshnikov.

World premiere: Alvin Ailey Dance Theatre, City Center, New York City, May 11, 1976 (Alvin Ailey Dance Theatre Spring Gala).

PAS DE QUATRE

Choreography: Keith Lester. Music: Cesare Pugni, arranged and orchestrated by Leighton Lucas. Costumes after the 1845 "Pas de Quatre" lithograph by Chalon and Maguire.

Premiere: Royal Opera House, Covent Garden, London, August 26, 1946.

Dancers: Alicia Alonso (Marie Taglioni), Nora Kaye (Carlotta Grisi), Barbara Fallis (Lucile Grahn), Lucia Chase (Fanny Cerrito).

New York premiere by Ballet Theatre: Broadway Theatre, October 8, 1946.
Same dancers as above.

World premiere: Markova-Dolin Ballet, Opera House, Manchester, England, May 27, 1936.

Dancers: Molly Lake, Diana Gould, Kathleen Crofton, Prudence Hyman.

Previous production by Ballet Theatre:

Choreography: Anton Dolin from the original of Keith Lester.

Premiere: Majestic Theatre, New York City, February 16, 1941.

Dancers: Nana Gollner, Alicia Alonso, Nina Stroganova, Katherine Sergava.

Lester imagined what occurred when the four great romantic ballerinas appeared together in a gala performance in London in 1845 in a pas de quatre choreographed by Jules Perrot.

PAS DE TROIS

Choreography: Valentina Pereyaslavec. Music: Franz Schubert, orchestrated by Albert Boss.

World premiere: Ballet Theatre Workshop, Phoenix Theatre, New York City, May 20, 1957.

Dancers: Jillana Williams, Conrad Ludlow, Nancee Charles.

PAS ET LIGNES
(PAS DE DEUX)

Choreography: Serge Lifar. Music: Claude Debussy ("Petite suite," orchestrated by Henri Büsser).

U.S. premiere: Metropolitan Opera House, New York City, April 19, 1960.

Dancers: Claude Bessy and Royes Fernandez.

World premiere: Paris Opéra Ballet, Geneva, March 15, 1957.

Dancers: Claude Bessy and Max Bozzoni.

LE PASSAGE ENCHANTÉ

Choreography: Ron Sequio. Music: Serge Prokofiev (Violin Concerto No. 1 in D). Scenery: Mel Juan. Moving light projections devised by Jerry Hochberg. Libretto suggested by paintings of Marc Chagall.

World premiere: Ballet Theatre Workshop, Hunter College Playhouse, New York City, May 11, 1964.

Principal dancers: Sallie Wilson, Gayle Young, Camille Crosby, Rosemary Jourdan, Mary Stone, Peter Saul.

With the aid of light projections, the paintings of Marc Chagall are represented in dance form.

LES PATINEURS

Choreography: Frederick Ashton. Music: Giacomo Meyerbeer (selections from the operas "Le Prophète" and "L'Etoile du nord," arranged and orchestrated by Constant Lambert). Scenery and costumes: Cecil Beaton.

U.S. premiere: Broadway Theatre, New York City, October 2, 1946.

Principal dancers: Cynthia Riseley and Barbara Fallis (Girl in Pink, Girl in Yellow), John Kriza (Boy in Green), Nora Kaye and Hugh Laing (Lovers), Diana Adams and Anna Cheselka (Friends).

World premiere: Vic-Wells Ballet, Sadler's Wells Theatre, London, February 16, 1937. Scenery and costumes: William Chappell.

Principal dancers: Mary Honer and Elizabeth Miller, Harold Turner, Margot Fonteyn and Robert Helpmann, Pamela May and June Brae.

PETER AND THE WOLF

Choreography: Adolph Bolm. Music and libretto: Serge Prokofiev. Scenery and costumes: Lucinda Ballard.

World premiere: Center Theatre, New York City, January 13, 1940.

Dancers: Eugene Loring (Peter), Viola Essen (Bird), Karen Conrad (Duck), Nina Stroganova (Cat), Edward Caton (Grandfather), William Dollar (Wolf).

PETROUCHKA

Choreography: Michel Fokine, rehearsed after his death by Dimitri Romanoff and Yura Lazovsky. Music: Igor Stravinsky. Scenery and costumes: Alexandre Benois (adapted by Oliver Smith). Libretto: Igor Stravinsky and Alexandre Benois.

Premiere: New York State Theater, New York City, June 19, 1970.

Principal dancers: Eleanor D'Antuono (Ballerina), Ted Kivitt (Petrouchka), Bruce Marks (Blackamoor), Dennis Nahat (Charlatan), Sallie Wilson (Chief Nursemaid), Marcos Paredes (Chief Coachman), Diana Weber and Zhandra Rodriguez (Street Dancers).

World premiere: Les Ballets Russes de Diaghilev, Théâtre du Châtelet, Paris, June 13, 1911.

Principal dancers: Tamara Karsavina, Vaslav Nijinsky, Alexandre Orlov, Enrico Cecchetti; Bronislava Nijinska and Ludmila Schollar (Street Dancers).

Previous production by Ballet Theatre:
Palacio de Bellas Artes, Mexico City, August 27, 1942.

Choreography: Michel Fokine (staged by him personally).

Principal dancers: Irina Baronova (Ballerina), Yura Lazovsky (Petrouchka), David Nillo (Blackamoor), Simon Semenoff (Charlatan), Jeanette Lauret (Chief Nursemaid), George Skibine (Chief Coachman); Jerome Robbins and Nicholas Orloff (Grooms), Rosella Hightower and Jean Hunt (Street Dancers).

U.S. premiere by Ballet Theatre: Metropolitan Opera House, New York City, October 8, 1942.

Same principals as above except Richard Reed (Charlatan) and Ian Gibson for Robbins (Groom).

PILLAR OF FIRE

Choreography: Antony Tudor. Music: Arnold Schönberg ("Verklärte Nacht"). Scenery and costumes: Jo Mielziner.

World premiere: Metropolitan Opera House, New York City, April 8, 1942.

Dancers: Nora Kaye (Hagar); Lucia Chase (Eldest Sister); Annabelle Lyon (Youngest Sister); Antony Tudor (The Friend); Hugh Laing (The Young Man from the House Opposite); Maria Karnilova, Charles Dickson, Jean Davidson, John Kriza, Virginia Wilcox, Nicholas Orloff, Jean Hunt, Barbara Fallis (Lovers-in-Innocence); Sono Osato, Rosella Hightower, Muriel Bentley, Jerome Robbins, Donald Saddler, Frank Hobi (Lovers-in-Experience); Galina Razoumova and Roszika Sabo (Maiden Ladies Out Walking).

Hagar, fearful lest she remain unmarried like her older sister, gives herself to a man of lust and later finds forgiveness and happiness with the one she has always loved.

POINTS ON JAZZ

Choreography: Dania Krupska. Music: Dave Brubeck. Scenery and costumes: Oliver Smith.

World premiere: Bushnell Auditorium, Hartford, Connecticut, January 16, 1961.

Principal dancers: Elisabeth Carroll (Girl), Scott Douglas (Boy), Sallie Wilson (Other Woman).

New York premiere: Broadway Theatre, April 26, 1961.
Same principal dancers as above.

POLYANDRION

Choreography: Tomm Ruud. Music: Aaron Copland ("Dance Symphony"). Costumes: Steven Rubin.

World premiere: New York State Theater, New York City, July 6, 1973.

Principal dancers: Karena Brock, Dennis Nahat, Terry Orr, Deborah Dobson, Kim Highton; Warren Conover, John Sowinski, Charles Ward.

PREVAILING WESTERLIES

Choreography: Richard Wagner. Music: Alexander Scriabin ("Poem of Ecstasy").

World premiere: Ballet Theatre Workshop, Hunter College Playhouse, New York City, December 17, 1963.

Cast: Richard Wagner (First Boy), Karen Krych and Joseph Carow (Young Couple), Ted Kivitt and Basil Thompson (Two Brothers), Hester FitzGerald and Peter Saul (Married Couple).

A PROMISE
(PAS DE DEUX)

Choreography: Robert Weiss. Music: Craig Steven Shuler. Costumes: Susan Tammany.

World premiere: New York State Theater, New York City, July 28, 1975.

Dancers: Gelsey Kirkland and Ivan Nagy.

PULCINELLA VARIATIONS

Choreography: Michael Smuin. Music: Igor Stravinsky (selections from "Pulcinella"). Scenery: Jack Owen Brown. Costumes: Stanley Simmons.

World premiere: Metropolitan Opera House, New York City, July 11, 1968.

Principal dancers: Susan Casey, Ellen Everett, Georgina Vidal, Diana Weber; Ian Horvath, Terry Orr, Michael Smuin, John Sowinski.

PUSH COMES TO SHOVE

Choreography: Twyla Tharp. Music: Joseph Lamb ("Bohemia Rag") and Franz Joseph Haydn (Symphony No. 82 in C). Costumes: Santo Loquasto.

World premiere: Uris Theatre, New York City, January 9, 1976.

Principal dancers: Mikhail Baryshnikov, Martine van Hamel, Marianna Tcherkassky; Clark Tippet.

QUINTET
OR THE ADVENTURES OF DON AND DOLORES FROM NEW YORK TO HOLLYWOOD AND BACK

Choreography: Anton Dolin. Music: Raymond Scott. Scenery and costumes: Lucinda Ballard.

World premiere: Center Theatre, New York City, February 1, 1940.

Principal dancers: Patricia Bowman (Sister), Anton Dolin (Brother), David Nillo (Indian Chief), Nina Stroganova (Prostitute), Anne Wilson (Fortuneteller), Hugh Laing (Caballero), Leon Danielian (Dictator), Miriam Golden (Mrs. Tourist / La Marquise), Edward Caton (Mr. Tourist / L'Abbé), Lucia Chase (Film Star / L'Etoile), Dimitri Romanoff (Director).

Two young dancers travel across the country in search of fame in the movies.

RAYMONDA

Choreography: Rudolf Nureyev, revised from the original by Marius Petipa. Music: Alexander Glazunov. Scenery and costumes: Nicholas Georgiadis.

Premiere: Jones Hall, Houston, Texas, June 26, 1975.

Principal dancers: Cynthia Gregory (Raymonda), Rudolf Nureyev (Jean de Brienne), Erik Bruhn (Abdul-Rakhman), Karena Brock (Henriette), Martine van Hamel (Clemance), Charles Ward (Bernard), Clark Tippet (Beranger), Bonnie Mathis (Sybille de Doris), William Carter (King of Hungary), Jolinda Menendez and John Prinz (Saracen Couple), Hilda Morales and Dennis Wayne (Spanish Couple).

New York premiere: New York State Theater, July 1, 1975.
Same principal dancers as above.

World premiere of Nureyev version: Royal Ballet Touring Company, Teatro Nuovo, Spoleto, Italy (Festival of Two Worlds), July 11, 1964. Designer: Beni Montresor.

Principal dancers: Doreen Wells (Raymonda), Rudolf Nureyev (Jean de Brienne), Ian Hamilton (Abdul-Rakhman). Cast also included Deirdre O'Conaire, Michael Coleman, Gary Sherwood, David Wall.

Count Jean de Brienne and Saracen knight Abdul-Rakhman contend for the hand of Raymonda. Jean wins and his marriage to Raymonda is celebrated in the third and last act.

RENDEZVOUS
(PAS DE DEUX)

Choreography: Bronislava Nijinska. Music: Sergei Rachmaninoff ("Polka by V.R.," orchestrated by Antal Dorati). Costumes: Enid Gilbert.

World premiere: Metropolitan Opera House, New York City, April 20, 1945.

Dancers: Lucia Chase, Dimitri Romanoff.

RIB OF EVE

Choreography: Agnes de Mille. Music: Morton Gould. Scenery: Oliver Smith. Costumes: Irene Sharaff.

World premiere: Metropolitan Opera House, New York City, April 25, 1956.

Principal dancers: Nora Kaye (Hostess), James Mitchell (Her Husband), Barbara Lloyd (Her Best Friend).

Through a series of parties and their aftermath, members of the social set demonstrate the futility of their existence.

RICERCARE
(PAS DE DEUX)

Choreography: Glen Tetley. Music: Mordecai Seter. Scenery and costumes: Rouben Ter-Arutunian.

World premiere: New York State Theater, New York City, January 25, 1966.

Dancers: Mary Hinkson and Scott Douglas.

THE RIVER

Choreography: Alvin Ailey. Music: Duke Ellington. Costumes: Frank Thompson.

World premiere: New York State Theater, New York City, June 25, 1970.

Principal dancers: Spring—John Prinz; Vortex—Eleanor D'Antuono; Falls—Richard Cammack, William Carter, Robert Gladstein, Vane Vest; Lake—Cynthia Gregory and Ivan Nagy; Riba—Dennis Nahat; Two Cities—Sallie Wilson and Keith Lee.

SLAVONIKA IAN GIBSON, SONO OSATO.

SCHUBERTIADE D'ANTUONO, ORR, GREGORY, YOUNG, WILSON, PAREDES, WEBER, PRINZ.

THE TAMING JOHN KRIZA.

RODEO

Choreography: Agnes de Mille. Music: Aaron Copland. Scenery: Oliver Smith. Costumes: Saul Bolasni.

Premiere: Hessisches Staatstheater, Wiesbaden, Germany, August 14, 1950.

Principal dancers: Allyn McLerie (Cowgirl), John Kriza (Champion Roper), James Mitchell (Head Wrangler), Charlyne Baker (Ranch Owner's Daughter); Ruth Ann Koesun, Paula Lloyd, Dorothy Scott (Her Eastern Friends from Kansas City).

First New York performance by Ballet Theatre: Metropolitan Opera House, January 9, 1951.
Same cast as above.

World premiere: Ballet Russe de Monte Carlo, Metropolitan Opera House, October 16, 1942.

Principal dancers: Agnes de Mille, Frederic Franklin, Casimir Kokitch, Milada Mladova; Eleanora Marra, Dorothy Etheridge, Ruth Riekman.

A tomboy discards her boots and jeans and dons a party dress to get her man.

ROMANTIC AGE

Choreography: Anton Dolin. Music: Vincenzo Bellini, arranged by Antal Dorati. Scenery and costumes: Carlos Merida.

World premiere: Metropolitan Opera House, New York City, October 23, 1942.

Principal dancers: Alicia Markova (Elora, a Nymph); Anton Dolin (A Youth); Karen Conrad (Cupid); John Kriza (Faun); Miriam Golden, Maria Karnilova, Sono Osato (Muses); Donald Saddler, David Nillo, Wallace Seibert (Friends of the Youth).

A faun and a youth are rivals for the love of a nymph who cannot dance until she is struck by Cupid's arrow.

ROMEO AND JULIET

Choreography: Antony Tudor. Music: Frederick Delius (A Walk to Paradise Garden from "A Village Romeo and Juliet," Eventyr, Over the Hills and Far Away, Brigg Fair, arranged by Antal Dorati). Scenery and costumes: Eugene Berman. Libretto based on the play by Shakespeare.

World premiere: Metropolitan Opera House, New York City, April 6, 1943. (The ballet was performed as scheduled, though Tudor had not finished it. The complete production was presented four nights later.)

Principal dancers: Hugh Laing (Romeo), Alicia Markova (Juliet), Nicholas Orloff (Mercutio), Jerome Robbins (Benvolio), Antony Tudor (Tybalt), Lucia Chase (Nurse to Juliet), Dimitri Romanoff (Friar Laurence), Sono Osato (Rosaline), Borislav Runanine (Montague), Miriam Golden (Lady Montague), John Taras (Capulet), Galina Razoumova (Lady Capulet), Richard Reed (Paris).

Shakespeare's plot condensed into a single act.

ROMEO AND JULIET (PAS DE DEUX)

Choreography: Erik Bruhn. Music: Serge Prokofiev.

New York premiere: New York State Theater, May 10, 1967.

Dancers: Carla Fracci and Erik Bruhn.

World premiere: Il Teatro dell'Opera, Rome, March 1966.

A ROSE FOR MISS EMILY

Choreography: Agnes de Mille. Music: Alan Hovhaness. Scenery and costumes: Christina Giannini. Libretto suggested by William Faulkner's story "A Rose for Emily."

New York premiere: City Center, December 30, 1970.

Principal dancers: Sallie Wilson (Miss Emily), Gayle Young (Her Lover), Zhandra Rodriguez and Carol Bryan (Children of Her Youth), Zhandra Rodriguez and Betty Chamberlin (Children of Her Old Age).

World premiere: North Carolina School of the Arts, Winston-Salem. Performed by students of the school, October 22, 1970.

RUSSIAN SOLDIER

Choreography: Michel Fokine. Music: Serge Prokofiev ("Lieutenant Kije Suite"). Scenery and costumes: Mstislav Dobujinsky.

World premiere: Boston Opera House, Boston, January 23, 1942.

Principal dancers: Yura Lazovsky (Russian Soldier), Nicholas Orloff (Drum Major), Galina Razoumova (Bride), Shirley Eckl (Mother), Simon Semenoff (Father), John Duane (Doctor), Donald Saddler (Death).

New York premiere: Metropolitan Opera House, April 6, 1942.
Same principal dancers as above.

A nineteenth-century Russian soldier, dying on the battlefield, recalls events of his life.

LE SACRE DU PRINTEMPS

Choreography: Glen Tetley. Music: Igor Stravinsky. Scenery and costumes: Nadine Baylis.

U.S. premiere: Metropolitan Opera House, New York City, June 21, 1976.

Principal dancers: Mikhail Baryshnikov, Martine van Hamel, Clark Tippet; Nanette Glushak, Rebecca Wright, Frank Smith, Charles Ward.

World premiere: Bavarian State Opera Ballet, Munich, April 17, 1974.

Principal dancers: Ferenc Barbay, Konstanza Vernon, Frederic Werner.

SARGASSO

Choreography: Glen Tetley. Music: Ernst Křenek (Symphonic Elegy for String Orchestra). Scenery and costumes: Rouben Ter-Arutunian.

U.S. premiere: New York State Theater, New York City, March 24, 1965.

Dancers: I. Sallie Wilson, Bruce Marks, Richard Zelens; II. Camille Crosby, Virginia Griffee, Marie Paquet, Barbara Remington, Rosanna Seravalli; III. Robert Holloway, Marcos Paredes, Paul Sutherland.

World premiere: Nederlands Dans Theater, Royal Theater, The Hague, July 7, 1964. Scenery and costumes: Nicholas Wijnberg.

Principal female dancer: Willy de la Bye.

SCHERZO FOR MASSAH JACK

Choreography: Lar Lubovitch. Music: Charles Ives (Trio for Violin, Cello, and Piano). Costumes: John Dayger.

World premiere: City Center, New York City, January 17, 1973.

Dancers: Susan Jones, Bonnie Mathis, Ruth Mayer, Zhandra Rodriguez, Christine Sarry; William Carter, Warren Conover, Ian Horvath, Keith Lee, Daniel Levans, John Sowinski, Clark Tippet, Charles Ward.

SCHUBERTIADE

Choreography: Michael Smuin. Music: Franz Schubert (piano pieces). Scenery: William Pitkin. Costumes: Marcos Paredes.

Premiere: City Center, New York City, January 1, 1971.

Principal dancers: Eleanor D'Antuono, Cynthia Gregory, Diana Weber, Sallie Wilson; Terry Orr, Marcos Paredes, John Prinz, Gayle Young.

World premiere: San Francisco Ballet, War Memorial Opera House, San Francisco, spring 1970.

SCHUMANN CONCERTO

Choreography: Bronislava Nijinska. Music: Robert Schumann (Concerto in A Minor for Piano and Orchestra). Scenery and costumes: Stewart Chaney.

World premiere: Metropolitan Opera House, New York City, September 27, 1951.

Principal dancers: Alicia Alonso and Igor Youskevitch; Ruth Ann Koesun, Barbara Lloyd; Eric Braun, Erik Bruhn, Royes Fernandez.

SEA-CHANGE

Choreography: Alvin Ailey. Music: Benjamin Britten (Four Sea Interludes from "Peter Grimes"). Costumes: Frank Thompson.

World premiere: Kennedy Center, Washington, D.C., October 26, 1972.

Dancers: Sallie Wilson and Royes Fernandez; Amy Blaisdell, Christine Busch, Zola Dishong, Deborah Dobson, Ingrid Fraley, Nanette Glushak, Rhodie Jorgenson, Janet Shibata; Robert Brassel, Richard Cammack, Daniel Levans, Dennis Marshall, Richard Schafer, Frank Smith, Clark Tippet, Charles Ward, Buddy Balough, Fernando Bujones, Warren Conover.

New York premiere: City Center, January 9, 1973.
Same dancers as above except Keith Lee for Robert Brassel.

SEBASTIAN

Choreography: Agnes de Mille. Music and libretto: Gian Carlo Menotti.

World premiere: Ballet Theater Previews, Phoenix Theatre, New York City, May 27, 1957.

Principal dancers: Nora Kaye (Princess), Darrel Notara (Prince), John Kriza (Sebastian, Their Moorish Slave), Lupe Serrano (A Courtesan), Enrique Martinez (A Cutthroat).

A Moorish slave allows himself to be killed in place of the courtesan he loves.

SEVEN FACES OF LOVE

Choreography: John Butler. Music: Stan Kenton and Duke Ellington.

World premiere: Ballet Theatre Workshop, Phoenix Theatre, New York City, May 20, 1957.

Dancers: Sono Osato, Buzz Miller, Lee Becker; Loren Hightower, Edythe Udane, Bruce Carlisle, Tom Hasson.

SHADOW OF THE WIND

Choreography: Antony Tudor. Music: Gustav Mahler ("Das Lied von der Erde"). Scenery and costumes: Jo Mielziner.

World premiere: Metropolitan Opera House, New York City, April 14, 1948.

Principal dancers: I. Igor Youskevitch, Hugh Laing, Dimitri Romanoff; II. Alicia Alonso, John Kriza, Mary Burr; III. Ruth Ann Koesun, Crandall Diehl; IV. Diana Adams, Zachary Solov; V. Hugh Laing; VI. Nana Gollner, Hugh Laing, Dimitri Romanoff.

The poems of Li Po are depicted in mime and dance.

SHADOWPLAY

Choreography: Antony Tudor. Music: Charles Koechlin ("Les Bandar-Log," op. 176, and two fragments from "La Course de printemps," op. 95). Scenery and costumes: Michael Annals. Libretto based on a theme from Rudyard Kipling's "Jungle Book."

Premiere: New York State Theater, New York City, July 23, 1975.

Principal dancers: Mikhail Baryshnikov (Boy with Matted Hair), Gelsey Kirkland (Celestial), Jonas Kage (Terrestrial).

World premiere: Royal Ballet, Royal Opera House, Covent Garden, London, January 25, 1967.

Principal dancers: Anthony Dowell, Merle Park, Derek Rencher.

SLAVONIKA

Choreography: Vania Psota. Music: Antonín Dvořák ("Slavonic Dances"). Costumes: Alvin Colt.

World premiere: Palacio de Bellas Artes, Mexico City, October 24, 1941.

Principal dancers: Irina Baronova (Slavonika), George Skibine (Jan), Lucia Chase (Marushia), Vania Psota (Vashek), Yura Lazovsky and Ian Gibson (Friends of Jan), Sono Osato and Nora Kaye (Friends of Slavonika).

U.S. premiere: Forty-fourth Street Theatre, New York City, November 21, 1941.
Same principals as above.

THE SLEEPING BEAUTY

Choreography: Mary Skeaping from the original of Marius Petipa and the staging of Nicholas Sergeyev. Music: Peter Ilyich Tchaikovsky. Designer: Oliver Messel. Libretto based on the tale by Charles Perrault.

Premiere: Metropolitan Opera House, New York City, June 15, 1976.

Principal dancers: Natalia Makarova (Princess Aurora), Mikhail Baryshnikov (Prince Florimund), Martine van Hamel (Lilac Fairy), Dennis Nahat (Carabosse), Jolinda Menendez (Fairy of the Crystal Fountain), Kristine Elliott (Fairy of the Enchanted Garden), Marianna Tcherkassky (Fairy of the Woodland Glades), Rebecca Wright (Fairy of the Song Birds), Karena Brock (Fairy of the Golden Vine), Fernando Bujones (Bluebird), Yoko Morishita (Princess Floride).

World premiere: Maryinsky Theater, Saint Petersburg, January 15, 1890.

Principal dancers: Carlotta Brianza (Princess Aurora), Pavel Gerdt (Prince Charming), Enrico Cecchetti (Carabosse), Marie Petipa (Lilac Fairy), Enrico Cecchetti and Barbara Nikitina (Bluebird pas de deux).

Previous productions by Ballet Theatre:

Bluebird pas de deux. Choreography: Anton Dolin.

Premiere: Robin Hood Dell, Philadelphia, June 24, 1940. Dancers: Karen Conrad and Anton Dolin.

Princess Aurora (A suite of divertissements from Petipa's full-length SLEEPING BEAUTY)

Choreography: Anton Dolin. Scenery and costumes: Léon Bakst.

World premiere: Palacio de Bellas Artes, Mexico City, October 23, 1941.

Principal dancers: Irina Baronova (Princess Aurora), Anton Dolin (Prince Charming), Nina Popova, Lucia Chase, Sono Osato, Karen Conrad, Nora Kaye, Annabelle Lyon, Irina Baronova (Seven Variations), Nora Kaye, Rosella Hightower, and Charles Dickson (Pas de Trois), Lucia Chase and Simon Semenoff (Cats), Karen Conrad and Ian Gibson (Bluebird pas de deux).

New York premiere: Forty-fourth Street Theatre, New York City, November 27, 1941.

Principal dancers: Same as world premiere except: Rosella Hightower, Karen Conrad, Lucia Chase, Sono Osato, Nora Kaye, Annabelle Lyon, Irina Baronova (Seven Variations).

The Sleeping Beauty Act III. Choreography: David Blair from the original of Marius Petipa. Scenery: Oliver Smith. Costumes: Miles White.

Premiere: New York State Theater, New York City, July 2, 1974.

Principal dancers: Cynthia Gregory (Princess Aurora), Bruce Marks (Prince Florimund), Jolinda Menendez (Lilac Fairy), Fernando Bujones and Natalia Makarova (Bluebird pas de deux).

A SOLDIER'S TALE

Choreography: Eliot Feld. Music: Igor Stravinsky ("L'Histoire du soldat," 1923 concert-suite version). Costumes: Frank Thompson.

World premiere: Kennedy Center, Washington, D.C., December 28, 1971.

Cast: Daniel Levans (Soldier), Eliot Feld (Pimp), Sallie Wilson and Paula Tracy (Whores), Buddy Balough, Robert Brassel, Richard Cammack, David Coll, Warren Conover, Rory Foster, Frank Smith, Bojan Spassoff, Luis Villanueva (Soldiers).

New York premiere: City Center, January 7, 1972.
Same cast as above.

SOLITAIRE (PAS DE DEUX)

Choreography: Kenneth MacMillan. Music: Malcolm Arnold.

Premiere: Kennedy Center, Washington, D.C., October 3, 1975.

Dancers: Martine van Hamel and Clark Tippet.

World premiere: Western Theatre Ballet, Theatre Royal, Bristol, England, June 24, 1963.

Dancers: Joan Lindsay and Simon Mottram.

SOME TIMES

Choreography: Dennis Nahat. Music: Claus Ogerman. Scenery and costumes: Rouben Ter-Arutunian.

World premiere: New York State Theater, New York City, July 14, 1972.

Dancers: Karena Brock, Kim Highton, Mimi Paul, Zhandra Rodriguez, Christine Sarry, Naomi Sorkin, Martine van Hamel; Ian Horvath, Jonas Kage, Dennis Nahat.

THE TRAITOR WILLIAM CARTER, ROYES FERNANDEZ, ROBERT GLADSTEIN, VANE VEST, MARCOS PAREDES.

TEXAS FOURTH REBECCA WRIGHT, ERIC NESBITT.

TROPICAL PAS DE DEUX ALICIA ALONSO, IGOR YOUSKEVITCH.

SPECTRE DE LA ROSE
(PAS DE DEUX)

Choreography: Michel Fokine. Music: Carl Maria von Weber ("Invitation to the Dance"). Scenery and costumes: Léon Bakst. Libretto: Jean Louis Vaudoyer.

Premiere: Palacio de Bellas Artes, Mexico City, October 31, 1941.

Dancers: Annabelle Lyon (Young Girl), Ian Gibson (title role).

U.S. premiere by Ballet Theatre: Forty-fourth Street Theatre, New York City, December 4, 1941.
Same dancers as above.

World premiere: Les Ballets Russes de Diaghilev, Théâtre de Monte Carlo, Monaco, April 19, 1911.

Dancers: Tamara Karsavina and Vaslav Nijinsky.

A young girl, returning from her first ball, dreams she is dancing with the spirit of the rose she wore.

THE SPHINX

Choreography: David Lichine. Music: Henri Sauguet. Scenery and costumes: Christian Bérard. Libretto: Boris Kochno.

U.S. premiere: Metropolitan Opera House, New York City, April 21, 1955.

Cast: Nora Kaye (Sphinx); Igor Youskevitch (Oedipus); Sharon Enoch, Joan Fisher, Leslie Franzos (Women).

World premiere (under the title LA RENCONTRE): Les Ballets des Champs-Elysées, Théâtre des Champs-Elysées, Paris, November 8, 1948.

Cast: Leslie Caron, Jean Babilée; Hélène Sadovska, Michèle Hoffer, Alexandra Hirschler.

Oedipus solves the riddles posed by the Sphinx.

A STREETCAR NAMED DESIRE

Choreography: Valerie Bettis. Music: Alex North, adapted and orchestrated by Rayburn Wright. Scenery: Peter Larkin. Costumes: Saul Bolasni. Libretto based on Tennessee Williams' play.

Premiere: McCarter Theatre, Princeton, New Jersey, October 26, 1954.

Principal dancers: Valerie Bettis (Blanche), Igor Youskevitch (Stanley), Christine Mayer (Stella), Scott Douglas (Mitch), Catherine Horn (Flower Vendor), Joan Fisher (Woman from Upstairs), Leslie Franzos (Neighbor), George Tomal (Man from Upstairs).

New York premiere by Ballet Theatre: Metropolitan Opera House, April 13, 1955.
Same principal dancers as above except Nora Kaye (Blanche).

World premiere: Slavenska-Franklin Ballet, Her Majesty's Theatre, Montreal, Canada, October 9, 1952.

Principal dancers: Mia Slavenska (Blanche), Frederic Franklin (Stanley), Lois Ellyn (Stella), Marvin Krauter (Mitch).

Blanche's encounter with Stanley Kowalski drives her deeper into the world of fantasy.

STREETCORNER ROYALTY

Choreography: Job Sanders. Music: Jack Montrose.

World premiere: Ballet Theatre Workshop, Phoenix Theatre, New York City, May 7, 1956.

Principal dancers: Sonia Arova (Woman), Jerry Ruffner (Leader), Ernest Parham (Musician), Bill Guske (Lieutenant).

An incident with a gang of juvenile delinquents.

SUMMER DAY
(PAS DE DEUX)

Choreography: Jerome Robbins. Music: Serge Prokofiev ("Music for Children"). Costumes and properties: John Boyt.

Premiere: City Center, New York City, December 2, 1947.

Dancers: Ruth Ann Koesun and John Kriza.

World premiere: American-Soviet Musical Society, City Center, New York City, May 12, 1947.

Dancers: Annabelle Lyon and Jerome Robbins.

SWAN LAKE

Choreography: David Blair, from the original by Marius Petipa and Lev Ivanov. Music: Peter Ilyich Tchaikovsky. Scenery: Oliver Smith. Costumes: Freddy Wittop. Libretto: Vladimir Begichev and Vasily Geltzer.

Premiere: Civic Opera House, Chicago, February 16, 1967.

Principal dancers: Nadia Nerina (Odette-Odile), Royes Fernandez (Prince Siegfried), Lucia Chase (Princess-Mother), Paul Sutherland (Benno), Tom Adair (Von Rothbart), Enrique Martinez (Wolfgang, the tutor).

New York premiere: New York State Theater, May 9, 1967.
Same principal dancers as above except Toni Lander (Odette-Odile) and Bruce Marks (Prince Siegfried).

World premiere: Maryinsky Theater, Saint Petersburg, January 27, 1876.

Principal dancers: Pierina Legnani (Odette-Odile), Pavel Gerdt (Prince Siegfried), Aleksandr Oblakov (Benno), Aleksei Bulgakov (Von Rothbart).

Act II of this production was first presented at the New York State Theater, New York City, January 18, 1966, with the same cast as above except Lupe Serrano (Odette-Odile).

Previous productions by Ballet Theatre:
SWAN LAKE ACT II

Choreography: Anton Dolin. Scenery: Augustus Vincent Tack and Lee Simonson. Costumes: Lucinda Ballard.

Premiere: Center Theatre, New York City, January 16, 1940.

Principal dancers: Patricia Bowman (Odette), Anton Dolin (Prince Siegfried), Hugh Laing (Benno), Gregor Taksa (Von Rothbart).

BLACK SWAN PAS DE DEUX, ACT III

Choreography: Anton Dolin. Costumes: Barbara Karinska.

Premiere: Metropolitan Opera House, New York City, October 23, 1944.

Dancers: Tamara Toumanova and Anton Dolin.

LA SYLPHIDE

Choreography: Harald Lander, from original by August Bournonville. Music: Hermann Løwenskjold, with additional music by Edgar Cosma. Scenery and costumes: Robert O'Hearn.

Premiere: Municipal Auditorium, San Antonio, Texas, November 11, 1964.

Principal dancers: Toni Lander (Sylphide), Royes Fernandez (James), Christine Mayer (Effie), Basil Thompson (Gurn), Rosanna Seravalli (Madge), Eliot Feld and William Glassman (Two Farmboys), Ted Kivitt (First Variation).

New York premiere: New York State Theater, March 13, 1965.
Same principal dancers as above.
The Lander version was restaged and partially revised by Erik Bruhn, and was first presented at the New York State Theater, New York City, July 7, 1971, with Carla Fracci (Sylphide) and Ted Kivitt (James).

Original production (under the title SYLPHIDEN): Royal Danish Ballet, Royal Theater, Copenhagen, November 28, 1836.

Principal dancers: Lucile Grahn and August Bournonville.

World premiere of Lander's staging: Le Grand Ballet du Marquis de Cuevas, Théâtre de l'Empire, December 9, 1953. Designer: Bernard Daydé.

Principal dancers: Rosella Hightower and Serge Golovine.

James, who has made an enemy of the witch Madge, deserts Effie, his fiancée, to pursue the Sylph. Madge gives him a poisoned veil which when wrapped around the Sylph causes her to die as her wings fall off. The witch jeers at James as Effie passes on the way to her wedding with his rival, Gurn.

LES SYLPHIDES

Choreography: Michel Fokine. Music: Frédéric Chopin. Scenery: Augustus Vincent Tack. Costumes: Lucinda Ballard.

Premiere: Center Theatre, New York City, January 11, 1940.

Principal dancers: Karen Conrad, Nina Stroganova, Lucia Chase, William Dollar.

World premiere of this version: Théâtre du Châtelet, Paris, June 2, 1909. Scenery and costumes: Alexandre Benois.

Principal dancers: Anna Pavlova, Tamara Karsavina, Maria Baldina, Vaslav Nijinsky. (Fokine's first version was performed in Saint Petersburg, on March 21, 1908, under the title CHOPINIANA. The dancers were members of the Imperial Ballet.)

SYLVIA PAS DE DEUX

Choreography: George Balanchine. Music: Léo Delibes.

Premiere: Teatro Municipal, Rio de Janeiro, August 20, 1964.

Dancers: Sonia Arova and Royes Fernandez.

New York premiere by Ballet Theatre: New York State Theater, March 17, 1965.
Same dancers as above.

World premiere: New York City Ballet, City Center, New York City, December 1, 1950. Costumes: Barbara Karinska.

Dancers: Maria Tallchief and Nicholas Magallanes.

TALES OF HOFFMANN

Choreography: Peter Darrell. Music: Jacques Offenbach, arranged and orchestrated by John Lanchbery (selections from "Les Contes d'Hoffmann" and other works). Scenery and costumes: Peter Docherty. Libretto based on the stories by E. T. A. Hoffmann and the scenario of the opera.

U.S. premiere: New York State Theater, New York City, July 12, 1973.

Principal dancers: Jonas Kage (Hoffmann); Cynthia Gregory (La Stella / Olympia / Antonia / Giulietta); Gayle Young (Spalanzani / Doctor Miracle / Dapertutto); Ellen Everett, Zhandra Rodriguez, Marianna Tcherkassky (Vision pas de trois); Nanette Glushak, Kim Highton, Clark Tippet, Charles Ward (Entertainers, Act III); David Coll and Warren Conover (Mignons).

World premiere: Scottish Theatre Ballet, Kings Theatre, Edinburgh, Scotland, April 6, 1972. Designer: Alistair Livingstone.

Principal dancers: Peter Cazalet (Hoffmann), Patricia Rianne (La Stella), Hilary Debden (Olympia), Marian St. Claire (Antonia), Elaine McDonald (Giulietta).

The libretto closely follows the plot of the opera, tracing the adventures of Hoffmann with La Stella, Olympia, Antonia, and Giuletta.

TALLY-HO;
OR THE FRAIL QUARRY

Choreography: Agnes de Mille. Music: Christoph Willibald Gluck, arranged by Paul Nordoff. Scenery and costumes: Motley.

World premiere: Philharmonic Auditorium, Los Angeles, February 25, 1944.

Principal dancers: Agnes de Mille (Wife), Hugh Laing (Her Husband, a genius), Anton Dolin (Prince), Maria Karnilova (A Lady, no better than she should be), Muriel Bentley and Miriam Golden (Two Others, somewhat worse), Lucia Chase (The Innocent).

New York premiere: Metropolitan Opera House, April 11, 1944.
Same principal dancers as above.
(Revived by American Ballet Theatre, April 2, 1965, under the title THE FRAIL QUARRY.)

The bored wife of a scholastic genius flirts with a predatory prince in the course of a hunting party in eighteenth-century France.

THE TAMING
(PAS DE DEUX)

Choreography: Job Sanders. Music: Paul Creston.

Premiere: Wisconsin Union Theatre, Madison, December 18, 1962.

Dancers: Sallie Wilson and John Kriza.

World premiere: Jacob's Pillow Dance Festival, Lee, Massachusetts, August 7, 1962.

Dancers: Sonia Arova and Glen Tetley.

An animal trainer is attacked by a black panther.

TCHAIKOVSKY PAS DE DEUX

Choreography: George Balanchine. Music: Peter Ilyich Tchaikovsky (original music for the Pas de Deux from Act III of SWAN LAKE). Costumes: Barbara Karinska.

Premiere: The public square, Festival, Santander, Spain, August 11, 1970.

Dancers: Mimi Paul and Bruce Marks.

World premiere: New York City Ballet, City Center, New York City, March 29, 1960.

Dancers: Violette Verdy and Conrad Ludlow.

TEXAS FOURTH

Choreography: Agnes de Mille. Music: Traditional; songs by Harvey Schmidt, arranged by David Baker. Scenery: Oliver Smith. Costumes: Christina Giannini.

Premiere: New York State Theater, New York City, July 8, 1976.

Principal dancers: Dennis Nahat (Fiddler-Caller / Head Batonist), William Carter (Buck and Wing), Rebecca Wright (Girl), Eric Nesbitt (Boy), George de la Pena (Piano Player), Buddy Balough (Trumpet Player), Ruth Mayer (Ghost of the Mother).

World premiere: Agnes de Mille Heritage Dance Theatre, Reynolds Auditorium, North Carolina School of the Arts, Winston-Salem, April 26, 1973.

THEATRE

Choreography: Eliot Feld. Music: Richard Strauss (Burleske in D for Piano and Orchestra). Costumes: Frank Thompson.

Premiere: City Center, New York City, January 6, 1972.

Principal dancers: Eliot Feld (Pierrot), Christine Sarry (Colombina), Terry Orr (Arlecchino), Vane Vest (Brighella), Frank Smith (Pulcinello).

World premiere: American Ballet Company [Feld's], Academy of Music, Brooklyn, April 24, 1971.

Principal dancers: Eliot Feld, Elizabeth Lee, Edward Verso, A. J. Brothers, Edward Henkel.

THEME AND VARIATIONS

Choreography: George Balanchine. Music: Peter Ilyich Tchaikovsky (Suite No. 3 for Orchestra, final movement). Scenery and costumes: Woodman Thompson.

World premiere: City Center, New York City, November 26, 1947.

Principal dancers: Alicia Alonso and Igor Youskevitch; Melissa Hayden, Paula Lloyd, Cynthia Riseley, Anna Cheselka; Fernando Alonso, Fernand Nault, Zachary Solov, Eric Braun.

THE THIEF WHO LOVED A GHOST

Choreography: Herbert Ross and John Ward. Music: Carl Maria von Weber, orchestrated by Hershy Kay. Scenery and costumes: John Ward.

Premiere: Metropolitan Opera House, New York City, April 11, 1951.

Cast: John Kriza (Thief), Ruth Ann Koesun (Isobelle / The Ghost), Ilona Murai (Mme. Carlotta), Lucia Chase (Fiona), Eric Braun and Jack Beaber (Detectives), Ralph McWilliams and William Inglis (Policemen).

World premiere: Ross-Ward Ballet d'Action, Ramapo Lyric Festival, Ramapo, New Jersey, August 1950. Music: Julian Freedman.

Isobelle plays the role of a ghost in an attempt to catch the Thief, but instead she falls in love with him.

THIS PROPERTY IS CONDEMNED

Choreography: Donald Saddler. Music: Genevieve Pitot. Costumes: Stanley Simmons. Libretto based on the play by Tennessee Williams.

World premiere: Ballet Theatre Workshop, Phoenix Theatre, New York City, May 13, 1957.

Cast: Ruth Ann Koesun (Willie), Ralph McWilliams (Tom), Beverly Barsanti (Alva), Fritza Hess (Conductor), John Grigas (Fireman), Joe Layton (Superintendent).

A love encounter of a pair who live by the railroad tracks.

UNFINISHED SYMPHONY
MICHAEL DENARD.

LA VENTANA RUDOLF NUREYEV, CYNTHIA GREGORY, ERIK BRUHN.

THE WANDERER
ANTON DOLIN, VERA ZORINA.

THREE-CORNERED HAT

Choreography: Leonide Massine. Music: Manuel de Falla. Scenery and costumes: Pablo Picasso. Libretto: Martinez Sierra, after a story of Pedro Antonio de Alarcón.

Premiere: Metropolitan Opera House, New York City, April 11, 1943.

Principal dancers: Leonide Massine (Miller), Argentinita (Miller's Wife), Simon Semenoff (Governor), Virginia Wilcox (Governor's Wife), Michael Kidd (Dandy).

World premiere (under the title LE TRICORNE): Les Ballets Russes de Diaghilev, Alhambra Theatre, London, July 22, 1919.

Principal dancers: Leonide Massine, Tamara Karsavina, Leon Woizikowski, Alice Alanova, Stanislas Idzikowski.

The unhappy adventures of a Spanish governor who flirts with a miller's wife.

THREE ESSAYS

Choreography: Lar Lubovitch. Music: Charles Ives ("Second Orchestra Set"). Scenery: William Pitkin. Costumes: John Dayger.

World premiere: City Center, New York City, January 15, 1974.

Principal dancers: (I) Marie Johansson, Warren Conover; (II) Christine Sarry, Clark Tippet; (III) Bonnie Mathis, Ian Horvath, Keith Lee.

THREE VIRGINS AND A DEVIL

Choreography: Agnes de Mille. Music: Ottorino Respighi ("Antiche danze ed arie"). Scenery: Arne Lundborg, after sketches by Sophie Harris. Costumes: Motley. Libretto: Ramon Reed, after a story of Boccaccio.

Premiere: Majestic Theatre, New York City, February 11, 1941.

Dancers: Agnes de Mille (Priggish Virgin), Lucia Chase (Greedy Virgin), Annabelle Lyon (Lustful Virgin), Eugene Loring (Devil), Jerome Robbins (Youth).

World premiere: Palace Theatre, London, in the revue "Why Not Tonight?," April 24, 1934. Music: Walford Hyden.

Dancers: Greta Nissen (First Novice), Margaret Braithwaite (Second Novice), Elizabeth Schooling (Third Novice), Stanislas Idzikowski (Devil), Walter Crisham (Dandy).

A devil seduces three virgins into hell by playing upon their weaknesses: lust, greed, and priggishness.

TIL EULENSPIEGEL

Choreography: Jean Babilée. Music: Richard Strauss ("Till Eulenspiegels lustige Streiche"). Scenery: Tom Keogh. Costumes: Helene Pons.

U.S. premiere: Metropolitan Opera House, New York City, September 25, 1951.

Principal dancers: Jean Babilée (Til), Ruth Ann Koesun (Nell), Angela Velez (First Lady), Eric Braun (Gentleman), Barbara Lloyd (His Lady).

World premiere: Les Ballets des Champs-Elysées, Théâtre des Champs-Elysées, Paris, November 9, 1949. Scenery and costumes: Tom Keogh.

Principal dancers: Jean Babilée, Elise Vallée, Danielle Darmance, Deryk Mendel, Hélène Constantine.

The rogue Til beats and cheats the gullible peasants but is saved from execution by his love for Nell.

TIMES PAST

Choreography: Keith Lee. Music: Cole Porter, orchestrated by William Bolcom (music originally written in 1923 for Jean Börlin's ballet WITHIN THE QUOTA). Scenery adapted from Gerald Murphy's 1923 designs. Costumes: Marcos Paredes.

World premiere: City Center, New York City, July 1, 1970.

Principal dancers: Sallie Wilson; Han Ebbelaar, Ted Kivitt, John Prinz, Michael Smuin.

THE TRAITOR

Choreography: José Limón. Music: Gunther Schuller ("Symphony for Brasses"). Scenery: Paul Trautvetter. Costumes: Charles Tomlinson.

Premiere: New York State Theater, New York City, June 30, 1970.

Cast: Royes Fernandez (The Leader); Robert Brassel, William Carter, Robert Gladstein, Keith Lee, Dennis Nahat, Marcos Paredes, Frank Smith, Vane Vest (His Followers); Bruce Marks (The Traitor).

World premiere: José Limón and Company, Palmer Auditorium, Connecticut College, New London (Seventh American Dance Festival), August 19, 1954. Costumes: Pauline Laurence.

Principal dancers: Lucas Hoving (The Leader), José Limón (The Traitor).

A modern retelling of the betrayal of Christ by Judas Iscariot.

TRIPTYCH

Choreography: Edward Caton. Music: Johannes Brahms (piano pieces, arranged and orchestrated by Joseph Levine).

World premiere: Metropolitan Opera House, New York City, October 2, 1952.

Cast: I. Hungarian Dances—Liane Plane, Jenny Workman, Jack Beaber, William Burdick, Enrique Martinez. II. Impromptu—Irma Grant, Barbara Lloyd, Vernon Lusby, Fernand Nault, Vernon Wendorf. III. Waltzes—Paula Lloyd, Anna Cheselka, Dorothy Scott, Liane Plane, Lila Popper, Isabel Mirrow, Rochelle Balzer, Kelly Brown, Scott Douglas, Robert Hanlin, Eugene Tanner, Leo Duggan, Ivan Allen.

TRISTAN
(PAS DE DEUX)

Choreography: Herbert Ross. Music: Richard Wagner. Scenery: Oliver Smith. Costumes: Miles White. Libretto based on the story "Tristan" by Thomas Mann.

World premiere: Metropolitan Opera House, New York City, September 23, 1958.

Dancers: Nora Kaye and Erik Bruhn.

Love in a tuberculosis sanitorium.

TROPICAL PAS DE DEUX

Choreography: Enrique Martinez. Music: Amadeo Roldan ("Oriental" and "Fiesta Negra" from "Tres Pequenas Poemas"). Costumes: Saul Bolasni.

World premiere: Metropolitan Opera House, New York City, April 27, 1951.

Dancers: Alicia Alonso and Igor Youskevitch.

UNDERTOW

Choreography: Antony Tudor. Music: William Schuman. Scenery and costumes: Raymond Breinin. Libretto: Antony Tudor, based on a suggestion by John van Druten.

World premiere: Metropolitan Opera House, New York City, April 10, 1945.

Cast: Hugh Laing (Transgressor); Diana Adams (Cybele); John Kriza (Pollux); Shirley Eckl (Volupia); Lucia Chase (Polyhymnia); Alicia Alonso (Ate); Patricia Barker (Aganippe); Roszika Sabo (Nemesis); Cynthia Riseley (Pudicitia); Janet Reed (Hera); Nana Gollner (Medusa); Dick Beard (Hymen); Regis Powers and Stanley Herbertt (Sileni); Michael Kidd, Fernando Alonso, Roy Tobias, Kenneth Davis (Satyrisci); Marjorie Tallchief, June Morris, Mildred Ferguson (Bacchantes).

Early distasteful contacts and experiences with sex condition a young man to commit murder when he is attacked by a predatory female.

UNFINISHED SYMPHONY
(PAS DE DEUX)

Choreography: Peter van Dijk. Music: Franz Schubert (Symphony no. 8 in E minor). Costumes: Kalinowski.

Premiere: New York State Theater, New York City, July 18, 1972.

Dancers: Cynthia Gregory and Michael Denard.

World premiere (under the title LA SYMPHONIE INACHEVÉE): Grand Théâtre de Rheims, Rheims, France, November 27, 1958.

Dancers: Jacqueline Rayet and Peter Van Dijk.

US
(PAS DE DEUX)

Choreography: Keith Lee. Music: Gustav Mahler (Symphony No. 5, "Adagietto"). Costumes: Marcos Paredes.

World premiere: Ballet Theatre Players, University of Massachusetts, Amherst, May 6, 1970.

Dancers: Alexandra Radius and Han Ebbelaar.

VARIATIONS FOR FOUR

Choreography: Anton Dolin. Music: Marguerite Keogh, orchestrated by Richard Savage. Costumes: Tom Lingwood.

U.S. premiere: Metropolitan Opera House, New York City, September 25, 1958.

Dancers: John Kriza, Erik Bruhn, Scott Douglas, Royes Fernandez.

World premiere: Festival Ballet, Royal Festival Hall, London, September 5, 1957.

Dancers: John Gilpin, Flemming Flindt, Louis Godfrey, André Prokovsky.

LA VENTANA
(PAS DE TROIS)

Choreography: Erik Bruhn, from the original by August Bournonville. Music: Hans Christian Lumbye.

Premiere: New York State Theater, New York City, July 28, 1975.

Dancers: Cynthia Gregory, Erik Bruhn, Rudolf Nureyev.

World premiere of the complete ballet: Royal Danish Ballet, Royal Theater, Copenhagen, 1854.

VESTRIS
(SOLO)

Choreography: Leonid Jacobson. Music: Genaidi Banschikov. Costume: Marcos Paredes.

U.S. premiere: Kennedy Center, Washington, D.C., May 20, 1975.

Dancer: Mikhail Baryshnikov.

New York premiere: New York State Theater, July 28, 1975.

World premiere: International Ballet Competitions, Moscow, June 1969.

VOICES OF SPRING

Choreography and libretto: Mikhail Mordkin. Music: Johann Strauss, arranged by Mois Zlatin. Scenery and costumes: Lee Simonson.

Premiere: Center Theatre, New York City, January 11, 1940.

Principal dancers: Karen Conrad (The Flirt), Dimitri Romanoff (Boy in Gray), Nina Stroganova (Flower Vendor), Patricia Bowman (The Toast of Vienna), Leon Danielian (Lamplighter), Edward Caton (General).

World premiere: Mordkin Ballet, Alvin Theatre, New York City, November 10, 1938.

Principal dancers: Karen Conrad, Dimitri Romanoff, Nina Stroganova, Patricia Bowman, Savva Andreieff, Mikhail Mordkin.

Flirtations abound during a springtime evening in a Viennese park.

VOLUNTARIES

Choreography: Glen Tetley. Music: Francis Poulenc ("Concerto for Organ, Strings and Timpani"). Scenery and costumes: Rouben Ter-Arutunian.

Premiere: Music Hall, Cleveland, February 4, 1977.

Principal dancers: Cynthia Gregory and Charles Ward; Martine van Hamel, Michael Owen, Richard Schafer.

New York premiere by American Ballet Theatre: Metropolitan Opera House, May 2, 1977.

Principal dancers: Natalia Makarova and Clark Tippet; Leslie Browne, Michael Owen, Richard Schafer.

World premiere: Stuttgart Ballet, Württembergische Staatstheater, Stuttgart, December 22, 1973.

Principal dancers: Marcia Haydée and Richard Cragun; Birgit Keil, Reid Anderson, Jan Stripling.

WALTZ ACADEMY

Choreography: George Balanchine. Music: Vittorio Rieti. Scenery: Oliver Smith. Costumes: Alvin Colt.

World premiere: Boston Opera House, Boston, October 5, 1944.

Dancers: Margaret Banks, Mildred Ferguson, Barbara Fallis, Roszika Sabo, June Morris, Fern Whitney (Pas de Six); Janet Reed, Albia Kavan, Harold Lang, Fernando Alonso (Pas de Quatre); Miriam Golden, Diana Adams, John Kriza (Pas de Trois); Nora Kaye, John Taras, Rex Cooper (Pas de Trois); Nana Gollner and Paul Petroff (Pas de Deux); entire ensemble (Finale).

New York premiere: Metropolitan Opera House, October 11, 1944.

Same dancers as above except Shirley Eckl for Mildred Ferguson.

THE WANDERER

Choreography: George Balanchine. Music: Franz Schubert ("Wanderer-Fantasie," transcribed by Franz Liszt, orchestrated by Charles Koechlin). Scenery and costumes: Pavel Tchelitchev.

Premiere: Metropolitan Opera House, New York City, May 21, 1943.

Principal dancers: Vera Zorina, Anton Dolin, Hugh Laing, Albia Kavan, Galina Razoumova.

World premiere (under the title ERRANTE): Les Ballets 1933, Théâtre des Champs-Elysées, Paris, June 10, 1933.

Principal dancers included Tilly Losch, Roman Jasinsky, Sergei Ismailoff, Pearl Argyle, and Elizabeth Schooling.

The Wanderer enters a community bringing with her what the critic John Martin analyzed as "many vague but apparently pressing emotional problems."

WAY OUT

Choreography: Robert Gladstein. Music: Jacques Ibert and George Reidel. Costumes: Athena Kalimos.

World premiere: Ballet Theatre Players, University of Massachusetts, Amherst, May 6, 1970.

Dancers: Karena Brock, Diana Weber, Han Ebbelaar, Terry Orr.

THE WIND IN THE MOUNTAINS

Choreography: Agnes de Mille. Music: Laurence Rosenthal (score based largely on early American songs and folk tunes). Scenery: Jean Rosenthal. Costumes: Stanley Simmons.

World premiere: New York State Theater, New York City, March 17, 1965.

Principal dancers: Gayle Young (Young Man), Karen Krych (Young Woman), Eliot Feld and Ted Kivitt (Two Skaters), Joseph Carow (Pathfinder), William Glassman (Stranger), Judith Lerner (Diversion).

WINTER'S EVE

Choreography: Kenneth MacMillan. Music: Benjamin Britten (Variations on a Theme of Frank Bridge). Scenery and costumes: Nicholas Georgiadis. Libretto after a theme by Carson McCullers.

World premiere: Teatro Nacional de São Carlos, Lisbon, Portugal, January 16, 1957.

Principal dancers: Nora Kaye (Blind Girl), John Kriza (Young Man), Ray Barra, Enrique Martinez.

U.S. premiere: Metropolitan Opera House, New York City, February 10, 1957.

Same principal dancers as above.

A blind girl inadvertently blinds her lover.

WORKOUT

Choreography: Robert Joffrey. Music: Robert McBride.

World premiere: Ballet Theatre Workshop, Phoenix Theatre, New York City, May 7, 1956.

Cast: Jacqueline Cecil, Diane Consoer, Françoise Martinet, Sandra Northrop, Brunilda Ruiz, Dot Virden; Gerald Arpino, Richard Beaty, Anthony Mordente, Michael Sears.

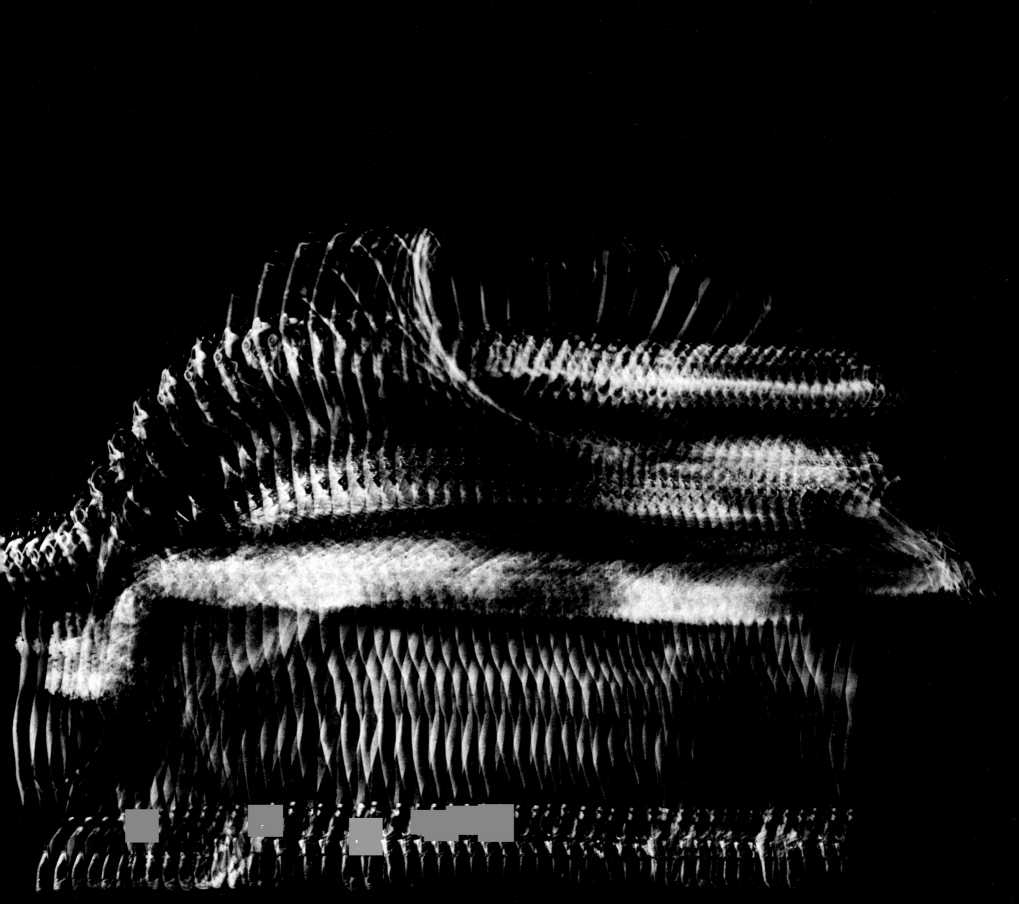

Ballet Theatre was founded when there were resident in New York a number of photographers whose interest in ballet exceeded that of the public in general and of the directors of the news media in particular. Thus it was that Albanian-born Gjon Mili, on the basis of his position as one of Life magazine's most valued photographers, was able to persuade his resisting editors to give him the assignment of making picture essays on the dance, and to finance special and very expensive photo sessions on stage. Because of Life's powerful influence on American taste, Mili's photographs were an important factor in drawing audiences to sample the ballet, an art form with which they were largely unfamiliar. Pioneering in strobe lighting he was able to freeze fast dance action with slow film—all that was available at that time. Mr. Mili has covered the highlights of Ballet Theatre history from its earliest GISELLE (page 336) to its production of LES NOCES (page 212).

In Chicago, Maurice Seymour (a Russian born in Bucovina) was introduced to Colonel de Basil in the foyer of the Civic Opera House, and soon the chauvinistic Russian director was sending his Russian dancers to be photographed by a Russian photographer. Thereafter, whenever a ballet company was in town, Seymour made himself available, cancelling other appointments and meeting with the dancers at their convenience, sometimes late into the night after performances. He photographed Ballet Theatre (and the Mordkin Ballet before it) during its customary Christmas layoffs in Chicago. His innovative lighting and skillful retouching produced photographs that revealed the dancers at their most beautiful, glamorous, and svelte, and his prints were of such clarity that they were eagerly accepted by newspaper editors who had only poor quality newsprint on which to reproduce them. When distributed throughout the country, Seymour photographs—such as that of Baronova with Skibine in PRINCESS AURORA (page 67)—conveyed to the general public the elegance of ballet.

Arriving in New York from Vienna during the year of Ballet Theatre's birth, Fred Fehl soon transformed what had been a hobby—candid photography at the theater—into a full-time professional occupation. He now maintains an archive of more than one hundred thousand photographs of live performances of theater, opera, and dance. Of ballet he has said, "Nothing is as gratifying as photographing in action, because a performance alone offers the flow of movement as well as the artist's highest emotional expression." He must have been gratified indeed with the flow of motion his lens captured during Baryshnikov's performance in COPPÉLIA (page 346).

The renowned photographer from Budapest, Hungary, André Kertész, was also in New York for Ballet Theatre's debut. His experiences with the company were for the most part frustrating, as the hectic activity of the initial season left little time for the dancers to collaborate with photographers. However, in several hastily arranged sessions, he was able to photograph groups on the roof of Radio City and on the rooftop farm of the Children's Aid Society in Hell's Kitchen on New York's West Side (pages 28–9).

Foremost of American photographers was George Platt Lynes, who produced his first ballet photographs for the American Ballet in collaboration with George Balanchine and Lincoln Kirstein. He began photographing the dancers of Ballet Theatre in 1950 and continued to supply the portraits for the souvenir program until his last illness in 1955. Lynes was almost unique in his ability to inspire sitters to assume poses of relaxed simplicity while at the same time projecting dramatic intensity. In the twin portraits of Jean Babilée and his wife Nathalie Phillipart (pages 190 and 191), for example, he succeeded in revealing a sulphurous quality in the usually placid Nathalie and an unaccustomed placidity in the often sulphuric Jean.

When Richard Avedon photographed the Ballet Theatre company for the 1949 edition of the souvenir program, he was in the early stages of his brilliant career as a photographer whose portraits make a penetrating psychological and social comment. His photographs of Janet Reed (page 161) and of the group in the waiting room of the Pennsylvania Station (page 123) looked at ballet from a fresh viewpoint, while his portrait on page 49 of John Kriza (taken on the stage of the old Metropolitan Opera House) was more traditional but equally beautiful.

Irving Penn, whose photographs were featured in the leading fashion magazines, also turned his attention to the ballet and produced the unique group portrait (later imitated) that appears on pages 132–3.

Performers who wished to be photographed at their most glamorous went to Marcus Blechman in New York or to George Hurrell in Hollywood. Ballet Theatre went to both: Hurrell is represented by his FANCY FREE series on pages 98–9; Blechman by his gallery of ballerinas on page 153.

Alfred Valente might well be called the Maurice Seymour of New York. He produced photographs of high artistic quality that were at the same time of a clarity ideal for newspaper reproduction. Louis Melançon, Sedge Leblang, and James Heffernan, successively the official photographers of the Metropolitan Opera Association, have photographed the company during the four decades it has performed on the stages of the old and the new houses. Richard Tucker, who took pictures of the opening night performance at the Center Theatre (pages 50 and 51), later photographed the company whenever it performed in the Boston Opera House.

During its tours abroad, Ballet Theatre was pictured by numerous foreign photographers, the first of whom called himself simply Semo and brought his camera to the stage of the Palacio de Bellas Artes in Mexico when the company was in residence there in 1943. Typical of the pictures he posed in front of scenery is the grouping of the cast of PILLAR OF FIRE (page 87).

During its visits to England in 1946 and 1950, Ballet Theatre took advantage of the more moderate wages paid stagehands there and scheduled photographic sessions in which a ballet could be performed with scenery and costumes for the sole benefit of a camera mounted on a tripod in the middle of the auditorium. It was thus able to obtain full-stage photographs (obtainable in American theaters only at dress rehearsals) such as those of ROMEO AND JULIET (pages 88 and 89). They were taken by Baron Nahum, who called himself simply Baron, and who by 1950 had become the official photographer for Buckingham Palace (his darkroom assistant was Anthony Armstrong Jones). Similar photographs were taken in London by Roger Wood (RODEO, page 171, for example), in Paris by Serge Lido, in Vienna by Yoichi R. Okamoto (who later became the official photographer for the White House under President Lyndon Johnson), and in Bulgaria and the Soviet Union by nameless state employees. Also, during its several visits to South America, the company enjoyed being the subject of photographic studies (for instance, that of Lupe Serrano, page 179) by the eminent ballet photographer Annemarie Heinrich.

(PREVIOUS PAGE) STROBOSCOPIC PHOTOGRAPH OF NORA KAYE BY GJON MILI.

In 1946, Cecil Beaton made some of the souvenir-program pictures of the company in the New York studio of Vogue and the balance in the magazine's London studio; a final photograph of the artistic committee (page 146) was taken in one of the suites Beaton had redecorated for the Plaza Hotel.

During the late 1950s, a new generation of American photographers turned its attention to ballet. Among the earliest was Martha Swope, who took her first dance photos while still a student at the School of American Ballet. When she became a professional in theater photography, she was named official photographer of the New York City Ballet and was later accorded the same designation by Ballet Theatre. Unlike her predecessors who specialized either in snapping action shots during actual performances or in taking posed pictures in their own studios, she did and does both — superbly well. She has kept the Ballet Theatre press department supplied with photographs, and for several seasons she produced the portraits for the souvenir programs. Jack Mitchell performed the same functions brilliantly for a decade until his interest shifted to portraiture with a clientele made up predominantly of opera singers. His successor at the start of the seventies was Kenn Duncan, who like Swope had begun his career as a dancer: he appeared as The Executioner in the Ballet Theatre Workshop performance of THE ENCHANTED.

The extraordinary increase in the ballet public during the 1970s has been accompanied by a proliferation of professional and amateur ballet photographers. At times the number of those who wished to photograph a performance could not be accommodated in the seats set aside for that purpose, and those who could not be seated officially had to find their own vantage points. The individuality and special quality of each photographer's work was further affected by his viewpoint in the theater: Kenn Duncan from the wings on stage, Louis Péres with his telephoto lens in the standing room, Beverley Gallegos in the front rows of the orchestra, James Heffernan from the broadcast booth of the Met (behind two panes of plate glass), and Dr. Michael Truppin, who can sit and shoot from anywhere because his silent camera (enclosed in a unique soundproof box) does not disturb those in neighboring seats.

The quality of ballet photographs is often influenced by factors beyond dancing or photographic technique. It is not by accident, for example, that Bil Leidersdorf has produced some of the finest pictures of Cynthia Gregory (as on page 357). The confidence she feels in her favorite photographer induces an easy relaxation conducive to unstrained photographic results. Nor is it coincidental that Dina Makarova excels in photographing Natalia Makarova (as in LA SYLPHIDE, page 298). The Rochester-born photographer, equally fluent in both Russian and English, has had a pleasant and useful association with the ballerina (to whom she is not related) from Natalia's first arrival in the United States.

Sixty-six photographers took the some five hundred and fifty photographs chosen for reproduction in this book after at least twenty times that number of prints, contact sheets, and negatives had been assembled and examined by Charles Payne and Robert Gottlieb. The author and the publishers would like to thank both Ballet Theatre and the Dance Collection, the Library and Museum of the Performing Arts, the New York Public Library at Lincoln Center, for permission to reproduce photographs from their archives. The names of all the individual photographers who could be identified are listed below.

GORDON ANTHONY
MARIA AUSTRIA
RICHARD AVEDON
CONSTANCE BANNISTER
BARON [NAHUM]
RADFORD BASCOME
JOAN BAUM
CECIL BEATON
BERTERO
MARCUS BLECHMAN
LUCIA CHASE
LARRY COLWELL
J. COOKE
CONSTANTINE
COSMOS-SILVO
COSTAS
ANTHONY CRICKMAY
EILEEN DARBY
DELAR
KENN DUNCAN
FRED FEHL
HERB FLATOW
BEVERLEY GALLEGOS
DWIGHT GODWIN
JAMES HEFFERNAN
ANNE-MARIE HEINRICH
IRA HILL
GEORGE HURRELL
HUSTON
GEORGE KARGER
ANDRÉ KERTÉSZ
G. MAILLARD KESSLERE
JOHN KRIZA

SEDGE LEBLANG
BIL LEIDERSDORF
SERGE LIDO
LISEG
GEORGE PLATT LYNES
LIPNITZKI
DINA MAKAROVA
LOUIS MELANÇON
GJON MILI
JACK MITCHELL
RIGMOR MYDTSKOV
YOICHI R. OKAMOTO
WALTER E. OWEN
CHARLES PAYNE
IRVING PENN
LOUIS PÉRES
PRITCHARD
PAUL RADKAI
WILL RAPPORT
ROY ROUND
SEMO
MAURICE SEYMOUR
SHARLAND
D. RICHARD STATILE
MARTHA SWOPE
DR. MICHAEL TRUPPIN
RICHARD TUCKER
ALFREDO VALENTE
CARL VAN VECHTEN
VOSS
ALDEN WEEKS
G. B. L. WILSON
ROGER WOOD

68-9 (LEFT) WOOD; (BOTTOM RIGHT) VALENTE; (OTHERS) SEYMOUR
70 SEYMOUR
71 (TOP LEFT) SEMO; (BOTTOM LEFT) CONSTANTINE; (RIGHT) SEMO
72-3 (LEFT) MILI; (OTHERS) BARON
74-5 (TOP, FROM LEFT) MILI, BARON, SEMO, SEMO; (BOTTOM) SEMO
76 SEMO
77 (TOP LEFT) CONSTANTINE; (TOP RIGHT) FEHL; (BOTTOM LEFT) SEMO; (BOTTOM RIGHT) VALENTE
78 LYNES
79 LYNES
80 (TOP, FROM LEFT) FEHL, LYNES, FEHL; (BOTTOM) MELANÇON
81 (TOP) LYNES; (BOTTOM) MELANÇON
82 (TOP) VALENTE; (BOTTOM) SEYMOUR
83 (LEFT) TUCKER; (RIGHT) SEYMOUR
84-5 (LEFT) COLWELL; (OTHERS) BLECHMAN
86-7 (LEFT) MILI; (RIGHT) SEMO
88-9 (TOP) VALENTE; (BOTTOM) BARON
90 COLWELL
91 (BOTTOM RIGHT) HUSTON; (OTHERS) WOOD
92 COLWELL
93 (LEFT) LYNES, (OTHERS) VALENTE
94 BARON
95 AUSTRIA
96 MELANÇON
97 (TOP) VALENTE; (BOTTOM) WOOD
98-9 HURRELL
100 (TOP CENTER) KARGER; (BOTTOM) BARON; (OTHERS) VALENTE
101 (TOP LEFT) BEATON; (TOP RIGHT) VALENTE; (OTHERS) BARON
102 KERTÉSZ
103 FEHL
104-5 (TOP) WEEKS; (BOTTOM) MELANÇON
107 JOHN KRIZA COLLECTION
110 CHASE
111 VALENTE
113 LYNES
114 (TOP) SEYMOUR; (BOTTOM) LYNES
115 (TOP) SEMO; (BOTTOM) LYNES
116 SEMO
117 HEINRICH
119 (LEFT) SEMO; (RIGHT) TUCKER
120 BALLET THEATRE ARCHIVES
121 TUCKER
123 AVEDON; (INSETS) KRIZA
124 TUCKER
125 CONSTANTINE
126 (BOTTOM RIGHT) SEYMOUR; (OTHERS) VALENTE
127 FEHL
128 BARON
129 BALLET THEATRE ARCHIVES
131 TUCKER
132-3 PENN
137 MILI
138 MILI
141 LYNES
144 WILSON
146 BEATON
148 FEHL
149 COOKE
151 MILI
153 BLECHMAN
156 THE SCOTSMAN PUBLICATIONS, MARY CLARKE COLLECTION
158 AVEDON
161 (BOTTOM RIGHT) LYNES; (OTHERS) AVEDON
162 NEWS PHOTO FROM BALLET THEATRE ARCHIVES
164 BLECHMAN

165 LYNES
167 MITCHELL
168 LEBLANG
169 LYNES
170 FEHL
171 WOOD
172-3 WOOD
174-5 (BOTTOM CENTER) DARBY; (OTHERS) FEHL
176 LYNES
177 LYNES
178-9 HEINRICH
180 LYNES
181 (TOP) SHARLAND; (BOTTOM RIGHT) VALENTE; (OTHERS) BARON
182-3 (TOP, FROM LEFT) FEHL, FEHL, BASCOME; (BOTTOM, FROM LEFT) KARGER, KARGER, SWOPE
184 AUSTRIA
185 LYNES
186 LIPNITZKI
187 LIPNITZKI
188 LEBLANG
189 LEBLANG
190 LYNES
191 LYNES
192 VALENTE
193 MITCHELL
194-5 (LEFT) MITCHELL; (TOP CENTER AND RIGHT) FEHL; (BOTTOM) HEINRICH
196-7 (LEFT) LEBLANG; (OTHERS) FEHL
198 PAYNE
199 (LEFT) UNITED STATES AIR FORCE PHOTO FROM BALLET THEATRE ARCHIVES; (RIGHT) BERTERO
200-1 OKAMOTO
202 MITCHELL
203 MYDTSKOV
204 LIPNITZKI
205 FEHL
206 (LEFT) MITCHELL; (RIGHT) BALLET THEATRE ARCHIVES
208 (TOP) ROUND; (BOTTOM) UNITED STATES NAVY PHOTO FROM BALLET THEATRE ARCHIVES
209 LEIDERSDORF
210 MITCHELL
211 MITCHELL
212-13 (LEFT) MILI; (TOP RIGHT) MITCHELL; (OTHERS) SWOPE
214-15 MITCHELL
216-17 (TOP, FROM LEFT) FEHL, SWOPE, FEHL, SWOPE; (BOTTOM, FROM LEFT) MITCHELL, FEHL
218-19 MITCHELL
220 SWOPE
221 MITCHELL
222-3 (TOP, FROM LEFT) FEHL, SOVIET PHOTO FROM BALLET THEATRE ARCHIVES, MITCHELL; (BOTTOM, FROM LEFT) MITCHELL, SWOPE; (CENTER RIGHT) FEHL
224-5 (TOP CENTER, BOTH PAGES) FEHL; (OTHERS) SWOPE
226-7 (LEFT) MILI; (RIGHT) MITCHELL
228 (BOTTOM RIGHT) FEHL; (OTHERS) MITCHELL
229 (TOP) PÉRES; (BOTTOM) FEHL
230-1 MITCHELL
232-3 (CENTER) FEHL; (OTHERS) PÉRES
234 DUNCAN
235 (TOP) LEIDERSDORF; (BOTTOM) PÉRES
236 NEWS PHOTO FROM BALLET THEATER ARCHIVES
237 MITCHELL
238 MITCHELL
241 SWOPE
243 SWOPE

244-5 MITCHELL
247 PÉRES
249 SWOPE
250 SWOPE
251 FEHL
252-3 (LEFT) GALLEGOS; (TOP CENTER) FEHL; (BOTTOM CENTER) SWOPE; (OTHERS) PÉRES
254-5 (CENTER) DUNCAN; (OTHERS) SWOPE
256 PÉRES
257 (TOP RIGHT) LEIDERSDORF; (BOTTOM RIGHT) DUNCAN; (OTHERS) PÉRES
258-9 (TOP, FROM LEFT) FEHL, HEFFERNAN, GALLEGOS; (BOTTOM, FROM LEFT) COSTAS, HEFFERNAN, GALLEGOS
260 SWOPE
261 (TOP LEFT) FEHL; (TOP RIGHT) LEIDERSDORF; (BOTTOM LEFT) PÉRES; (BOTTOM RIGHT) SWOPE
262-3 (BOTTOM LEFT) PÉRES; (OTHERS) SWOPE
264-5 (TOP, FROM LEFT) SWOPE, SWOPE, COSTAS, MAKAROVA; (BOTTOM LEFT) SWOPE; (BOTTOM RIGHT) MAKAROVA
266-7 (TOP CENTER) SWOPE; (BOTTOM CENTER) PÉRES; (BOTTOM RIGHT) FEHL; (OTHERS) LEIDERSDORF
268-9 SWOPE
270 (CENTER) DUNCAN; (OTHERS) MAKAROVA
271 PÉRES
272-3 (LEFT AND BOTTOM RIGHT) HEFFERNAN; (OTHERS) SWOPE
274 SWOPE
275 SWOPE
276 DUNCAN
277 DUNCAN
278 (TOP RIGHT) MITCHELL; (OTHERS) DUNCAN
279 DUNCAN
280-1 (TOP, FROM LEFT) GALLEGOS, DUNCAN, MAKAROVA; (BOTTOM, FROM LEFT) FEHL, SWOPE, LEIDERSDORF
282-3 MITCHELL
285 DUNCAN
286-7 (TOP, FROM LEFT) SWOPE, FEHL, SWOPE, MAKAROVA; (BOTTOM, FROM LEFT) PÉRES, DUNCAN, SWOPE
288-9 (TOP, FROM LEFT) VAN VECHTEN, BANNISTER, VAN VECHTEN, DUNCAN, MITCHELL; (BOTTOM LEFT AND RIGHT) MITCHELL
290 (TOP LEFT) DUNCAN; (BOTTOM LEFT) PÉRES; (RIGHT) FEHL
291 (TOP LEFT) SWOPE; (OTHERS) PÉRES
292-3 (TOP, FROM LEFT) HEFFERNAN, FEHL, BAUM; (BOTTOM CENTER) HEFFERNAN; (BOTTOM RIGHT) FEHL
294 (TOP LEFT) SWOPE; (BOTTOM LEFT) PÉRES; (RIGHT) GALLEGOS
295 (TOP) SWOPE; (BOTTOM LEFT) PÉRES; (BOTTOM RIGHT) GALLEGOS
296 (TOP LEFT) TRUPPIN; (TOP RIGHT) SWOPE; (BOTTOM) FEHL
297 (TOP RIGHT) HEFFERNAN; (OTHERS) SWOPE
298-9 (TOP) HEFFERNAN; (BOTTOM, FROM LEFT) MAKAROVA, PÉRES, HEFFERNAN, PÉRES
300 (TOP RIGHT) HEFFERNAN; (OTHERS) SWOPE
301 (BOTTOM) HEFFERNAN; (OTHERS) SWOPE

302 (TOP RIGHT) LEIDERSDORF; (OTHERS) SWOPE
303 (TOP LEFT) SWOPE; (OTHERS) LEIDERSDORF
304 (TOP LEFT) DUNCAN; (OTHERS) SWOPE
305 (BOTTOM) SWOPE; (OTHERS) MITCHELL
306 SWOPE
307 SWOPE
308 MITCHELL
309 AVEDON
311 (TOP) FEHL; (CENTER, FROM LEFT) VALENTE, VAN VECHTEN, BLECHMAN; VALENTE; (BOTTOM, FROM LEFT) CONSTANTINE, BARON
312 (TOP, FROM LEFT) SEYMOUR, SEMO, VALENTE; (CENTER LEFT AND RIGHT) VALENTE; (BOTTOM LEFT AND BOTTOM) FEHL
313 (TOP, FROM LEFT) SEYMOUR, VALENTE, VALENTE; (CENTER LEFT) DARBY; (CENTER AND BOTTOM LEFT) FEHL; (BOTTOM RIGHT) RAPPORT
315 (TOP LEFT) HEINRICH; (BOTTOM LEFT) VALENTE; (OTHERS) SEYMOUR
317 LYNES
319 (BOTTOM) DANCE COLLECTION; (OTHERS) MYDTSKOV
320 (BOTTOM) FEHL; (OTHERS) SEYMOUR
322 FLATOW
323 FEHL
324 FEHL
328 (LEFT) SEYMOUR; (RIGHT) VALENTE
329 SEYMOUR
330-1 (LEFT) FEHL; (RIGHT) SWOPE
333 BEATON
335 (TOP LEFT) COURTESY OF ALONSO; (OTHERS) FEHL
336 MILI
337 (LEFT) TUCKER; (RIGHT) CONSTANTINE
338 (TOP LEFT) BARON; (BOTTOM RIGHT) OWEN; (OTHERS) FEHL
339 FEHL
340 SEYMOUR
341 (TOP) GODWIN; (BOTTOM) FEHL
343 BEATON
345 SEYMOUR
346 FEHL
347 MILI
349 BALLET THEATRE ARCHIVES
350 ANTHONY
352 (RIGHT) RADKAI; (OTHERS) HEINRICH
353 BEATON
355 SWOPE
357 LEIDERSDORF
358 (FROM LEFT) FEHL, CONSTANTINE, FEHL
359 (FROM LEFT) SWOPE, FEHL, MILI
360 (FROM LEFT) LEBLANG, BALLET THEATRE ARCHIVES, FEHL
361 (FROM LEFT) CRICKMAY, PÉRES, SWOPE
362 (FROM LEFT) LEIDERSDORF, MITCHELL, MITCHELL
363 (FROM LEFT) MITCHELL, KERTÉSZ, FEHL
364 (FROM LEFT) MITCHELL, SWOPE, SWOPE
365 (FROM LEFT) SEYMOUR, FEHL, FEHL
366 (FROM LEFT) SEYMOUR, SWOPE, MITCHELL
367 (FROM LEFT) PÉRES, SWOPE, LEBLANG
368 (FROM LEFT) DUNCAN, FEHL, VALENTE
369 MILI
373 SWOPE

(OPPOSITE PAGE) NATALIA MAKAROVA IN OTHER DANCES.

INDEX

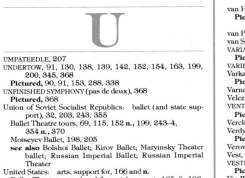

GRAPHICS CREDITS

The text of this book—as well as all display type— was set in ITC Tiffany, a modern combination of Ronaldson and Caxton, two significant typefaces not favored in many years. The MacKellar, Smiths, and Jordan foundry cut Ronaldson in 1884; the American Type Founders Company issued Caxton about twenty years later. Caxton, an excellent face in its own right, was eclipsed by the popularity of the various Goudy types. Ed Benguiat designed ITC Tiffany to blend the best features of these two unique styles; in doing so, he developed a refined and entirely novel typeface.

This book was photo-composed in film on the VIP by Monotype Composition Company, Inc., Baltimore, Maryland, and by TypoGraphics Communications, Inc., New York City; the two-color and three-color reproduction was carried out by Rapoport Printing Corporation, also of New York City, using both their Stonetone and a halftone process. The four-color work was produced by Sanders Printing Corporation of New York City. The book was bound by A. Horowitz & Son, Bookbinders, Fairfield, New Jersey.

Ellen McNeilly directed the production and manufacturing. Neal T. Jones supervised the copy editing and proofreading. R. D. Scudellari designed the book and directed the graphics.